THE RAPE OF SERBIA

THE RAPE
OF SERBIA

THE RAPE OF SERBIA

The British Role in Tito's Grab for Power
1943–1944

MICHAEL LEES

HARCOURT BRACE JOVANOVICH, PUBLISHERS

San Diego   New York   London

Library of Congress Cataloging-in-Publication Data
Lees, Michael, 1921–
    The rape of Serbia: the British role in Tito's grab for power/
Michael Lees.—1st ed.
        p. cm.
    Includes bibliographical references.
    ISBN 0-15-195910-2
    1. Yugoslavia—Foreign relations—Great Britain. 2. Great
Britain—Foreign relations—Yugoslavia. 3. World War, 1939–1945—
Yugoslavia. 4. Tito, Josip Broz, 1892–1980. 5. Mihailović, Draža,
1893–1946. 6. Yugoslavia—History—Axis occupation, 1941–1945.
I. Title.
DR1258.G7L44   1990
940.53'497—dc20   89-29495

Printed in the United States of America

First edition
ABCDE

This book is dedicated to the memory of the victims of the mur-
ders and massacres perpetrated by the Soviet-bloc despots, aided
by their lackeys and dupes. May those truly patriotic Loyalists
who were slaughtered in Yugoslavia in the name of revolutionary
liberation rest more peacefully now that the true nature of the
communist swindle is at last becoming exposed and generally accepted. We cannot restore their lives but we can, and must, ac-
cord them their proper place in history.

It would be intolerable if the official history of SOE activities
now being written just repeated the hitherto accepted version of
history, which had its origin in communist-inspired disinformation. The authoritative version must take account of the new information and analyses coming to light all the time, both in
Yugoslavia and overseas.

CONTENTS

CONTENTS

ACKNOWLEDGMENTS

Already in my previous memoir I paid tribute to Basil Davidson for his account of the frivolous shenanigans in the SOE Cairo (MO4) office in January 1943, which possibly determined the tragic fate of the Yugoslav peoples. This saga, together with his unkind review of Nora Beloff's excellent book *Tito's Flawed Legacy*, drove me to undertake an in-depth study of the secret SOE files that had found their way surprisingly into the Public Records Office in Kew Gardens, London, England. I wanted to find out what really happened to cause the U-turn in British wartime policy in regard to Yugoslavia. I also wanted to know why we British liaison officers dropped to Mihailović were treated as fall guys and untrustworthy pariahs.

Thorsons has kindly agreed to inclusion of material previously published in my war memoir, *Special Operations Executed*. I am indebted to Gollancz and the author for permission to quote from Davidson's *Special Operations Europe*. My thanks are due for permission to quote from Sir William Deakin's book *The Embattled Mountain,* and I am grateful for his replies to questions I put to him in correspondence. Similarly, I am grateful to Sir Fitzroy Maclean, Bart., for permission to quote from *Eastern Approaches.* I also acknowledge permission to quote from Bickham Sweet-Escott's *Baker Street Irregular,* from Vane Ivanović's *LX Memoirs of a Yugoslav,* and from David Martin's *Patriot or Traitor: The Case of General Mihailovich.* Crown-copyright material in the British Public Records Office is reproduced by kind permission of the controller of Her Majesty's Stationery Office.

Although I must stress that those to whom I pay tribute do not necessarily agree with my conclusions, opinions, and emphasis, I greatly appreciated the advice of Stevan K. Pavlowitch, one of the most impressive and totally objective authorities on Yugoslavia, and the help of Richard Clogg, the well-known historian of modern Greece, who permitted me to study George Taylor's papers in his office at the University of London.

I am also indebted to the university for their publication recording the so-called Auty-Clogg symposium, formally titled "British Policy Towards Wartime Resistance in Yugoslavia and Greece." At this very exclusive meeting, in an almost unbelievable way, the lengthy dissertations about Yugoslavia uniformly evaded the only issue of importance, namely: Should Great Britain have been in the business of enthusiastically helping a gang of ruthless communist revolutionaries to exploit Allied recognition and massive logistical aid in order to kill other Yugoslav patriots in an out-and-out civil war, while the Germans made good their strategic withdrawal? But no one thought to disturb the prestigious ambience with such a vulgar, pragmatic question.

I also record my thanks to Nora Beloff, Roger Scruton, Milan Deroc, Dominic Flessati, Nikola Pašić, the Reverend James Coombes, and Charles Crighton, all of whom studied one or another of my drafts and made valuable, detailed observations. My brother-in-law, Chips Selby-Bennet, kindly skimmed through my first draft and reacted as brothers-in-law do, which was fair enough because that first draft was very rough and excessively aggressive, reflecting my fury at what I had found in the PRO files. But

"Boadicea" cut me down to size with withering comments and coerced me to write more soberly on such a tragic subject.

Archie Jack, a very active participant at the Loyalist head-quarters in Yugoslavia, read at least two drafts, contributed a mass of material, kept up an encouraging correspondence, and consti-tuted a steadfast father figure throughout. With David Martin, the real guru, who has fought the disinformation put out against the Loyalist patriots for nearly forty-five years, I have had a con-stant and massive exchange of material and ideas.

I received great help from Sava Bosnić, Heather Williams, and Staniša Vlahović. The last, with his encyclopedic knowledge of the location of key documents in the PRO, saved me months of research. My erstwhile skin-diving companion, Vane Ivanović, gave me very effective assistance in connection with publication.

The Right Honourable Sir Ian Percival, Sir Richard Keane, Bart., and Ljubo Sirc also very kindly read a draft manuscript and gave their general comments.

My thanks are due to Sir Brooks Richards, president of the Special Forces Club, for his patience and tolerance; to Chris Woods, until recently custodian of the official SOE files and now chairman of the Special Forces Club historical subcommittee; to Peter Lee, the former committee chairman and now librarian; and to Gervase Cowell, Chris Woods's successor as SOE advisor at the Foreign Office.

My heartfelt thanks go to Mary O'Sullivan of Barryroe, who tirelessly typed at least three drafts in her spare time, and to Catherine Nagle of CMOS Computers, Clonakilty, who is one of those all-too-rare beings who can actually make a word processor do what it is meant to. Also to Alan Davies.

My wife served as an officer in the signals-planning section of SOE Cairo and in Bari and knew many of the people men-tioned in this book. Her recollections have been invaluable.

In conclusion, I want to place on record that I have greatly enjoyed swapping material and views with Mark Wheeler, the official historian for SOE activities in Yugoslavia nominated by the British Cabinet Office. I wish him every success in his task. Whatever else, it is, I fear, a highly controversial and thankless

ACKNOWLEDGMENTS

one. *"Courage, mon vieux"* and "Take the self-serving blarney with a grain of salt" are probably the best counsel I can give him. I would like to feel that I have followed the latter maxim myself in this attempt to tell in unequivocal language some unpalatable, but irrefutable, truths that have been covered up far too long. In doing so I hope to contribute toward setting the historical record straight. This is vital for the defense of democracy against future totalitarian hoodwinking.

May those hundreds of thousands, mostly but by no means exclusively Serbs, who died in Yugoslavia in fratricidal strife, fanned by the whims of the leaders of the Great Powers, at least inspire us to insist: never, never again. The Serbs, a brave and superbly patriotic people, suffered a holocaust in measure not so greatly less than that suffered by the Jews: twice, in 1914–18 and again in 1941–46. In truth their only sin was being in the wrong place at the wrong time and, on the second occasion, trusting the Western Allies. Have we no shame?

SERBO-CROAT PRONUNCIATIONS

c is pronounced like **ts** in fats

č like the **ch** in beach

ć is a similar sound; the difference is imperceptible to most Anglo-Saxon ears.

š is like **sh** in shock

ž is like the **s** in pleasure

j is like **y** in yet

ai and **aj** are like the **i** in white

SERBO-CROAT PRONUNCIATIONS

Generally, Serbo-Croat spelling is used in this book. Exceptions are commonly known names such as Yugoslavia (instead of Jugoslavija) and Belgrade (instead of Beograd). Also I use Četniks as the plural (rather than Četnići, which would be correct) because of its common use.

AUTHOR'S NOTE

This book deals with the Yugoslav civil war—a highly controversial subject. It links my personal eyewitness account of experiences in 1943–44 with my extensive research of the official records forty years later. My experiences and conclusions are sharply at odds with what might best be described as "the British Yugoslav Establishment view" or, perhaps more aptly, "the victor's history." This version has been assiduously built up over the years by the communist historians in Belgrade and the protagonists, supporters, and sponsors of the Tito regime elsewhere, principally in the United Kingdom. Some time ago I started using the expression *received wisdom* to denote this fanciful and distorted mixture of history, mythology, and left-wing dogma. *Perceived history* is, I suppose, semantically more correct. But *received wisdom* it is here—and I intend to knock some big holes in it.

AUTHOR'S NOTE

I have also coined the term *Loyalist* or *Loyalist Četniks* to identify the noncommunist national resistance movement commanded by Gen. Draža Mihailović. The misrepresentation of the centuries-old term *Četnik* by communist propagandists, by Axis disinformation, and by opportunists and bandits seeking to legitimize themselves obliges us to use something other than "Četnik" alone. Rather late in the day, General Mihailović, the minister of war for the legitimate Yugoslav government in exile, endeavored to call his forces the "Yugoslav Army of the Homeland," but the term never caught on because Tito had preempted him by calling his communist-led Partisans the "National Liberation Army." The Mihailović forces also at times used the term *Royalist*, but the communists immediately seized on this name as proof that the Mihailović movement was pan-Serb, which it was not. So "Loyalist" it is in this book, and I believe that this is an appropriate term.

My main source of materials was the Public Records Office; references given in the text relate to documents in the PRO unless stated to the contrary.

PART I
The Antecedents

CHAPTER
1
SOE

■

THE INIQUITY OF IT ALL

In future, Mihailović forces will be described not as patriots but as terrorist gangs; we shall also drop the phrase "red bandits," as applied to [Tito's] partisans, and substitute "freedom fighters."—British government directive, early 1944

In the dark, narrow hallway serving as cloakroom and passageway to the back quarters of the Special Forces Club in London hang the portraits of Winston Churchill, Marshal Tito, and Gen. Draža Mihailović.

The portrait of Mihailović—a youthful but studious and contemplative face—is in the middle, and that is fitting. For this was the man who was caught in the middle between the two titans who destroyed him and condemned him to extinction.

It is also fitting that this group of portraits be relegated to a fusty corner, symbolic of the fudging, the falsifying, the covering up of history that has taken place for nearly half a century.

Mihailović was the brave Serbian patriot who in May 1941 first raised the flag of large-scale resistance against Hitler in occupied Europe. For eighteen months he and his Loyalist Četniks enjoyed acclaim from the free world as an example to other enslaved peoples. Yet in 1944 Churchill and Tito between them obliterated the Yugoslav Loyalist movement. Thanks primarily to British recognition, British propaganda, and overwhelming Allied logistical and air support, and under the guise of resisting the German occupation, Tito was able to turn his British and American guns on his pro-Western countrymen. In an out-and-out civil war, he grabbed power.

Disregarding all of the promises he had made to his British sponsors, Tito then introduced a brutal, repressive, Stalinist-style regime accompanied by mass killings and atrocities. Already in the autumn and winter of 1944, when the Partisan armies invaded Serbia, helped by the Red Army and the Bulgars, impromptu massacres had taken place. Even Loyalist guerrilla forces fighting alongside the Red Army against the retreating Germans were later disarmed by their Russian comrades and handed over to Tito's commissars for disposal. In the case of the officers, that generally meant execution out of hand. Any opposition, actual or potential, in the towns or villages in Serbia was crushed ruthlessly.

In May and June 1945 the atrocities reached their peak. The conscience of the world has recently been stirred by the story—told all too late—of the deviously conducted forcible repatriation of 35,000 Croatian and Slovenian home guards and Serbian Četniks, together with women and children, which was carried out by the British in Austria. These people, refugees who had been accepted as such by their captors, were told that they were being transferred to a refugee camp at Palmanova in Italy. They eagerly entrained for the journey, only to find after the doors had been bolted that they were being handed over to Partisan guards and shunted to Slovenia.

It is now known that they perished at the hands of Tito's communists. They were systematically and sadistically slaugh-

4

tered by specially formed execution squads who had worked out techniques to ensure that they died and were interred without trace, most of them in the terrible pit at Kočevje. As with other Stalinist-inspired massacres in Russia and Poland, everything was organized in a highly professional manner. No doubt Tito called in NKVD experts. The purpose was to ensure that the outside world would not learn what was going on. The experts clearly gave highly professional advice; the cover-up was successful for a very long time.

Recently there has been much publicity about the 35,000 because of allegations that Harold Macmillan, who later became the British prime minister, was responsible for the repatriations. But that publicity has diverted attention from the horrible fact that this 35,000 represented only the tip of the iceberg. There are no available records or authoritative estimates of the political killings performed by the communists in Yugoslavia. The officials and historians in Belgrade have suffered amnesia in this regard. They would, wouldn't they? But from what is available from the very few sources that have had the temerity to touch on this taboo subject, it appears that a quarter of a million souls in all might be a realistic figure. That is not a scholar's figure nor a figure that can in any way be substantiated. A betting man might even call it too low. At a Communist Party caucus meeting late in 1945 Tito called for an end to the mass killings, which were still going on six months after the war had ended. He did so not out of mercy or any other "bourgeois" weakness but rather because, in his own words, "no one fears death anymore." Killing had become counterproductive.

For a nation of fewer than 16 million people at the time, a quarter of a million dead in secret political killings—after the deaths on the battlefield—is statistically horrifying. In order to establish some sort of comparison, imagine a million executions in the United Kingdom or 4 million in the United States.

Those were the silent killings motivated in part by sadistic settling of old scores by the hardened communists and in part by the desire to eliminate any possible focus of opposition to Tito's intended permanent takeover of power and the establishment of a totalitarian state on Stalin's model.

These secretive, illegal executions were followed by the much-publicized trials for which a framework of legality was cobbled together. Again the Stalinist technique was copied. The object, of course, was to massage history, to establish the glorious record of Tito and his movement, and to carry out a public-relations assassination of rival ideologies. The established ideologies were, of course, the Serbian Orthodox and royalist traditions in Serbia and the Roman Catholic church in Slovenia and Croatia. So Mihailović and Archbishop Stepinac, the Roman Catholic primate of Yugoslavia, were ideal victims, and their arraignment was stage-managed in a glare of publicity. All the stops were pulled out in order to condemn, in the eyes of the world, Mihailović and everything he stood for.

It is a shameful fact that Clement Attlee, the British prime minister from 1945 to 1951, declined a request in 1946 by a disillusioned and remorseful Churchill, his predecessor, that the British government should press for a fair trial for Mihailović. Attlee told Ernest Bevin, his foreign minister, that he could see no advantage for the British Labour Party in acceding to Churchill's request. Mihailović, the erstwhile hero and ally, went alone and abandoned to his grave. He was executed by firing squad on July 17, 1946, on a Belgrade golf course.

It is even more shameful that, incredibly, Tito achieved some measure of success with this Stalinist-style public-relations exercise and that much of the so-called evidence dished up by the prosecution at the Mihailović trial has found its way into the *received wisdom*.

Churchill's remorse had come too late. Too late for Mihailović, too late for a free Yugoslavia. Tito had hoodwinked the British, and he made no bones about it. "I have outsmarted and deceived that old fox Churchill," Tito publicly boasted after the war.

How had Churchill, cleverest of politicians and strategists, been so deluded?

Who sold Churchill the idea that Mihailović—the man Hitler termed an "uncompromising enemy," whose annihilation was the key to Axis success in southeastern Europe—was a German collaborator? Who accepted Tito's claims of troop strength and battle victories—claims so preposterous that even Stalin cautioned Tito against exaggerations too outlandish—and delivered them to Churchill as fact? And who, conversely, delayed and buried pro-Mihailović intelligence reports so effectively that there is no evidence that they ever reached Churchill?

Are we to disbelieve Tito's postwar ambassador to Britain who—years later and with no ax to grind then—gave an amusing account of how he had "indoctrinated" the British intelligence officer who had Churchill's ear on matters Balkan? Are we to ignore Heinrich Himmler's statement that Tito had "fooled and humiliated the British and Americans in a most comical way"?

Here a note about the Americans is appropriate. They were not nearly as gullible as the British. But in the Balkans, a British sphere of influence, they deferred to Churchill's judgment, however unwillingly. "The U.S. government," Churchill wrote in March 1945, "have never been enthusiastic about our pro-Partisan policy and it has always been with great difficulty that we have dragged them reluctantly behind us." Churchill, at that time, had just begun to realize how completely Tito had fooled him. He plaintively mentions the embarrassing chore of having to explain to the Americans "that after all Tito has not turned out to be what we hoped for."

At least the Americans tried to atone for their acquiescence. A U.S. commission of inquiry fully exonerated Mihailović, and in 1948 President Harry S Truman awarded him the Legion of Merit.

The British have not been so quick to admit the mistake. Some find it hard to accept, apparently, that our great wartime leader could have been taken in by a guerrilla from the Balkan backwoods. Yes, in this matter Churchill was naïve. It was not until May 25, 1945—nearly two years after he had rolled out the welcome mat for Tito—that it occurred to Churchill to request a full dossier on him. "Is it true," Churchill asked in his request memo, "that he was educated at a communist college?"

It was the British who were deceived and who are clearly accountable for helping Tito grab power. The Soviets were too far away to supply Tito during the decisive period—the year 1943 and the first nine months of 1944. But their agents were working overtime on Tito's behalf. So were, unfortunately, fellow travelers and gullible admirers in the West, including some in British government agencies and secret services. The deception had its origins in a Soviet-inspired and Soviet-orchestrated misinformation campaign started in 1942.

Once set on a course, Churchill was always hard to deflect. Evidently he began to lean strongly toward Tito early in 1943. The firm decision was reached at the end of 1943 when he ordered the abandonment of Mihailović after Tito issued the ultimatum: "It's him or me."

It seems incredible that a leader of Churchill's character and resolution could have let himself be steamrollered in this way.

After the decision was made, it had to be justified. Mihailović, the patriot and hero of 1941 and 1942, was first portrayed as ineffective, then as a collaborator. The communists provided "evidence" of Loyalist peccadilloes while concealing their own flagrant, large-scale strategic collaboration with the Germans. Only a month before the first British mission (team) had contacted them, three leading members of the Tito clique spent some weeks wining and dining the Germans in Sarajevo and Zagreb. The two sides had agreed on a truce to enable the communists to concentrate on the critical civil-war battle against the Četnik Loyalists on the Neretva River. In addition to the truce, the negotiators had discussed a strategic long-term plan whereby the Germans would help Tito to establish a free zone in the Sandžak Mountains to the west of Serbia, which was a Loyalist stronghold, in exchange for Partisan support against an expected Western Allied landing on the coast of Dalmatia. This plan was vetoed by Hitler personally. He refused to deal with "communist bandits." But the British leadership was about to do just that.

In May 1944 the Germans had mounted a parachute assault against Tito's headquarters, capturing his main base. It was only thanks to the prescience and quick action of Col. Vivian Street, the chief staff officer of the British mission to the Partisans, that Tito escaped capture. Together with his mistress and his dog, he was flown out to the British base at Brindisi, Italy. Although he was supposed to be a resistance leader, he was accommodated comfortably and safely under British military protection on the island of Vis. Vis was formally Yugoslav territory—a fact useful for face-saving purposes.

Tito expressed his gratitude in typical communist fashion—with contempt. Without a word to his British allies and protectors, he sneaked off one fine day in a Russian-piloted plane to Moscow in order to see the puppet master, Stalin. Tito's purpose was to have Red Army divisions diverted into Serbia to drive out the Axis troops, to forestall the Loyalists, and to pave the way for communist seizure of power in postwar Yugoslavia.

Having obtained Stalin's help, Tito became more aggressive toward his Western Allies every day. In the spring of 1945 he tried to annex Austrian and Italian territories. These efforts were thwarted, but they heralded the shape of things to come. Churchill's "great guerrilla" ally of 1943 had become Stalin's satellite of 1945. And there was nothing the Western Allies could do about it. By then Yugoslavia was safely behind the Iron Curtain, which had divided Europe and which permitted the new Red dictators to ply their despotic trade.

The train of events set in motion by the 1943 decision to ditch Mihailović and his Loyalist resistance was inexorable. The hoped-for united resistance of the Yugoslav peoples under Tito against the German occupation proved the bankrupt illusion it had always been. The massive Allied support given to Tito was used primarily to conquer the patriotic Loyalist bastion in the Serbian heartland. Serbs recruited or conscripted by Tito from outside Serbia fought their Serbian brothers while the German army carried out a more or less orderly withdrawal. Had the British directed all support to the Serbian Loyalists—or at least coordinated the two resistance movements so that they refrained from fighting each other—this orderly German retreat could never have been possible. But British policy now openly fostered civil war. The BBC, which had heralded Mihailović as a patriot and hero in 1941 and 1942, was already early in 1944 denouncing the Yugoslav Loyalist patriots as collaborators and traitors. The subsequent abandonment of the legitimate exiled royalist government, and of the monarchy itself, were the inevitable consequences.

In Moscow, Tito had solicited Stalin's help to draw in the Bulgarians, as well as the Soviet army, to suppress the Serbian Loyalists. The Bulgarian army, which had served the German occupation in Serbia since 1941, became "liberators" overnight.

By the spring of 1945 Churchill, at long last, was totally disillusioned with Tito. But he lost power to the Labour Party, and the incoming socialists had neither the time nor the inclination to worry about the end of a monarchy and the introduction of Soviet socialism in Yugoslavia. It was a long way away, and in May 1945 the Western mood was one of euphoria. The Soviets were still comrades in arms and allies. The West closed its eyes to the unpleasant developments in Eastern Europe.

In Belgrade, the communist government consolidated its totalitarian power, crushing all opposition. In true Marxist-Leninist style it then set about rewriting history to suit itself. In the West—and particularly in Britain—the supporters of the Tito regime wrote their heroic versions of what had happened, and their books became gospel. Titomania became literarily profitable. Over the years, through constant repetition, the myths and legends became accepted as fact. In Yugoslavia the few remaining Loyalists were hunted down. Dissent was silenced. The Tito lobby, inspired and fostered by the Belgrade communists but enthusiastically supported by their erstwhile Western sponsors, shouted down any other versions of history. All of the usual public-relations gimmicks were called into play. Symposiums were organized and packed with Tito sympathizers. The Loyalist case—and the simple truth—went by default.

This warping of history could not have persisted without the events of 1948. That was when Tito quarreled with Stalin. This rift in the Soviet united front had nothing to do with ideology but had everything to do with personalities. Tito simply got too big for his boots, and Stalin tried to slap him down. To Tito's good fortune—or maybe it was his brilliant political instinct—this occurred when the cold war was at its worst. Western vision, clouded by wishful thinking, saw a rift in the Iron Curtain that could be exploited. Tito received considerable financial and moral help from the West. The rift also gave an enormous boost to the Titoist public-relations machine in London, which immediately sprang into action, claiming that Tito's differences with Stalin were the direct result of the wartime support given to Tito by the West. Thus Titomania was revitalized. Yet any serious student of communism in general and Tito in particular realizes that Tito's split with Stalin was not derived from gratitude to the West. That claim is patently bogus.

The first cracks in the monolithic Titoist gospel appeared not in the West but in Belgrade itself, early in the 1950s. Milovan Djilas, one of Tito's closest collaborators in the wartime hierarchy and later a vice-president of Yugoslavia, turned revisionist. Vlada Dedijer, Tito's personal biographer, joined him. More recently Veselin Djuretić, a younger-generation historian, published a revealing work that explained precisely how Tito and his clique deceived the Western Allies. Still more recently, a war historian in Belgrade, Miso Leković, published a book entitled *The March Negotiations,* which recounts with amazing frankness details of Tito's collaboration with the Germans in 1943—precisely at the time that Churchill was being pressured to support the communist Partisans and abandon the Loyalists.

Yet in England, Titomania has persisted. As recently as January 1989 an eminent member of the Special Forces Club in London suggested that the portrait of "that traitor" Mihailović be taken down so as not to offend the Yugoslav ambassador. It might have been more in the spirit of these times to suggest that Tito's portrait be removed, for who's to say that he and his despotic regime will not become officially discredited in Belgrade, as is happening with Stalinism in Soviet Russia?

This book was born in 1986 when I first visited the British Public Records Office (PRO) in Kew Gardens, London. I had served with the Loyalist Četnik forces from June 1943 till May 1944. From my own experiences I knew that the Titoist gospel was grotesquely false. But the wall of sponsored Titoite propaganda was impenetrable. I, and the few other Britons who knew the truth and tried to tell it, were simply shouted down. Then I published my War memoirs, *British Operations Executed,* which I had actually written in 1949–50 and which told of my experiences in Serbia with the Loyalists. Because my account gave the lie to the accepted Titoite gospel, I felt it prudent to search the records for *official* documentation that would refute any attempt by the Ti-tomaniacs to discredit my story.

In the public records in Kew I found a gold mine. In Britain, secret-service records are classified and kept under wraps for an indefinite period. The secret services include the Special Intelligence Services (SIS), also known as MI6; the Counter-Intelligence Service (MI5), and the Special Operations Executive (SOE). In the PRO's War Office section, for reasons unexplained, there is a substantial batch of SOE Cairo files dealing with Yugoslavia during the key period—from September 1943 onward. These files seem to have slipped through the classification net. Ironically, they may well be unauthorized copies removed from the Cairo SOE office by James Klugmann. Klugmann was a British officer and an ardent communist, the man said by some to have recruited the notorious traitor Anthony Blunt for the NKVD (Narodnyi Komissariat Vnutrennikh Del) in the 1930s. He was most certainly a communist wartime mole.

Most importantly, these files contain a day-by-day operational log. It includes most of the signals exchanged between the missions (British teams) in Yugoslavia and the Cairo SOE headquarters. The log starts in September 1943 and continues into 1944. The files also contain most of the reports written by the SOE's British liaison officers (BLOs) on their assignments with both the Loyalists and the Partisans. They show policy memorandums and policy documents. I was able to find my own reports and signals, along with those of others, detailing sabotage successes and expressing bitter frustration at the lack of support and supplies given us operatives with Mihailović's Loyalists. I was able to see the difference between this shoddy treatment and that accorded our missions to Tito's Partisans. Reading these SOE files and the Foreign Office files that were released in the normal way, I was able to build up a very full picture of what really happened in 1943. This picture was enormously enhanced by a study of Churchill's own papers, which are filed under the name "Premier Series" in the PRO. These show very clearly how the British leader was misled. Most importantly, I found conclusive evidence of our missions being lied to by SOE Cairo, of deceptions, and of "dirty tricks."

In 1987 the British Cabinet Office decided to appoint an "official historian" to write a formal history of the SOE's activities in Yugoslavia during the war. The appointment was to be made by the cabinet office's chief mandarin, then Sir Robert Armstrong, who became famous for admitting, during litigation in Australia aimed at suppressing Peter Wright's book *Spycatcher*, that he had been "economical with the truth." Wright was telling about dirty tricks in MI5. The desperate efforts made to muzzle him gave me, and others interested in Yugoslavia, cause for concern that similar efforts might be made to cover up the appalling shenanigans that took place in SOE Cairo in 1943 and the almost unbelievable distortion of history that has been perpetrated ever since. One had the feeling that the British establishment would be relieved if the skeletons stayed in their cupboards, thus avoiding further public disillusionment about communist and fellow-traveler influence in the secret services.

But they are not going to. In one way or another the truth must out. The revelations in this book, shocking as they are, do not give the complete picture. That can come only from a study of *all* of the secret files. The official historian has access to them. Truth should be served.

The main purpose of this book is to right a terrible wrong. Mihailović was not a collaborator, as Tito and his British sponsors have repeatedly claimed. He was a true patriot—far more so than his communist rivals. Where he failed was in politics and public relations. In those fields he was totally outclassed by the Comintern-trained Tito and his mentor and master, Stalin. Tito won the Yugoslav civil war with the political help of the Soviets and their military presence in the autumn of 1944. But it is my own honest belief that he could never have done so without the British logistical help and recognition he received in 1943 and the first nine months of 1944. He was enormously aided by moles in the secret services and by self-serving or gullible British protagonists who set out deliberately to help—or were tricked into helping—Tito gain power. Above all, Tito was successful in catching Churchill's eye when the latter was in an adventuristic mood. Those who put Tito into power and their disciples may have wished to justify their actions, but in the name of humanity can't they shut up now? The pro-communist bandwagon has had its day. The widows and children of loyal, patriotic Serbian soldiers have had to live with the false allegations for more than forty years. It is time that they saw justice done. If the Soviet people deserve *glasnost,* can't we have it too?

The second purpose of this book is to record the truth for the sake of the future. At the time of writing Gorbimania is the order of the day. May he succeed in eradicating Stalinism and bring the Soviet people out of the evil darkness. But the West should have no illusions about the spymasters in the KGB. Those men are professionals paid their salaries to do a job. Their job certainly includes planting moles in our institutions ready for activation in five, ten, or twenty years' time.

There is still plenty of potential pro-Soviet material around in circles of woolly-headed elitists and among gullible or self-seeking individuals of all political hues. These dupes can be triggered to provide pro-Soviet background clamor should the Soviet leadership so desire. The gullibility of so many Western progressives did terrible harm in the Stalinist era. Can we not learn from past mistakes? Unrelenting watchfulness and hard-nosed skepticism are essential for the maintenance of our freedoms.

MISSION HENBURY/FUGUE

It was in March 1943 that I found myself a member of SOE Cairo, then known as MO4. I had literally talked my way into the organization. SOE Cairo security was abysmal at the time, and I heard of MO4 under the pseudonym of "the Tweed Cap Boys" from a drunken officer in the bar of Shepheard's Hotel. The barman, who knew it all, directed me to the MO4 offices. Fortuitously, I found that a colonel to whom I had an introduction in connection with a totally different matter worked for MO4. I visited him and learned that he was going away on operations. So I returned a few days later to MO4 and claimed that I had been introduced by him with a view to my recruitment into the organization. I was fobbed off twice. The third time it worked, and I found myself allocated to the Yugoslav section of MO4.

I had come from an airborne brigade and needed no parachute training. With other prospective agents I was sent on a course to Camp 102 at Ramat David near Haifa in Palestine. There we were instructed in the use of most of the small arms available during the war by a delightful, highly efficient, and virtually incomprehensible Pole, Stan Lazarewicz. We also had a very good practical series of classes in explosives and demolitions.

I was intrigued and a little disturbed, however, by the character and physical-fitness tests. On a night's forced march that was little more than a stroll for me, hardened as I was by the tough training in my parachute regiment, I was surprised to find that only 50 percent of the trainees completed the march—and that no one seemed particularly concerned. In another exercise, two-man teams were sent on the road with instructions to cover a little over 100 miles on foot in four days, stage a reconnaissance of secret installations en route, and, at the end of the march, break into a defended headquarters.

I was shocked that after two days my companion and I were the only two still following the route. The others had all hitched a lift home by then. My companion, a game but relatively old veteran of the First World War, went lame on the third day, and I finished the exercise alone, carrying out the break-in undetected. I had to telephone to be collected: the instructors had not expected anyone to finish. This lack of fitness and determination of the recruits appeared not to disturb the staff at all, and I found myself wondering whether I had been wrong in regarding the exercise as a test of determination and stamina. Perhaps, I thought, it had been a test of ingenuity and duplicity—in which case I was the only failure! Later, nothing surprised me in SOE. I frequently had cause to remember the words of Micky Thomas, second in command of the 156th Parachute Battalion, on hearing that I was joining MO4: "If you want to get yourself killed, Mike, that's your own affair, but don't cry if you get let down. These people have a very bad reputation for doing that if it suits them."

In Cairo the GSO2 (general staff officer grade 2) of the MO4 Yugoslav section was Maj. Basil Davidson, a tall, clean-cut, classically good-looking man, with considerable charisma. His appearance fitted the part. He seemed a straightforward staff officer, not a regular soldier but a good enough imitation of one. He briefed me in the most general terms. I had already taken a three-week crash course in Serbo-Croat, and my instructor had also given me quite a good background of the wartime developments in Yugoslavia. From Davidson I learned that I was to be dropped as a BLO into southern Yugoslavia, east of Priština, whence I was to travel south to Macedonia. I was to replace a Major Morgan, who had been dropped "blind" shortly before; that is, he had been dropped without a prearranged reception party. Morgan had disappeared and was presumed captured.

I learned that the guerrillas in my area formed part of the Loyalist Četnik organization based on the traditional Serbian Četnik village militia. They were loosely controlled by Gen. Draža Mihailović, the officially recognized national leader of the resistance forces in Yugoslavia.

I was given to understand that SOE policy was one of full support for Mihailović, who had been widely hailed as the first great leader of overt resistance to the Axis in occupied Europe. I learned that a considerable number of SOE missions were being dropped to his commanders throughout Serbia. The existence of other resistance groups not under Mihailović—outside Serbia and principally in Croatia and Slovenia—was mentioned only as background detail. I do remember some reference to communist "partisans" controlled by a leader called Tito.

In a last briefing Davidson and his intelligence officer, a Capt. F. W. D. Deakin (now Col. Sir William Deakin) indicated that there might be some of these "partisans" in Macedonia and that at some stage the question of helping them too might arise. But no mention was made of the communist Croats already being dropped as advance parties to make contact with Tito's Partisans in Slovenia and Croatia; this I did not learn about until more than forty years later. Of course, there was no mention either of the efforts then underway to make direct contact with Tito's main headquarters, which were at that time moving down into Montenegro from Bosnia.

I do remember very clearly that my briefing contained no reservations about continued full support of Mihailović and his Loyalist Četniks. Indeed, the whole atmosphere of my briefing made the possibility of the Allies changing horses in midstream unthinkable. I was told that serious aircraft shortages had inhibited support of Mihailović's forces, but that additional long-range Halifax bombers had been allocated and we could count on regular supplies and support. With the substantial number of missions dropping to Mihailović's commanders, and further proposed missions, we had no reason to doubt that we were part of an ongoing operation, with the straightforward task of supplying and training Loyalists in sabotage and demolitions and leading or assisting them in these operations. The political angle hardly came into my official briefing. Such political and historical knowledge as I took with me I obtained principally from my Serbo-Croat instructor.

It was also made rather clear to me that it was firm SOE policy to try to exert the direct control of SOE Cairo over the resistance movements, and even to take a degree of command where possible. General Mihailović was the formal leader of the Loyalist forces throughout Yugoslavia, and the British had a colonel attached to him, but we were given no signal plans for communicating with the British mission at his headquarters; all of our communications were to be funneled through the Yugoslav section in Cairo, to which we would report and to which we would be responsible.

Captain Deakin, Major Davidson's second in command in the Yugoslav section in Cairo, was an unobtrusive and quiet-spoken individual, evidently an intellectual. The third member, then a lieutenant but shortly to be promoted to captain, was a rotund, rather scruffily turned-out individual, James Klugmann. Klugmann, seemingly a very human person, fussed around us like a mother hen. He was charming, solicitous, and enormously helpful in tending to all our needs: for louse powder, for cyanide suicide pills, for secret maps, and for any other paraphernalia that we required or that he thought to be necessary. Walking around with a cigarette permanently attached to his lower lip, he inspired great affection and had an encyclopedic knowledge of almost every subject. I was flabbergasted later when I learned of his true affiliations and the utter ruthlessness of his underlying character.

Before setting out on my mission, I met the two senior officers at SOE in Cairo: Col. Guy Tamplin, who by coincidence had been in my regiment, the Queen's Own Dorset Yeomanry, and Brig. C. M. "Bolo" Keble, the chief of operations of SOE, a bouncy, domineering individual who gave me a pep talk. It all seemed very straightforward and very military, and had I thought back to Micky Thomas's warning, I would probably have wondered what the hell he was moaning about.

I gathered together my team, and, one of nine or so such missions, we traveled up to Derna, boarded a Halifax, and dropped into Serbia on the moonlit night of June 1 or 2, 1943. We started our adventure in blissful ignorance of the turmoil going on just below the surface in the Yugoslav section of MO4.

THE PARTISAN-ČETNIK MO4 OFFICE WAR

Forty-two years after my drop into Serbia I read a rather offensive review of Nora Beloff's perceptive book *Tito's Flawed Legacy* in *The New Statesman*. The review, by the selfsame Basil Davidson, the handsome and charismatic staff officer in charge of the Yugoslav section of MO4 in the spring of 1943, angered me so much that I started a study of just what had happened in Yugoslavia in 1943 and, perhaps more importantly, just what MO4 in Cairo had been up to in orchestrating events.

On my mission to Yugoslavia I had, of course, experienced the cataclysmic changes that occurred there, though Tito's communist Partisans were only in very limited evidence in Serbia. I had already left the Balkans when the communist takeover of the country was consummated, substantially aided by the Red Army as in Poland, and only rumors of the misery and massacres that marred the liberation from Axis control reached me. Then, in the summer of 1946, I learned with sadness of the hunting down in the mountains, the mock trial, and the subsequent execution of General Mihailović. The chase had taken more than a year despite the desperate efforts of OZNA, Tito's secret police, to eliminate Mihailović as a possible focus of revolt. From afar I watched the Stalinization of Yugoslav society. I also observed, with regret but without surprise, the anti-Western stand taken by Tito in the years immediately after the war—so removed from the almost embarrassingly strong pro-British attitude of the people of Serbia in 1943. Stalinization in the guise of Titoism made Yugoslavia in those years as antidemocratic as any country in the Soviet bloc.

When Tito squabbled with Stalin in 1948 and Yugoslavia became isolated from her communist allies, I watched the astute manner in which Tito reharnessed his wartime connections with the West, again taking advantage of Western and, in particular, British gullibility until thirty years later he had successfully extracted some 20 billion dollars from Western banks while giving nothing in return. Instead he became, like Cuba's Castro, a fomenter of anti-Western trouble in the Third World.

Over the years I observed the whole sorry story unfold, but until Basil Davidson's review, which reawakened my interest, I had never really appreciated what caused it all. Then I happened to come across Davidson's 1980 book *Special Operations Europe*. While I could not help admiring the wit and vividness of Davidson's style, my overall reaction was a mixture of surprise, fury, and disgust. With horror at my own gullibility I recoiled at his flippant account of the shenanigans that had occurred in the Yugoslav section of MO4 in the last weeks of 1942, just before I joined. I realized with revulsion that these shenanigans must have been still reverberating as my team and others were dispatched by Cairo to the Četniks as if nothing had occurred and no changes were planned.

Unbeknown to me and, I believe, to most or all of the others subsequently sent off to join Mihailović, the leading figures of the Yugoslav section, together with the director of operations, Brigadier Keble, had pulled off a major coup over the heads of the entire intervening hierarchy. They had enlisted the help of

Churchill himself, who was on a visit to Cairo, and obtained his direct authority to modify the policy of giving support exclusively to the Yugoslav government in exile and its minister of war, General Mihailović. They obtained Churchill's permission to take up contact with Tito.

To contact other resistance groups and particularly those outside Serbia, the home ground of the Mihailović Loyalists, was entirely reasonable. It was the motivation, the manner, and the atmosphere of the doing of it that appalled me in Davidson's account.

In fifty stunning pages, Davidson tells his version of what he calls the "Partisan-Četnik struggle" in Rustem Buildings, the headquarters of SOE Cairo, then known as MO4. It appears from his story that there was an in-house war involving a large number of staff of all ranks: from the strange, old-fashioned archivist, Miss Flannery, from her brash opponent in the filing department, a senior sergeant, right up to the chief of staff in charge of operations, Brigadier Keble himself. Although Davidson modestly describes himself only as "a well-marked Partisan supporter," his account indicates that he either was orchestrating this office struggle or at least would like the reader to think that he was doing so, and that he was ably supported by Captain Deakin and, in particular, by Lieutenant Klugmann. But the biggest joker in the pack was Brigadier Keble himself, who had been placed in charge of the operational sections of SOE Cairo late in 1942.

In my opinion Davidson shows himself in this book and other postwar writings to be unashamedly—indeed, proudly—of a strongly left-wing persuasion. Nevertheless, he attaches no political virtue to Keble's espousal of the Partisan cause. Indeed, he attributes to Keble much baser motives, namely, ruthless exploitation of the situation in order to further personal ambition. Davidson claims that Deakin was already in 1942 in favor of helping the Partisans. Moreover, Klugmann was evidently a major factor in this whole situation, as is hardly surprising.

The evident objective of the "Partisan protagonists" in MO4 was to switch support from "that silly old goat Mihadge-lo-vitch," as Miss Flannery described the Yugoslav commander in chief, to

Tito. It is clear from Davidson's book, if not from the mass of other circumstantial but convincing evidence, that the atmosphere in SOE Cairo in the closing weeks of 1942, and in particular the attitudes of the individuals directly involved in the Yugoslav section, were fundamental to what happened in Yugoslavia itself in 1943 and constituted a major factor in shaping the future of Yugoslavia and indeed of the entire Balkans.

SOE security at the time was a sham. How otherwise could I have talked my way in? But SOE, like its sister organization SIS, also known as MI6, was a top-secret outfit. Its memorandums and reports were restricted to the highest military and political levels, and, as tends to happen in such circumstances, they acquired a gospel authenticity that, "on security grounds," could not be questioned.

There was a compelling mystique about all of the secret organizations that made it possible for almost anything to be said and done without accountability; and the attribution to "most secret sources"—a euphemism for SIS—allowed tendentious and politically devious material to be fed into the intelligence reports and into the decision-making machine by those who had a mind to do so. These included not only those dedicated Soviet moles such as the infamous Kim Philby—at that time an influential member of SIS—and left-wing agents of lesser standing in the socialist hierarchy, but also what one might call amateurs in the left-wing progressive political spectrum. Yet even today "most secret sources" wartime memorandums, which make dogmatic assertions without supporting evidence, are quoted by historians as "fact."

An example of this "top-secret" mystique begetting unchallenged historical "fact" is the story that Keble was privy to deciphered German signals that revealed the great importance and massive anti-Axis activity of the Partisans and collaboration with the Germans by the Četniks. Keble certainly did receive some intercepts, but nowhere can be found precise detail of what they contained or how the wide-sweeping conclusions were reached. We do not know whether there were other intercepts proving the opposite. Nor is there a plausible explanation of how Keble managed to get on the superexclusive circulation list for these deciphered signals. Even to this day the original signals are not available, and we are simply told the conclusions as indisputable facts. Over the years these "facts" have been repeated and fed into history and have thus become accepted as gospel. The "evidence" of the intercepts was the decisive argument used by the pro-Partisan faction in Cairo in January 1943. According to Davidson, it was the major factor in Captain Deakin's talk with the prime minister, to which I will shortly refer. Careful study of this segment of history will show that wherever there is a lacuna in logic, nebulous "intercepts" are traded out as the clinching argument.

I have gone to some trouble to delve into the question of the intercepts. It is still largely a closed book, but the little I glean from persons involved leads me to question very strongly indeed the significance attributed to this material in relation to Yugoslavia. I have been told that only about six "Enigma" signals—so named for the German coding machine, the secrets of which were discovered by the Allies—relating to Yugoslavia were translated and circulated. It is hardly conceivable that six signals—or indeed sixty—not dealing directly with the subject from a political-analysis viewpoint but only with German troop movements and the effect on them of resistance activity, could have built up a picture on which major decisions affecting strategic plans could be based.

Basil Davidson makes no secret at all of his loyalties in Cairo's Partisan-Četnik conflict. I do not impute base motives to him. I am sure he was convinced that the Partisans were the people to back and that it was his military duty to do so. After all, he stated in an interview with the Yugoslav paper *Danas*, "Any national liberation movement must also be a revolutionary movement. A movement that is not revolutionary is in its essence not liberational: it just exchanges one yoke for another." If what took place later in 1943 in Cairo was wrong, tragically wrong—as it is the purpose of this book to reveal—it was more a question of the wrong men for the job, and of course a lack of control and abysmal lack of security in MO4. Nonetheless, the main responsibility for the decisive first act in this office play must surely be attached to Basil Davidson.

Davidson's book reveals what led to Churchill's dramatic modification of the Yugoslav policy when he passed through Cairo in January 1943. Davidson tells us that "several facts appear." He states that Captain Deakin, Davidson's immediate subordinate in the Yugoslav section, was a personal friend of Churchill, knew all of the information in the intercepts, and was in favor of helping the Partisans. As regards his own role, Davidson says that he discussed an idea with Deakin: "One cannot order one's junior to go to the prime minister over all the intervening hierarchy, but there is no law against encouraging two friends to meet; nor is there any limit, if one of them happens to be prime minister, upon what they may legitimately talk about."

Davidson goes on to explain that, following a social meeting with Deakin, Churchill sent for Brigadier Keble, who handed the prime minister a memorandum. Davidson does not state it explicitly, but it seems rather likely that he, or Deakin and he together, wrote the memorandum, which, in Davidson's words, was "shrewdly composed." It recommended that the British go on supporting Mihailović and the Četniks in Serbia but that support be given to other evidently effective resistance forces in other parts of Yugoslavia, notably Slovenia and Croatia, which deserved support and were getting none. It was suggested that this move was desirable in order to preempt the Russians or Americans taking an interest in them, and that for this purpose the allocation of more long-range aircraft to support SOE's "four limping Liberators" was necessary.

As Davidson states, the memorandum itself, which appears in the Public Records Office in Kew under reference FO 37579, was not an alarming document. But that was not the point of it! Indeed, that was not the point of this charade at all.

The document seemed to be based solely on the desire to solicit the prime minister's intervention in order to obtain sorely needed aircraft. Almost certainly that was the main motivation in Keble's mind. But, in my opinion, for the key Partisan sympathizers in Cairo—and surely for the communist Klugmann—it involved something of much greater importance. It represented the thin end of the wedge: an authorization to contact Tito's communist Partisans under the guise of supporting "other effective resistance forces in Croatia and Slovenia" in addition to Mihailović and his Loyalists in Serbia.

Of subtler—but eventually just as great—significance was the reestablishment of a working relationship between Churchill and Deakin, right over the heads of the proper channels.

Above all, this meeting effectively demonstrated Churchill's intent to take over supervision of the Yugoslav file. As is well known, Churchill had a particular, almost sentimental attachment to the Balkans, stemming perhaps from his Gallipoli involvement in the First World War; and his South African experiences made any guerrilla operation a matter of interest to him. He was an adventurist by nature, and he had recently been dissuaded by his chief of the general staff, later Viscount Alanbrooke, from a rash plan to invade Norway. The Yugoslav affair must have fascinated him; it was the only war theater with substantial guerrilla activity at that stage.

To what extent Churchill's assumption of a degree of direct interest in SOE Yugoslav affairs was realized by Lord Glenconner, the titular and political head of the Special Operations Executive in Cairo, and by SOE London headquarters is not clear. But it is from this point on that SOE London and the Foreign Office increasingly became mere spectators on the scene. If Davidson's account is true—and there is no reason to doubt it—the real center of developments became the self-propelled operational Yugoslav section in Cairo, under the orders of the chief of operations, Brigadier Keble. The section became increasingly the self-nominated champion of the Tito Partisans and underminer of "that silly old goat Mihadge-lo-vitch" and his Loyalists.

For 1943, the year of decision, the Foreign Office files in the Public Records Office are massive. They contain detailed memorandums and discussions of all aspects of the Yugoslav situation. Decisions were taken, advice was sent, protests were made, conclusions were reached. But much of this was futile and superfluous, removed from reality. The real game was being played out by MO4, which exercised remarkable influence over political and military developments through its control of its missions and through encouragement, or de facto recognition, of one or the other of the resistance groups. MO4 had day-to-day control over the allocation of the drops of stores, arms, and communications equipment; it also determined the priority given to agents' messages by the cipher department. A comparison of the PRO's SOE files with the Foreign Office files leads to the conclusion that many times, on many matters, the Foreign Office did not even know what SOE Cairo was doing. SOE Cairo decided what to tell the Foreign Office, and more often than not Cairo was plowing its own distinctive furrow.

The Minister of State's Office in Cairo was charged with representing the interests of the Foreign Office and the British Cabinet. From the attitude the Minister of State's Office adopted throughout 1943, as reflected in the Foreign Office files, it must have gotten the message loud and clear that the Yugoslav section in MO4 was following a line agreed with, and based on the authority of, the prime minister. In January the key meetings with Churchill took place under the auspices of the minister of state, and we have only to guess that he, too, got a nod and a wink from the Great Man.

At this stage of affairs the wishes of the military had little bearing on the picture. And where Lord Glenconner fitted into the unofficial but very real pattern is not clear. It would probably not be far from the mark to conclude that his role was largely decorative; his name was used where convenient, and he got no credit but was useful for taking the knocks.

Thus the Partisan sympathizers had a fair wind.

THE PERSONALITIES AND THEIR IMPACT ON EVENTS

Although at a later stage other personalities and organizations became dominant in the British role in Yugoslavia, as will be clear already from my account of the direct contact established with Prime Minister Churchill by Captain Deakin and Brigadier Keble in the last days of January 1943, MO4 and its Yugoslav section exerted a profound influence on what happened in enemy-occupied Yugoslavia during the decisive period. This was the ten months between early February and December 10, 1943. During this relatively short span British policy switched from one of recognizing the Yugoslav resistance forces commanded by the minister of defense, General Mihailović, to completely abandoning them and throwing massive support behind Tito's previously outlawed communist movement.

A small handful of people in MO4 had a profound influence on these developments. In this section I delineate the dramatis personae and the manner in which they affected events.

Deakin: Churchill's Protégé

Fate placed F. W. D. "Bill" Deakin in the hot seat in Yugoslavia. He has also himself contributed significantly to the historical record. As Churchill's literary secretary, he had helped to research the prime minister's historical book on the duke of Marlborough and had evidently made a favorable impression. After joining SOE London, Deakin was sent to America in 1941 to organize anti-Axis work in Latin America. This work was vetoed by U.S. authorities and Deakin returned to London.

In November 1942 Deakin was sent to Cairo. The plan was to drop him into Yugoslavia to discover the identity of resistance bands outside Serbia "hopefully organised by the non-Communist Croat peasant party and by Mihailović's commander in Slovenia, Novak," as Deakin himself wrote later. There was no plan, and no authority at this time, to drop British liaison officers to other resistance groups. That first came in a directive to SOE by the chiefs of staff in March 1943. To prepare for such a widening of the field, however, was a natural and prudent measure.

Following the Deakin-Keble approach to Churchill in Cairo, the prime minister on his return to London gave orders on February 12 to Lord Selborne, the cabinet minister responsible for SOE, that he considered it "a matter of the greatest importance" to establish the desired closer contacts with the other Yugoslav leaders. To quote again from Davidson: "With, that is, the leaders of the Partisans whose locations we had fixed on the map we had assembled from the SD [Sicherheitsdienst, the German intelligence service] intercepts."

Those "Partisans" were, of course, the communist Partisans, and the leader was Tito, as was already known to those concerned.

Davidson writes that while the Foreign Office might have been "considering" contact with the Partisans, Keble in Cairo was doing a lot more than mere considering. If guerrilla war in the Balkans needed "tuning up," he knew how to do it. Besides, Keble possessed from the prime minister an authority to go ahead and do it that nothing could cancel as long as the order was not withdrawn: "And it was not withdrawn."

Indeed it was not. Churchill was so hooked on the idea that he informed the Turkish foreign minister of his plans even before he advised SOE London and the War Cabinet.

In April, the first exploratory missions were dropped into Croatia, and one of them quickly made contact with a Partisan headquarters. Tito indicated his willingness to receive a British mission, and Captain Deakin was selected to represent SOE. He parachuted into Yugoslavia and made contact with Tito's headquarters on May 28, 1943.

Basil Davidson tells us that Deakin was pro-Partisan already at the end of 1942—*before* his January 1943 meeting with Churchill. When I put this to him in correspondence in 1988, Deakin replied, "As to my being pro-Partisan this could be fairly said after the first British mission to Tito—in the military sense. . . ." Deakin also advised me that "as to my views on Yugoslav matters in early 1943 Basil Davidson's book is not a gospel source."

At the start Deakin may not have been as dedicated a member of the pro-Partisan movement in Cairo as Davidson implied, and his role may have been limited to carrying out Davidson's instructions. But this is not the impression one gains from Davidson's book. He paints his pictures in striking colors, and Deakin appears in a central role.

Surprisingly, in his own book *The Embattled Mountain,* Deakin makes no reference to approaching Churchill on behalf of the Cairo Partisan faction. He mentions Churchill's decision to increase the number of aircraft available to SOE, but there is no word about meeting with the prime minister or enlisting his help in authorizing contact with the Partisans. Rather, Deakin states that the decision to "make contacts in Partisan territory" was made by the British general headquarters in Cairo on March 23 and that it was not even known where the main headquarters of the Partisan movement were situated. Davidson, by contrast, states specifically that the identity and location of the Partisans were known from SD intercepts.

It is all very confusing. Deakin's January meeting with Churchill was perhaps the most decisive factor in determining the future of Yugoslavia. Yet it merited no mention in his book. Is that not taking modesty a little too far?

The waters are further muddied by this passage from Deakin's book: "By chance I had written a personal note through our Embassy in Cairo to Mr. Churchill, with whom I had worked as literary secretary before the war, merely telling him that I was about to leave on a mission to Yugoslavia." The context implies that the note was written in May, not January, and that it constituted Deakin's first approach to the prime minister. That's even more confusing.

This personal note precipitated the Algiers incident, which demonstrated the extraordinary situation that had developed following Churchill's visit to Cairo and the assumption by MO4 that it had been given carte blanche.

On receipt of Deakin's letter, Churchill, who was preparing to visit North Africa in June, promptly asked that Deakin come to Algiers to report to him on affairs in Yugoslavia. The Minister of State's Office had to advise Algiers that Deakin had just dropped into Yugoslavia, but it used the opportunity to forward two memorandums—emanating from MO4—for the prime minister's personal attention. These memorandums, in Deakin's words, "implied a clear departure from existing policy of exclusive support for Mihailović."

But this, too, is an odd statement, because the policy of exclusive support for Mihailović had already been abandoned in January by fiat of the prime minister. The abandonment was the victory of the pro-Partisan side in the Cairo office war.

These two memorandums, which were known only to MO4

and the Minister of State's Office, went much further. They hammered in the wedge put in place in January. So radical was the proposed further change of policy implied that Desmond Morton, the prime minister's intelligence advisor, actually blocked the papers before they could get to Churchill.

This incident created an uproar in the Foreign Office. It demonstrated very dramatically the independent line being taken by SOE Cairo at the operational level as a result of the unofficial "authority" given to Keble by Churchill and MO4's broad interpretation of that authority. It also demonstrated the support given them in this action by the Minister of State's Office. It reflected the evident nod and wink given by Churchill to the minister of state in January indicating his personal desire to back the Partisans and if necessary to ignore the views of the proper channels, namely, the Foreign Office and the military chiefs.

The message to the prime minister that his erstwhile literary secretary was in Yugoslavia reinforced his interest in the Yugoslav situation, and he called for regular news of Deakin's progress. For his part, Deakin started sending eulogistic signals about the Partisans' prowess. These signals, or the main contents of them, went to the prime minister. Inevitably, a momentum developed. While credit (or perhaps, better said, the main responsibility) must go to Basil Davidson for initiating and winning the Partisan-Četnik office war in Cairo, at this stage Deakin effectively took over the baton. Operating mostly in the background, he became a key, and frequently *the* key, figure in the British sponsorship of the Partisan movement and thus of the communist takeover in Yugoslavia. He has also remained a key influence in the unquestioning support given by historical and academic circles in England to the Belgrade public-relations machine in its propagation of the myths and legends created by the Tito movement.

Vane Ivanović, a Yugoslav shipowner, consul general for Monaco in London, and a man of stature, has written very succinctly about Deakin's role in obtaining recognition of Tito as the leader of Yugoslav resistance and in the creation of the subsequent historical record. In his book *Memoirs of a Yugoslav* he acknowledges his personal friendship for and indebtedness to Deakin, with whom he attended school at Westminster. He clearly wishes to be very fair. He states that it was unquestionably Deakin who was decisive in persuading Churchill to initiate the shift in policy in January 1943 and to authorize an independent mission to the Partisans "without reference to SOE London." He goes on to point out that Deakin's subsequent reports were based exclusively on Partisan sources except for what he himself saw in the Mount Durmitor battle—"in which he acquitted himself valiantly." Ivanović goes on to point out that "Whatever its reliability, it was Deakin's military information and assessment that Maclean [Brig. Fitzroy Maclean] accepted in toto when he arrived at Partisan headquarters in the following September for his first stay, for, then, by his own account in *Eastern Approaches,* he himself saw no warfare."

It was following this first stay of less than three weeks that Maclean recommended to Churchill not only that the Partisans be given massive support but also that the Allies abandon Mihailović.

Deakin wrote of his own December 1943 report to Churchill, "As I talked I knew that I was compiling the elements of a hostile brief which would play a decisive part in any future break between the British government and Mihailović." But Deakin was reporting to Churchill what he had learned from Tito Partisan sources. And Tito wanted Mihailović abandoned and liquidated at all costs because he represented the one obstacle that could prevent Tito from snatching power after the war.

Ivanović writes further, "I cannot, especially writing today, dismiss this evidence that the military evaluation so made by Deakin and Maclean (through which the meanest intelligence staff officer could have driven a coach and four) was, or could have been, the SOLE ground for the acceptance of the partisans as a fully fledged fighting force. The whole operation reminds one of the Runciman mission sent to Czechoslovakia before Munich in 1938."

Following his return to Cairo in early December 1943, where he again met Churchill, Deakin became head of the Yugoslav section of MO4, then renamed Force 133. Later he dealt with

Yugoslav affairs, advising the new, specially formed, British-commanded Balkan Air Force and working with the political representative of the commanding officer of the Allied Mediterranean Forces. The base headquarters of the Maclean mission with Tito, then called 37 Military Mission, and the Yugoslav section of SOE also came under operational command of the Balkan Air Force in June 1944. So Deakin remained very much at the heart of Yugoslav affairs.

Subsequently Deakin went to Belgrade, where he became first secretary with the British embassy. To quote from Ivanović again:

> He stayed, I think, till the end of 1945, if not longer. During this period the newly formed Tito government disregarded all the promises made to the British and other Allied Governments to let the peoples of Yugoslavia choose their postwar Constitution or Government. . . . Perhaps Foreign Office documents of the period, still to be released, will throw light on Deakin's own role in Belgrade at that time, so decisive for us in the consolidation of Communist power.
>
> There has been no symposium or discussion in Great Britain or elsewhere in Europe on the role of SOE in the last war in which Deakin has not taken a prominent part. In each of these, the version of events in Yugoslavia that has been aired is that of the victorious pro-partisan faction inside SOE. On the British side, I have not come across any views or interpretations of the other side within SOE.
>
> If any individuals on the British side can be selected as decisive in the choice of the Partisans as the guerrilla force to be backed, they are Churchill and Deakin. The dogged and the pitiless role of carrying this policy through to the bitter end was Maclean's.

Maybe Vane Ivanović underestimates the role of Davidson, a more dominant character and, according to my reading of his book, the initiator of the Cairo Partisan-Četnik office war. He was also Deakin's superior officer at the time. Whatever Deakin's influence was with Churchill and whatever pitiless role was played by Maclean later, to Davidson must—on the basis of his own account—go the prime credit of it all. The irony of it is that Maclean was accorded very special recognition by Tito. Deakin, who—as Ivanović points out—did a great deal for the Tito regime both during and after the war, has had only limited recognition, while the man who seems to have started it all, Basil Davidson, has received the least of the three.

Davidson spent about fifteen months in a nerve-wracking British liaison officer's job in a really dangerous area. Deakin spent a few spectacular weeks in the Mount Durmitor battle but saw little more fighting. And Maclean's books reveal that he saw very little action at all with the Partisans. His job was mostly at the high headquarters level. Grounds for thought?

Klugmann and His Canadian Communist Croats

James Klugmann attended Gresham's, one of the smaller British public schools. Also at Gresham's at various times were Donald Maclean, later to become a notorious traitor, and two other very conventional, apolitical individuals. The first, Terence Airey, was to become Gen. Sir Terence, a distinguished soldier. The other, Archie Jack, had only a brief association with Gresham's, in that he attended its preparatory school, but it is intriguing to bring in his name here because it was he who, in September and October 1943, carried out with Mihailović Loyalist help the demolition of five railway bridges, including the 450-foot single-span bridge over the Drina River near Višegrad. This really important sabotage took place at a time that Klugmann, in MO4, was doing his utmost to paint Mihailović as a collaborator and replace him with his communist rival Tito.

After Gresham's, Klugmann gained a double first in modern languages at Cambridge University. Intellectually he was brilliant. He was also a dedicated member of the Communist Party. He joined in 1933 and remained in the party until his death in 1977. He was the main architect and organizer of the left-wing student movement, and not only in Cambridge. With Guy Burgess, the spy, he recruited for the Oxford communist cell as well. He was also secretary of the Rassemblement Mondial des Étudiants (the Student World Assembly) based in Paris, and in this role he became involved in recruiting for the International Brigades, the military units formed to serve with the republican forces in the Spanish Civil War and comprising idealists, socialists, and a strong sprinkling of communists.

Klugmann's activities have been dealt with extensively by Andrew Boyle in *The Climate of Treason,* by Barrie Penrose and Simon Freeman in *Conspiracy of Silence,* and by many others who have written about the Cambridge set. It is clear from their accounts that he was not only an overt communist, he was also a central figure in putting together the covert communist organization that penetrated the British secret agencies and even the Foreign Service. He acted as recruiting sergeant for David Haden-Guest, a dominant figure in the extreme left-wing circles at Cambridge. He worked closely with Burgess, and it has been claimed that together they recruited Anthony Blunt, who later turned traitor. Klugmann was also close to Donald Maclean, both at Gresham's and at Cambridge. Klugmann's sister Kitty was engaged to Maurice Cornforth, another well-known left-winger, and there is a story that she acted as communist courier carrying messages to her brother in her panties. Among many others he allegedly recruited was John Cairncross, who worked for General Communications Headquarters (GCHQ) on intercepts and for SIS on Yugoslav affairs. Klugmann was no dilettante playing at communism because it was fashionable. He was a professional, totally dedicated and enormously hardworking. He may have been the best man the Soviets had, even including Philby, because he had no weak spots. He was outwardly charming and human, but inwardly he was a hard man.

Klugmann went to Cairo as an enlisted soldier in the Pioneer Corps, the British army's auxiliary labor force. Whether his open membership in the Communist Party prevented him from gaining a commission earlier, I do not know. There is a story that a fire at Wormwood Scrubs destroyed official records that classified him. In Cairo he was spotted by Terence Airey, working in the Special Intelligence Branch, who recognized Klugmann's brilliance and helped him gain a commission in SOE in February 1942. He made captain in May 1943 and major in the spring of 1944, when he was transferred to Bari, Italy.

He was the one staff officer involved in policy, intelligence, and operational briefings who remained in the Yugoslav section throughout. He was in a key position dealing with the British liaison officers and their signals, supplies, and reports. After Davidson left in August 1943, Klugmann must have been greatly in demand to advise higher authority and to draft top-level memorandums. He was the anchor pin of the section with his unrivaled background knowledge and his remarkable intellectual and linguistic abilities.

Basil Davidson, in his review of Nora Beloff's book, poured scorn on the theory that Klugmann could have had any influence on the decision to contact the Partisans: "That . . . a second lieutenant could have exercised any operational influence whatsoever is almost as daft as supposing that the 'key people' were engaged in subversive conspiracy." But the former proposition is not daft at all, as Davidson himself made abundantly clear in *Special Operations Europe*. In this epic of the bureaucratic war in SOE Cairo we meet James Klugmann already on page 83, and the following four pages are devoted to what can only be described as eulogy extolling the intellectual capacity, the politics, and the key role of James Klugmann. Writes Davidson: "It could even be called the Klugmann period and it changed a great deal."

Klugmann reappears for the whole of page 100, then on pages 111, 112, and 114. We are told of the strange friendship—considering the difference in rank—between Keble and Klugmann. On page 122, Klugmann the lieutenant is pushed into the lavatory by Keble the brigadier to hide him from security personnel, who are looking for him for some unspecified reason. It's hardly the story of someone without influence.

Apart from making himself useful as the source of all knowledge, Klugmann was very special because it was he who was looking after the Canadian communist Croats. Now this is one of the SOE mysteries that I have struggled to unravel without total success. British policy until January 1943 was firmly linked to the exclusive support of the Loyalist forces of General Mihailović. There was no authority to have anything to do with other forces until Churchill's Cairo visit in January 1943, and there was not even any discussion of backing the communist-led Partisans before mid-1942. Yet at the end of 1941 Col. S. W. Bailey, an old hand who had been in SOE from the beginning and with its predecessor organization in Yugoslavia before the German invasion, goes off to North America and rapidly gets caught up in a program of recruiting Croatian-born members of the Communist Party from the Canadian mining community. In this he worked closely with the Canadian Communist Party and its general secretary, Tim Buck. A special SOE training camp, called Camp X, had been set up in Canada, and these Croatian communists were trained there for dropping into Yugoslavia.

This recruitment was intended to bring in one hundred recruits. In the end about thirty went off to Cairo. They immediately came under the control and assiduous care of James Klugmann. Davidson says the Croats idolized Klugmann.

Helping Colonel Bailey in Canada was Capt. William Stuart. Stuart had been in the British consulate in Zagreb before the war. In Canada he was recruiting the Croats for SIS. He was dropped into Yugoslavia together with Captain Deakin. He was killed by a bomb a few days later. Deakin and Tito were both slightly wounded by the same bomb.

Stuart was replaced in Canada late in 1942 by another SIS man, Maj. Robert Lethbridge, who gave his name to the Lethbridge Mission, a villa in Cairo where the Croatian communists were subsequently housed. This setup was looked after by James Klugmann, and he was helped by Didi Stuart, Captain Stuart's widow. "Lethbridge" is also the classification given in the Public Records Office in Kew to the batch of SOE files that, mysteriously, landed there through War Office channels and thus became released to the public under the Thirty-Year Rule when the main SOE files remained classified, and still so remain. It seems probable that these were actually Klugmann's own copies. They start around September 1943, that is, just after Basil Davidson left on a mission and at the time that Klugmann moved up a peg in the Yugoslav section hierarchy. They are relatively comprehensive. If these were indeed Klugmann's files, that confirms not only that MO4 security was lax but also that Klugmann was in an absolutely key position in the MO4 organization from September 1943 onward.

As I mentioned earlier, Captain Deakin was in New York on another mission early in 1942, and Vane Ivanović, in his *Memoirs of a Yugoslav*, states that Deakin was working with Bailey and Stuart in Canada on the recruitment of the young communists of Croat origin. Surprisingly, in a recent letter to me Deakin categorically denied having any knowledge of "the Canadian project" until he learned of it in Cairo at the end of 1942—though he had met Bailey and Stuart in New York earlier that year.

Deakin was in SOE London after returning from New York. It is strange that he learned nothing of the Canadian communist Croat recruitment even in London. But the whole affair was so alien to official policy that one wonders whether anyone in London knew of it.

The first recruits arrived at Camp X on July 22, 1942. Allowing for the establishment of relations with Tim Buck, the Communist Party leader, the project must have been thought up sometime in the spring of 1942, if not earlier. There had indeed been a plan in 1941 in SOE London to recruit former Yugoslav members of the International Brigade who had ceased to be communists, in order to send them on a mission to find out who Tito really was.

But such a plan would not encompass the recruitment of the communist Croats. These men had not been serving in the International Brigades in Spain. They were mostly miners who had emigrated to Canada. Furthermore, they had not ceased to be communists. On the contrary, they remained fervent members of the party.

Although Klugmann became their minder in Cairo, the decision to recruit them was taken elsewhere, in London or conceivably in Canada, and certainly not by Klugmann or for that matter by Keble or Davidson. The project is said to have been one of the subjects of a secret meeting on August 8, 1942, involving SOE, SIS, and the Foreign Office. But recruits were already in the pipeline long before then. Had someone, somewhere, planned it all a long way ahead? If so, on whose authority? There was certainly no authorization through the proper channels to recruit a whole raft of communists at a time when the British government was committed to supporting the Loyalists.

The new Croatian government's genocide program against the Serbs in 1941 had caused the question of Serbian-Croatian relations to become highly sensitive both within Yugoslavia and outside. Mihailović's movement was predominantly Serb. The recruitment of communist Croats raised an explosive ethnic question in an already touchy political situation. Bailey must have known this, as must have SOE London.

SIS, was, of course, most secret. It was a pure intelligence organization, supposedly without political function. But in fact it was deeply penetrated by communists and communist sympathizers. The Yugoslav desk of SIS in its Broadway headquarters in London, known as ISLD (Inter-Services Liaison Department), was occupied by John Ennals. The Cairo desk of ISLD was manned by James Miller. Both Ennals and Miller had been at Cambridge in the 1930s. Ennals, for one, was very forthright about his allegiance. When he left his desk job at ISLD to drop into Yugoslavia, he said he felt his task had been completed. It had, indeed. Yugoslavia had been secured for communism by then.

It is just conceivable that a plan to recruit Croats—of any persuasion—was formulated at SIS and later expanded to include SOE. It is also conceivable that Bailey in his muddled way drifted into looking for *communist* Croats, as the easiest to recruit, on his own responsibility. Bailey's vagaries and arbitrary nature are striking. More on this later.

The mass recruitment of the Canadian communist Croats remains a puzzle and raises unanswered questions. If it was not part of a sinister plan, then someone, somewhere, apart from Bailey was being very maladroit. Who thought of the plan? Why? And who authorized it? These questions remain unanswered. They are key questions because the case of the communist Croats is symptomatic of the unquestioning pro-Partisan atmosphere that seems to have pervaded MO4 even before Deakin dropped to

Tito. Even if it turns out, as it very well may, that it was all an incompetent muddle, we still need verification that this was the case. History requires this information from the SOE files.

James Klugmann became the mother superior of the thirty Canadian communist Croats when they arrived in Cairo, and, as will already be obvious, he was the ideal round peg in a round hole. Basil Davidson tells us also about Klugmann's "brilliant" handling of the rough-hewn Croatian miners. I urge the reader to beg, borrow, or steal a copy of *Special Operations Europe,* which will tell him in a very readable, though flippant, manner all about this and much else. Although my views on Yugoslavia, on politics, and probably on much else differ from those of Basil Davidson, I would be happy if his book were made compulsory reading for students of politics and more especially for those studying the rise and fall—and the ethics and morality—of the liberational revolutionary illusion promoted by the communists to further Soviet imperialism. It is a very interesting subject in these days, when the beautiful but sensitive flower of *glasnost* is peeping through the surface of the fifty-year-old swamp of Stalinist brainwashing.

The Kremlin knew all about the communist Croats, a leading member of the Croatian team told *Borba,* a Yugoslav daily, after the war. The relevation in the spring of 1942 that the British secret services were recruiting communist-inclined agents on this scale must have been music to the ears of Moscow. It obviously gave encouragement to the communist Partisans in Yugoslavia. Vladimir Velebit, a leading member of the postwar Yugoslav government and later ambassador to Britain, has publicly said that Tito's inner circle was amazed at the number of communists in the British secret services. He was not, one assumes, referring only to the Canadian-Croatian miners.

It was probably no coincidence that it was at this juncture— the Croat recruitment—that Moscow came down off the fence and started spreading pro-Tito and anti-Mihailović propaganda through its public-relations agents around the world. As has been explained vividly by Milovan Djilas, then number three in the Partisan hierarchy, the Russians were very careful not to frighten the Western Allies off. Until the middle of 1942, they took pains to pretend that they knew nothing of Tito's setup. They had even established relations with the royal Yugoslav government and made noises about sending a mission to Mihailović. In the summer of 1942, however, the radio station Voice of Free Yugoslavia (also known as Radio Free Yugoslavia), which operated from southern Russia, started to attack Mihailović.

Once the communist Croats had been recruited and shipped to Cairo, they had to be put to use. That was obvious. It was also obvious that their political persuasion made them suitable to support only one resistance group—Tito's. The decision by the chiefs of staff in March 1943 to contact "hopefully non-communist" resistance groups was circumvented. Rapidly, three teams were deployed to the Tito Partisans. This was not exactly what the chiefs of staff wanted. But it was what they got. These Croats formed the spearhead of the missions to Tito. Strangely, their signals and reports were later given credence far beyond those of us apolitical British officers attached to the Loyalists. No one seems to have taken their political tendencies into account when assessing their evidence. One of them, Steve Serdar, later contributed substantially to dossiers alleging collaboration by Mihailović. No one thought to question Serdar's politics.

Deakin's interpreter was another of the communist Croats, one Ivan (John) Starčević. In *The Embattled Mountain* Deakin tells us, "I was ill-qualified in Serbo-Croat and he was nominally allotted to me as interpreter. If he had any other duties, I never discovered them. There were many times during the coming months when I was grateful for his presence." One asks the precise significance of "nominally allotted." One also asks why a noncommissioned interpreter should have "other duties" unknown to the mission commander.

Whoever authorized it, and whatever the precise motivation, the decision to recruit these men was a milestone on the road to abandoning the Loyalists.

The freedom given Klugmann, a known leading communist, to read the secret MO4 signals, to brief and debrief agents, and to wander off in the evenings holding political meetings with the

Croats recruited through the Communist Party is amazing. It is all the more extraordinary in light of the seven-year sentence given Lt. R. N. Uren, a junior officer in the SOE London Balkans section, for transmitting secret information from the SOE archives to the Communist Party in Great Britain. This draconian treatment of a petty communist contrasts strangely with the leeway given Klugmann, who was to play an increasingly influential and sinister role later in 1943 and in 1944.

Klugmann was directly involved in the Yugoslav section of MO4 and its successor organization Force 133, and then in 37 Military Mission, the base headquarters of Brigadier Maclean's mission to Tito, until the end of the war. He then went to Yugoslavia working for U.N.R.R.A. (the United Nations Relief and Rehabilitation Agency). After that job finished, he worked in London for the British Communist Party, organizing strikes in British industry. Peter Wright tells how John Cairncross was offered a chance to return to the United Kingdom without prosecution if he could make Klugmann talk to MI5 about the communists in the 1930s. But Klugmann was a hard man and laughed at him. Having substantially contributed to Tito's grab for power, he turned against Tito on Soviet orders, writing a book against him in 1948. Later, when the Soviets relented, he recanted. In 1977 he died while writing a book on British communism. He was the total apparatchik.

Bailey: The Enigma

While Davidson, Deakin, and Klugmann were the three key officers in the Yugoslav section, this rundown of personalities would not be complete without bringing in Colonel Bailey. S. W. "Bill" Bailey was an old SOE hand who came to North America from Istanbul and Jerusalem. Before the war he had worked for the Trepća Mines in Yugoslavia and was fluent in Serbo-Croat. He was a man of considerable literacy, and his dispatches show he knew more about politics than about soldiering. It was not surprising that he, as the doyen of the Balkan contingent, was named head of the mission with Mihailović.

Bailey is the enigma, the mystery man, in the whole strange

process whereby the Yugoslav section of MO4 Cairo became involved in the Yugoslav revolutionary movement. Basil Davidson, as he tells us in his book, was caught in the ripples and swept along, himself helping substantially in the buildup of this movement. But the movement had started earlier, at least as early as the Canadian project.

How could Bailey, with his knowledge of the political and ethnic situation in Yugoslavia, let himself become involved in the massive recruitment of Croatian communists—let alone initiate it? It just does not make sense. He was a soldier under orders, but that does not answer the question either. The scope of his orders issued on December 31, 1941, included the selection and vetting of recruits from the Balkan émigré groups for training in subversive work in occupied Europe. The files show that London had an exchange with him about the vetting of some earlier recruits found in the United States and he had confirmed that he was checking their personal histories "from the national political point of view." So why does he move to Canada, make contact with the Communist Party, and recruit a bunch of Croatian communists who would surely not pass muster from any "national political point of view"?

William Stevenson's book *The Man Called Intrepid* tells the story of the "quiet Canadian," Sir William Stephenson, who was the chief of the joint SIS/SOE operation in North America, known as British Security Co-ordination (BSC), and to whom Bailey was acting as political advisor. Stevenson eulogizes the Tito movement and deals in general terms with the recruitment of Croatians and their training at Camp X in Canada. Before Bailey moved to Canada from the United States the agents recruited by him came through a contact of "Wild Bill" Donovan, head of OSS, the American Office of Strategic Services, precursor to the CIA. Did Stephenson or Donovan introduce Bailey to the Comintern agent Nikola Kovačević or the Canadian Communist Party's secretary general, Tim Buck, and did Stephenson fail to consult London? The recruitment of communists on this scale in early 1942 could hardly have happened had SOE London realized what was being done. According to the Foreign Office files SOE and the Foreign Office were forthrightly opposed to supporting the Tito Partisans right through to about April 1943.

In *Spycatcher,* Peter Wright states that the Soviets were operating a number of agents inside BSC in New York. One of them he names as Charles Ellis, who was Stephenson's SIS deputy there "for most of the war." Was Ellis the key in this mystery? Did Ellis introduce Buck and persuade Stephenson to overrule London?

Ellis is also mentioned extensively by Chapman Pincher in his book *Too Secret for Too Long.* The book alleges that he spied for both the Germans and the Russians and that he enjoyed the protection of the head of SIS Security, none other than the notorious Kim Philby.

Vladimir Velebit, Tito's main contact with the British both during and after the war, wrote in his memoirs that the Canadian communist Croats were recruited through the influence of "leftist elements in the British intelligence services." SOE London, which was formally responsible, was headed by Sir Charles Hambro along with Col. George Taylor, Maj. Peter Boughey, and Colonel Pearson. Other than Pearson I knew them all and can say that it would be hard to find individuals less likely to be described as "leftist elements." As for Pearson, it is clear from Foreign Office correspondence with SOE that he was the most conservative of them all. So if the "leftists" were not in SOE London, then where were they?

Later in this book I recount how Fitzroy Maclean tells a story of a signal that was dispatched from Cairo to the prime minister falsely using the signature of General Wilson, commander in chief of the British forces in the Middle East, when MO4 was trying to sabotage Maclean's appointment as liaison officer to Tito. Did some leftist element in London forge a signal under the name of Sir Charles Hambro or George Taylor, countermanding Bailey's instructions to vet recruits from a "national political" point of view and directing him instead to switch to communists? It may read fancifully, but as this story develops, it will be seen that far dirtier tricks were perpetrated in the Yugoslav affair.

From Canada Bailey was sent to Cairo to join Mihailović and to replace Maj. Bill Hudson, who had been in Yugoslavia since

September 1941. It was planned to drop Bailey in August 1942, but he contracted malaria and did not go until Christmas Eve. One has to ask: What did Bailey think of it all in Cairo between August and December 1942? How did he reconcile the atmosphere in MO4, as reflected in Davidson's account of the doing-down of "that silly old goat Mihadge-lo-vitch" in the Partisan-Četnik office war, with his own mission to the Yugoslav commander in chief?

It seems inconceivable that Mihailović was not aware of Bailey's activities in North America. He had communications with the government in exile, which would have known what was going on in the émigré communities. The recruitment and training of a substantial number of émigré Croats could hardly have escaped notice. The Kremlin certainly knew!

In his book *Camp X,* David Stafford states explicitly that several meetings were held between Bailey and top leaders of the Communist Party in Canada. On being asked why he was only seeking communists, the book recounts, Bailey replied that only the communists were really fighting. One can imagine a ludicrous scenario. Bailey drops into the Loyalist headquarters a couple of months later: "How do you do, General Mihailović. I've come to help you. I've just been recruiting communists for Tito because only the communists are really fighting."

Bailey's voluminous signals and reports after he parachuted to Mihailović make it evident—by lack of mention—that his Canadian venture was never brought up between him and Mihailović. Bailey's reports do show, however, that his relations with Mihailović were not on a colleague-to-colleague basis. Mihailović, who surely knew of the British recruitment of the communist Croats and Bailey's close involvement with it, must have been very suspicious of him personally from the start, particularly when Bailey failed to come clean about it.

Nevertheless, Bailey's arrival must have raised Mihailović's hopes of receiving some real support. In the fifteen months from his first contact with the British until Bailey's drop, the Loyalists had received less than thirty tons of supplies. When Bailey arrived, Mihailović had every reason to be optimistic, particularly following the tremendous BBC buildup of his movement in the earlier part of 1942.

Actually, the BBC hype did more harm than good in Britain because it awoke unattainable expectations of massive operational activity by the Loyalists. It also went counter to the instructions given to Mihailović by his government, and the advice by SOE, to avoid fighting that could provoke reprisals until the time was ripe for a general uprising. Quite specifically, the Yugoslav government—presumably with the approval of the Foreign Office and of the Political Warfare Executive (PWE)—broadcast a message on the BBC in November 1942 telling Mihailović to conserve his forces and his energy. This was a thoroughly correct attitude in the light of Hitler's order in October 1941 to execute 100 Yugoslavs for every German killed and 50 for every German wounded. An October 1941 massacre at Kragujevac included all students at the local high school. The Germans admitted to 2,300. Yugoslav literature claims 7,000. The total number of Serbs shot in the 1941 uprising exceeded 35,000. The Germans even took hostages in advance and stored them up for execution when the quota called for it.

Significantly, the BBC broadcast advising Mihailović to conserve his forces was made in November 1942—the very time that Keble, Davidson, and even the Foreign Office were wondering whether resistance could not be gingered up. It may be a case of the left hand not knowing what the right was doing. But it could also have been a very astute move by left-wing influences in the BBC or the PWE, encouraging the broadcast in order to throw doubt on the efficacy of the Loyalists at a time when attention was becoming centered on Yugoslav resistance.

It is also possibly significant that Guy Burgess had an advisory role at the BBC and was a member of the Joint Broadcasting Committee from January 1941 to June 1944. He also had free run of the ministry of information and the PWE. Brendan Bracken, the information minister, was close to Churchill, and through him Burgess had a channel to drop the odd hint at the highest level.

There are references in the Foreign Office files showing concern about the Yugoslav slant of the BBC, and the false attribution of Loyalist operations in September through November 1943 to the Partisans did untold harm to our relations with the Loyalists, as I myself came to experience.

Whether or not there was manipulation of the advice broadcast to him, Mihailović was the recipient of virtually no material support, despite being the hero of the resistance and the minister of war of the exiled government. Sadly, Bailey's arrival changed nothing, which must have been a very considerable disappointment to Mihailović.

Only two drops were made between Christmas 1942 and a fateful christening party in Lipovo in February 1943, attended by Mihailović's headquarters staff. This party represented another milestone on the road to the abandonment of the Loyalists. As was not abnormal on such occasions, everyone had a good booze-up and Mihailović made a controversial speech. In it he complained bitterly of the lack of support and referred to the communists and the Croatian *ustaša* as his worst enemies. This was quite reasonable. The *ustaša*—the Croatian equivalent of the German SS (Schutzstaffel)—had committed massive genocide against the Serbian minority in Croatia. Now it was totally allied with the Germans. As for the communists, they eventually took over the country and carried out judicial murder against Mihailović personally. The speech was therefore both correct and prescient.

It is significant that Mihailović bracketed the *ustaša* and the communists together. The *ustaša* and the communists had cooperated before the war when they were both illegal organizations dedicated to the overthrow of the Yugoslav government—"that creature of Versailles," as the communists called it. Tito's public-relations men have always concealed this historical fact. This prewar communist-*ustaša* link made it easy for *ustaši* (the members of the *ustaša*) to change sides and join the Partisans when it became obvious that the Germans would be defeated.

It was typical of Bailey that he, instead of quietly suggesting to Mihailović that his words were a bit strong—or even ignoring the incident entirely—wrote a voluminous report about the incident, building it into an issue. Arriving in Cairo at the precise moment that the MO4 pro-Partisan faction had just gotten at the prime minister, this report came as if sent from heaven. It was seized on, blown up, and copied to the secretary of state, to the Foreign Office, and even to the Cabinet. A justified but un-diplomatic comment became a turning point. Of such is history made.

It sounds almost incredible, but, in addition to his adverse report, Bailey ordered supplies stopped. This order was largely cosmetic, because the very lack of supplies had been the cause of the squabble. But psychologically, it was extremely important. Resumption of supplies was approved only after a rebuke to Mi-hailović had been extracted from the Yugoslav government in London. This was just one of a series of incidents, misunder-standings, and problems between Bailey and Mihailović.

There is a significant reference in one of Bailey's reports to Mihailović's insistence that without five loads of supplies being de-livered he could not regard the British as serious supporters. It was a fair comment. But it is noteworthy that Mihailović needed to make the comment at all. When they were supporting Tito in the subsequent civil war against Mihailović, the British on one occasion had sixty supply planes in the air at one time.

Throughout his period in Yugoslavia from Christmas 1942 till early 1944, Bailey seems never to have established a satisfac-tory working relationship with Mihailović in spite of his very con-siderable qualifications. We shall see, as this account unfolds, that Bailey had to contend with a shocking lack of support from his base as well as a considerable ambiguity in his position. But a study of the files shows that Bailey tended always to exaggerate and thus exacerbate the problems.

The Serbs tend to be a hard-living, hard-drinking, courageous people. Mihailović himself was a regular soldier and a fierce tra-ditionalist. I only met him once, in sad circumstances, and I can claim no personal knowledge of him. Nevertheless, from what I have heard I believe that the Loyalists would have responded better to a charismatic, dashing personality as a liaison officer, someone who could have caught their imagination and overcome their inevitable suspicions. In this area Bailey obviously failed.

His contribution was a voluminous mass of political analyses and reports that, by reason of their length, were never acted upon before events had overtaken them. One feels that he was more concerned with impressing his superiors than with helping Mihailović, or even killing Germans.

This state of affairs contrasted dramatically with the situation at Tito's headquarters in June 1943. The Partisan main army of about 15,000 men, which had been trying to penetrate the Loyalist-held Sandžak area, was encircled near Mount Durmitor by an Axis offensive directed against both resistance movements. Captain Deakin arrived in the middle of the fray—fortuitously for both him personally and the Partisans. There started a personal attachment that became a blood-brother relationship when Tito and Deakin were both slightly wounded by a bomb, which killed Stuart. Tito was formally no more than the leader of a band of outlaws, who at that stage were condemned by the Yugoslav government and not even recognized by the British, but support was thrust upon him enthusiastically and unconditionally. In the words of Bickham Sweet-Escott in his book *Baker Street Irregular*, Deakin, "though wounded . . . had begun to send out a series of brilliant messages to Cairo which left no doubt as to the military value of Tito's movement."

While Bailey wagged his finger at Mihailović and stopped supplies, messages of encouragement poured in to Tito. No one thought to tell him what to do or what not to do. All the stops were pulled out to build a relationship with him, even though he was openly attacking the officially recognized resistance movement. The stated SOE policy was to make contact with other resistance groups "willing to fight the enemy and willing *to undertake not to fight civil wars*," but MO4 Cairo was primarily interested in consolidating in the field the war already won in the Cairo office—the Partisan-Četnik war.

In truth, the military value of Tito's movement was extremely questionable at that time. According to his own colleague Milovan Djilas, Tito's main force was at that stage little more than a disorganized rabble fleeing from Montenegro, suffering desperate casualties, forced to abandon its wounded. With the greatest difficulty they had slipped out of an Axis encirclement. Big words were used to describe this near-disaster. The Axis attempts to corner the Partisans were described grandiloquently as the "Fourth" or "Fifth" Offensive." The flights were described as "breakouts." But that was the Partisan propaganda style.

Neither then nor later did the British representatives dare to insist to Tito that he stop fighting the forces of Mihailović, the legal army of the recognized government. Without a card in his hand, when he desperately needed materiel and Allied recognition, Tito made it clear from the start that his was a sovereign movement, that Mihailović and his Loyalist forces were the enemy, and that his purpose was to eliminate them and conquer their homeland, Serbia—take it or leave it! From the very start the British with Tito took this message without protest, and they went on taking it; and in due course they provided the means for Tito to fulfill every one of his stated ambitions, including his main ambition—to win the civil war and establish a communist dictatorship.

Contrast this with the treatment of Mihailović. At no stage whatsoever did he get such encouragement. With the left-inclined atmosphere that existed from January 1943 on in MO4, not to speak of the prevailing winds in MI6, in the Political Warfare Executive, and in the Political Intelligence Branch, Mihailović probably never had much of a chance. But Bailey failed to exploit what opportunities there were, and his voluminous reports dwelled at length on all of the Loyalist movement's shortcomings. They reflected his own failure to come to grips with the Loyalists' problems, and they also provided considerable ammunition for those in Cairo and London who were—for whatever reasons—inclined to favor the Partisans.

Bailey served at Mihailović's headquarters from Christmas 1942 until the end of 1943. Both he and Bill Hudson—the first British liaison officer with Mihailović—were separately received by the prime minister in the spring of 1944. Both Bailey and Hudson said later that Churchill then told them unequivocally that he had been misled by SOE concerning some aspects of the situation in Yugoslavia. This anecdote may possibly be apocryphal. I have it, nevertheless, from two very reliable sources. Furthermore, since I completed this whole story I have convinced myself that if Churchill was misled, it was because at the time he wanted to be misled and encouraged his protégés to recommend what he wanted to hear. Truly he "led with his chin." Later things were quite different, and he recognized that he had made his greatest mistake of the war. But his full conversion did not begin until after Tito had bamboozled him personally in the late summer of 1944.

When he was in London in the spring of 1944, Bailey put forward a complicated plan for the personal replacement of Mihailović and for the geographical segregation of the two resistance movements. But it was ludicrously naïve to believe that the imposition of another leader—even if such a change were possible—would mitigate Tito's all-out drive to bring the whole of Yugoslavia under communist domination. I believe this idea was deliberately put around by the communists to split the Loyalists and confuse the British. At that stage any plan to influence the march of events was too little and too late. The plan is only of interest in telling us about Bailey himself. He was either utterly naïve or very deep and devious.

In my studies I have observed time and again that with a friend like Bailey, Mihailović needed no enemies. And in the extraordinary context of the whole Yugoslav affair I have to ask myself: Could Bailey have been a mole?

In fairness I must stress that others who were with the Mihailović forces and who knew Bailey personally far better than I did find it impossible to entertain such suspicions. Furthermore, his writings as well as his verbose signals and reports have the character of a right-wing establishment bureaucrat. Politically one would have expected Bailey to be a conservative—a "wet," or ready-to-compromise, conservative in today's terms, not a radical of the right or left.

But then, Kim Philby's colleagues in the Foreign Office refused to entertain the concept that he was a traitor right up to the point that it became undeniable. To me Bailey remains an enigma. Whatever he was, there is no doubt that he did untold harm to Mihailović and the Loyalist cause.

Davidson: "A well-marked Partisan supporter"

Let me turn now to a totally different and very straightforward character in Cairo, Basil Davidson. He exuded charm and, in the Cairo scene, he could have been taken for a dashing staff officer in the regular army. I realize that this description would probably appall him. The very opposite to Bailey, Davidson could not be mistaken for a conservative—wet or dry. His book tells us that he started life as a journalist before the war and was recruited into Section D, a predecessor organization to SOE. He was sent to Hungary, where he ran a news service with the British mission as cover for the preparation of postoccupation sabotage. When the Germans and Hungarians invaded Yugoslavia, Davidson escaped via Belgrade and Albania. Together with other British diplomatic staff he was interned briefly by the Italians and then released. He returned to the United Kingdom via the south of France, Spain, and Portugal. Transferred to the Middle East, Davidson served for a time in Istanbul, trying to make contact with Hungary. Then he was carrying explosives between Palestine and Istanbul before he was put in charge of the Yugoslav section of MO4 in Cairo in September 1942.

Davidson remained in charge of the section until August 1943, when he parachuted to Tito's headquarters in Bosnia with the task of making contact with the Hungarian resistance and establishing himself in Hungary from a base in the Yugoslav Bačka region. That proved impossible. He remained for more than a year with the Partisans in the Bačka and in the Vojvodina, the area between the rivers Sava and Danube. This war was very different from that of the mass formations. With no big mountains and woods to retreat into, the small units to which he attached himself lived in the plains, concealing themselves in hiding places in the villages during the winter and in the maize fields during summer. I have spent some fascinating hours reading Davidson's signals from his mission, which was code-named Savannah. The intensity of Davidson's politics and his obsession with liberational revolution disturb me. So does his unquestioning acceptance of every Partisan claim. But I have to admire his personal courage on the Savannah operation. Just what he achieved militarily, as opposed to politically, I do not know. But he had remarkable guts and stamina. Davidson was no ordinary man, in more ways than one.

Vladimir Velebit, Tito's postwar ambassador to Britain, wrote of Davidson in his memoirs that he was a journalist and a writer with pronounced leftist sympathies and that he was very close to the Communist Party.

The Partisan-Četnik war in the Cairo office in January 1943, when Davidson was in charge of the Yugoslav section, certainly becomes more comprehensible—if not any less regrettable—when one studies *Special Operations Europe* and other books he has written about Africa since the war. His writings clearly define his philosophy. Sadly, I believe, his efforts in Yugoslavia were for the wrong cause. But this is no reflection on his personal qualities. He was a fighter for his causes. I approve of fighters. He was also refreshingly open about his radical opinions.

Seton-Watson: The Meddling Guru

Also in Cairo at that time was the accepted expert in Balkan matters, Hugh Seton-Watson. He was special advisor to SOE on Yugoslav and Bulgarian affairs. His father had been the leading Balkan expert before him. Seton-Watson capitalized on his father's reputation, and his word on Balkan matters was gospel in Cairo. I believe that he finished his life as a conservative and merits great respect for his later opinions on other eastern countries and their problems. Nevertheless, his views as a university undergraduate had been hard-left socialist if not forthrightly pro-communist. There is no doubt that, during the period 1942 to 1944, he was still a fervent left-winger and outspokenly in favor of the revolutionary adventure in Yugoslavia.

Together with Klugmann, with whom he was very friendly, Seton-Watson was deeply involved in an energetically pursued but ill-fated endeavor to organize a Bulgarian communist resistance using a dedicated, romantic, card-carrying communist, a young man named Frank Thompson. This disastrous mission, code-named Claridges, is described in Stowers Johnson's book *Agents Extraordinary.*

Frank Thompson and Seton-Watson had been at Winchester together and were firm friends. Whereas I have seen no evidence to indicate that Seton-Watson was actually a member of the Communist Party before the war, Frank Thompson certainly was, and he flaunted his politics.

The organization and direction from Cairo of the Claridges mission appear to have been Seton-Watson's only venture into the operational side. It is clear that he and Klugmann played a substantial role in the planning. There were two preparatory missions involved, which appear in the operational log under the code names Mulligatawny and Monkey Wrench. The original mission dropped into Albania near Lake Ohrid in August or September 1943. It was officially scheduled to cross Macedonia and act as reception for Frank Thompson, who was to make contact with Bulgarian communists and start a resistance movement there. The main preparatory mission, under Maj. Mostyn Davies, a well-connected and brave officer, was top secret, and it was given absolutely overriding priority.

Tito would not permit British missions to be dropped to Partisans in Serbia before the break with Mihailović at the end of 1943. Wisely, Tito was concerned about the heartland Serbs' perception of the communist Partisans, and he feared that British liaison officers on the two sides might get together and work out a local truce. This was the last thing he wanted. Nevertheless, one of Tito's top henchmen—a man who went by the name of Vukmanović-Tempo—met Mostyn Davies in Macedonia and traveled with him to southeastern Serbia, just south of where my own mission was located and adjacent to that of another British liaison officer with the Mihailović forces, Capt. Robert Purvis. The operational log shows that Mulligatawny and Monkey Wrench enjoyed such a priority from MO4 that a substantial proportion of all drops to Yugoslavia in the last three months of 1943 were going to those missions. This was so extraordinary that I wonder whether Brigadier Maclean at Tito's headquarters knew what was going on. I found no signals between MO4 and the Maclean mission to indicate that he did. Whether or not Klugmann and Seton-Watson were operating with the knowledge of Maclean, the massive deliveries of arms into Macedonia had nothing to do with the buildup of a Bulgarian resistance. That may have been the excuse for the priority given to Mostyn Davies's mission, and it was certainly the excuse Cairo used when it fervently denied that the mission existed at all. (To Cairo's embarrassment, Davies made contact with Robert Purvis. This blew it.) The fact is that these massive drops were being made to enable Vukmanović-Tempo to recruit a Partisan force from the mixed population of Arnautis (Muslim Albanians living in Serbia) and disaffected Serbs in preparation for the planned conquest of Serbia. This force, in due course, drove up from the south.

I believe that the exploitation of the proposed reconnaissance into Bulgaria by Frank Thompson was organized by Klugmann on his own initiative; no doubt he spun a good yarn to Brigadier Keble. It helped enormously in the communist war against the Loyalists in Serbia. Undoubtedly the involvement of Seton-Watson lent weight to the plan and facilitated the evident priority given to the Davies mission.

Frank Thompson was killed in Bulgaria. His mission was exploratory, and it is inconceivable that he needed, or could have transported, the massive amounts of arms dropped into the Bulgarian-annexed zone of southeastern Serbia, which had little indigenous Bulgarian population. The whole Claridges/Monkey Wrench/Mulligatawny affair provides added evidence of the freedom enjoyed by Klugmann, Seton-Watson, and others to operate their own private policies.

Not surprisingly, Seton-Watson's immediate postwar writings confirm his wartime stance. His views had contributed substantially to the pro-Partisan atmosphere in Cairo. They must have influenced the Minister of State's Office and the Middle East Command because of his unique academic standing. Whether in continuing conviction, or for self-justification, he did a great deal after the war to color the *received wisdom* Red.

An angle on Seton-Watson and his attitude is revealed in the diary of Vladimir Dedijer, a leading member of Tito's hierarchy and close comrade of Deakin in the battle on Mount Durmitor. Dedijer came to Cairo with the delegation brought out by Maclean and Deakin in December 1943. The diary records advice given to another member of the delegation, a man called Milojević.

"Hugh, the son of Seton-Watson, asked him (Milojević) to be sure to tell the journalists, who were about to interview him, that the Partisans really cared for animals. If you could somehow supply photographs of dogs and cats, you would win over many people in England, added Seton-Watson." Thus the British public was to be bamboozled. Even intellectual integrity went by the board in Seton-Watson's blinkered enthusiasm for the Partisan cause.

On January 26, 1943, at the time of the MO4 Partisan-Četnik office war and shortly before Churchill was snookered, Seton-Watson published an article in *The Spectator* attacking Mihailović. Yet he was supposed to be an objective advisor, and Mihailović had been appointed minister of defense for a friendly government. Had an ordinary officer like me done that, I would have been instantly court-martialed. But in MO4 his views were in vogue.

Seton-Watson worked closely with Klugmann. He was evidently sold on abandoning the Loyalists. But I would not want to suggest for a moment that he was part of a Soviet-inspired conspiracy or that his first loyalty was to the U.S.S.R., as that of Klugmann undoubtedly was. Rather, I believe that, like so many other arrogant intellectual elitists, he could be almost frivolous in pursuing a pet ideological cause without adequately assessing, or subsequently monitoring, the practical implications of, and the damage caused by, the policies he so enthusiastically advocated.

Keble: Klugmann's Disciple and Protector

The next key player in the MO4 scenario was Brig. C. M. "Bolo" Keble, who, when a colonel, was placed in charge of the operational sections of MO4 in 1942. In *Special Operations Europe*, Basil Davidson is less than charitable about Keble's personal characteristics. He implies that Keble was a lecher, with a nickname TIM ("Touch I Must"), of aggressive physical bearing and inclined to ruthless, ambitious maneuvering. Whatever his motivations, Keble was evidently a forceful individual, determined to put MO4 on the map. He was a regular from a line regiment and staff-trained. He had previously done a stint with military intelligence. His qualifications were thus impeccable for the job of turning MO4 from semi-spymaster's organization into a paramilitary machine supplying guerrilla foot-slogging operations.

Keble's arrival as operational chief followed the appointment of Lord Glenconner as head of SOE Cairo and an awakening interest on the part of military command in the Middle East in the disruptive potential of paramilitary resistance behind the enemy lines.

Bickham Sweet-Escott writes about the SOE chain of command in *Baker Street Irregular*. SOE was answerable to the chiefs of staff in London and, for policy, to the Foreign Office. Where political affairs and military strategies conflicted, SOE found itself between two fires. In Cairo, the situation was more complicated still because SOE Cairo was answerable to SOE London on both counts. In theory the military decisions were taken by the London chiefs of staff advising the Cabinet, advised in turn by the Joint Intelligence Committee. The Foreign Office controlled the political decisions, and the PWE exercised influence both in London and in Cairo. But increasingly the Foreign Office agency in Cairo—the Minister of State's Office—came into play, as did the military Middle East Command, which serviced MO4 for materiel, airfields, and aircraft drops.

The files reflect the bureaucratic complications. Writing in impeccable style, analyzing the long- and short-term political and military implications of the messages coming in from the field, the officials would take their time and call for the views of the numerous offices involved. They spent days at a time discussing the merits of, and office responsibility for, the various issues. It is all very far removed from the guerrillas sleeping rough in the mountains, constantly threatened by enemies creeping up behind them in the mist and snow with grenades and knives in their hands.

The complexity of MO4's organization should have led to operational paralysis, and in some areas it did. But the near-total lack of control provided the opportunity for independent initiative, and an excuse for it, even if it involved playing both ends against the middle.

Keble did just that. When Churchill accepted his January

1943 memorandum that advocated support for other resistance movements, Keble seems to have taken this as carte blanche to initiate and carry out policy at the operational level without asking London. It is not clear to what extent Keble sought sanction from Lord Glenconner, his chief, for his initiatives. Certainly the latter accepted responsibility for everything that happened in Cairo, but it was in the nature of the man to back up his men or sack them; and Glenconner and Keble left at the same time in November 1943.

Keble was another natural conservative who has come under suspicion as a committed ally of the left. I can only write about Yugoslav affairs, but he also had Albania and Greece in his bailiwick, and certainly very odd things happened in the control of operations in those two countries.

In Yugoslavia the odd things were legion. First there is the interpretation of Churchill's wishes following the fateful meetings in January 1943. The formal instruction was quite clear. It was that Mihailović and his forces should be supported in Serbia but that endeavors should be made to contact other resistance groups, notably in Croatia and Slovenia, which, as Deakin wrote me in 1988, were "hopefully organised by the non-Communist Croat Peasant Party, and by Mihailović's commander in Slovenia, Novak."

But whatever the London policy, the victors in the Cairo office war were in no mind to mess around with the "hopefully non-Communist Croat Peasant Party" or with "Mihailović's commander in Slovenia." They intended, as Davidson makes clear in his book, to contact Tito, and steps were soon under way to make such a contact by dropping some of Klugmann's communist Croats.

As I have already written, the Croats did indeed make contact with Tito as MO4 intended they should. And Tito immediately agreed to receive a British mission. Deakin was chosen for SOE, while SIS sent Captain Stuart.

Deakin wrote of his mission, "Such an operation originated in the directive to SOE of the Chiefs of Staff in March 43—to report on all Resistance groups in Yugoslavia." Actually the mission was sent deliberately to establish relations with Tito.

Deakin added that further reason for this formal decision had been the disclosure from German intercepts, and similar information from Bailey, that Mihailović was heavily engaged alongside the Italians—and parallel to the Germans—in the fourth offensive against Tito's Partisans.

Now, this comment is significant in its reference to Mihailović's engagement against Tito's Partisans. The truth can have another interpretation. What was really happening was that Tito and his main force had moved from Bosnia down into Montenegro partly because of German pressure against them in Bosnia and partly by design: the move fitted into the framework of Tito's ambition to conquer Mihailović's territory in Montenegro and the Sandžak and eventually to turn east into the heart of Serbia and south into Macedonia. This was not an attack by Mihailović on Tito, as stated by Deakin. It was a move by the Partisans against Mihailović territory. Furthermore, it was a move that was at first approved by the Germans, who were in talks with Tito's delegates in Zagreb. (I deal with this in detail in a later chapter on collaboration.) Subsequently, when Hitler ordered that no deals be done with bandits, the Germans mounted a major cleanup operation against all guerrillas. The Mihailović forces, which bore the first brunt of the German cleanup operation, were simply endeavoring to defend their own territory. They would not have been involved in this fighting at all had Tito not initiated the move toward the Mihailović homeland.

During Keble's time in MO4 there seems to have been little inclination to ask whether Tito was willing to avoid civil war. Not a bit of it. Whereas Bailey stopped arms supplies and made an issue of Mihailović's emotional verbal attack on the communists, MO4 Cairo seems seldom to have questioned Tito's right to fight Mihailović and his Loyalists and to invade Mihailović territory as and when he wished; and any Mihailović defense constituted an "offensive." Evidently Keble had decided that Tito was to be given total support and that this support was not conditional on anything. This decision made civil war inevitable. Yet in the meantime the British missions to outlying Loyalist units were sent on their way by Keble unbriefed about what was going on at their base and about how little support they could expect. With forty-five years' hindsight this is hardly credible. It is certainly inexcusable.

Sadly, the Public Records Office has no SOE files for the period before September 1943, and we have to rely on the Foreign Office files for official information about this period. We therefore only see what MO4 and the Minister of State's Office in Cairo thought fit to pass on to the Foreign Office. Under Keble's guidance they probably told London what suited their pro-Partisan policy and nothing more.

Keble remained in charge of MO4 operations throughout the summer of 1943, and he enhanced his reputation for vigorous management. Some might call it ruthless. He was in operational charge when the now-notorious May 29 Glenconner signal was sent to Mihailović.

This signal was the next milestone on the road to the destruction of the Loyalist movement. Following the christening-party incident, the Yugoslav government had been constrained to reproach Mihailović. The reproof, and Mihailović's acceptance of it, took about three months, during the greater part of which Bailey withheld supplies and arms from Mihailović. Within days of that matter being settled, MO4 sent Bailey, for transmission to Mihailović, a policy signal in Lord Glenconner's name which, paraphrased, read:

> General Mihailović does not represent a fighting force of any importance West of Kopaonik [a mountain in southern Serbia]. His units in Montenegro, Herzegovina and Bosnia are already annihilated or else in close co-operation with the axis. It is also difficult to say that his units exist in Croatia, Slovenia and Slavonia. The Partisans represent a good and effective fighting force in all parts whereas only the Quislings represent General Mihailovic . . . you will advise General Mihailovic that he immediately go to Kopaonik with all his faithful officers and men; if necessary he is to break through by armed force . . . in the future the Supreme Commander will consider the districts under his command and influence to be bordered on the West by the fighting

elements already existing on the right bank of the Ibar river and towards the South to Skoplje.

To understand how shocking this signal was, one must remember that there was still in force the official British policy of giving full support to Mihailović. Officially, MO4 was authorized only to examine whether other resistance groups merited support—which hinged on the strict condition that they not undertake to use it for civil-war purposes.

Mihailović himself had not even been informed that there was any consideration being given to dropping agents to other groups, whether communist or otherwise, let alone to assisting or recognizing them. Yet here we have MO4 invoking the supreme commander and telling Mihailović to withdraw his forces to a small corner of Yugoslavia and to hand over the rest to groups regarded by him as communist outlaws.

The Foreign Office was appalled. Douglas Howard, head of the office's southern department, wrote in a memorandum dated June 15, 1943,

In one way or another SOE have excelled themselves in their handling of this question.

First Lord Glenconner goes and sends Bailey a telegram off his own bat and completely at variance with our own policy and with the telegram sent to Mihailovic a week before. . . .

We have suggested to the Chiefs of Staff that the disastrous telegram be rescinded. Unless we do that, we shall have ruined any chance of coming to any agreement with Mihailovic. Even if it is withdrawn so much bad blood will now have been spilt, that it may be very difficult to come to terms.

Bailey had protested to MO4 on receipt of the signal. Nevertheless, he passed the message on to Mihailović without waiting for a response. As Bailey expected, Mihailović's reaction was fierce. Eventually the signal was rescinded, but the harm had been done, as Douglas Howard had predicted.

Compare this whole scenario with the situation a month or two later when the Foreign Office suggested mildly through Fitzroy Maclean that Tito be requested not to attack the Loyalists. Maclean refused to pass on the signal on the grounds that Tito had made clear his intentions to invade Serbia and liquidate Mihailović, and that passing the signal would damage relations.

The Glenconner signal, which went out a couple of days after Deakin was trying to drop to the Tito Partisans, was clearly all part of the MO4 policy in Cairo to build up Tito. It was probably cobbled together fast in order to take the tactical pressure off the Partisans and to give them a route to break out of the German encirclement.

But there's another interesting angle. Davidson and Deakin have both claimed that the latter was privy to intercepts and clearly implied that these included Enigma signals. It was a strict rule that nobody privy to Enigma should risk capture. Yet Deakin was dropped into a highly dangerous situation. This is an enigma in itself. What is the explanation of the apparent flouting by MO4 of a strict rule? Did Deakin really see Enigma traffic, or were the famous intercepts on which the January change of policy was based just run-of-the-mill stuff? And if he did indeed see Enigma signals, why was he allowed to drop into what was undoubtedly the most perilous situation faced by the Partisans? Maybe we will learn the answer to this puzzle when the official history of the Balkan operations is written.

It was pure coincidence that my own mission, named Henbury, was dropped by MO4 to a Mihailović Loyalist unit in southeastern Serbia on June 2, 1943—only three days after the bombshell Glenconner signal to Mihailović. Our arrival, coming on the heels of a signal telling the head of the movement to which we were accredited that his forces were "quislings" and that he was no longer persona grata, was not auspicious. Furthermore, our drop took place only a couple of days before the Algiers incident. In this extraordinary affair, which I recounted earlier, MO4 endeavored again to modify policy to Mihailović's disadvantage. And MO4 had blithely sent my mission and eight others into enemy-occupied territory while cutting the ground from under our feet by alienating Mihailović. Who bears the responsibility? Keble was in charge, whoever was advising him.

Keble was chief of staff of MO4 throughout the summer of 1943, during which time MO4 was shaken by left-right dissension. In Greece, due to the energetic attitude of the king and Churchill's support for him, the political drive by the communist elements was held in check. But in Albania, less in the spotlight, MO4 policies certainly helped the Enver Hoxha communist movement gain power; and this movement's progress was greatly helped by the events in Yugoslavia and by assistance from Tito.

To what extent Keble consciously favored the left is hard to say. Probably he was not left-inclined but just got caught up in the leftward momentum in MO4. He was probably also influenced by the January incident in which Churchill had gone over the heads of the hierarchy and given his blessing to a new policy for Yugoslavia.

On September 29, Keble signed an extraordinary memorandum that favored dropping all support of nationalist or royalist resistance movements and building up left-wing movements *as a matter of principle*. This, he suggested, would achieve stable postwar republican governments— and the possibility of restored constitutional monarchies in some cases— as opposed to communism. The argument was both mad and bad. It failed to point out that, in the Balkans, the left-wing resistance movements were without exception communist and that the proposed policies could only lead to a rapid communist takeover of the whole Balkans. This sinister document was almost certainly drafted by Klugmann for Keble. But the fact that Keble signed such a blatantly Marxist-Leninist paper indicates that at best he was rather muddled.

Keble was replaced in November 1943 in the reorganization of MO4, in which Lord Glenconner also resigned. The trigger point seems to have been an uproar about Greece involving a Greek delegation of resistance figures brought out for consultations. The delegates included communists who opened their innings by putting the king's future in question. There was a monumental row and SOE was blamed for the fiasco.

But it is also said that Fitzroy Maclean had a part in Keble's departure, and the story of how "Bolo" Keble crossed swords with Fitzroy is relevant. Sir Fitzroy's own account can be found in his book *Eastern Approaches*. It also formed the theme of a paper he presented at the 1975 London University symposium called British Policy Towards Wartime Resistance in Yugoslavia and Greece—the so-called Auty-Clogg symposium. Maclean says he had put out feelers while in Cairo about going into Greece. He was told that he was to be sent to Yugoslavia and was summoned to London to report to the prime minister immediately. That was in July 1943. Churchill explained to him that he had his doubts about Mihailović's contribution to the war effort, that he wanted to know about Tito, and that he wanted Maclean to find out "who was killing the most Germans" and how he could help them kill more. Politics was to be a secondary consideration:

> He wished me to command the mission with the rank of Brigadier and also to be his own personal representative with the Partisan command . . . what was important was that I should be dropped in as soon as possible. This would be done under the auspices of SOE and he had given them instructions to afford all possible assistance.
>
> I accordingly went round to Baker Street to make my mark and ask them to get me on the first plane to Cairo, which they undertook to do. A week or so later I rang up to ask when I was going and was told that, owing to bad weather, there had been no flying. A day or two after that I was sent for to number 10 Downing Street to see the Prime Minister. He showed me a signal he had had from General Wilson the Commander in Chief Middle East. This said that he considered me totally unsuitable for the job. I was somewhat pained at this as General Wilson happened to be an old friend. . . . Churchill then showed me the reply he had sent General Wilson over his private link. This said fairly abruptly that the Commander in Chief was to do what he was told and not argue.

Maclean goes on to claim that SOE in London tried to sabotage his air passage and that Lord Selborne, the cabinet minister in charge of SOE, suggested to him that he take an oath of loyalty to SOE and had dangled the Distinguished Service Order in front of him as an inducement. Maclean says that the Wilson signal had not been sent by the general at all, and someone else must have drafted it. There is a clear implication that it was Keble. Maclean then recounts a meeting with General Wilson in which he learned that SOE had employed a Colonel Vellacott to spread misinformation about him; and there is again a clear implication that this had been organized by Keble.

Maclean's account is rather damning to Keble, but the Foreign Office files appear to show that Maclean's memory about the first part of his story is not too good. They show that he was brought home by the Foreign Office—not Churchill—and the purpose was to brief him as political advisor to the head of the mission. A July 26 signal from the Foreign Office to the deputy minister of state in Cairo states very specifically that Maclean was to act as second in command of the SOE mission and as political advisor furnishing the head of his mission with reports on political matters. This signal makes it clear that Lieutenant Colonel Maclean and Colonel Bailey were to be the political advisors to the brigadier to be accredited to Tito and to the brigadier to be accredited to Mihailović. The files also show that a Brigadier Orr had already been nominated by General Wilson for the job with Tito and that SOE had yet another brigadier as a reserve candidate. There is nothing in the files to confirm Maclean's claim that he was brought home specifically to head up the mission.

But Maclean did manage to see Churchill. He spent a weekend at Chequers in late July. On July 28 the prime minister wrote a personal memo indicating that he wanted Maclean to do both the political and military jobs with the rank of brigadier.

Lord Selborne, minister of economic warfare, and Sir Charles Hambro, head of SOE London, both pleaded for the original plan of having the military and political functions separate. Sir Orme Sargent of the Foreign Office agreed with them at first. Subsequently, he wrote,

After talking the matter over with Sir C. Hambro I accepted his arguments, but I have now seen Colonel Maclean who has been informed by SOE of this new development, and he tells me that he personally would be in favour of the Prime Minister's proposal. His reasons are that he would be afraid that C in C Middle East are not really interested in this Yugoslav venture and that their name is being taken in vain by SOE, who, in order to magnify their position, are planning to send out a number of inefficient officers, many of whom will be senior to Colonel Maclean, and that it would be difficult for him to work with them satisfactorily. He suspects that the officers who SOE are to obtain from the Middle East are not chosen because of their suitability for this particular work, but are merely rejects from the army which Headquarters wish to get rid of.

That was a pretty ruthless spiel, and it certainly presaged the high-powered methods used subsequently by Maclean in aid of Tito. It fixed the opposition in London.

The argument rumbled on for a few days, but naturally in the end the Old Man got his way and General Wilson was so informed.

Maclean subsequently seems to have concentrated his efforts entirely on supplying Tito with military hardware and moral support. All of the political tasks that were laid down in the original brief to him were apparently forgotten. These political objectives included one specifying that the Partisans should undertake not to fight General Mihailović's forces except in self-defense. "Our first aim," the instructions stated,

is . . . to endeavour to bring about the co-ordination of the military activities of General Mihailovic and the Partisans (and any other resistance elements in Yugoslavia) under the direction of the Commander in Chief Middle East. . . .

At the same time the ultimate aim of His Majesty's Government is to endeavour to reconcile all such groups to each other and to persuade them to subordinate the racial religious and ideological differences which separate them today, so that Yugoslav unity may be preserved and the political, economic and constitutional problems which today confront the country may be settled by the free will of the people.

It is indeed sad that the unquestionably spectacular energy and talents of Fitzroy Maclean were not concentrated on the political side and on trying to stop the Yugoslav civil war. Instead, those remarkable talents and stratospheric drive resulted in tremendous Allied support for Tito—and for Tito's ambitions. Regrettably, Tito's first and foremost ambition was to destroy Mihailović and the royal Yugoslav government through an out-and-out civil war.

Whatever happened in London, there is no doubt that Brigadier Keble, and Colonel Tamplin too, attempted to block the appointment of Maclean as military and political head of the mission. A memo written by Maclean on September 3 (FO 371/37612) deals with a meeting between Maclean and Lord Glenconner that could best be described as cold. Lord Glenconner had evidently called the meeting in an effort to bury the hatchet. It would perhaps be a little ingenuous to say that the meeting was successful. "Lord Glenconner observed that we now had reached deadlock."

This row, together with the row about the Greek delegation of resistance figures mentioned earlier, brought about the Foreign Office recommendation that MO4 be placed under command of General Headquarters Middle East. In due course this happened, and MO4 was renamed Force 133. For whatever reasons, it seems to have become accepted that MO4, and perhaps Brigadier Keble in particular, were operating their own policies.

It is ironic that in Yugoslavia the policy operated by Brigadier Keble from January to November 1943 prepared the ground, created the atmosphere, and opened the floodgates for Brigadier Maclean's brilliantly implemented program of total support for Tito. But Keble became a casualty. It was a straight personality clash, nothing to do with policy. Maclean intended to run his show himself with no interference from anyone. There was no room in that scenario for cooperation with the dynamic and dominant Keble.

The downfall of Keble is ascribed in Basil Davidson's *Special*

Operations Europe, in the author's usual colorful manner, to his crossing swords with Fitzroy Maclean and specifically to his alleged instruction to Colonel Vellacott to confide in all useful ears around the best bars in Cairo the deliberate lie that Maclean was a hopeless drunk, an active homosexual, and a consistent coward. Davidson presumably gleaned this story from Maclean's own writings. But the fanciful impression given by Davidson that Keble was fired almost at once—"and that was pretty much the end of Keble . . . this was really the last that was heard of the man who got the intercepts and used them, and a few months later he was dead"—is factually inaccurate. Keble's regimental records show that, after he had worked away for nearly three months more in MO4, he was transerred to another job as chief of staff maintaining his rank as temporary brigadier, received the Order of the British Empire for his SOE work, stayed in the army, and died in 1948 aged forty-four. The truth is duller than Davidson's colorful "faction." But, as Davidson records, nothing about Keble's era in SOE was dull.

In another colorful passage of *Special Operations Europe* Basil Davidson asserts,

A top level meeting called by General Wilson launched yet another purge of SOE Cairo, and all obstacles were removed. But well forewarned now, Maclean took another step to win the war. Happening to have the right connections, he provided himself with a separate and secret radio link by wave length and code, between himself in Yugoslavia and General Wilson in Cairo, as well as with the Prime Minister in London. So that later on, as he told us thirty years later, "when I found that Churchill was not receiving signals from me [at Tito's Headquarters] that had been duly despatched [via SOE Cairo] and acknowledged, I was fortunately able to repeat them to him in full by another [radio] channel."

It makes a good story. But it also faithfully reflects the atmosphere and practice of SOE Cairo in 1943. Because he had the imprimatur of the prime minister, Maclean was able to deal with MO4 and Brigadier Keble. But the British liaison officers with Mihailović had no imprimatur from Churchill. We were on our own with hosts who were being deceived, betrayed, and denounced as enemies by our own headquarters. Our requests and our signals were being ignored. Our successes were being attributed to the Partisans, not to our hosts, the Loyalists. While we can laugh today about MO4 snarling up with Brigadier Maclean and getting a bloody nose, MO4's shenanigans were no laughing matter for us BLOs who had no court of appeal or ultimate recourse. So we should now leave the Keble era in Cairo. Whatever it was at the start, in the autumn of 1943 it became an era of undisguised skulduggery.

Et Al.

There were, of course, many others in MO4 Cairo. I recollect a charming old Etonian, Denis Ionides. He was a fairly junior officer concerned chiefly with administration. He stayed junior, probably because he was so decent, but he saw everything that went on. He died some years back just after David Martin brought out his book *Patriot or Traitor: The Case of General Mihailovich*. He was no longer able to read, but his wife recorded how he clutched the book, happy in the thought that at last someone had spoken out.

Even if this anecdote is apocryphal, it still fits very precisely with the whole scene and with my own affectionate memory of Ionides.

There were various captains and majors and even a lieutenant colonel in the Yugoslav section in the summer and autumn of 1943, but they came and they went, and it is very clear that the changing nature of the personnel enabled those who were permanent to determine policy. The characters who left their mark in MO4 Cairo were of course Davidson, Deakin, Klugmann, Seton-Watson, and Keble. Bailey left no mark in Cairo but a very mysterious trail in Canada and in Yugoslavia itself.

And what about the delightful, old-fashioned archivist, Miss Flannery? Did she exist in the flesh or was she just an apocryphal figure? You may recall her being mentioned in Basil Davidson's fifty stunning pages on the Partisan-Četnik office war. Was she real or mythical? Either way, it's a good story.

From June 1943 onward it was obvious—if it had not been so earlier—that Mihailović was going to be dumped sooner or later and that support of the Partisans was the bandwagon to jump on. Once Maclean was appointed by the prime minister in early August, there was only one possible way that things could go. The policy acquired an unstoppable momentum. But it was MO4 that blazed the trail ensuring that Tito would be given Allied support in his bid to replace the Yugoslav people's cruel Axis yoke with the even crueler Stalinist yoke. With the possible exception of Klugmann, the team members, in their gung-ho enthusiasm for Tito, surely failed to foresee the horrifying massacres, the misery, and the economic destitution that communism would bring to Yugoslavia.

CHAPTER
2
Yugoslavia
■

**THE YUGOSLAV ARMY OF THE HOMELAND: THE LOYALISTS
AND OTHER "ČETNIKS"**

The Germans attacked Yugoslavia on April 6, 1941, starting with
an air bombardment of Belgrade that killed more than 10,000.
The German offensive followed tortuous political maneuvering
in which the Germans brought considerable pressure to bear on
the Yugoslav regent, Prince Paul, and the government to adhere
to the Axis. Under this pressure the Yugoslav prime minister
signed a protocol of adherence to the Tripartite Pact on March
25 in Vienna. This resulted in a military coup against the government and Prince Paul. Young King Peter, who was just under
age, was proclaimed of age and placed on the throne. The coup
was led by an air force general named Simović. Churchill declared that Yugoslavia "had found her soul." The new Yugoslav

government tried to placate the Germans, but Hitler was determined to attack Greece and liquidate Yugoslavia as a state.

The Yugoslavs were wrong-footed. The Nazi propaganda set the Croats and the Serbs against each other, and it was effectively over within a week. The government and the king fled the country. Croatia seceded from Yugoslavia to form a new state under German sponsorship led by Ante Pavelić and his *ustaša* fascists. The Croatians taken by the German army were allowed to return home, while a large number of Serbian officers and soldiers who had been captured were shipped off to prisoner-of-war camps. Nevertheless, a substantial portion of the army escaped capture and made its way home or took refuge in the mountains. Many of them took their arms with them.

The country was dismembered. Slovenia in the north was split between Greater Germany and Italy. The *ustaša*-controlled Independent State of Croatia (known as the NDH) incorporated the greater part of Bosnia and Herzegovina and was itself split between Italian and German zones of control and influence. Various bits and pieces of the Yugoslav territory were split off, to Hungary in the northeast and to Bulgaria and to Italian-occupied Albania in the south, while important parts of the coastal province of Dalmatia went to Italy. The main part of Serbia— that is, what was left after the bits and pieces had been chipped off—came under direct German military rule. A Serbian government under General Nedić was appointed to control administration of this remaining rump for the Germans. Unlike Ante Pavelić, the *poglavnik* (dictator) of the new Independent State of Croatia, Nedić was no fascist. Like General Pétain in France, he was a patriotic collaborator who felt that this course was the best means to save something of his country and his people. Nedić formed a paramilitary organization, a Serbian state guard, to police German-occupied Serbia.

The *ustaša* had been an outlawed terrorist organization before the war, with its main refuge in Italy. It was responsible for the murder of King Alexander in Marseilles on October 9, 1934. It was distinctly fascist in nature, and its paramilitary forces were similar to the SS. Immediately on gaining power in the new Independent State of Croatia, these forces started a reign of terror.

It was directed principally against the Serbian minority with the declared intention of driving out one-third, converting one-third from the Orthodox to the Roman Catholic faith, and killing one-third. I doubt that the conversion program achieved its 33 percent, but certainly a very substantial proportion of the population became refugees, fleeing into Serbia or into the mountains. There was also massive genocide. Estimates of the numbers killed vary greatly; according to the Serbs it may well have reached several hundreds of thousands. There were reports of rivers literally running red with blood. The *ustaša* program enormously intensified the historical strife between the Serbs and the Croats and became a major factor in what happened later. So did the flow of refugees into the mountains.

It was as a direct consequence of the events in Croatia that a great proportion of those sheltering in the woods and mountains in Croatia and Bosnia, and some even in Serbia itself, were Serbs driven from their homes and unable to return. The Serbs as a people were experienced in guerrilla warfare after a long history of struggle against foreign oppression, and these Serb refugees constituted the main source of fighting men for the resistance movements.

Thus in Yugoslavia there was a large pool of manpower represented by the soldiers who had avoided capture, by the refugees from towns, and by the Serbian refugees from the genocide in Croatia. To this group—and most importantly—were to be added the refugees from reprisals, which caused the pool of manpower to become self-replenishing. The resistance forces, mobile and living off the land, clashed with the occupation forces. When the occupation forces carried out reprisals, the villagers fled and joined the mobile forces. Thus the whole cycle started anew. This pattern was fundamental to the growth of the communist Partisan movement. I believe that it was rather cynically exploited by them in order to strengthen their numbers on the one hand and destroy the established order in the villages on the other. Certainly, reprisals were neither deliberately avoided nor regretted by the communist elite, who just made noble noises about necessary sacrifices.

But there were also the "Četniks." The whole Četnik concept—even the very term itself—enormously complicated the resistance picture. The term derives from *četa*, or band. For centuries the villages had formed these bands for their own protection against foreign invaders. In Western European terms they were a form of home guard or militia. As a result of this tradition, armed bands of *all* types tended to be called by the very loose term *Četniks*. They included bands of various political complexions and even straightforward bandit gangs. Confusing the issue further, the term came to be both approbatory and pejorative, depending on the speaker.

Because of widespread support from Četnik groups the Mihailović movement became known loosely as "the Četniks"; and it was always known as such by the Allies. I am not clear whether Mihailović himself used the term for his movement at an earlier stage, but later the main Mihailović forces called themselves "the Yugoslav Army of the Homeland." I think the term was coined because the communists had seen and exploited the propaganda value of calling every noncommunist grouping—regardless of its political affiliation—Četnik and then accusing its members of collaboration. In this manner—by association—Mihailović was accused of collaboration.

Yugoslavia is a large and enormously varied country with a diversity of peoples: from the Slovenes in the north with an Austro-Hungarian culture; via the Croatians with an Austro-Hungarian overlay on a Slav peasant background; through Bosnia, where there were substantial Serb and Muslim populations; through the Serbian heartland with its fiercely individualistic Serbian character, Slav but something quite individual and special; through Montenegro, another unique area with a fierce mountain Serbian type but a bit different from the Serb of the flatter agricultural land; down to Macedonia, where Bulgar and Greek influences were felt. In this hodgepodge, which had unified itself spontaneously as a reaction to domination by the surrounding powers and which was proclaimed a state on December 1, 1918, there were inevitably many cultures, many groupings, many affiliations, and many loyalties. No wonder there were so many different četas and Četniks, and some of them had to be collaborators.

It is primarily, but not exclusively, for this reason that I use the term *Loyalists* to denote Mihailović's regular mobile forces and his committed nonmobile reserves. The term reflects their rather simple loyalty to their nation and their king.

Regrettably, as things developed in Yugoslavia, the Yugoslav Army of the Homeland never really got off the ground as a national movement, and for this the British must bear a very considerable responsibility. While Mihailović struggled to establish control over the Četnik units dispersed from Slovenia in the north to Macedonia in the south, the MO4 policy—the consequences of which were probably never really thought through—was to drop liaison officers only to Serbia, where the Mihailović movement was already predominant and well organized. This meant that the Mihailović movement was never given the help it needed to build up elsewhere.

Furthermore, MO4 insisted that the British liaison officers report directly back to MO4 in Cairo. Generally they had no wireless communications with the chief liaison officer at Mihailović's headquarters. This lack of central control within Yugoslav territory of the Mihailović BLOs derived from the SOE policy of wishing to control resistance movements directly and to use them ultimately as an arm of military strategy. The policy added enormously to Mihailović's own problems of control. MO4 on the one hand was trying to tell his subcommanders—through us BLOs— what to do and on the other blaming Mihailović for what the outlying areas did or did not do. Similarly, MO4 even dictated the distribution of supplies so that Mihailović's control of his subordinates was weakened and, even worse, was seen to be weakened. In addition, MO4 eventually exploited its direct contact with BLOs in the outlying commands in order to gather alleged evidence against Mihailović and thus to create dissension in the movement.

It is worth digressing here to consider the influence of the BBC and other radio networks, and the subject of misinformation generally. (The word "disinformation" to denote intentional misleading is a modern term, somehow inapplicable in this World War II narrative. But that is the meaning I have in mind when using "misinformation.")

In the early days, the BBC was fulsome in its praise of Mihailović and his Loyalists. Too fulsome, in fact. His movement was built up to such a ludicrous extent that it raised hopes that could not possibly be justified, and incidentally caused the Germans to intensify their brutal reprisals. Claiming editorial freedom as its prerogative and accepting only general guidance, the BBC seems not to have realized that every broadcast would be picked up, studied, and perhaps acted on: in the Axis camp, in the Allied camp, and in the Yugoslav territory itself.

By contrast, every German news broadcast was drafted to serve specific purposes defined by the military and political leaders. Sometimes it was cleverly done; frequently not so cleverly; but the military and political direction was clear. And it prevailed. Not so with the BBC. It was so, however, with the Voice of Free Yugoslavia programs broadcast from southern Russia from mid-1942. These broadcasts, purporting to come from a free and purely Yugoslav station, were in fact coordinated between the Soviet leadership and Tito and directed solely toward building up the Partisan movement.

Until mid-1942 the BBC had a clear field and encouraged patriots—and opportunists—to subscribe to the Loyalist movement. Before the beginning of 1943 the broadcasts started to become equivocal, wittingly or unwittingly supporting the Free Yugoslavia line, and throughout 1943 the left-wing bias became more and more marked. Later, when in December 1943 the British government finally decided to turn up the heat, the BBC unleashed a barrage of anti-Mihailović and pro-Tito propaganda. That some 100 Allied servicemen were in the hands of the Loyalists did not deter the BBC.

In fact, already in the late summer and autumn of 1943, the BBC news was being heavily doctored. Whether this was by influence of SOE Cairo, the Minister of State's Office, or possibly the PWE, I do not know. The official policy as laid down in June 1943 by the chiefs of staff, and specifically spelled out in their cable quoted a little later, was that radio propaganda would be brought into line with the policy of fairly supporting both Mihailović and other groups fighting the Axis.

Even so, the left-wing doctoring was flagrant. In September 1943 a large bridge near Višegrad, probably the largest blown by resistance movements in the Balkans, was demolished by Major Archie Jack, covered by Mihailović forces and watched by the chief BLO with Mihailović, Brigadier Armstrong. The BBC announced this as a *Partisan* success. Similarly, my own first sabotage operation, on the night of September 30, 1943, which involved the destruction of a length of line on the main Belgrade-Salonika railway, about one kilometer long and demolished at every joint, and which blocked traffic for seven to ten days, was, within forty-eight hours of my reporting it to Cairo, attributed by the BBC to the Partisans. Thus the British misinformation campaign in favor of the communists was already in gear well before December 1943.

With all of this misinformation it is indeed amazing that, six months after the British had denounced Mihailović and mounted a massive pro-Partisan campaign, the bulk of Serbia still remained totally under Mihailović's influence, resisting the Germans and Bulgars. We were able to travel from our operational area in southeastern Serbia in the spring of 1944 some 150 miles in a large column in daylight to Pranjani near Čačak for evacuation from an airstrip near Mihailović's headquarters without encountering a single Partisan unit.

But when we arrived in Bari we found that the maps in the SOE office showed the areas we had passed through and lodged in as being firmly in Partisan hands. That demonstrated graphically the extent of misinformation inside SOE. There was an incident in which one BLO, a very responsible individual with a civil-service background, was so incensed that he struck the pins off the map. From then on the ex-Mihailović BLOs were forbidden access to the map room.

I must ask here: Could the maps, which were allegedly prepared from "most secret sources" intercepts and claimed to have been decisive in persuading Churchill to approve contact with the Tito Partisans in his Cairo meetings in early 1943, have been as erroneous as the demonstrably false maps in Bari in June 1944?

MO4 maps were decisive on another occasion: the critical

meeting on December 10, 1943, in the prime minister's bed-room, at which he effectively abandoned Mihailović. There is a most revealing memo (PREM 3 510/10 5) to Churchill from his intelligence advisor, Desmond Morton. It is dated December 2, 1943. It reads,

> SOE Cairo has given me for you a copy of their MOST SE-CRET MAP showing the disposition of the Partisan forces and Mihailović as at 8 A.M. this morning December 2nd. . . . This map shows the position much better than the one you receive daily in London. The London version suggests that the Germans hold most of the country with the Partisans hiding in inaccessible districts. Cairo's operational map, which is corrected daily from the large number of operational telegrams which they receive from the field, shows almost the reverse to be the position. The Germans are holding all the main lines of communications but the greater part of the country is in Partisan hands. The Cairo map also shows the very small districts now held by Mihailovic.

If further proof were needed that someone in Cairo was cooking the books late in 1943, this is conclusive. The London maps were prepared by objective intelligence officers from various sources, *including, of course, all of the intercepts.* The Cairo map claimed to be based on information from the field. But the real information from the field demonstrated that virtually all Serbia, all Serbian territory annexed to Albania and Bulgaria, and, at that stage, the Sandžak, together with substantial areas of Montenegro and even parts of Bosnia were Mihailović territory. Can I prove this? Yes. All of the Partisan propaganda in the world cannot wish away the operational log in the Public Records Office. The log contains the reports from the field to which Desmond Morton refers, and they tell a different story of Mihailović's strength. As to those areas which were indeed under Tito's control, Cairo was receiving signals from only a small number of missions, maybe five or so, spread over huge areas, and the BLOs with the Partisans were transmitting Partisan-source information. That map was "cooked," and there are no two ways about it. It so happens that Klugmann had a clear field on December 2, 1943, the day the bogus map was first seen by Desmond Morton. Keble had just left on November 27 and Deakin did not arrive till December 9.

Deakin, who then took over the Yugoslav section on December 13, had just come directly from the field and had, shortly before, had a narrow escape when his plane was bombed on the ground. The pressures and the preparation of his famous collaboration dossier about alleged Mihailović misdoings clearly preoccupied his attention so that he had no time to check maps, and it has to be assumed that the map referred to by Desmond Morton was used at the fateful meeting with the prime minister on December 10, 1943.

In the later map incident in Bari in June 1944 it was actually Maj. Jasper Rootham, who had been private secretary to Neville Chamberlain before the war, who struck the pins off the map. Jasper and Archie Jack visited the map room together and were aghast that large areas they had just covered as BLOs to Mihailović were shown in Partisan hands. They knew this to be false because they had moved around freely and had encountered no Partisans. The officer in charge of the map room told them that they were misinformed, whereupon Rootham swung at the map. They were so upset that Archie Jack called a meeting of a number of Mihailović BLOs and insisted that Klugmann attend. Klugmann's explanation was a pathetic amalgam of excuses: that the decisions came from above and had to be obeyed; that there was lack of effective office staff, lack of cypher clerks, and so on. He was most apologetic and conciliatory, and the BLOs believed him. At that stage Klugmann's true nature was not realized.

The Cairo map given to Desmond Morton in December 1943 was allegedly prepared from operational signals, and it suited the Partisan case much better than the maps in London prepared from all sources, including, of course, all of the intercepts. Yet the previous map served up by MO4 to Churchill—which, according to Davidson, was crucial to the decisions made in January 1943—was prepared just from the intercepts to which Keble was privy. It all sounds like an awfully selective use of information.

Misinformation about what was happening was the major factor in the Yugoslav civil war. It was widespread at base and in the field.

From the end of 1942, when Colonel Bailey dropped to Mihailović but failed to bring any material support or encouragement, it must have become increasingly clear both to Mihailović himself and to his outlying commanders that the British were manipulating the movement. From the middle of 1943, when the British missions were dropped to the Tito Partisans and started to give them massive supplies, it must have been obvious to all that the Loyalist movement was in danger of being dumped.

In particular, it is incredible and shameful that SOE Cairo started dropping missions to the Partisans and pouring in supplies to them without any prior consultation with Mihailović. Was he not bound to suspect that the British missions being dropped to his local commanders were no more than spies?

The Mihailović movement would have had great potential had it been able to draw on the huge manpower loyal to the king and wanting to join, particularly in Serbia. With coordination between Mihailović, his local commanders, and BLOs properly dispersed throughout the country both within and outside Serbia, his movement could have met any demands by Cairo or London for carefully planned, timed, and organized sabotage. Moreover, they could have been coordinated with Middle East Command strategies far better than could be achieved by Tito's lumbering mobile columns, which were, in any case, serving another master—communism.

If we had stayed with Mihailović, we could have secured the total defection of the Nedić state guards in 1944 when the *ustanak*—the great uprising—was called. The Allies had no qualms about trying to turn the Vichy French, an exactly parallel case. This would have brought arms and men to the Allied side and would have been considerably less offensive ethically than the turning, and use against Serbs, of the brutal Bulgarians, achieved by Tito with the help of the Soviets late in 1944.

Mihailović enjoyed great popular support with the ordinary people. I can only speak for the peasants in the southeastern

Serbian mountains, and from what I heard secondhand from other areas, but based on these sources the support in Serbia itself for the Loyalist movement, for the king, and for Mihailović personally was astonishingly strong.

Tragically, Mihailović was a bad organizer—indeed, rather a bumbling bureaucrat—and he had poor advisors. He was also vulnerable through his association with the exiled government. As in many other countries, there was a hard core of disaffection with the prewar regime. None of this would have mattered if the British had helped him take a real grip on his forces, and if the British had not reviled him, cheated him, and eventually put a knife in his back.

In spite of the equivocal and devious attitude of MO4 regarding the Mihailović movement, the BLOs throughout were treated as allies and even friends by the Loyalists. I know of no case in which a British serviceman was mishandled or even rudely treated, or restricted in any way from going where he wanted. Many of us traveled around entirely on our own volition, and I for one arbitrarily changed from one Loyalist unit to another according to the possibilities of getting sabotage carried out. Escaped prisoners of war were succored, as were crashed aircrews, and nothing was asked in return. The same applied to Yugoslav nationals under the formal or informal protection of the British missions.

There were about 500 total, mostly American, crashed aircrewmen, scattered like confetti over thousands of square miles, safely passed from Loyalist village to Loyalist village to the evacuation rendezvous. It would be fascinating to compare the numbers of aircrewmen evacuated by the Loyalists with those helped by the Partisans. I believe that such a comparison would demonstrate the much larger area in Loyalist hands until late in 1944. Attention should also be drawn to the manner of treatment dealt out by the two armies. There are many complaints from Americans about their treatment by the Partisans.

Mihailović and his commanders maintained a pedantically correct and friendly attitude to the British missions right up to our departure at the end of May 1944. This is truly remarkable when it is considered that we had withdrawn support from him

THE RAPE OF SERBIA

at the end of 1943 and had even before then poured thousands of tons of supplies into his enemy's hands.

In the light of the courteous treatment of the missions by Mihailović and his observance of diplomatic niceties regarding their Yugoslav members, one reads with a sense of shame a signal in which Brigadier Maclean at Tito's headquarters outlined the procedure to be followed in the event that Tito forces captured British missions with Mihailović. It was agreed that the British members of the missions would be given safe-conduct directly out of the country, but members of Yugoslav origin would be first arrested and then treated according to the findings of the Partisans. We all have a good idea what those findings would have been. This took place while the British were providing Tito with the arms that he was using to attack Mihailović, and while the official policy of the Joint Chiefs of Staff was still that Partisan units could be supported only if they pledged not to use arms against Mihailović units.

In the late summer of 1941, about six months after the start of Yugoslav resistance, a spontaneous uprising took place in Serbia and Montenegro, as a result of which the Germans carried out massive reprisals against the civilian population in Serbia. Although his forces became drawn into this uprising, Mihailović and the exiled royal government, as well as SOE London, were all opposed in principle to arbitrary general resistance on the grounds that it was quite unsustainable at that stage of the war and that it was bound to result in the destruction of the nation and particularly of the Serbian people. The Serbs had suffered massively in the First World War, losing 1.5 million from a population of about 6 million, and they were again being massacred in the genocide program that was still being carried out by the *ustaša* in Croatia.

As a trained soldier and a student of guerrilla-warfare tactics— and as a veteran of the very harsh Serbian experiences in the First World War— Mihailović recognized that general uprisings by inadequately armed, half-trained guerrillas were wasteful and unproductive. Rather, he believed honestly and passionately that the right course was to build up in the mountains a numerically strong force, to obtain arms for them from the Allies, and to prepare for a general uprising to coincide with an Allied landing on the Adriatic coast or Greece, or—as actually did happen—with the entry of the Red Army. In the meantime he felt that all attacks on the Axis or sabotage had to be weighed in each individual case by the value of the action against its probable cost in reprisals.

In preferring this policy, Mihailović was doing no more and no less than other European resistance movements, counseled precisely along these lines by SOE as he was. Both SOE and the royal government in exile specifically instructed him in 1941 to follow this strategy. Actually, in 1941 and 1942 extensive sabotage was carried out by Mihailović's forces. Very little was known about this activity in Allied circles, partly because of his lack of communications with the Allies and partly because of his lamentably negligent attitude regarding public relations. In this he was totally outgunned by the communist dialectical materialists.

The Germans were actually more threatened by the bide-your-time policy than by one of haphazard aggression. If the guerrillas came into the open and pitted themselves against the German regular forces, defeat and subsequent reprisals were inevitable. But the threat of guerrillas in the mountains, dispersed over huge areas and able to appear anywhere, tied down substantial Axis forces. It should be recorded that more enemy divisions were deployed in Yugoslavia, guarding the towns, the mineral resources, and the communications, in 1941–42 than were deployed late in 1944 when Tito had received massive Allied support. The reason, of course, was that Tito was using the vast bulk of his resources and forces not against the Germans but in civil war.

It is fascinating to note how Tito apologists among the historians will try to demonstrate how there were very few German units in Serbia, thus implying that the Loyalists were not resisting. But when they come to talk about Tito "liberating Serbia," suddenly from nowhere the German enemy becomes predominant. As always, the Partisans' apologists want everything all ways.

THE NATIONAL LIBERATION ARMY (PEOPLE'S LIBERATION ARMY): THE COMMUNIST TITO AND HIS PARTISANS

The Partisan organization was totally different from that of the Loyalists. It had fundamentally different origins. As I have explained, the Mihailović movement sprang up spontaneously and represented at best nothing more than an alliance of patriotic elements loosely linked together in a common desire to resist the invader. By contrast, the Partisan organization grew out of a prewar undercover communist scheme. Tito, the Croatian Josip Broz, had spent virtually all of his adult life as a servant of the Comintern. He served in the Austrian army in Russia during the First World War. He was wounded and he stayed in Russia, marrying a Russian and working there for a time. He returned to Yugoslavia to organize on behalf of the Comintern, the Moscow-dominated international organization linking Communist parties. He served a prison term for his political activities. He survived Stalin's purges in the late 1930s and had become the unchallenged leader of Yugoslav communism before the outbreak of the Second World War. He was a totally committed Stalinist communist.

Partisan mythology has it that the Partisan movement started to resist when the Germans invaded Yugoslavia in April 1941, but this is communist special pleading. The Partisans followed the instructions of their Soviet masters to the letter and did not appear as resisters and patriots until Germany attacked Soviet Russia. Indeed, Sava Bosnić, a well-known historian, recently gave a paper in Canada revealing how the Gestapo helped to return Yugoslav communists from Spain in 1940. The communists were tolerated by the Germans until June 22, 1941, when the SS ordered the arrest of communists previously protected by the Nazi-Soviet pact. Even then Tito did not exactly jump into the fray. In fact, he needed a reminder from Moscow on July 4 to call for partisans to join the general uprising (for more on this subject see Milan Deroc, *Special Operations Explored*).

Already before the war the communists had a network of cells throughout most of Yugoslavia. Their aims had nothing whatsoever to do with Yugoslav patriotism, although to be fair it must be said that many Yugoslav communists later exhibited great patriotism. The communist cells had to do with plotting, planning, and organizing the breakdown of the established order. They also had to follow the tactical dictates of the Comintern.

Tito's ideas in 1941 were very different from Mihailović's, and they are clearly on record thanks to the books written by Milovan Djilas, number three in the Partisan hierarchy and postwar vice-president of Yugoslavia, and by Vladimir Dedijer, Tito's personal biographer. Both have turned revisionist. The Partisans were not overly worried about reprisals against the civil population, as is loud and clear from Djilas's writings. The victims were just casualties of "the great struggle for freedom," as they were wont to put it. Tito was foremost concerned with meeting the imperious demands of his master Stalin for action, any action, and immediate action to relieve in any way, however small, the pressure of the German armies invading Russia and threatening Moscow. Considerations such as avoiding reprisals against his countrymen were secondary. He was, of course, also concerned with getting ready to grab power.

Tito was, furthermore, particularly interested in building up his own numbers in order to achieve superiority over the Loyalists and to broaden his political base. As I have already written, the German reprisals increased the flow of men into the woods and mountains. These refugees tended to join the Partisans because they had mobile forces moving through and on, out of the devastated areas.

This was the essential difference: Tito's forces were largely mobile; they had no permanent home base. They occupied territory and moved on when Axis pressure became too great or when their political objectives required them to take over new areas. They left a degree of devastation behind, but they also left a strengthened communist political organization wherever they went. They made a point of destroying the civil administration and the municipal or village records and of liquidating any potential political rivals. Thus, in true Marxist-Leninist style, the Partisans were at every opportunity creating chaos which could be exploited politically at a later date, even when they had to flee before German military action against them.

Tito's concern right from the start was to make his movement a national one and to gain power throughout the country. This was almost an obsession with him, as was his having been driven out of Serbia by the Germans after the 1941 uprising. The need to get back into Serbia dominated his policy. Astutely he called his movement the National Liberation Army or the People's Liberation Army, thus underlining the nonsectarian nature of his movement.

In 1942 the term "partisan," like the term "Četnik," was often used loosely to describe any guerrilla group. Resistance groups right across the political spectrum were called partisans. This led to quite some misunderstanding in the British agencies and to the attribution of the extensive Loyalist activities in 1941 and 1942 to "partisans" and thus, by association, to Tito's Partisans. It does not explain or excuse, however, the BBC giving undue credit to the Partisans—with a capital *P*—in 1943. By that time, the distinction was quite clear.

Tito's main columns plodded backward and forward from Užice in western Serbia west through Bosnia as far as Bihać. They also marched south through Herzegovina into Montenegro and back again. In their moves into Montenegro they were set on first destroying the Montenegrin Četniks and then turning east into Sandžak and Serbia. They moved in long, single-file columns. This exhausting process was neither economical nor productive. Casualties were horrendous. As a general rule the wounded could not be left in friendly areas—the traditional guerrilla method, which was favored by the Loyalists—but had to be carried, suffering, until they recovered or died or had to be abandoned. In the famous rout from Mount Durmitor, proclaimed by communist propaganda as a victorious breakout from the fifth Axis offensive, Tito was cornered and only escaped by abandoning his wounded, by jettisoning a large proportion of his armament, and by leaving fairly substantial forces to their fate with orders to give cover to the Partisan headquarters staff and their main forces— which were running for their lives.

In the areas of Bosnia, Herzegovina, and Croatia where these Partisan forces lumbered back and forth there were of course frequent clashes with Axis troops. Communications were sabotaged but not in accordance with any strategic plan. Rather, they were broken to protect Partisan retreats; and the movements were practically always retreats. Furthermore, the area in which all this movement went on was not really vital to the Axis. What were important to the Germans were the main rail lines and mines— and they went on operating both.

While the military advantages derived from the Partisan mode of operation are questionable, the political advantages were not. The areas through which the forces traveled were being prepared as first priority for communist takeover. When from time to time the Axis area commander decided the ploy had gone far enough, he moved against Partisan units. Such retaliations became the "second," "third," and "fourth" offensives in Partisan propaganda and mythology. The miserable transport of suffering humanity, dragged and carried behind the fleeing Partisans, created the Partisan legend that "wounded were never abandoned." In fact they were, but it all gave the impression of huge numbers and great glory.

These tactics also affected the intercepts. To read historians of the Partisan school and persuasion one obtains the impression that the intercepted German signals spelled out details of intense Partisan resistance effort and of Četnik collaboration. No such thing. The intercepts chiefly carried reports of "bandit" sightings and of movements of Axis forces. For a long time the Germans referred to all resistance as "bandit activity." Generally they did not specify what brand of bandit. But Partisan apologists have been assiduous in claiming all "bandit activity" mentioned in intercepts as Partisan activity.

The bravery of the Partisans cannot be gainsaid. It was breathtaking. But this had nothing to do with Tito or communism. It was quite simply a quality of the Serbs. Forced to flee their homes, seized and indoctrinated by the communist elite and well led, often by Spanish Civil War veterans, the Serbian qualities shone out. Had we BLOs with the Mihailović forces been allowed to arm, and above all to encourage, the massive numbers of Serbs in the Serbian heartland, then totally under the influence of Mihailović and royalist sentiment, Yugoslavia might well be a democracy today.

The ruthlessness with which the Partisan movement and the

population were manipulated by the ruling clique stands out in Djilas's writings. Even as he was using commissars to indoctrinate the recruits in communist ideology, Tito publicly portrayed the whole movement as a patriotic one. He kept its direction and support by the Soviets very much in the background. In his book *Wartime* Djilas tells us how Stalin more than once told Tito to be careful that the West did not catch on to the Soviet orchestration of the situation.

Tito brilliantly fostered the concept of the integrity of a whole Yugoslavia without sacrificing the special identities of its many nationalities and tribes. This ploy, which suited Soviet Comintern theory, enabled Tito's propagandists to portray Mihailović and the Loyalists as pan-Serb fascists concerned only with Serbian interests and a postwar strengthening of Serbian hegemony.

After the crushing of the 1941 uprising the Partisans lost their foothold in Serbia. Serbia and the neighboring Sandžak were, from a resistance viewpoint, Mihailović territory. Serbia's population was royalist, patriotic, and traditionally very militant against invaders. It was important territory in that the main north-south railway lines traveled the Ibar and Morava valleys and linked Belgrade and Salonika. It was the key rail link for moving German forces up and down from Greece. Serbia also held mineral resources important to Germany. Therefore, Serbia was not only the heartland of the Mihailović Loyalist movement but also strategically the most important area in all of Yugoslavia.

Eastern Bosnia, Montenegro, and Herzegovina were contested by Loyalists and Partisans, and these were the barren lands in which the two forces clashed time and again. Effectively, western Bosnia and Croatia were predominantly Partisan territories with no serious presence of forces loyal to or loosely associated with Mihailović.

Dalmatia in the west and Slovenia in the northwest were two other territories with both Partisan and Loyalist presences at the start. The development of events in these territories was illustrative of the different organization of Mihailović's and Tito's forces.

At the start, the Loyalist commanders in Slovenia and Dalmatia, Karlo Novak and Trifunović Birčanin, respectively, were strongly placed. Unfortunately, they received no support and no encouragement, and they were far removed from Mihailović through both distance and lack of communications. By contrast, Tito's organization exercised rigid control over the communist cells throughout Yugoslavia; excellent communication was maintained. The communist organization, which had existed since peacetime, worked superbly well. With a clear objective—exploitation of the wartime circumstances to destroy all anticommunist opposition—and with the benefit of substantial Allied material support as early as July 1943, Tito's outlying units inevitably overcame the Loyalist forces in Slovenia and Dalmatia, who received not one single planeload from the Allies at any time.

I have spelled out the areas of operations—inevitably in very general terms—in order to make the point that there was a fairly natural geographical division between the Partisan domain and the Loyalist heartland in Serbia. Only after the Allies had publicly denounced Mihailović and urged the Loyalists to switch their allegiance to Tito, and only after the massive logistical support for Tito demonstrated that this was not all communist propaganda, was Tito able to penetrate Serbia in a serious way.

Tito's overwhelming priority—a goal he made quite clear— was the conquest of the Serbian heartland, the "liberation" from the Loyalists. The tragedy is that we, the British, helped him succeed in attaining it.

Except for public-relations purposes, the Partisan war against Axis forces was secondary. It took place. The Axis was occupying Yugoslavia, and it was impossible to move around, particularly in large columns, without stumbling over Germans or Italians or Bulgars. But most of the fighting against the Axis by the Partisans took place in the legendary Axis "offensives"—when the Partisans were on the run and had little choice but to shoot back.

I stress that this section of my book is not written as history but is intended solely to give the lay reader some idea of the background before I come to the main story, which is what I saw with my own eyes in southeastern Serbia in 1943 and the blow-by-blow account of the undoing of Mihailović and the Loyalists.

I have already mentioned the total freedom enjoyed by BLOs

with Mihailović. In sabotage operations, we were free to observe, to help, or to lead. Major Archie Jack played the central role in Loyalist bridge-destruction operations in October 1943, and I personally placed the charges on railway lines together with Loyalist units on a number of occasions from September to December 1943. Even after the break with Mihailović, when we were awaiting evacuation and when he had been formally and publicly abandoned by the Allies, I derailed two more trains. Although they did not help me on the latter two occasions (only because I did not tell them what I was going to do), the Loyalist forces did nothing whatsoever to hinder me, nor did they protest as some of my "more responsible" colleagues, who condemned me, feared they might. Yet a few weeks previously we had publicly denounced them over the BBC as collaborators. Some collaboration!

Compare this with the treatment of the liaison officers by the Partisans. I think it is fair to say that few of them had freedom of movement without surveillance. Where they did not need interpreters they had minders. The American missions with the Partisans made this point after their return, and I have heard British confirm it. They were frequently caught up in the fighting, particularly on the march with the mobile columns, and, sadly, in the "liberation" of Serbia. Nevertheless, I have yet to read of a BLO with the Partisans regularly leading, or even accompanying, demolition teams in their day-to-day sabotage operations, though one or two reported being shown a demonstration. For sabotage reports, the BLOs had to take the Partisans' word. This is what they signaled through. Not all identified it as hearsay.

In contrast, the British with the Loyalists were able to make eyewitness reports truthfully and objectively. In the event that they reported a bit too explicitly in their moments of frustration, their reports were seized on by SOE Cairo and by the Minister of State's Office as justification for their negative view of Mihailović. After rereading my own signals from the field and remembering the circumstances, I am ashamed that I grumbled so much. My complaints provided ammunition that was used to considerable effect in the anti-Mihailović campaign.

Col. Bill "Marko" Hudson and Col. Bill Bailey at Mihailović's headquarters provided particularly valuable material for the critics. Their reports tended to be rather long, rather detailed, and sometimes rather complicated. They could be used selectively to prove almost anything. We did not know, of course, that our masters in Cairo would not just take our messages at face value and, in reading them, allow for the pressure that weighs on any man living in enemy territory. Moreover, I must point out that I for one had no idea that Cairo was not wholeheartedly behind the Mihailović movement. I did not even learn until several months after the fact that a mission had been dropped to Partisan headquarters. That MO4 should be seriously moving toward a break with Mihailović was quite unthinkable.

On the Partisan side it was different; very different indeed and much simpler. The Partisan commanders called the shots, and the Allied officers with their units appear to have mainly served the purpose of providing help. They appear to have had no say in strategy or tactics. The decisions were made by Tito and his subcommanders.

The attitude of the Partisans toward the British was typified by Tito's refusal to allow drops to Partisan units in Serbia. He obviously wanted to avoid the possibility that an independent-minded BLO might contact a BLO with the Loyalists and even organize a local truce arrangement, as I myself tried to do from the Mihailović side at one stage.

Then there was the sudden worsening of the Partisan attitude regarding the BLOs in the autumn of 1944. This is reflected in many reports I have read, and it took place not long after Tito had—in Churchill's word—"levanted" to Moscow to coordinate with the Russians the "liberation" of Serbia. Tito disappeared overnight from his headquarters on Vis, without even informing—much less consulting—the British mission, and he flew off in a Soviet plane or, more correctly, an American-built plane operated by the Soviet mission on Vis.

About this time or shortly afterward the British mission was advised that the liaison officers with the subordinate Partisan commands had to be withdrawn, leaving only the missions with the main commands. This, of course, was the time that the Partisans were preparing the coup de grace against the Loyalist forces, and it has to be assumed that this move reflected the need to camouflage from the British the ruthless measures planned for dealing with the Loyalists and all other potential opponents.

THE BRITISH FOSTERING OF THE CIVIL WAR

The different attitudes of the two movements with regard to the British missions were a logical corollary of their different natures. The Loyalists were led for the most part by regular officers who followed regular traditions and manners and by Serbs who had been allies of the British for decades. Although in fact they were let down, their nature was to continue to regard the British as allies and to treat them as such. The Loyalists, furthermore, were serving their government in exile and their king, who remained under British protection.

Mihailović had no revolutionary purpose. His movement's political aim was to free the country from the occupation; to save it from a communist takeover; and then to hold democratic elections with the help of the Western Allies. He wanted to restore the legitimate government under the monarchy and, last but not least, to restore the honor of the army after its ignominious April 1941 defeat. In pursuance of this general-resistance concept, the movement was prepared to cooperate with and accept direction from the Allies, provided that its leaders were satisfied that they were not being manipulated or asked to subject their people to reprisals without weighing the consequences and without a quid pro quo.

The Partisans, by contrast, set themselves up as a sovereign state with a national army. They pretended to this stature even when they were nothing more than a rabble of outlaws running from encirclement to encirclement. They admitted of no interference and pretended to be dealing militarily on a basis of army commander to army commander and politically on a basis of government to government.

The difference in the two relationships was really almost ludicrous. Mihailović was the minister of defense of a legitimate though exiled government. He was the leading political figure and commander of the forces in the Serbian homeland. Yet he was treated by MO4 as a lackey. Tito early in 1943 was staggering from rout to rout with mobile forces smaller than those of Mihailović and with reserves minuscule compared to those of the Loyalists. Yet Tito's movement was built up by MO4 without making any serious effort to achieve any degree of control.

While Tito was becoming confident and aggressive, what was happening psychologically to Mihailović? By June 1943 if not earlier he must have been strongly suspicious that, at best, the Allies intended to abandon him outside Serbia or, at worst, the Loyalists had been sold out to the Russians in some strategic superpower deal. He had been living in the mountains and the woods for more than two years, constantly under threat, with the responsibility for his movement and indeed for all of the people of Yugoslavia. He may have been limited in outlook, he may have been a bureaucrat, he may have been many things, but he was a very responsible human being with a great depth of feeling. He saw everything he had tried to achieve slipping away from him, and he saw the British, whom he had been brought up to respect and like, cheating him and treating him as a lackey without even justifying their actions.

The fundamentally different natures of the two resistance movements were mirrored by fundamental differences in the attitudes of the British liaison officers. "Marko" Hudson tried to mediate between Tito and Mihailović as early as 1941, and he earned not a little opprobrium from Mihailović for his endeavors. Bill Bailey was obliged to transmit to Mihailović messages that were at times unreasonable and at times outright offensive. He encountered Mihailović's anger—and not unreasonable anger—on a number of occasions, not least for what happened with the Italian Venezia Division at the time of the Italian capitulation—a shocking incident that I will chronicle a little later.

In the outlying missions we sought to prevent the Loyalists from fighting the Partisans. In my area the relative weakness of the Partisan forces created a complication because my commanders were tempted to clean them out before they became reinforced. It was largely due to pressure by the missions that they did not do so. The clashes we had with the detachment of Partisans based on Mount Radan near Leskovac, a mere couple of hundred strong, took place only when they entered our area or ambushed us as we were passing through the plains to attack the railway line. My own sabotage group suffered ambushes on two occasions. We did not retaliate.

Other BLOs with Mihailović also tried to restrain the Loyalists from attacking the Partisans, but the BLOs with the Partisans appear to have adopted an entirely different philosophy. Whether this stemmed from their own initiative, from MO4 instructions, or from Partisan pressure I do not know.

The official policy of seeking to prevent the two movements from fighting each other is shown in a telegram from the chiefs of staff (PREM 3 510/13) to the Middle East Defence Committee, dated June 27, 1943. Here are pertinent excerpts:

6. . . .We should continue to support Mihailovic, provided he accepts H.M.G.'s recent directive.
7. Croatian guerrillas and Communist Partisans should forthwith be supplied with war material, but Partisans operating in close proximity to Mihailovic's forces should first be required to give assurance to British Liaison Officers that no operations will be carried out against Mihailovic except in self-defence.
8. This policy will be open to reconsideration from time to time in light of your recommendations.
9. No definite territories should be allotted to different resistance movements with a view to supporting each of them only in those districts, but resistance groups of all kinds should be supported wherever they are able to undertake operations against the Axis, subject to proviso in para. 7.
10. Our ultimate object must be to unify all resistance movements throughout Yugoslavia. With this in view, instructions are being sent through SOE channel to Bailey and other British liaison officers to arrange, if possible, political nonaggression agreement between Mihailovic and Partisans.

11. Radio propaganda will be brought into line, and publicity extended to all groups which fight the Axis as soon as the Partisans and Mihailovic give the assurance required in paragraphs 6 and 7. . . .

Paragraph 7 is unequivocal in making support for Partisans contingent on their assurance to British liaison officers that they would not initiate conflict with Mihailović. The SOE operational logs for that period are not available in the Public Records Office, but the Foreign Office files show no evidence that these assurances were ever obtained. Indeed, there are repeated reminders from the Foreign Office to the Minister of State's Office in Cairo urging that such assurances should be obtained and complaining about the failure to do so. The responsibility for the failure to get assurances from the Partisans—or even ask for them—lay with Cairo. With SOE Cairo or with the Minister of State's Office in Cairo, or with both. It also lay, of course, with the British mission to Tito.

The policy of the Foreign Office was spelled out very clearly on July 22, 1943, in a document titled "Brief for Colonel Maclean." It states:

. . . Our first aim is, therefore, to endeavour to bring about the coordination of the military activities of General Mihailovic and Partisans (and any other resistance elements in Yugoslavia) under the direction of the Commander-in-Chief, Middle East.

Moreover, in our view negotiations for effecting political understandings between these various groups should not be rushed lest internal rivalries are thereby aggravated.

At the same time, the ultimate aim of His Majesty's Government is to endeavour to reconcile all such groups to each other and persuade them to subordinate the racial, religious and ideological differences which separate them to-day, so that Yugoslav unity may be preserved and the political, economic and constitutional problems which to-day confront the country may be settled by the free will of the people.

It is also the hope of His Majesty's Government that King Peter will return as the Constitutional monarch and it is believed that through him and with his assistance, the aims of His Majesty's Government can be realised.

When Maclean arrived in Yugoslavia on September 17, 1943, he had had eight weeks in which to study the above brief. Early in October he received a signal from Brigadier Keble of SOE instructing him to approach Tito with a view to stopping the fighting between the two resistance movements. Maclean declined to pass on the message on the grounds that Tito and the Partisan movement were determined to "liquidate" Mihailović and that giving Tito the message would cause a deterioration of relations at this early stage of his mission.

When Deakin dropped to Tito at the end of May 1943, the Partisan movement was in extremis. By the skin of its teeth it had extricated itself from the encirclement near Mount Durmitor. It desperately needed arms and supplies. Should such support not have been made dependent on arms not being used to attack Mihailović? This was the official government policy, and it was the only honorable policy for Great Britain with her commitment to the Loyalists.

Three months is a long time in a war, and if the table was never thumped before Maclean's arrival on September 17, obviously it was a bit harder for Maclean then. But the arrival of a senior head of mission, and the de facto recognition thus accorded, should have made Tito more amenable to discussions. Maclean, despite clear instructions from London in his brief, seems to have chosen not to exert pressure.

We do not know precisely what passed between Deakin and Maclean on one side and Tito on the other. Furthermore, we do not know whether Deakin and Maclean had received secret instructions from Churchill. But we do know what was the official government policy. Should not Deakin and Maclean have flatly told Tito to take the support on Allied terms or leave it? That is what Bailey and Armstrong were doing with Mihailović.

Tito needed the Allies far more than they needed him. The Germans had already rejected advances he made to them in the spring of 1943, and the Russians could not help at that time. Tito had nowhere else to go. Yet the British mission failed dismally to extract anything from him then; or indeed at any time, as far as can be seen from history and the records.

Deakin was an academic, not a businessman and understandably no power politician. But Maclean, with his experience in Russia before the war, should surely have been up to such a task. Indeed, his highest-level influence in British political and military circles demonstrated his ability to apply pressure where needed. Why oh why did he not use that talent, that drive, that power to steer Tito away from the civil war, and why oh why did he ignore his Foreign Office brief? He might have failed, but I have found no sign that he tried. The evidence seems to show that little table-thumping took place with Tito. Pressure, when it came—and it was very great pressure indeed—was all the other way: pressure on the British agencies to give Tito anything Tito wanted.

As I have already related, Bickham Sweet-Escott in his book *Baker Street Irregular* tells us that, immediately on his arrival in Yugoslavia in early June, Deakin started sending out a series of telegrams espousing the potential of the Tito movement. Maclean in his turn arrived with Tito on September 17 and already by November 6 had produced a voluminous report that sold the Partisan story effusively—on the basis of Partisan facts and figures. Many of the "facts" were tendentious. Most of the figures were false. The speed at which this material was produced absolutely precluded any study of the situation in detail on the ground, or any coordination with Colonel Bailey at Mihailović's headquarters, as was called for in the brief for Colonel Maclean.

But here the big question I have already hinted at has to be asked outright: Were things happening over the heads of the hierarchy and outside the official channels? Had a policy been established on an unofficial nod-and-wink basis when Churchill visited Cairo in January 1943 and held the fateful meetings with Deakin, Keble, and the minister of state? The files show unequivocally that Captain Maclean, as he was in July, was brought back from Cairo to the Foreign Office for briefing and appointment as political advisor to the brigadier who was to be named head of the military mission to Tito. But Maclean's own books and his paper to the Auty-Clogg symposium tell us quite specifically that he was brought back by the prime minister to head up the mission. It is all very confused and confusing. What is certain is that following the weekend at Chequers the prime minister wrote this personal memo (FO 371 37610) to the foreign secretary:

> Mr. Fitzroy Maclean, M.P. is a man of daring character with Parliamentary status and Foreign Office training. He is to go to Yugoslavia and work with Tito largely for S.O.E. The idea is that a Brigadier should be sent out to take command later on. In my view, we should plump for Maclean and make him the head of any Mission now contemplated, and give him a good military Staff officer under his authority. What we want is a daring Ambassador-Leader with these hardy and hunted guerillas.
>
> If you agree, please act in this sense with the War Office and S.O.E., and use my influence, for what it is worth.
>
> 28.7.43.

This memo may well have been dictated late at night and typed on the spot. The typing was untidy, and evidently the great man had to make two or three tries at the signature, which appears in the form of shaky initials repeated partly on top of themselves two or three times. Maybe he was very tired. But the memo set the pattern for what was going to happen in Yugoslavia.

In *Eastern Approaches* Maclean tells us that he warned Churchill in Cairo early in December that Tito was avowedly a communist and that the postwar system would inevitably be on Soviet lines and oriented toward the Soviet Union. According to Maclean's account, Churchill then asked, "Do you intend to make Yugoslavia your home after the war?" "No Sir." "Neither do I. And that being so, the less you and I worry about the form of Government they set up the better, that is for them to decide."

This comment by Churchill is significant because at that time he was publicly committed to doing his utmost to get the king back into Yugoslavia and to ensure free elections for the people of Yugoslavia after the war. In the subsequent months various diplomatic steps were taken to try to bring Tito and acceptable politicians together, with a view to getting a less extreme government and the desired free elections. Yet Churchill seems not really to have been sanguine about it or, if his remark was not unduly cynical, to have had his heart in it.

This sequence of events forces one to ask: Did something more happen at Chequers on the night of July 28? While advising the foreign secretary in his memo to plump for Maclean, did he mumble to Maclean, "See here, Maclean, I want also to plump for full support for Tito, whatever the consequences, and you have to supply me with the arguments to justify this course in Parliament"? Some such occurrence would explain a lot. It would explain nearly everything.

It is significant that Maclean insisted on having a direct line of communication not only to the Middle East commander in chief but also to the prime minister. Brigadier Sir Fitzroy Maclean is still very much with us, appearing on the television and writing fascinating travel and political commentaries. Will he one day tell all? Some of us would dearly like to know *in full* what happened on that fateful night at Chequers.

Eastern Approaches tells us of Maclean's first meeting with Tito and gives us impressive evidence of the failure of the British mission to do any table-thumping or indeed to make any use of this unique opportunity to try to check the civil war. Maclean tells how Tito made his position quite clear about Mihailović and the Loyalists. That position, including the claim that Mihailović was a collaborator, reflected the Partisan "facts" and interpretations put around in the Soviet-conducted misinformation campaign, which had been going on for more than a year. Maclean did not need to drop into Bosnia to hear that spiel. But *Eastern Approaches* says nothing about putting forth the Western Allied viewpoint or policy, *and nothing about asking for assurances or making supplies dependent on finding a modus vivendi with Mihailović. Tito stated his viewpoint. That was that.*

Reflecting the totally different attitude adopted by the British mission to Mihailović, a signal came in from Bailey in which he

reports giving another bludgeoning message to Mihailović—a
signal he pretended came from General Headquarters (GHQ)
Middle East, though actually he was its author. The message lists
a series of complaints, some of which may have been real but
some of which were certainly imaginary. The catalog of complaints included my own grumbles. They dealt with various sabotage projects and claimed that the local Loyalist commanders
were being obstructive or that they had not received instructions
from Mihailović. In reality it is probable that most if not all of
the problems arose from lack of communications between Mihailović and his subcommanders, from the outlying BLOs' lack of
direct communication with their chief at Mihailović's headquarters, and from the monumental delays in Cairo in deciphering
signals from Mihailović BLOs.

Specifically, Bailey's signal spoke of Maj. Radoslav Djurić, the
Mihailović commander in southeastern Serbia, "with three thousand men armed by the British during the past four months now
engaged fighting Partisans in his area to the detriment of anti-
axis effort."

Djurić never had 3,000 men armed by the British at any time.
Official statistics I quote elsewhere show that the whole Loyalist
movement received enough arms for only 1,500 men from June
to November 1943. Bailey must have known his signal was misleading. So did Mihailović.

The signal also claimed that forty drops had been planned
for Mihailović in September, that none of them would now be
delivered, and that there would be no resumption of supplies
until categorical and unambiguous instructions to remedy the
position had been issued by Mihailović and confirmed by the local commanders.

In reporting passing this message to Mihailović in the name
of GHQ Middle East, Bailey stated, "Possible not probable Mihailovic will reject ultimatum and break off relations but am
making no progress at moment. Therefore consider better have
rupture before (repeat before) arrival Brigadier so that future
line can be decided at highest level but in personal consultation
with him." Bailey amazingly went on to suggest that this "rupture" would help future relations between the brigadier and the

Loyalists. He also suggested that Mihailović might play the Americans off against the British. This resembled the specious argument used in Cairo in January 1943 that the Partisans had to be supported in order to forestall the Russians or the Americans from doing so.

Not surprisingly, the Foreign Office's reaction was unfavorable. There was also considerable anger at Bailey speaking in the name of GHQ Middle East. The ultimatum was withdrawn.

But the harm had been done. Once again Mihailović had been bludgeoned. While the Foreign Office did not subscribe to or support Bailey's initiative, someone seems to have followed Bailey's instructions and stopped supplies, because there is no evidence that forty planeloads went to Mihailović in September. Indeed, only two or three went to southeastern Serbia. MO4 would not have missed a chance like that to sabotage Mihailović. Not the opportunist Keble or the sinister Klugmann.

Shortly thereafter, however, Brigadier Armstrong arrived and brought with him a very encouraging letter from General Wilson, the Middle East commander in chief. This missive approached Mihailović diplomatically and assured him that the British were now in a position to give him adequate supplies. Mihailović's reaction was to cooperate in a spate of bridge-blowing carried out by Archie Jack and Brigadier Armstrong. Hundreds of Bulgars and Germans were killed. All went reasonably well until Mihailović was again shocked by the change in attitude following Maclean's drop to Tito and the subsequent cessation of supplies to the Loyalists. Coming so soon after an incident involving the Venezia Division in which the Loyalists were tricked out of their booty, this new disappointment angered Mihailović considerably. The final straw was the attribution by the BBC to the Partisans of the extensive Mihailović actions. Mihailović had to interpret this as Perfidious Albion at work.

The Venezia Division incident is particularly revealing in this general context. In September 1943 the capitulation of the Italians was eagerly awaited, and Colonel Bailey with a Loyalist force contacted the Italian Venezia Division, which was occupying Montenegro. Some days previously, in order to get to the town of Berane, where the division was based, this Loyalist force had taken the town of Prijepolje, killing about 200 Germans in the process. Colonel Bailey was present at the battle. The Loyalists proposed to disarm the Venezia Division and carry away their weapons, but Bailey requested that the Loyalist commander let him talk alone with the Italian general.

Bailey came out from this talk and announced that the Italians would keep their arms and coordinate action with the Loyalists. This was, of course, what the Italians wanted. The Loyalists did not like that at all: they wanted the arms. They submitted to Bailey's demand unwillingly. That they did so at all was symptomatic of the respect and trust with which the Loyalists treated the British. Regrettably, it was their undoing.

Cairo was fully informed of Bailey's movements, intentions, and actions. Indeed, the capture of Prijepolje, which was reported to Cairo, was announced by the BBC before the incident at Berane. True to the usual form, it was announced as a great success by the Yugoslav resistance and attributed not to the Loyalists but to their enemies, the Partisans. Cairo knew that Bailey's force was negotiating the Italian surrender. Why did Bailey stop the Loyalists from disarming them? Did he do so on his own initiative and, if he did so, why? And why did he take the Italian general aside out of the hearing of the Loyalist commander? The balance of probability must be that he did so on orders from Cairo. Indeed, his signal of October 14, 1943, says, "*at your instigation* [emphasis added] Colonel Bailey managed to persuade Mihailovic not to disarm the Italians in the Lim Valley."

What happened at Berane was of major importance in the Yugoslav civil war. Fortunately, Italian sources are available, in particular the book by Stefano Gestro, which was written with the cooperation of the Italian army's historical branch, *La Divisione italiana partigiana: Montenegro 1943–45*. Dominic Flessati, producer of a BBC program on SOE and author of a biography of "Marko" Hudson, gave me a summary.

The book shows that the Italian general, a man named Oxilia, behaved in a very dignified and courageous manner. When the Italian capitulation was announced, he determined to break away from the Germans and put his forces at the disposal of the

Allies. With other outlying forces that had moved in he had a very strong, well-equipped division with supporting arms—by far the most important individual Italian force on the Yugoslav mainland. His division also dominated an area of Montenegro leading south into Albania and Macedonia and east to Sandžak on the road to the Serbian heartland.

Bailey and the Četniks had moved in first, and Berane and its surrounding area were Loyalist territory. The Loyalists took over the civil administration of Berane, and on September 23 there was a joint Italo-Yugoslav ceremony. Tito then moved by throwing first the entire corps of one of his generals, Peko Dapčević, then part of the corps of another, Koča Popović, into securing Berane by force of arms. He signaled to Dapčević, "My plan is to concentrate the first corps and your second corps in the Sandžak and Metohija so as to move, at the right moment, toward Serbia and Macedonia."

General Oxilia tried to persuade the Partisans and Loyalists to cooperate and fight the Germans together. There was a great opportunity, he thought, to mount an offensive thrust toward Podgorica and the sea. But Dapčević refused and told Oxilia to keep out of Yugoslav internal affairs.

From September 23 until October 10 there was a struggle for the hearts and minds of the Italians, accompanied by Partisan attacks on the ground. In the political and psychological struggle the Partisans, as usual, outgunned the Loyalists, with the Partisans swearing that they were the representatives of the Allies. They had solid support in this from their BLO, a Major Hunter, and the argument that a British general (Maclean) had just joined them was very telling. So also was the BBC and its false claims attributing Loyalist successes to the Partisans. An outlying Italian unit had jumped the gun and joined the Partisans, and together they were attacking Loyalists. The BBC weighed in, calling the Loyalists "enemies," which greatly impressed the Italians. In the end the sheer weight of Partisan forces rushed down by Tito into Mihailović territory—and the support of the Partisans by the British—persuaded General Oxilia to throw in his lot with the Partisans. Nevertheless, he insisted on permitting the very much smaller Loyalist force to withdraw unharmed.

Bailey's behavior continued to be extraordinary. He accompanied the Loyalists in their successful drive to Berane. He intervened to stop the disarming of the Venezia Division by the Loyalists. He stayed for two days only and then set off back to Mihailović headquarters. Why? It seems he wanted to be there to meet Brigadier Armstrong, who dropped on September 24. But there were others who could just as well have met Armstrong. Furthermore, Armstrong went off on the bridge-blowing operations as soon as he arrived, and no one thought to go to Berane to stiffen up General Oxilia and to support the poor Loyalists who had taken the town in the first place. Berane was a pure Loyalist area with a strong contingent. They were destroyed by this incident.

The files also show that Armstrong and Bailey were insisting at the end of September that Mihailović refrain from sending more Loyalists westward to counter the Peko Dapčević offensive. Thus the British, and specifically Bailey, delivered Mihailović the most decisive blow he suffered in the Yugoslav civil war. Was Bailey manipulating the situation in order to favor the Partisans—either on his own or on secret instructions from MO4— or was he just being a sycophantic bureaucrat rushing back to impress the new chief?

It is extraordinary to note that with the arrival of Armstrong's team there were, at Mihailović's headquarters, Brigadier Armstrong; Colonel Howard, his new chief of staff; Colonel Bailey; Colonel Hudson; Major Greenlees; Major Jack; and Major Solly-Flood—seven senior officers. The failure to send someone back to Berane was not Armstrong's fault. He and Howard and Jack had just arrived, and he set out immediately on demolition operations. But surely Bailey or Hudson or Greenlees could have been spared for the vital argument going on in Berane, in order to support the Loyalists with General Oxilia.

Berane was in a strategic location as a starting point for eventually opening up a road to the coast. It also had a serviceable airfield. Did Bailey not see its military value? Did he ever discuss it with MO4?

This incident is of great significance. First, it demonstrated the Loyalists' obedience to British demands. It demonstrated the manipulation of the Loyalist forces by the British mission, whoever was responsible for it, Bailey or Cairo. It demonstrated the ruthless opportunism of the Partisan command. It demonstrated that the British mission with the Partisans had not taken steps to stop Partisan aggression against the Loyalists; possibly the subject had never been raised. It demonstrated once again the doctoring of news at some link in the chain of information via SOE Cairo, the Minister of State's Office, the PWE, and the BBC, which somewhere, somehow, resulted in the repeated attribution of Loyalist successes to the Partisans. Finally, the incident raises very serious questions about Bailey, his competence, and his attitude regarding the Loyalists to whom he was officially accredited.

Mihailović was furious. He would be, wouldn't he? There was the inexcusable news doctoring, which really made a difference. Then he lost the arms from the Venezia Division—arms and supplies for 10,000 to 15,000 men—representing five times the arms supplied to the Loyalists during the whole war. And he also lost Montenegro. It was a major disaster, the turning point on the ground in Yugoslavia.

There were numerous other instances of one law for Mihailović and another for Tito. Two stand out. As I have already related, in the first, muddles by the British mission with Djurić, Mihailović's area commander in southeastern Serbia, and my own naïveté in telling Cairo too much, resulted in Bailey's stopping supplies to Mihailović.

In the second, in November 1943, Col. Bill Cope and Maj. Rupert Raw, who had succeeded John Sehmer as liaison officers with Djurić and did not speak Serbo-Croat, failed to understand Djurić correctly, used a bad interpreter, or even were intentionally misled by Djurić. They "understood" that Djurić had received instructions from Mihailović to collaborate directly with the Germans; they rushed off a high-priority signal to MO4 to this effect. In fact, what Mihailović had ordered was that young volunteers should be sought out and encouraged to penetrate the Serbian state guard of General Nedić as spies, in order to defect to the Loyalists when instructed to do so, bringing with them their arms, supplies, and other defectors if possible. The

Loyalist units were also called on to resist Partisan encroachment on Loyalist territory in the Sandžak. The false interpretation was grabbed by Cairo and sent in an elaborate report by the Minister of State's Office to the Foreign Office. Thence it went to the foreign secretary himself and from him to the prime minister. The latter sent it to the American president and to Commonwealth prime ministers. Mr. Rose, an official in the southern department of the Foreign Office, suggested that perhaps Colonel Cope had had a bad interpreter. This was indeed the case. But no one listened to Mr. Rose. In the atmosphere at that stage the incident was a godsend to help justify the planned dumping of Mihailović. In due course the Minister of State's Office realized that an error had been made, but sent no "hold-it" signal. Someone just wrote a very low-level letter correcting the mistake, a letter that failed to reach the top echelons. Obviously it was not meant to. That sort of thing happened to Mihailović all the time.

That sort of thing never happened in the British mission to the Partisans. The available signal traffic seems to show that the mission did not concern itself with matters such as checking up on whether the Partisans were attacking the Loyalists and trying to stop them. The Loyalist forces were the main enemy of the Tito Partisans, and the British mission just got on with the job of treating the Partisans as a fully independent, allied army and giving them highly efficient and enthusiastic support.

Bill Deakin has written that the material he collected from the Partisans about Mihailović amounted to a "hostile brief" when he was reporting to the prime minister in Cairo on December 10, 1943. In my opinion it is incontestable that Deakin went to some trouble to gather information to support the Partisan claim that Mihailović was guilty of collaboration.

I deal with the general question of collaboration in a subsequent chapter, but one has to ask here: What was the effect on Tito and his staff of this assiduous collection of evidence against the Loyalists?

It was the official government policy to tell both Mihailović and Tito to cool it; to lay off the civil war and to concentrate on fighting the Axis. It was government policy to continue recognition of Mihailović as minister of defense and to give full support to his movement. Yet here we have the BLO to Tito gathering information from the communists to use against our ally. If he did not ask, at least he listened and wrote it all down.

Should he not have been telling Tito that he was not interested? That Mihailović was our ally and would Tito kindly shut up and get on with the war against the Axis? That was the line we BLOs with the Mihailović commanders took. But in my opinion it seems all too evident from the history and even from the writings of the British officers concerned that their attitude did nothing to discourage Tito from his conclusion that all he had to do was to push and keep pushing for the door to open and that his demand that the British betray their allies would be granted. In due course the British did just that.

THE LOST YEAR AND A HALF

Mihailović first established his headquarters on Ravna Gora Mountain in May 1941. The abortive summer 1941 uprisings in Serbia and Montenegro, which cost such heavy reprisals, were followed by a relatively quiet period. Contact having been established by couriers, and by radio from Malta, Capt. Bill "Marko" Hudson was infiltrated by submarine in September 1941 on the Montenegrin coast, where he reached a communist group that included Djilas. A great deal has been written about Hudson's adventures and tribulations, and I do not propose to trespass deeply onto this terrain. A very good and honestly researched account can be found in Milan Deroc's *Special Operations Explored*, recently published. Still, I want to make certain points about this period that are relevant here.

Hudson was fluent in Serbo-Croat and knew the country well from his experience as a mining engineer there before the war. He made his way from Montenegro to Tito's headquarters, where he stayed a little time before moving across to join Mihailović. Mihailović had been expecting him and was put out at the delay in his arrival, also at the questionable company he had been keeping. That was hardly Hudson's fault, but it was an inauspicious start.

Hudson's arrival coincided with a worsening of relations between Mihailović and Tito, and though he made valiant efforts to bring them together, events militated against him. Hudson, like others of us later, had constant communications problems. Whole chapters have been written about what happened or did not happen to his W/T sets, which were variously buried or stolen or borrowed by others. (For those of my readers born into the electronics age, W/T, or wireless telegraphy, sets in the Second World War were forty-pound, suitcase-sized radio transmitter-receivers using Morse Code—not voice—signals. They were powered by bulky, sixty-pound batteries. Sometimes they worked.)

Hudson was back with Tito again when the Germans launched their major attack. Following an altercation with Tito about when Tito was going to stop running and on which hill he was going to stand and fight, Hudson took off in disgust. He tried to rejoin Mihailović, only to find that the latter had gone walkabout too.

Hudson had vacillated about the choice between the Partisans and Mihailović. He was at first more impressed by the Partisans, but when he left Tito to rejoin Mihailović, he did so because he felt the latter to be the better prospect. The *received-wisdom* historians deal extensively with what happened with Tito, Mihailović, and Hudson in 1941. They try to prove that the break was all Mihailović's fault, but they gloss over Hudson's deliberate choice of Mihailović as the sounder proposition.

Ironically, Hudson was regarded by the Foreign Office as politically leaning to the left. The significance of his decision to leave Tito and rejoin Mihailović should not be discounted. Hudson shows himself in all his long reports and cables to be a very fair and humane man. He was particularly affected by the horror of the reprisals, which, of course, did not worry the Partisans.

The story goes that, sadly, Hudson found himself a rejected suitor. Mihailović would not have him back, and he spent a lonely, hard winter in 1941–42 with such help as he could get from peasants or with none. When he was allowed by Mihailović to rejoin the headquarters in the late spring of 1942, he had no means of communication and was unable to report to Cairo on a regular basis. Captain Robertson, a Yugoslav communist posing as a British officer, was dropped to him as a communicator in

July 1942, but his advent created many more problems than it solved. It is certainly the case that there were no regular exchanges that summer between the then-head of the British mission to Mihailović and MO4. Bailey was to have been dropped to relieve Hudson in August, because of the lack of proper communication with the latter and his supposed fatigue. But Bailey contracted malaria and did not fly till Christmas 1942. By then the shenanigans of the Cairo Partisan-Četnik office war had started. MO4 staff members, even down to the mysterious but fascinating Miss Flannery, were already denigrating their Loyalist ally as "that silly old goat Mihadge-lo-vitch" and preparing to throw him and the Loyalists overboard.

Thus the British, and especially the BBC, hailed Mihailović as a hero in the early days of 1941, even though they had virtually no contact with him and gave him virtually no supplies. The drops to Mihailović forces between the autumn of 1941 and Bailey's arrival fifteen months later totaled sixteen planeloads according to one source, twenty according to another, each amounting to one or two tons. And without a BLO in touch with Cairo, Mihailović hardly knew what Cairo wanted of him. Cairo probably did not know any too well what it wanted of him either, there were so many cooks stirring the broth.

Already in the autumn of 1941 there were differences with the British. When he had a confrontation with Mihailović about making terms with Tito, Hudson is supposed to have stopped a drop—according to one version of history. According to another, the drop did not materialize for technical reasons. Either way, it caused resentment.

This was one of a whole series of incidents that led to the strained relationship between Mihailović and Hudson. This tension persisted throughout Hudson's time in Yugoslavia. Hudson's reports, which were sent through after Bailey's arrival at Christmastime 1942, were clearly affected by these unfortunate circumstances. But the critical parts of the reports were seized on and built up by the elements in the British agencies who wanted to back the communists. The Partisan sympathizers and agitators in Cairo and London could not believe their luck.

Les absents ont toujours tort!

Then Colonel Bailey arrived on Christmas Eve 1942, duly recovered from his malaria. A colonel—that should change things, the Serbs thought. No doubt, as happened nine months later with Brigadier Armstrong's arrival, there was celebrating at Mihailović's headquarters. No doubt the *šljivovica* flowed, and why not? Now at last, they no doubt felt, we can come to grips with things, agree on attitudes and policies, and receive some goodies *caido del cielo*— fallen from heaven— too, and maybe do some sabotage without reopening the whole reprisals can of worms— that is, if they give us some ammunition to make the Germans think twice about taking reprisals.

It was not to be. In two long months two planes arrived. Then came the infamous christening party, the tipple, the exasperated speech by Mihailović—who, incidentally, was no roisterer but a studious introvert—and schoolmarm Bailey stopped even the single monthly drop. Nothing came to Mihailović headquarters for the next three months.

Regrettably, much verbiage came from the BLO mission at Mihailović headquarters. Bailey at least had W/T equipment and signalers. Lots of it and them. Voluminous, verbose signals poured out to Cairo. One of the first was a twenty- or thirty-page foolscap report that had been written in November by Hudson—way out of date in every sense by then—followed by an even longer message by Bailey commenting on Hudson's report. But all of this superbureaucratic stuff brought no supplies, no mutual understandings, and no action.

It did provide a mass of material for the Foreign Office and SOE to dissect, chew over, digest, and discuss, and the files in the PRO certainly show that this opportunity was seized upon avidly.

It is unfortunate that Bailey did not appreciate that with these reports he was digging Mihailović's grave and providing the ammunition needed by the Partisan faction in Cairo. Later, much later, he tried to reverse the process he had started, but by then, in the spring of 1944, it was too late.

But I have to ask: Did Bailey know full well what he was

doing, and did his 1944 initiative just stem from the need to cover his tracks?

Typically, in one of these reports Bailey related anecdotally how Mihailović relegated him to the end of the column when he was in disfavor. My reaction to that is: What sort of a man was he to permit that? No wonder he was in disfavor. And no wonder there was never a meeting of minds between him and Mihailović, though in his signals he tried to pretend there was.

As I have recorded earlier, no sooner had that embargo on supply drops been lifted than the notorious Glenconner signal of May 29 threw a spanner into the works. Then, after a brief peace between the British mission and Mihailović, Bailey slammed in the notorious message that he was subsequently ordered to withdraw on the intervention of the Foreign Office. As I wrote earlier, this message, actually drafted by Bailey, purported to come from GHQ, and Bailey used it deliberately in order to provoke another row with Mihailović. By the time it was withdrawn, the switch from support of the Loyalists to support of the Partisans was already virtually accomplished.

The *received-wisdom*, pro-Partisan propaganda has it that the British turned from Mihailović to the Partisans because he was doing nothing in spite of British support. The truth is that there was never, at any stage, effective British support for the Loyalists; that the planeloads dropped in two years to Mihailović's forces in the whole of Yugoslavia were less than the Partisans would be receiving on one dropping ground in a couple of nights when their turn came; that there was no moral support other than the unfortunate early 1942 BBC hype, which was too much and too soon; and that Mihailović had no British mission with proper communication telling him what MO4 wanted until Christmas 1942, at which time he had only one, which was constantly at cross-purposes with him.

What happened in that period with the Partisans? Djilas tells the story. It's simple. They went about their business exactly as planned from the start. Whereas Mihailović, anxious to avoid reprisals, with no clear policy from his own exiled government and

109

with no consistent and coherent lead from the British, adopted a defensive position awaiting events, the Partisans burrowed away at their long-term aim of politicizing as wide a territory as possible in preparation for taking over power.

Mihailović's overseas contact was his exiled government in London, the members of which were bitterly divided among themselves following the *ustaša* atrocities. The exiled government could do nothing for him and, by exasperating its British hosts, did a great deal to damage his cause by association. The Partisans, conversely, had the Soviets as their contact abroad, and it is now very clear from Partisan writers such as Djilas and Dedijer that the links between Tito and the Soviets were like those that existed between the Yugoslav Communist Party and the Comintern before the war but with the important difference that Stalin himself took a great personal interest. Very astutely, Stalin stressed time and again to Tito the vital need to cover up this Soviet orchestration. Moreover, in dealings with the Foreign Office the Russians took pains to pretend that they hardly knew who Tito was.

The Soviet international apparatus was hard at work preparing the ground for Tito. The misinformation campaign against Mihailović and the Loyalists conducted through the left-wing media in Western and neutral countries swung into action in the summer of 1942. There can be no doubt at all that the moles in the British agencies, notably in MI6/SIS, were tipped off. Left-wingers in other agencies such as PWE and the BBC, whether politically inspired by Soviet contacts or just observing the left-inclined media slant of those days, followed suit. The whole climate of opinion was nurtured and prepared.

There was no conservative action to counter or mitigate the massive leftist-inspired misinformation. There was no agency charged with putting the Loyalists' case. Although SOE London was steadfastly loyal to the official policy of supporting the Loyalists, SOE was a secret organization and employed no publicity agents to sell its ideas. Moreover, in the atmosphere of Russophilia that existed at the time, anyone opposing left-wing gullibility was on a losing wicket.

There is no doubt that the Partisans gained by having no

illusions to start with about getting help from the Western Allies. It was impossible for the Soviets to send them supplies. Thus the Partisans were forced to go out and take arms by force from wherever they could, from the Axis or Nedić or the *ustaša* or the Domobrans—or Četniks. They had no qualms about taking food and other supplies, with or without the goodwill of the population. They had no help, but they had clarity of purpose. It is undeniable that necessity hardened and helped the Partisans. However vile the ambitions of their leaders, they were no slouches in combat.

When in time the Allies contacted them, they found themselves almost embarrassed by the massive support they received. But, having been through hard times, they knew not to waste it. The level of support then given to the Partisans was made possible by increased aircraft availability in the summer of 1943 and, to a lesser extent, by the switch of all support away from Mihailović.

Only a month or two after MO4 began throwing massive support to the Partisans, the chief of the American OSS (Office of Strategic Services, the precursor of the CIA) in Bari, a Colonel Huot, set out to best the British with seaborne support and poured in 6,000 tons of supplies. The British, not to be outdone, trumped his ace, and before the end of 1943 the Partisans on the mainland and the islands had received a total of 18,000 tons in six months of contact—in comparison with Mihailović's 20 to 30 tons in the year and a half after his first contact with the British. A signal (WO 202/145) of December 20, 1943, shows that the Loyalists received only 653 rifles, 625 Bren guns, 51 antitank rifles, 4 antitank guns, 18 mortars, 3,346 grenades, and 14.6 tons of explosive between June and November 1943. That was enough to arm a maximum of 1,500 men and weighed about 30 tons in all. By June 1944 the Partisans had received 5,000 planeloads totaling 6,900 tons by air plus 22,000 tons by sea from British sources alone—in nine months.

This comparison is necessary to put the history into perspective. *Received wisdom*, Partisan-inspired, is notoriously vague about chronology and logistics and relies on vague generalizations. Even at the time of this writing, 1988, Sir Fitzroy still gave newspaper interviews stating flatly that Mihailović was a collaborator . . . was a collaborator . . . was a collaborator. Just that, nothing more. But history cannot be written with placards and labels.

It is entertaining to record that there is a furious cable from Brigadier Maclean, who had found out about Huot's oneupmanship when he arrived at the coast from Tito's headquarters. In dynamic style he agreed with Tito that Allied personnel appearing in Yugoslavia without prior clearance from Maclean would be arrested by the Partisans and that any Partisans in Italy not cleared by Tito would be arrested by the British. Tito must have been delighted. As usual, he won on both counts. The fact that the Partisans could arrest Allied personnel implied official recognition. The British were under obligation to arrest any Partisans coming to Italy. The term "Partisans" could cover a lot of ground—including, quite possibly, Loyalists. It gave Tito a useful lever.

The British government took the decision to abandon Mihailović and throw total support behind Tito shortly following the Tehran conference of the Big Three powers attended by Churchill, Stalin, and an ailing Roosevelt. Although Churchill and Stalin later in Moscow arbitrarily agreed on a division of interest in Yugoslavia on a fifty-fifty basis, whatever that might mean, Tehran was not, I believe, the precursor of that deal and the turning point in Yugoslav history, as some supporters of the Loyalists and the exiled government were inclined to believe.

What happened in Tehran was that the decision was made to give large-scale support to the resistance movement in Yugoslavia. But the position regarding the Loyalists was not settled formally and probably was not even discussed by the three leaders. Stalin knew quite well what was going on; he was pulling the strings. But the decision to abandon Mihailović was taken by Churchill and Churchill alone. It was justified by the collaboration accusations, but it was brought about by Tito's insistence and by Churchill's disinclination to call Tito's bluff. The two resistance movements could have coexisted if we had had the will to oblige them to do so, and there was no commitment vis-à-vis the Soviets that precluded supporting both movements.

The Foreign Office files show that already in the spring of 1943 there was hard talk of deciding between Mihailović and Tito. Sir Orme Sargent, a senior Foreign Service official, harked back to this point a number of times, stating that the choice was between a "short-term" policy for military considerations, which favored supporting Tito, and a "long-term" policy of favoring the Loyalists for the sake of postwar democracy and maintenance of the monarchy. The concept that there was a need for backing one movement only was, I believe, false and may have been the main cause of the decisions ultimately taken. It was pushed strongly by the Partisan faction and particularly by Tito himself.

Whether or not he was tipped off by sympathizers in the British agencies, Tito made it clear right from the first contact with the British that support for him had to be all or nothing, that he intended to liquidate the Loyalists, and that there would be no compromise, take it or leave it. Apparently without arguing, Deakin and Maclean advised Churchill to take it.

Either Tito was astute in discerning that he could get away with this ploy, or maybe he was advised by the Soviets or by sympathizers in the Western agencies to play a hard hand. We will probably never know the answer. That he played an uncompromisingly hard hand and that he made no secret whatsoever of his attitude is undeniable.

It is also clear that, whether or not he was tipped off, his treatment by the British mission must have told an old campaigner like Tito to push and keep on pushing. Push away, boys; the Brits are a pushover. So the British chose the "short-term" policy and condemned all of Yugoslavia to communism.

Did the "short-term" policy really bring military advantages? My personal experience in southeastern Serbia, astride the key Axis communications, convinces me that it did not.

The question opens up an enormous field on which I am not qualified to comment in detail because it covers all of 1944, while my experience is limited to the first half of that year. It is certainly the case that a huge volume of military materiel was poured into Yugoslavia late in 1943 and throughout 1944. A great deal of costly air supply and air close support was exploited by Tito for civil-war purposes. The strategy and tactics adopted inside

Yugoslavia were decided by Tito and his commanders alone. The British just gave support— shipping and dropping arms and supplies and carrying out air strikes when and where requested. For the British missions to Tito it was not theirs to reason why, it was just theirs to do or die. Mostly they did— as quartermasters and as conduits for Tito to put over his propaganda.

In theory, Tito took cognizance of the general strategy of the Anglo-American Mediterranean command. In practice, he did just what he wanted, eventually even threatening the invasion of Italian Venezia Giulia and Trieste, in which adventure he was thwarted not by his British mission but by the rapid action of General Freyberg and the New Zealand Division. He gave moral and logistical support to the successful communist takeover of Albania and the unsuccessful communist grab for power in Greece. Djilas in his writings states that the Albanian communists recognized Tito as their guru and leader.

It is also the case that the Germans continued to operate the main lines of communications, the rail lines from Salonika to Belgrade; the Danube waterway, except when it was interrupted by aerial mining; and most of the mining companies, until the Wehrmacht retreated before the advancing Russians. This German retreat was accomplished in reasonable order, right through Tito country. And it was the Red Army that liberated Belgrade, albeit accompanied by Partisans. It is furthermore the case that Tito's "liberation" of southern and southeastern Serbia from the Germans, from the Nedić state guard, and from the Loyalists still holding out in the mountains was materially assisted by the Bulgarian army. The Bulgar jackals had joined with the Germans in 1941 and annexed a substantial section of southeastern Serbia. They had helped the Germans in the occupation and protection of communications in the annexed territory and in the portion of Serbia under German control. But in 1944 they bolted and jumped on the Red bandwagon. Their help was immediately welcomed by Tito. No talk of Nuremberg-type trials of war criminals. The Bulgar, bitter enemy of yesterday, became the comrade of today. And the Bulgar army was used in the great communist roundup of the Yugoslav Loyalist resistance pockets still holding out.

As I said, this is a huge field of history and I am in no way qualified to examine it all. Nevertheless I have to comment that the silence of the Partisan-inspired *received wisdom* on these subjects is deafening. If you belong to the school that believed—and amazingly still argues—that the alliance of necessity with Soviet Russia after Barbarossa in 1941 necessitated a total abandonment of long-term Allied interests and an acceptance of anything Stalin wanted, including his continued efforts at subversion in the West, then the "short-term" policy may have been right.

But if you believe in all that, then you must believe in leprechauns too.

What would have happened had His Majesty's Government quietly implemented and continued the policy that was in force officially throughout 1943 until December 10? What if HMG had exercised a degree of control, made support for both sides dependent on both Mihailović and Tito eschewing or delaying the civil war; had specified more sabotage targets and provided materiel and British personnel to destroy them? What would have happened then?

In southeastern Serbia, far more effective sabotage of Axis communications could have been achieved by a clear demonstration of British support for the Loyalists, who were in virtual domination in the area throughout 1943 and who could have harnessed the massive potential reserves of Serbian peasants. The policy of abandoning and vilifying the Loyalists was morally and ethically wrong. Furthermore, it effectively stopped our nascent sabotage action on the vital Salonika-Belgrade railway line in the Morava Valley just as we were getting going.

Nothing was done against the Axis on that line throughout most of the important winter of 1943–44, while the Partisans concentrated on gathering their forces and equipping them with British arms in order to bring their civil war to Serbia.

COLLABORATION

What is collaboration? This term is used very loosely, and it means what its users choose it to mean. In war there has always been collaboration. Any truce is collaboration to those who wish to denounce it as such. The unofficial Christmas Day truces in the Flanders trenches, when the German and Allied soldiers climbed out and exchanged greetings, sweets, and cigarettes, would no doubt have been denounced by communist dialectical materialists as "collaboration by imperialist forces."

In March 1943 Tito's emissaries held a series of meetings with senior German officers. These meetings are described in detail by Milovan Djilas in his writings. Djilas and two other leading Partisan figures, Vladimir Velebit and Koča Popović, spent several weeks with senior German officers enjoying safe-conduct, transport, and accommodation provided by the Axis in Sarajevo and Zagreb.

Until very recently it was claimed by Partisan historians that these March 1943 meetings were held in order to discuss exchanges of prisoners of war. Neither the Partisans nor the Germans, however, were ever in the business of exchanging POWs in high-level negotiations. The Germans shot "bandits" as a matter of course, and the Partisans normally shot their enemies too, even when they were captured. Any such transaction would have been at platoon or company level—not at the level of Djilas and senior German officers.

The purpose of the meetings was, of course, to discuss the situation that at the time posed an agonizing problem for the Partisans. They certainly knew from the international communist spy network—if not from Klugmann in SOE Cairo, or Philby in MI6/SIS, or Burgess in one of his Foreign Office, PWE, or BBC roles—that the Middle East command was in a mood to "ginger up" resistance activities with increased supplies.

At that stage the Partisans were not on the list of potential recipients of supplies, whereas the Mihailović Loyalists supposedly were right at the top. Furthermore, higher resistance activity was the logical precursor to some invasion in the Mediterranean—perhaps on the Adriatic coast of Yugoslavia or in Greece. The Soviets, however, desperately wanted to gain postwar influence in the Balkans and to secure an Adriatic port in the postwar settlement.

Tito—and Stalin—had to be worried that a Western Allied

invasion through Greece or on the Adriatic coast, supported by the famous planned *ustanak*, or uprising, of the Serbian clans, which was the pivot of Mihailović's policy, would leave the communists with no possibility of success in their plans for insurrection, civil war, and eventual takeover of power.

There was even more to it than that. The negotiations represented one of Tito's most brilliant moves. His forces were faced on the Neretva River by the Montenegrin Stanišić and Djurišić Četniks, who were impeding his attempts to penetrate the Sandžak and enter southern Serbia. Furthermore, the Germans were driving down behind him. By instituting the negotiations and by agreeing to stop sabotage on the Zagreb-Belgrade line and other communications, he bought the respite he needed to concentrate his entire mobile forces against the well-organized Montenegrin Četniks. It was an inspired tactical move, but it was more flagrant collaboration with the Germans than anything Mihailović was ever accused of.

I am revealing no new discoveries here. Walter R. Roberts, in *Tito, Mihailović, and the Allies 1941–1945*, deals with the incident. So does Walter Hagen in *Die Geheime Front*. So does Milovan Djilas, with only minimal coverup, in *Wartime*. But there are purveyors of the *received wisdom* who paint the Neretva battle as something heroic. In truth it was a sordid civil-war maneuver.

What is also ignored by the Partisan purveyors of wisdom is the fact that these very same Četniks were interned in POW camps in Greece in the first stage of the next German cleanup operation. The Četniks surrounded, captured, and interned included 5,000 Stanišić and Djurišić Četniks taken in Kolašin and 2,000 taken in Sandžac between May 12 and 15. Once they were out of the way, German forces turned on the Partisans and encircled them in the Sutjecka Canyon about May 28. In other words, the famous fifth offensive of Partisan legend was first started against the Loyalists. Yet those purveyors of wisdom will have us believe that the Germans used the Loyalists in the offensive against the Partisans.

Djilas, Popović, and Velebit spun out their negotiations for some weeks, keeping the German pressure off the Partisans. The proposal being discussed, as Djilas admits, was that the Partisans should take over the Sandžak as recognized Partisan territory and back up the Germans holding the coastal strip against the Allies. It was not until April that Hitler rejected the deal on the grounds that he would not treat with bandits.

The Partisan negotiators spent a pleasant time in Zagreb. Velebit visited his parents. Djilas ran into an old female acquaintance. Koča Popović, French-educated and an almost paranoiac Anglophobe, practiced his language skills conversing with an equally vitriolic pommy-bashing German officer who spoke French too.

Perhaps most ironic of all was Tito's personal and private motive for the March negotiations. The Germans held Herthe Haas, Tito's second common-law wife and the mother of his child. Tito had actually abandoned her when she was pregnant in order to elope with another communist comrade twenty-five years his junior. Tito nevertheless arranged the release of Herthe Haas as a bonus in the negotiations. As they were bamboozled by the Partisan claim that it was the Loyalists and not the Partisans who were collaborating, so most British observers swallowed Tito's propaganda that the Mihailović forces were womanizers, overlooking the fact that Tito was accompanied throughout the war by a lady companion.

Actually the March 1943 negotiations were not the first between Tito and the Germans. Desultory contacts had commenced in August 1942 when the Partisans captured engineer Hans Ott in western Bosnia near Livno. Negotiations resumed on November 17, and further talks took place at the end of January 1943. Tito even agreed to meet Ante Pavelić's *ustaša* negotiating team on January 23, 1943, but the German offensive against the "republic" in Bihać put paid to that. Hans Ott became very friendly with Tito, who used him as a regular contact with the Germans; he stayed with the Partisans until the end of the war. Tito had no reservations about dealing with the enemy. He did, however, have the good sense not to be found out and to detract attention from his own collaboration by unleashing a propaganda campaign about alleged Loyalist collaboration. He also deemed it prudent to liquidate Hans Ott after the war.

Proof of the Partisan collaboration in March 1943 has been

provided by the Belgrade authorities. Tito became increasingly embarrassed by the rumors circulating about the March 1943 negotiations with the Germans, and an official military historian, Miso Leković, was authorized to research the tricky subject in detail. He published his book in 1985 after Tito's death. This book represents a total indictment of the extensive Partisan collaboration record, and it shows the enormous benefits derived therefrom. It also shows that Tito's sole concern was his civil war against the Četniks. This case is irrefutable. Leković is pure kosher: an official Partisan historian publishing in Belgrade. Sava Bosnić published a superb synopsis of the book in the *South Slav Journal*, which totally destroys the *received wisdom* hypocrisy on the collaboration issue.

Incidentally, there were also extensive negotiations between the SS and Tito's Partisans in Slovenia in July 1944. They were carried out by Tito's later personal secretary, Dr. Jose Vilfan, while Tito himself was living under British protection on Vis. These negotiations were an insurance policy against an Allied landing in Venezia Giulia. They are not relevant to this book, because by July 1944 Tito had gained the support of the British in his civil-war aims, and the negotiations were directed against the Western Allies, not the Serbian Loyalists. They merit mention because they underline the gullibility of those who believed the trumped-up allegations of collaboration by Mihailović.

In the light of all of this evidence, Deakin's obsession with Mihailović's supposed collaboration would be comical had it not led to such tragic results. I refer to the momentously important meeting of December 10, 1943, which resulted in Churchill's abandonment of Mihailović. I will examine this meeting in greater detail later on. But here I want to touch briefly on the role played by Deakin, who attended the meeting.

In his book *The Embattled Mountain*, Deakin recalls how the prime minister interrogated him for nearly two hours "as the Officer concerned with interpreting the evidence derived from captured German and Četnik documents concerning the links between Mihailović and his commanders with the Italians and the Germans." He writes, "As I talked I knew that I was compiling the elements of a hostile brief which would play a decisive part in any future breach between the British Government and Mihailović."

Deakin takes full responsibility for the brief to the prime minister in regard to alleged Mihailović collaboration and the interpretation of the evidence. The "captured documents," however, came substantially from the Partisans. They could only, couldn't they? And they would certainly be interpreted very aggressively by the Partisans, wouldn't they?

It is important to register that Deakin appears to imply that his case against Mihailović—his interpretation of Partisan-submitted documents claiming collaboration—was very material, perhaps decisive, in the finalization of the decision to denounce Mihailović. It is important because Churchill decided that same December 10 that he wanted Mihailović "removed" by the end of the month.

The question of alleged Loyalist Četnik collaboration has been the subject of massive research and writings. This is hardly surprising, because something had to be dug up to justify the cynical abandonment of Mihailović, of the exiled government, of the Loyalist resistance, and eventually of the king. The public record could hardly be allowed to state the truth, namely, that the British had abandoned their allies because it was expedient. Why was it expedient? Either it was because Tito said, "I am going to liquidate Mihailović, take it or leave it," and the British had not seen fit to call Tito's bluff; or it was all ordained since the January 1943 Cairo meetings, and Churchill had more or less made up his mind then, and all the rest was just a charade.

More than twenty British officers served with the Mihailović forces. Incidentally, nearly all of them were dropped after the January 1943 meetings. There was an equal or greater number of NCOs. There were some hundreds of crashed aircrew, British and American, who were rescued, succored, transported, and evacuated by Mihailović forces. I have met nearly all of the British liaison staff. Most of us were together at evacuation with a substantial number of aircrew. I have read the statements under oath of a number of the 500 Americans. To a man all of these people, if asked, "Was Mihailović a collaborator?" would reply firmly and unequivocally, "No."

Yet he was condemned and abandoned on the strength of the interpretation of evidence by Deakin without any counsel for the defense or any friendly spokesman present. In my opinion, *The Embattled Mountain* and Deakin's signals and reports in the PRO show irrefutably his total acceptance of the Partisans' views of the Loyalists. And we know from Fitzroy Maclean's own signals and reports that Tito had made clear his unswerving aim to "liquidate" Mihailović and that nothing would be allowed to stand in his way. Yet Tito's "evidence" was accepted without question. Isn't that ludicrous?

Several other factors have a bearing on the collaboration issue. The Germans, who had every possible interest in fostering the civil war and thus diverting the military effort that could otherwise be used against them, did a great deal to promote the theory that the Loyalists were collaborating with them. They even distributed photographs of friendly Četnik groups to the Yugoslav press to support their claim and discredit the genuine Loyalist forces in the eyes of the civil population.

Furthermore, there were so-called "legal" Četniks. In part these derived from a deliberate, legitimate move by Mihailović in November 1941 when, in the wake of the abortive Serbian uprising, he had to all but dissolve his mobile force and go into deep hiding with a small headquarters. He sent many of his men home. Others he encouraged to infiltrate the German-sponsored Nedić forces. They were to hold themselves ready to be called back into the mountains, bringing their arms with them. In 1943 both Archie Jack and I used such men to help us in setting up sabotage operations. These men were agents, not collaborators, but that was too fine a distinction for the Tito propagandists.

Then there was Kosta Pečanac, a Četnik hero from the First World War who raised a Četnik force and went over to support the Axis. He was not part of Mihailović's movement, and Mihailović had him executed. Yet the Partisans have used his name extensively to denigrate Mihailović by association.

———

The Yugoslav situation was typical of a resistance scenario. It existed in other countries, perhaps most notably in France, but it was natural to the Balkans. In Western European movements, resisters worked by day for the occupiers and did clandestine jobs at night. Although perhaps SOE did not comprehend the full sophisticated extent of what was happening in Yugoslavia prior to 1943, the potential was known and encouraged. It was the ideal scenario for the preparation of the *ustanak*, when a Serbian horde of some half a million warriors, in the tradition of old, would *at the right moment* rise and drive out the occupier, coordinating its move with an Allied invasion, whether from the west or from the east.

This plan could have worked. It could have worked very well indeed were it not for one Josip Broz, alias Tito, and his ruthless ambition to grab sole power for himself in Yugoslavia; and to cheat and lie and bamboozle however much he needed to. Like any confidence trickster, he only needed gullible victims. He found them, particularly among the British.

From quite early on there had clearly been accommodation between Četnik forces loosely associated with Mihailović and the Italians. This existed principally in Montenegro but also in Herzegovina and Dalmatia. It was a live-and-let-live collaboration. The Italians were glad of a bit of peace, and the Četniks were preparing to exploit this accommodation when the Italian collapse came. The Venezia Division incident referred to earlier corroborates this view. This accommodation was quite specifically known to, and approved by, SOE from the start, as is clearly shown by Col. George Taylor's report of March 11, 1943, which he made after a long visit to SOE Cairo and a thorough study of the Yugoslav situation. Colonel Taylor was the chief staff officer of SOE London and thus effectively Lord Glenconner's director in London. Capt. Nedjelko Plećaš, a Yugoslav air force officer who was dropped to Mihailović by the British in 1942, later wrote about the SOE policy condoning such collaboration, which he himself followed.

Nevertheless, when, in late November and early December 1943, the Foreign Office scented that the prime minister was leading up to a policy of total support of Tito and the abandonment of the Loyalists—and that he could no longer be headed off such a course and they would need to justify this policy change—Secretary of State Anthony Eden started condemning this earlier collaboration in Montenegro and denounced the evil of it, totally ignoring the fact that it had been encouraged by the British, and encouraged for entirely laudable reasons.

When the decision to abandon Mihailović had finally been taken and when Churchill was also no doubt seeking to rationalize it before his own conscience, he wrote on January 2, 1944, to the foreign secretary (PREM 3 511/2):

> There is no doubt in my mind whatever that Mihailovic is in collaboration with the enemy. This was confirmed not only by people like Deakin who have come back from Tito's forces but by many of the officers now serving in the Mihailovic area. I have been convinced by the arguments of the men I know and trust that Mihailovic is a millstone tied round the neck of the Little King and he has no chance till he gets rid of him.
>
> As an instance of the follies into which the King has been dragged Deakin showed me a photograph of one of Mihailovic's commanders being entertained by the Italian general, against whom he was supposed to be fighting, at a banquet to celebrate the grant to him of a decoration from King Peter and the Yugoslav Government.

While showing Churchill the photo from his Mihailović collaboration dossier, Deakin evidently omitted to apprise him of the background just related—the fact that tactical accommodation with the Italians in Montenegro had been known to and approved by SOE from the start. Furthermore, the prime minister's claim that many of the officers serving in the Mihailović area had confirmed Mihailović's collaboration was grotesquely false and hypocritical. No BLOs had come out to report. The inept Cope-Raw misunderstanding of Mihailović's instructions to Djurić, and the absurd claim that they constituted collaboration with the Germans, had been corrected. It is, of course, possible—indeed, almost certain—that the correction was not passed on to Churchill by MO4 or the Minister of State's Office.

A "most secret" report dated December 10, 1943, obviously prepared by the Yugoslav section for that day's meeting with the prime minister, quotes "extracts from reports by British Liaison Officers with Mihailović Forces—15th Nov. to 10th Dec. 1943." These were condensations culled selectively from half a dozen signals. They contain short statements by captains More and Wade and (once again) Colonel Cope. They refer to hypothetical bargaining with the Nedić people about eventual cooperation against the Partisans, and contain Cope's, Wade's, and More's personal perceptions of the attitudes of the Loyalist commanders. In the light of Tito's announced intention to liquidate the Loyalists and the Partisan offensives already under way at that time in Sandžak and western Serbia, there was nothing surprising and definitely nothing that could be reasonably complained about in these extracts. They constituted the subjective speculation and opinions of frustrated BLOs, all of whom relied on interpreters. We know that Cope's interpreter got things wrong. Yet the Yugoslav section built up this straightforward tittle-tattle into a big deal. Any intelligence officer worth his salt would have relegated them to the ash can. There were even three signals from a Captain Hargreaves complaining about low Četnik morale and lack of help for his mission. I wonder who was to blame for that. Cairo or Hargreaves himself? Hardly the Loyalists, who knew that they were being betrayed.

F. H. Hinsley, now Sir Harry, is the recognized authority on British intelligence in the Second World War. He refers to reports critical of Mihailović sent by "Captain Robertson." Hinsley evidently does not appreciate that "Captain Robertson," real name either Dragi Radivojević or Branko Radojević, was a communist spy controlled by Klugmann and sent by MO4 into Mihailović headquarters with the purpose of spying on both Mihailović and the chief BLO, Captain Hudson. I tell his full story later. Maybe MO4 showed Robertson's reports to Churchill. That would have been a typical Keble-Klugmann "dirty trick."

Churchill's January 2, 1944 rationalization of the decision to dump Mihailović had been prompted by a signal (PREM 3 511/2) from the foreign secretary of December 29, 1943, the fifth paragraph of which states, "I am doubtful whether we should tell Tito that we are prepared to have no further dealings with Mihailovic first because we here at any rate have not yet got conclusive evidence of his misbehaviour."

Without consulting the foreign secretary, however, Churchill had made his decision to get rid of Mihailović, and even Tito was informed of the "general way things were going" and specifically that the BLOs with Mihailović were being instructed to try to cross to the Partisans. The PREM series in the Public Records Office for this period shows that the prime minister had been worked up into a quite vitriolic state of mind about Mihailović, and he wrote of him almost as a monster. It is almost incredible today to read how Tito put over this propaganda without ever having left his Yugoslav headquarters.

Between Eden's December 29 message and Churchill's January 2 rationalization there was another intriguing exchange between the two. On December 30, Churchill wrote, "Everything Deakin and Maclean said and all the reports received showed that he had been in active collaboration with the Germans." Eden replied on January 1, "As regards Mihailovic I do not recall any decision in Cairo to demand his dismissal before the end of the year. Maybe this was after I left."

Then came Churchill's January 2 message, from which I have already quoted. Here is another passage from that message: "I still feel that the only chance for the King is to dismiss Mihailovic and muzzle his anti-Tito propaganda. In this way alone can he free himself from the growing antagonism. Once Mihailovic is dismissed I believe that Maclean and Randolph [Churchill's son] will have a chance to work on Tito for a return of the King to his country."

It is in the light of these signals that the collaboration case against Mihailović has to be viewed. Tito had persuaded Maclean that Mihailović had to go. The prime minister had bent his knee to Tito's blackmail in the hope of getting the king back into the country. Then it became imperative to justify the decision to abandon Mihailović, and, whatever it contained, Deakin's dossier had to be regarded as damning. Lie or not, the Yugoslav section claim that we BLOs with Mihailović had reported him as being in active collaboration with the Germans had to be accepted. The falsely interpreted Mihailović signal to Djurić passed to Cairo by Cope had to be regarded as valid and the correction suppressed. The collaboration issue was as simple as that.

Although Foreign Secretary Eden adopted a hypocritical attitude about Mihailović's accommodations with the Italians when Churchill's absolute determination to sacrifice the Loyalists became clear, he was never happy about the decision, as can be seen in a memo from him to Sir Orme Sargent (FO 371 44273) on June 20, 1944. He wrote, "I find this report most disturbing. Brigadier Armstrong does not bear out the oft-repeated tale of Mihailovic's collaboration with the enemy. Yet he was with him all the time wasn't he? I have never understood on what the evidence rests tho I have asked a score of times."

The Partisan campaign of tendentious accusations against Mihailović of collaboration was enormously helped by the pro-Partisan atmosphere that increasingly came to rule in the British agencies. Starting in SOE Cairo, firmly catching hold in the Minister of State's Office in Cairo, it spread—if it was not previously established there—to PWE and the Political Intelligence Centre and eventually even to the military in the Middle East. As people saw the way the wind was blowing, they jumped on the bandwagon until Četnik bashing became the main sport of the Yugoslav section in Italy during 1944.

As I have related earlier, some of our signals sent in moments of frustration were taken out of context and used by those in Cairo who were determined to undermine the Loyalists. Evidently these presentations reached the prime minister. Nevertheless, I am sure that none of the BLOs in retrospect will say that the Loyalists were quislings.

The Germans, despite their campaign to portray Četniks as friendly to them, regarded Mihailović as anything but a friend or collaborator. We have been treated to a surfeit of claims about the intercepts that supposedly support the Partisan case but about which we have no specific details. Yet on July 17, 1942, Hitler signaled one of his lieutenants, "The basis of every success in

Serbia and the entire south-east of Europe lies in the annihilation of Mihailović." On February 9, 1943, an intercepted signal from a German general reported, "The movement of General Mihailović remains in the first place with regard to leadership, armament, organization, and activity."

At the end of February 1943 Hitler wrote to Mussolini, "Your Second Army [should] regard Mihailović and his movement as uncompromising enemies of the Axis powers." Yet it was at this very time that Churchill was being persuaded by SOE Cairo that Tito's forces were of overriding importance. How could this possibly have come about? Sir Harry Hinsley states that in August 1943 "Enigma left no doubt, at least at the highest level, that the Germans remained set on Mihailovic's destruction."

The Partisans and their publicists have made great play of the German poster with a photograph of Tito and the reward of 100,000 reichsmarks for his capture, dead or alive. They have insulted the intelligence of their readers by cutting off the picture of Mihailović which appeared on the same poster side by side with Tito's, with an identical price on his head. It was typical of the time and the attitudes that many of the Partisan allies in the British agencies merited the insult by swallowing the fraud. In a court of law a silly ploy like that would destroy a case. Not so in the *received wisdom*. The Titoites continue to use the picture of Tito alone, relying on the use of noise, more noise, and more noise still to make the Titomania case.

Great play is also made of Loyalists fighting the Partisans while the Germans were doing so. This is perhaps the most tendentious claim of all. Such fighting nearly always occurred when the Germans moved against the Partisans and the latter, on the run, invaded Mihailović territory. In the famous Mount Durmitor battle, for instance, the Partisans attacked Mihailović in his territory when the Germans and the Italians came up behind them. In the Durmitor offensive the Germans first captured the main Montenegrin Četnik force.

It must be stressed that the Partisans made no secret of their utter determination to destroy the Loyalists in preference to destroying Axis forces. Inevitably they clashed with both at the same time.

The purveyors of the Tito propaganda also conveniently telescope events, paying little attention to chronology. In the autumn of 1944 the tastelessly named "Ratweek" attacks by the Partisans, driving into Serbia with enormous logistic and air support from the British, pushed some surviving Loyalist units literally into the arms of the enemy, in some cases into enemy redoubts. This was then alleged to be "Četnik collaboration" and treated as if it had been happening continuously since 1941.

What were the Loyalists supposed to do? Commit suicide?

If he had been a collaborator like Nedić, Mihailović would have fled with the Germans in 1945. He did not do so, and though he was down to a "hiding to nothing"—a no-win situation—he called the *ustanak* in September 1944 against the retreating Germans. It was, predictably, a half-baked affair, nearly a year after he had been abandoned by the West and stood alone. But he did it, and he made contact with the Red Army, who promptly handed over the Loyalist units involved to the Partisans for "disposal." The officers were, of course, shot.

How many sources and how much evidence does one have to trot out to show that Mihailović was not a collaborator?

Yet Deakin, relying largely on communist source documents and on "evidence" from BLOs' signals extracted selectively by Partisan sympathizers in MO4, presented Churchill with a two-hour hostile brief. No one from the mission to Mihailović was there to represent the other view. That meeting sealed Mihailović's fate. It helped split the Serbian warrior nation. A true tragedy.

As I wrote at the start of this section, in wars collaboration in the pedantic sense of the word always takes place from time to time—in guerrilla war even more so. In Yugoslavia prior to December 1943 the Partisans collaborated with the Axis infinitely more extensively and profitably than anything Mihailović was accused of. Mihailović scorned a public-relations exercise to build a case against the Partisans, and the British did nothing to help him build one. The Partisans, by contrast, used their vastly superior publicity machine to fabricate a case against Mihailović. The British grabbed the case and publicized it because they needed justification for their decision to abandon Mihailović. It's as simple as that.

THE EXILED GOVERNMENT AND KING PETER

The story of King Peter and the Yugoslav government in exile is a book unto itself. I am in no way qualified to write on this complex subject, and I will therefore limit myself to a few general points that have a bearing on the theme of this book.

When he had decided to abandon the Loyalists at the end of 1943, Churchill wrote that he had been convinced by the arguments "of the men I know and trust" that Mihailović was a "millstone tied round the neck of the Little King." I believe it would be fairer to comment that the "Little King's" exiled government became a heavy cross for Mihailović and the Loyalist movement to bear. The reasons were various. First, there was the inevitable dissention that arose between the Serbs and the Croats in the government following the reports from Yugoslavia of *ustaša* atrocities and the genocide of the Serbian minorities in Croatia. Then the Slovene elements in the government seem to have fished in troubled waters. Certainly the Slovene vice-premier, Miha Krek, was instrumental in spreading to British agencies Partisan-inspired rumors about Mihailović collaboration in 1941.

The differences, problems, and squabbles of the exiled government exasperated the British, as did the machinations of young King Peter's prospective mother-in-law. Similarly, King Peter's determination to get married at a time when others felt he should be thinking more of his people and of the problems of his country did little to endear the Loyalist cause to British government circles.

Communicating with his government must have taken an inordinate amount of Mihailović's time and caused him great annoyance and frustration. Added to this was the problem of the communications themselves. When he managed to establish regular W/T contact with British help, through the so-called Villa Resta series, his signals passed, in order, through SOE Cairo and the British ambassador to the exiled government in London, Sir George Rendel, before they reached their destination. This was a slow process, and even at the start the signals enjoyed a rather low priority. Worse, Sir George decided at his sole discretion which signals should or should not be passed on to the Yugoslav government. Thus the British censored Mihailović's signals. This was truly extraordinary behavior vis-à-vis an Allied government.

Later, however, an even more extraordinary situation prevailed. The signals came into and went out from SOE Cairo to Mihailović's headquarters. Incoming signals were then passed on to the Minister of State's Office in Cairo, which had assumed the role of embassy to the exiled government when King Peter and his ministers moved to Cairo late in the summer of 1943. Whereas Sir George Rendel in London had been a good friend to the Yugoslav government and, as far can be seen from the files, had adopted as fair and correct an attitude as was possible in his role as censor, the Minister of State's Office in Cairo seems to have been predisposed to favor the MO4 pro-Partisan line from early in 1943. The office adopted an attitude verging on open hostility to Mihailović. Mihailović's signals to his government and his king became subject to unsympathetic and arbitrary censorship. Furthermore, they were treated by MO4 in a cavalier manner.

The Public Records Office has a series of communications (file WO 202/144) between the British embassy to Yugoslavia and MO4 in October 1943. These reveal that MO4 let Villa Resta signals accumulate "to the tune of a hundred or so twice within the last three months." A letter to MO4 from an embassy official named Philip Broad dated October 22, 1943, states, ". . . enclosing copies of further Villa Resta messages. I note that one of these is dated 29th December, 1942 whereas the most recent is dated 1st July of this year. We should obviously get into appalling trouble with the Yugoslavs. if we were to pass these on to them now. I think the best thing would be for us just to pigeon-hole them, but in case the Yugoslavs spot the gap and attack us, could you please be so good as to let me know why these messages have only come through now?"

On October 26, Broad states, "As I have mentioned before it is out of the question for us to send these on now."

The same day, Colonel Davidson of MO4 (not Basil Davidson but a successor) writes back, "To hand over ancient messages to the Jug Government would certainly provoke a scream. If enquiries are made I will produce an answer."

Though devious, all of this is more cockup or coverup than conspiracy. But it certainly constitutes Perfidious Albion at work again.

An objective reading of the Foreign Office files in the Public Records Office brings out the difference between the attitudes of our ambassador to Tito on the one hand and our ambassador to the royal Yugoslav government on the other. Our ambassador to Tito was Fitzroy Maclean, and he seems to have become Tito's mouthpiece with the British government rather than the British government's mouthpiece with Tito. He was loath to pass on messages that Tito did not want to hear, but he readily advised Tito how to put his case to the British. In his legendary report after his first visit to Tito, nicknamed "the blockbuster" in the Foreign Office, Maclean put Tito's case himself with spectacular emphasis and lucidity. It may sound apocryphal, but it is said that he even used to help Tito draft his messages to Churchill.

I would dearly love to know whether he drafted Tito's message complaining in the most intemperate and dictatorial manner about the BBC, a message sent just a few days after Maclean dropped. Although the message constituted a direct challenge to the British government, it was written in the most beautiful Foreign Office prose. Hardly the style one would expect from an international revolutionary.

Conversely, the ambassador to the royal Yugoslav government, in his communications with the Foreign Office and his attitude to Mihailović, caused Douglas Howard, head of the southern department, and Sir Orme Sargent, his superior, to comment in a memo that the Minister of State's Office in Cairo appeared "not to want agreement to be reached with Mihailović."

In practice the embassy to the royal Yugoslav government seems to have been much more concerned with assisting Maclean and the Tito Partisans than the government to which it was accredited and its minister of defense, Mihailović. This paradox was further underlined by the extraordinary organizational arrangement under which the Minister of State's Office in Cairo acted as rear link for the mission to Tito on political matters while also providing the ambassador to the royal Yugoslav government in Cairo. With Tito sworn to liquidate the government and Mihailović, it would have taken a Solomon to carry out the two tasks fairly and simultaneously; and Ralph Skrine Stevenson and his assistant, Philip Broad, though no doubt admirable and experienced Foreign Office officials, were certainly no miracle workers or Solomons. It was an anomalous and crazy setup. Mihailović was in a trap, with the obligation to report to his government via MO4 and with the embassy censoring and holding up his signals. Furthermore, those signals went through the deciphering office, which was open to the officers in MO4, including the international communist guru and doyen of the Cambridge set, James Klugmann. It would be naïve to disregard the possibility that the signals were subject not only to censorship by the embassy and to cavalier treatment in the deciphering office of MO4 but also to leaking to the Partisans via the communist agency in Cairo, with which Klugmann was surely in contact.

How much better off Mihailović would have been had he had no exiled government to report to! He was subordinated to an authority with which the British were exasperated and bored; and with whose failings, real and imaginary, Mihailović became associated. Beyond that, how much better off might Mihailović have been without a British mission and British signals?

PART II
The Action

■

CHAPTER
3
"U Sumu"
(Into the Woods)

■

We had traveled by slow train from Cairo to Derna, where the MO4 airfield was located. The climate was hot and I had a cold. We were lucky in not being delayed, and though I knew nothing of it at the time, we must have just missed Deakin on the airfield. Perhaps I flew in the same Halifax on its next trip. I remember that there were only two functional that night.

Not only did I know nothing of Deakin's flight, I knew nothing of *any* British mission being dropped to the Partisans. I knew virtually nothing of the Partisans. From our briefing I recollect no instructions other than those about supplying the Loyalists and preparing sabotage on the main north-south railway line. There had been some slight mention of possible Partisan bands in Macedonia, but the mention had been incidental. There was nothing actual, nothing pressing.

My eardrums popped and hurt abominably from the inflammation caused by my cold in the unpressurized Halifax. After some six or seven hours I was glad to hear the aircrew member in charge of us say that we were passing Priština; shortly thereafter he opened the hatch. The slipstream whistled in. I positioned myself at the rear of the open hole in the floor with "Tommy" Tomlinson facing me. Tommy was to be my second-in-command. The red light shone, then the green, and I was down and away before the airman had dropped his hand and shouted "Go!"

The still night air as I fell out of the slipstream, the moisture in the atmosphere after the dust and dryness of Derna, immediately impressed itself on my senses. We had been dropped high, and I landed near the bottom of a steep ravine after quite a long spell in the air. I found myself near a path on its side, and, swallowing to clear my clogged eardrums, I felt relief and pleasure as the rushing and roaring waters of a mountain stream below made themselves audible at last.

The moon was bright, and the ravine lay in gently mountainous country deeply clothed in beech forests, interspersed with oaks, covering practically the whole area in view. It was stunningly beautiful.

Quite rapidly I made contact with the reception party organized by Maj. John Sehmer, who had dropped a few weeks previously. He was accredited to Maj. Radoslav Djurić, the commander responsible for the area known as Jablanica, northeast of Priština, which stretched east to the old Bulgarian border, south to Vranje in the Bulgarian-annexed part of Serbia, and north to the Niš-Leskovac plains.

Djurić had a number of commanders under him in the Jablanica area. His full command had about 3,000 fully mobile troops plus 10,000 or more peasant reserves, perhaps one-third of whom were armed. Djurić's area stretched farther west and north; but Jablanica was the part that came to concern me after my original plans had to be changed, following the disaster that befell our missions shortly thereafter.

Major Djurić was a regular soldier of some forty years of age. He was tall, with the rather flat features of Central Asian peoples, and a bit fleshy in build. Although he was friendly, he failed to inspire confidence in me from the start. Nonetheless, he appeared very much in command as we gathered around in the dropping area, where the signal fires were already extinguished and the turf, which had been cut out earlier, was being replaced in order to hide all signs of them.

John Sehmer was a gnomelike little man about five feet three or four in height. He sported a pair of smart riding breeches, a service dress-uniform jacket, amazingly a genuine Sam Browne belt, which he used to festoon himself with a multitude of handguns, ammunition, and grenades, and a Yugoslav peasant cap on top of it all. His round, boyish face was adorned with a couple of days' ginger stubble, and he peered shortsightedly through steel-rimmed spectacles. He sucked a meerschaum pipe and carried an alpenstock. He was actually of part German origin, as his name signified, and he looked it. He conversed with Djurić in reasonably fluent but heavily accented German. From time to time he switched to French with an equally bad accent. His Serbo-Croat was and remained similar. But he fitted in well and neither expected nor looked for comforts, sleeping on the floor and sharing the lice with the rest of us. Although he made some mistakes that cost dear, he was a good man and the type who went well for guerrilla warfare. Sadly, he was later captured and killed on a mission to Czechoslovakia.

Sehmer was accompanied by a Captain Hawksworth, who was, I believe, an officer in the Royal Engineers and who had also dropped very recently. Hawksworth was dark, with piercing eyes and a rather conspiratorial manner. I never quite understood Hawksworth's role; whether he was a sabotage expert for Sehmer or a commander of a sub-mission. Combined with his manner was a romantic turn of mind, and at one stage he requisitioned a crossbow for killing sentries, black uniforms to enable him to form a special task force, and rubber stamps for marking with a black hawk the faces of sentries killed with the crossbow. I remember hearing rumors of these plans at the time and was fascinated to find some signals about them in the Public Records Office forty years later. The ideas were entertaining and harmless, and at least they reflected a desire to do what we had come for, namely, kill Germans. Hawksworth was an entertaining fellow. I believe that he carried out more than one operation against the Axis. I recollect that I heard about a daring attack on a railway station north of Leskovac that was partly successful, and he may have undertaken other jobs that I did not hear about.

Sehmer and Hawksworth's group included two W/T operators, a Sergeant Blackmore and a Sergeant Leban, the latter a Slovenian, along with two New Zealanders, Sergeants Lindstrom and Harvey. My group comprised lieutenants Tomlinson and Smith, who were newly commissioned Royal Engineers officers included as explosives experts, and Leading-Aircraftman Thompson, an excellent W/T operator and, as I had found in the few days we had been together, an extremely pleasant individual.

Lieutenant Smith had been sent to join Sehmer, while Tomlinson and Thompson were to accompany me into Macedonia south of Skoplje, where we were to replace Major Morgan's mission. Morgan had been captured shortly before by the Bulgars after he had dropped blind into that area. Vojvoda Trbić, the local organizer of the resistance south of Skoplje, had been contacted by Djurić and had come up to the Jablanica area to guide my party south.

In the dropping zone there was hectic activity. The other members of my party had collected together and were swapping stories of their drop. Tomlinson had suffered minor injury to his back but was not in serious condition, and the other two were fine. Peasants dressed in broadly cut jodhpur-style breeches and square-waisted jackets, all of heavy homespun material, were carrying in the twelve or so containers dropped from our Halifax and loading them onto bullock carts. These were driven by their womenfolk, and as soon as they had their load up, they rumbled off into the darkness. Djurić explained that everything was being hurried because the dropping ground had been used twice before and it was feared that the Bulgarian occupation forces were wise to it.

My first impression was one of remarkable organization. No one stood around. Everyone seemed to know his task and to get on with it, though they all had time to greet us, embrace us, and make us feel welcome. The relatively few mobile troops guarding the dropping zone were dressed for the most part in peasant gear, though some of them wore battle-dress jackets. The officers mostly wore Yugoslav military clothing and equipment, and most of them carried Schmeisser submachine guns; I learned that the possession of one of these was a sign of considerable prestige. In all, the Loyalists were a motley lot in their clothing and equipment.

What struck me most was the integration of the peasantry and these Loyalist Četniks. The peasants, a proportion of whom were carrying long, ancient rifles slung across their backs, acted as runners, supplied the bullock carts and transport, and brought food and drink. Some of them, evidently local leaders, talked to Djurić and his officers on an equal basis. There was no servility and certainly no hostility. In that clearing we were seeing a little bit of national custom stemming from the history of the Serbs. We were watching a traditional četa (a local band or group) in operation, like the četas that through the centuries had fought other wars and other occupations, German, Bulgar, and Turk. It all seemed so natural, and one could feel that it had been going on for a long time.

In that country of gentle mountains and woodland, which stretched mile after mile with only an occasional track and no paved roads at all, the peasant holdings were often separated by one or two ravines and usually by a mile or so as the crow flies. This distance could entail two or three hours' march on foot with one, two, or maybe more ascents and descents of hundreds of feet each time. Each holding was independent and virtually self-supporting. There was usually barley or wheat corn and grazing for livestock. There were cattle, sometimes sheep, bullocks for transport, small, sturdy horses, but very few mules. Pigs and chickens ran around the homesteads, and the warm summer climate favored peppers and other semiexotic vegetables. Beans formed the main item of the staple diet. No holding was without its plum trees for making the potent *rakija* or *šljivovica*, and many had pear and apple trees as well. The women worked with the men on the land, and after cooking the food, they wove all of the material they needed on

139

their own looms; they also made all of the clothing, some of which was of fine quality, design, and appearance. The footwear was formed from rectangles of rawhide wrapped around the foot and known as *opanake*.

The houses were built of mud with home-fired tiled roofs. In the mountains they were universally single-storied. A two-storied house was regarded as a sign of enormous prestige and fortune, and was to be found only in the foothills and plains. But even in the mountains, most of the houses had a cellar, or *podrun*, which served the vital purpose of storing the *rakija*. Chimneys were a rarity; the smoke from the open fire in the center of the floor filtered through a hole in the peak of the roof. There was usually just one bed in the house, reserved for the mating couple. Grandparents, children, and others slept on mats on the floor, where we would join them in due course. There would be a low, round table and a few small stools and, apart from the looms, no other furniture. The reserves of food, mostly dried, hung from hooks in the ceiling.

The homesteads were simple. The holdings seemed limited only by the amount of land the members of the family were physically able to cultivate; there were large areas of unexploited woodland between each settlement. The families were almost entirely self-supporting. Some produce was carried up to ten, fifteen, or more hours' journey—an average distance to the nearest village or township—and sold in order to purchase needles, sugar, or salt, which were the articles most in demand. While the life was rugged and hard, the mountain peasants in that area were proud and fiercely individualistic, and they loved their *svojina*— their home and land. As long as their health held, they had all that they wanted, and provided they had a good woman who bore them a strong son, they could pass their old age pondering the past and testing last year's *šljivovica*. For the man born to it, with the necessary stamina, it was an idyllic existence. It was in Yugoslavia that I determined that I myself would become a peasant with my own *svojina* before I finished my days.

All around one could feel the history of these mountain folk. One could understand why they had formed their četas to protect their houses. One marveled at the distances they traveled to join together; and in the year ahead I was amazed time and again at the news-carrying service—the bush telegraph—that functioned automatically, without conscious organization. Each family would send a courier on to the next, to pass on any item of news, and it was literally all done on the run.

These peasants had few riches in the monetary sense and virtually no assets or valuables other than their homesteads and their stock. They had no machinery and worked largely with wooden plows drawn by bullocks. Yet they had a unique way of life, and nowhere in those mountains did I find a desire for change. They wanted to hold what they had and to live as their forebears had. They were prepared to fight for that, as had been their ancestors, and in the mountains of southeastern Serbia there were hundreds of thousands of them. They constituted an extraordinary potential for a guerrilla army.

In a year in those mountains, not once did I hear those peasants expressing support for communism or for the Partisans. They were Royalists to a man; and they swore total support for "Uncle Draža" Mihailović. *Autres temps, autres moeurs.* Things may have changed later. But when we left that area in March 1944, nothing had changed. And no amount of propaganda will persuade me that it did.

Those Serbs were opposed to any invader. This was their history. One felt totally confident moving around without guides through those mountains. The territory was friendly; the people knew who we were; the bush telegraph signaled our coming, and the bush telegraphers would come running to tell us what was happening elsewhere and where the invader was. When we were there, "invader" meant not only Axis troops but also any Partisan group that encroached on the territory. This happened very little in the mountains themselves, but on the one or two occasions that Partisan patrols pushed up, the peasants made it very clear to them that they too were without business there.

The potential of the territory as a safe base for Četnik-style guerrilla warfare was fantastic. All they needed was support—arms and equipment. The relatively gentle terrain of the mountains over large areas provided virtually unlimited possibilities for dropping zones.

To the east lay the valley of the Morava. From Vranje in the southeastern corner of the Jablanica command area north to Grdelica, the railway and road ran for the most part through the mountains, dropping down into the Morava Valley. In that part the valley was narrow and precipitous. Then to the north it opened up into the Leskovac plains. To the west were many more miles of mountain and *suma*—woodland—before the Ibar Valley was reached.

In the Leskovac plains to the north the pattern of country and life changed. Falling to the foothills, the sparsely populated woods and mountains gave way to small villages surrounded by rich farmland. The homesteads became small hamlets. Churches, far apart in the mountains, appeared in the larger hamlets. The barley, oats, and wheat of the mountains became replaced by maize on the flatlands, and the staple bread there was maize-based and of doughy consistency. The people changed too, not very much yet in the hamlets in the foothills; but already one got the feeling that other eyes and ears were watching and listening, and that one could not be sure of the loyalties.

Moving farther into the plains, one came across bigger villages, still depending on agriculture but with larger farms, many of them evidently prosperous. In these villages one began to feel the influence of the towns, of the politicians, and of the proletariat. And, of course, in the villages the occupation was more noticeably present, and patrols were regularly passing through. Yes, in the plains it was different.

It was the second morning after our drop that the surprise attack took place. We had passed the first night in a peasant homestead and rejoined the main party the next day in another clearing, where the stores were being distributed. News had come in of Bulgarian and German columns approaching, and it was evident that an Axis cleanup operation was starting. Trbić counseled against trying to start our journey south over the Bulgarian border, and we buried some of our W/T equipment. With runners coming in, advising us of the movement of the enemy columns, we moved off into the woods with Djurić's headquarters platoon of about thirty men.

It was early June, and it coincided with the Axis encirclement of the Partisans on Mount Durmitor far to the west of us,
in which attack Deakin and Tito shared splinters from the same
bomb. It was a general cleanup by Axis forces of all guerrilla-
held mountain areas, and they were after the Loyalists just as
much as they were after the Partisans. But Partisan mythology
has it that the Loyalists were collaborating with the Axis in this
cleanup. I did not feel as if I had the Axis on my side in those
next few days. The shared bomb that slightly wounded Tito and
Deakin became earthshaking news. What happened to the Mihailović BLOs did not even merit a footnote.

We spent the day in the woods with rumors coming in. We
experienced a nasty introduction to the bitterness of internecine
strife when Sergeant Leban, the W/T operator of Slovenian ex-
traction, told me that three Croats sent out as spies by the Germans, who had been caught and held prisoner, had been quietly
dispatched as the enemy got closer and their guarding became
more onerous and insecure. It was logical enough, but disturbing
to our Western minds. More disturbing to us was the manner of
their execution: their throats were slit. But we were going to experience a lot worse.

Late at night we moved into a tiny hamlet consisting of two
homesteads, which was clear of enemy troops, and settled in for
the night. We were awakened at dawn by the peasant woman's
cries of "Idi brzo. Brzo. Bugari su tu." (Go quickly, quickly. The
Bulgars are here.) An advance Bulgarian platoon, clearly aware
of our location, had made a dawn attack and set up a machine
gun covering the house. Before I could get my boots on, it was
firing bursts.

My life was probably saved by the speed with which Radoslav Djurić made his exit. First through the door and with no
thought for his command, he left behind his strongbox, which
contained a heavy bag of gold sovereigns I had brought with me.
I am a peasant by nature and mean about money, and I did not
really like the idea of those sovereigns being seized by the Bulgars. By the time I had shot off the lock of the strongbox, which
was too heavy to carry, and extricated the bag of gold, I was
alone in the house and bursts were coming through the wall.

Through the window I could see a second machine gun being mounted. Sehmer and the others had gone with Djurić or followed after him. No one else was in sight. As the front of the house was under steady fire, I made my way out through the back window. I had to cover about thirty yards of open ground to reach the safety of the woods below. As I neared cover at full gallop, the Bulgars saw me and I narrowly escaped a burst, jumping over the body of a Serb who had been less lucky.

I saw no other sign of life until I ran into Sehmer. He seemed fully confident that the others were just ahead in two groups, one with Djurić and the other with his adjutant, a man named Vlada. We went on and caught up with Djurić, who had six of his men with him, along with Harvey and Leban from our party. The rest of my team was missing. He assured us that they were with Vlada. I was not too happy about the manner of his reply, but he was very confident. With hindsight I now regret deeply that we did not attempt a counterattack, but with hindsight I also know that I could not have forced Djurić to do so; and even if we had, the Bulgars had two machine guns mounted. I had seen them in position before I left the back of the house, and we had nothing to counter them. Djurić had a Schmeisser and I had a Sten, but the rest had only rifles or handguns. So we would have had no chance; and the Bulgars were efficient infantry soldiers.

All the same . . .

We found out later that the Bulgars had caught the other members of the British team as they ran from the front of the house following Djurić and Sehmer toward the forest. Lieutenant Tomlinson, my number two, was wounded in the arm but escaped into the forest. Thompson, the W/T operator, was killed instantly. Three more men were hit: Lieutenant Smith, one of the explosives experts; Sergeant Blackmore, Sehmer's W/T operator; and Lindstrom, one of the New Zealanders. Lindstrom and Smith were shot on the ground by the Bulgars. Smith feigned death. Blackmore, with four bullets in his chest, had fainted. Having taken their boots and valuables, the Bulgars left them for dead. We recovered Smith and Blackmore, but they both died a day or two later.

Djurić had acquitted himself badly. His sentries were inadequate, and he was the first to run. He was a devious individual, and in the months ahead we frequently had cause to distrust him. When Bill Cope took over the mission from Sehmer, Djurić manipulated him and his number two, Rupert Raw, taking advantage of their lack of Serbo-Croat on a number of occasions. It's quite possible that he intentionally misled them, for example, on the occasion of the Mihailović "collaboration" signal. Why Djurić would behave thus is not certain, but it is possible that he was at that stage trying to replace Mihailović in British favor. Mihailović never really trusted him, and on other occasions there were misunderstandings between them.

Whatever the truth of that, later on Djurić became distracted by something more personal and evidently more pressing for him. He took up with a notorious ex–Gestapo spy, a prewar communist, Vera Pešić, recently a German general's mistress. She was captured and taken to Djurić to be interrogated and shot. But he made her his mistress instead. This liaison went on for some time, and Rupert Raw was instructed by MO4 to find out about it. He wrote an entertaining and salacious report, which can be found in the PRO together with the other BLO reports (WO 202 162).

Shortly after the British mission withdrew in March 1944, Mihailović sent orders to one of Djurić's subcommanders, Jovo Stefanović, to arrest Djurić and send him under escort to the Mihailović headquarters. Stefanović did arrest Djurić, but unfortunately he made a great error in judgment by accepting his "parole," his word not to escape, and allowing him out of the building to answer the call of nature. Obviously in some doubt about his prisoner's sincerity, Stefanović obliged him to go out without his trousers. It was not the wisest of moves. Djurić, bare bottom and all, bolted. He made it to the Partisans.

The modern reader may not understand the truly binding nature of parole for an officer at that time. To give one's parole in the first place would be extraordinary. To break it was unthinkable. But to do so was Djurić's style.

This, of course, is not the story Djurić tells. He claims that Mihailović had him arrested because he wanted to join the Partisans but that he was allowed to keep his Schmeisser and, seizing an opportunity, he shot his way out. He would claim that, wouldn't he? And would even dear, gentlemanly, naïve Jovo Stefanović let him keep a submachine gun?

I accept the first version. Not because it makes a good story but because it happens to be true. Milovan Djilas, Tito's close colleague, supports it in his writings, though he should have every reason to support Djurić's own version, as Djurić promptly issued a long and passionate broadcast from Partisan headquarters urging Četniks to desert to the Partisans. For his pains Djurić was given an immediate senior-staff appointment, and he never looked back under the red banner. Like the Bulgars and many ustaši, he became a useful comrade. He died not long ago, a revered, pensioned senior officer.

Fitzroy Maclean wrote of Djurić, "While I was in Serbia I was to meet Radoslav Djurić, until recently one of Mihajlovic's best known commanders and now chief of staff to a Partisan division. This amusing, somewhat cynical character seemed to have been received by the Partisans with open arms although in the past he had always been known, even among the Četniks, for the ruthless brutality with which he had waged war against them." Other British officers with the Partisans mentioned Djurić in their reports. He seems to have impressed them as an entertaining and urbane individual. For me he was the ultimate nasty bit of work.

Jovo Stefanović was a great friend of mine, and in my book *Special Operations Executed* I describe him as a true gentleman. But he should have known better than to accept Djurić's parole. Mihailović suffered from the same shortcoming; he was a gentleman too. Regrettably, there was no room for gentlemen in this conflict. A civil war is the bitterest and worst of all wars, and what was happening in Yugoslavia was a civil war, with the war against the Axis little more than an overlay. The British decision-makers never clearly understood this situation, and the *received wisdom* denies it or glosses it over. We did not know it either in June 1943.

Although they must have known or suspected a lot more than we did, our Loyalist Četnik hosts—at that stage—also probably did not appreciate the full extent of the communist determination to take over Yugoslavia. The communists had been surrounded and very near total extinction in the Axis encirclement of Tito's main force near Mount Durmitor in Montenegro the month before. With missions dropping to them in Serbia like confetti at a wedding, the Loyalist Četniks cannot have believed that the British decision-makers were going to abandon them for the communists, leaving the British missions as hostages to fortune and to having their throats cut.

When I read and reread my well-thumbed pages 83–136 of Basil Davidson's *Special Operations Europe* describing the Četnik-Partisan office war in Cairo; and when I read of the conviction of the head of the Yugoslav section of MO4 that liberation movements should be revolutionary to be viable; and when I read on page 109 how this selfsame section head describes himself as "a well-marked Partisan supporter"; and when I learn now all about the involvement of the MO4 head of operations and Davidson's boss, Brigadier Keble, and the astonishing influence of the hardened Cambridge set leader and communist guru James Klugmann; and when I see Tito reverently referred to as "this gigantic guerrilla"; and when I read the sinister memorandum in the Public Records Office signed by Keble, whoever drafted it, on September 29, 1943, in which he recommends supporting only revolutionary movements throughout the Balkans; and when I know as I do know now the attitudes at MO4 in June 1943—I can understand bloody well what was going to happen to us BLOs in the next twelve months. But I certainly had no inkling at the time.

While understanding now why it happened and understanding that, with Cairo in that mood, it *had to* happen, I cannot forgive or forget the astounding cynicism that delivered us innocents into that situation and that used the British missions to pull the wool over the Loyalists' eyes in that critical period.

Unwittingly we BLOs with Mihailović perpetrated a monstrous fraud. Those we tricked by our mere presence, including my friends Stefanović and Andrejević, were massacred in due course, almost certainly by their Serbian countrymen in Partisan uniforms supplied by the British and using British bullets—or, more probably, British commando knives.

There are two techniques. The throat slit, like killing a pig. The other more merciful. The knife goes in above the rib cage at the side of the neck, forward and down into the heart. Regrettably, the former was more common.

Furthermore, I cannot forgive or forget the double standards: the almost hysterical manner in which we were adjured by MO4 to stop the Loyalists from fighting the Partisans—even in defense of their own territory; while the Foreign Office in London bleated away impotently asking for assurances from MO4 that the Partisans would not attack the Loyalists, which yammering was generally ignored by MO4 and the British mission with the Partisans but no doubt raised a belly laugh from Tito—if the matter was ever raised with him, that is.

The Bulgar massacre was a major setback. Worst of all, Sehmer and I lost our good radio operators, Blackmore and Thompson. With Thompson dead and Tomlinson recovering from his wound in the care of the Loyalist peasants, and with the Axis cleanup operation in full progress, my scheduled journey south with Trbić was out of the question. Sehmer's W/T equipment had been destroyed by the Bulgars on the morning of the massacre, and between us all we had left was the set I had buried, a small hand generator and one battery. To work them we had the Slovene, Leban, who was only half-trained as an operator, temperamental, and unaccustomed to our specialized equipment. After some days' bitter work with the hand generator, we managed at last to get through to Cairo and explain our position. Orders came for Sehmer to proceed with Djurić, who was moving northeast, and for me to move to an area on the western slope of Mount Kukavica, taking Leban with me. The surviving New Zealander, Harvey, came with me too, to lend a hand until Tomlinson recovered. Trbić had already returned south, and the mission to Skoplje was canceled by Cairo. I was to remain in the Kukavica-Barje-Oruglica area and prepare to sabotage the Niš-Skoplje railway in the Morava Valley.

In the Oruglica area were three active or semimobile brigades. The largest and most mobile was the Leteći Brigade, commanded by an air force officer, Capt. Bora Manić. This unit was based directly on Mount Kukavica, the large mountain overlooking the Morava Valley from the west.

The Vranjska Brigade, as its name signified, reached down to Vranje and included the whole area beyond the new wartime Bulgarian border, that is, the territory annexed to Bulgaria. This brigade was commanded by Capt. Jovo Stefanović, a regular officer of the Royal Horse Guards.

The third brigade, to which I attached myself frequently, was the Leskovačka Brigade of Lt. Mile Andrejević, which took in the foothills and plains stretching toward Leskovac and Lebane to the north and west.

There were two other brigades formally included in the Jablanica area—the Jablanica Brigade, commanded by Capt. Ilja Janović, which was stationed in the mountains to the west, and the Gnilanska Brigade, commanded by Lt. Joško Popović, which took in the area over the new border in that part of Serbia annexed to Albania. This was the land of the Arnautis, who were a curious, often hostile folk of Muslim religion and Albanian ethnic origin.

In the Bulgar attack Popović, another regular officer, had been wounded with a bullet through the ankle. I had taken off his boot and bandaged the ankle, the bone of which had been penetrated by the bullet. All that day and the next Joško marched on that ankle. I was dumbfounded at the bravery and tenacity of the man. The physical courage of the Serbs and their capacity to endure suffering are truly remarkable. These qualities, of course, added to the ferocity of the civil war, in which Serbs fought on both sides.

I spent the month of June and part of July with Jovo Stefanović. Jovo was a regular officer. His parents had been reasonably well-to-do peasants. He had done well at school and gone on to the military academy, whence he had obtained a commission in the Royal Horse Guards. He had a brother who was a doctor and another who was a civil servant. Jovo was a thoroughly decent man. A regime and country that allowed a peasant family to progress in this way cannot have been all bad, as the revolutionaries and gurus of the left pretended.

Jovo had formed part of the secret group of officers who had overthrown the government on March 27, 1941. After the capitulation he had been taken prisoner by the Germans but had escaped and returned home. He had been summoned by Mihailović to join the Loyalists and given command of a brigade.

Of medium height, with a fierce mustache, wiry and good-looking, Jovo epitomized the type of Serb regular officers who had acquitted themselves so well in the First World War. Like all of his caste, he was a natural ally of the British, and that he should have been or become a collaborator was to me then, and is still to me today, quite unthinkable. I know he was killed by the Partisans sometime late in 1944 after we left, whether in battle or in a massacre I do not know. The world is poorer for the passing of the officer-and-gentleman type in the Balkans, men like Jovo. He was a brave and good soldier, he was liked by his troops, and he was greatly revered by the peasants, who happily served as reservists. His ideas and attitudes were straightforward. He served his country and his king. He did not pretend that everything had been wonderful or the best of all possible worlds in Yugoslavia before the war, but he believed that, on the whole, the way of life in Serbia had been good enough for the bulk of the population and, after the years of tribulation through which the country had gone, was not to be jettisoned lightly.

Jovo felt bitter, as did all Serbs, about the suffering of his countrymen in Croatia and Bosnia, where the Serbs had been subjected to the *ustaša* terrorism and genocide; but he did not call for a holy war against the Croats. Rather, like most Serbs, he felt that, in the event of a return to the old form of Yugoslavia, ways had to be devised to build up the Croatian Peasant Party of Vladko Maček as the best bulwark against fascist and communist ideologies.

In many ways Jovo Stefanović, with his homeland Serbia, his peasant background, and his officer-class training, epitomized the opposition in Yugoslavia to the Croatian fascist *ustaša*, which had allied itself to the Axis and to the other totalitarianism, the emerging communist front. The communists had recruited their main forces among the Serbian refugees from the genocide in Croatia, Bosnia, and Herzegovina, among urban refugees, and among some industrial centers; and of course among the natives of Croatian and Slovenian ethnic origin. They had very little support from the Serbian peasants in Serbia proper and virtually none in the southeastern corner, where the population was fervently nationalist and loyal to the king.

This southeastern corner sat astride the vital north-south rail link to Salonika, and it was my area of operation.

In the summer of 1943 the sole Partisan unit in our part of the country was situated on Mount Radan to the west of Leskovac, and it comprised at that time only about 200 men. Although the communists enjoyed some limited support in the town of Leskovac itself, which was a significant industrial center, in the villages, even in the plains, the feeling was predominantly pro-Loyalist. Even after the British propaganda switched to favor the Partisans, the Partisan buildup, though aggressively pushed, was slow. But at this time, in the summer of 1943, the disparity was even greater. The 200 Partisans compared with 3,000 to 5,000 mobile Četniks in the Jablanica area alone. And Jablanica was only a tiny part of Serbia as a whole and of Mihailović's total forces.

As soon as I had settled the mission into Oruglica, Harvey and I set off together with Jovo Stefanović, all of us disguised in Serbian peasant clothing, to reconnoiter the bridges on the railway line from Vranje to Grdelica. It was a long, hard march, lasting nearly a week. Wearing the hard rawhide *opanake* for the very first time, our feet suffered desperately, and on many days I abandoned them and walked barefoot. We reconnoitered the rail bridges, passing close alongside them, and mixed with the peasants when we had to cross road bridges. These were often watched.

On the way back Jovo and I had to pass through a village that had been turned into a Bulgar camp. We had to walk right up the main street with the soldiers lounging or sitting on each side of the road. Other soldiers busied themselves carrying cooking materials. Some glanced at us curiously. Jovo quietly took my arm and whispered to me to keep going straight on. He managed matters with remarkable sangfroid, a coolness that I was forced to demonstrate but that inside of me I did not share.

Nodding greetings to the Bulgar soldiers in their brown uniform jackets and shorts, I had to wonder if these were the same troops who had shot my colleagues in cold blood on the ground a fortnight before.

After returning over the frontier to Oruglica I went down with a bad bout of malaria. It was fairly prevalent in that part of the Balkans, and it was a rather dangerous variety. I became seriously ill and delirious at times and had no quinine, atropine, or other antimalaria drugs. The fever recurred on a number of occasions, and then only my considerable physical strength enabled me to keep going.

Through late June and early July 1943 we suffered frustration and some problems caused by internecine strife between Stefanović and Bora Manić. Manić was very different from Stefanović. A younger man, maybe twenty-eight, he had been a lieutenant in the air force and had served at Mihailović's headquarters before being sent to his current command. He was a tall, athletically built man of striking good looks, though his finely cut features, well-drilled physique, and thin, cruel mouth gave him a Prussian appearance. He was immensely competitive, and I remember thinking at the time that he was the type who goes to the top or to jail. He was not a man to retire after a quiet career and grow roses.

Bora Manić machinated and manipulated and caused me problems, but he was a character, and he could have been a great guerrilla had we been able to support him. I regret very much that we did not meet again to swap stories. I am sure he could contribute much to this account. I recollect that he had a particularly vitriolic hatred of the Partisans, and he too had little use for Djurić, even before the latter defected. I suspect Manić saw through him. Manić would not have accepted his parole. Manić was a cynic.

My problems with Manić arose from his passionate jealousy of Stefanović, who was the senior officer. Manić wanted very keenly to form a Jablanica corps, comprising all of the area brigades, with himself as commander. With the British support that was then promised and still confidently expected, and with the huge manpower potential of the Loyalist peasant reserves, this could have become a potent force.

There was friendship between Manić and the third brigade commander, Mile Andrejević. The latter was very noncompetitive. A soft-spoken, small, and sparse individual, impeccably dressed even in difficult circumstances, he was a man of quiet strength and great reason and tolerance. He had been a regular, like Stefanović (in his case, an engineer subaltern in the guards division), and he and Jovo were close friends. He acted at times as peacemaker when Manić and Stefanović came near to blows— or to shooting each other.

I spent time with all three brigades. Without scruples or hesitation I played the commanders off against each other in order to get sabotage done in spite of my inability to bring in the anticipated and promised drops. I traveled freely around the country, frequently, indeed nearly always, by myself. I decided to which command I would attach myself and what action should be taken. The idea that they might attach a minder to me, or tell me what to do or where to go, was unthinkable. Even so, I would not for a moment pretend that my Serbian commanders would take orders from me. They respected my integrity and independence, and I respected theirs. I had to negotiate my wishes, and frequently—indeed generally, but not always—my ambitions regarding action were fulfilled only in part, and sometimes not at all. But there was no question whatsoever of my being in any way under their command.

I have commented on the difference in the relations between ourselves and the Loyalists on the one hand, and the liaison officers with the Partisans and their hosts on the other, not in order to say that the Loyalists were right in their freer attitude or that the Partisans were wrong, but to stress that what we reported was what had happened and not what we were told had happened. We made our own assessments on the basis of what we had seen with our own eyes. They were not spelled out for us by our hosts.

The trouble between Manić and Stefanović started with my first planned supply drop. I was with Stefanović's brigade, and

Manić warned of a German attack coming in over Mount Kukavica against his positions. The warning, coming shortly after the previous Bulgar-German cleanup operation, made me naturally cautious, and I called the drop off. Subsequently I had grounds to suspect that Manić had fabricated the attack story in order to prevent Stefanović from getting the drop.

On the occasion of the next drop, a joint affair organized by the three brigades, there was an incident in which Manić was on the point of shooting Stefanović and I was obliged to knock Manić down. This was something I had never previously done to another officer, let alone to a member of a foreign allied force. Naïvely I mentioned the incident later when I returned to base, and it rapidly found its way into the *received-wisdom* mythology as an example of the "drunken, irresponsible behaviour" of Loyalist officers.

One needed to be awfully careful what one said or wrote or reported. Rather, one ought to have been awfully careful. We did not know that at the time, and sadly we were not careful; and the pro-Partisan "walls that had ears" used to write it all down.

Up to this point I had no cause for complaint at the service given to us by MO4. Our communications problems arose solely from the loss of W/T equipment in the Bulgar attack, and once we got a message through, MO4 responded quickly. My first drop was canceled by me, no fault of MO4's, and the next of two planes came very soon thereafter. Looking at the files forty years later, I found, interestingly, that this happened to be the honeymoon period in relations between Mihailović and Bailey. This honeymoon followed the formal withdrawal of the notorious Glenconner signal of May 29 and lasted until the next squabble between Bailey and Mihailović, which was triggered by the reports from our area that Djurić was refusing to cooperate. In this latter squabble Bailey told Mihailović that he was stopping drops "on orders from GHQ." It seems evident that MO4 seized the chance and took Bailey at his word.

But at this point, thanks to the honeymoon period, I got two planes in one night. Maybe there were other reasons, but that seems to be the logic of it.

The conclusion that MO4 exploited Bailey's stupid, provocative, and schoolmistresslike demarche is strengthened by a statement made to the 1973 Auty-Clogg symposium by Colonel Woodhouse, a former BLO in Greece: "The point that I am making here is that in the middle of 1943 Mihailović was in the doghouse and was therefore not being allowed any aircraft, and Tito had not yet become the rising star."

CHAPTER
4
Sabotage with the Loyalists

■

Sometime late in July or early in August 1943 I received a signal telling me to do my utmost to interrupt the Belgrade-Salonika railway, and this I assume was linked to the happenings in Sicily or Italy. The obvious target was the larger of the two bridges over the Morava near Vladički Han. I had reconnoitered this bridge with Jovo. It was very well guarded, also relatively close to the garrison in Vranje from which reinforcements could be brought quickly by road. We would have to capture the blockhouse guarding the bridge and do it quickly. For that I would need a substantial force with ten to twelve machine guns and, if possible, a mortar. Stefanović had not sufficient mobile troops readily available. Manić's brigade was my best bet.

At that stage the subcommanders had no general license from Mihailović to carry out sabotage without his consent, but in a long, hard night's conferring with a lot of *rakija* consumed and many promises of drops for his brigade—which I honestly felt entitled to make at that stage—I won Manić around, and he agreed to help without waiting for approval from Mihailović or Djurić. We set to immediately with our preparations, and Manić was co-operative and highly efficient. The operation was going to be a considerable undertaking, involving about 150 men in all. We had a long approach march over Mount Kukavica, and we had to cross the Bulgarian frontier. With such a large force, with horses carrying the machine guns and mortar, this march constituted a problem. Manić solved it by bringing the local Nedić state guard commander into play.

As I wrote earlier, the Nedić state guard was the semimilitary, semipolice force that supported the Axis-sponsored Nedić regime. As such it was fully collaborationist. The local commander of the guard had wanted for some time to desert and join Mihailović, but he had been requested by the Loyalist brigade commanders to stay with the Nedić forces until he was called over for the *ustanak* or until his position became untenable. The idea was that, when the time came, he would cross over to the Loyalists, bringing his men and arms with him. In the meantime he kept us informed as far as he could of Axis troop movements. The good sense of this policy was proved on this occasion because, without cooperation of the state guard, crossing the frontier with a substantial force without being spotted would have been virtually impossible. Once we were spotted, the attack on the bridge would have been impossible. With the guard commander's cooperation, however, everything was enormously facilitated for us. Not only did the state guard consent to look the other way but our friend proposed to invite his Bulgar opposite numbers across the border to a drinking session and thus make sure that both sides of the frontier would be unguarded at the same time and at the agreed point.

I got to know that state guard commander well—so well that I used a photograph showing him, me, and Jovo Stefanović in my book *Special Operations Executed*. Does that make me a collaborator too? This incident is typical of what went on not only in the Balkans but in virtually every occupied country. Things could not be judged in black-and-white terms. There were many shades of gray. It is just in Yugoslavia that the black-and-white

judgment has been made, and only because the British volte-face
had to be justified.

Major Archie Jack has told me that he was personally helped
by Nedić forces in reconnoitering targets for sabotage. On one
occasion a Nedić sergeant took him through the German sentry
posts and actually onto a bridge he wished to examine. Was Jack
collaborating? If so, I'm all for collaboration.

We were still planning the bridge job when my W/T gave up the
ghost. I concealed this from Manić. In a few days we were ready
to go. A matter of hours before we were due to start the approach march, Tommy and I were bathing in the stream below
Manić's house when two British sergeants appeared without
warning. They were unexpected reinforcements for the mission:
Sergeant Faithful of the army physical training corps, previously
a parachute instructor, who had been dropped in to help where
he could, and Sergeant Johnson, a W/T operator and mechanic.

While Johnson was particularly welcome to replace the Slovene Leban if and when we could get back on the air, a new set
and a motor charger would have been more appropriate and even
more welcome. It would also have been more to the point. But
that was not all, unfortunately. Sergeant Faithful brought an
abrupt but simple message from John Sehmer at Djurić headquarters. Base had told him to let me know that I should postpone operations against the railway line till further notice. That
and nothing more.

With that and nothing more the hopeful world around us
collapsed and stayed collapsed.

After the severe setback of the Bulgarian attack only thirty-
six hours after our drop; after losing half the mission; after our
enforced change of plans following that Axis drive against our
area; after completing the arduous and detailed reconnaissance
of railway targets; after evading a second Axis drive through our
area; after being caught up in the strife between Manić and Stefanović; after my several bouts of malaria; after and in spite of
all of these problems I had succeeded in setting up an attack
force to blow a major bridge on the most important rail route in
the Balkans. Furthermore, at this time the Germans were rush-

ing troops north from Greece to reinforce their garrisons in Italy. It was my chance to strike a significant blow for the Western Allied cause.

Now there came this abrupt message to "postpone" operations against the railway line till further notice. There is no doubt in my mind today that I made the biggest mistake of my life. I obeyed the order from Sehmer. It was a knee-jerk reaction of a young officer trained in a military tradition. A soldier obeys. He argues afterward. But I couldn't argue. I had no W/T.

It was a sorry error. The blowing of that important bridge on that key line at that vital stage would surely have had an impact on policy-making in London, if not in Cairo.

Or would it? After Brigadier Armstrong's arrival late in September, a total of five admittedly less important bridges were blown by Mihailović's Loyalists to the west under the guidance of Archie Jack and observed by Armstrong, and those demolitions scored only passing reference in a fortnightly report to London. And the Višegrad bridge, the important and large bridge over the Drina brought down by Archie with Loyalist help, resulted in a report by the BBC that the Partisans had blown it! And this lie has been carried forward into history. In his recent book *Waldheim: The Missing Years*, Robert Edwin Herzstein writes, "Adding to the confusion, the Partisans blew up a key bridge spanning the Drina river at Višegrad." Maybe the decision-makers in 1943 were lied to as well as the BBC.

Only the first of my subsequent railway sabotage operations merited mention in the reports from Cairo to London, though the majority of them were indeed signaled through and the signals acknowledged by SOE Cairo during the short September-October period during which my W/T worked before it gave out again. By then, however, with Maclean dropping in to Tito, Cairo was firmly locked on to a course leading to the abandonment of Mihailović and the need for justification of his betrayal. Railway sabotage by Loyalists did not fit into that scenario.

It is ironic that I finished my guerrilla career in SOE being badly wounded in an attack against a German corps headquarters in northern Italy and was blamed, reviled, and demoted for carrying out this important and successful attack contrary to orders.

But I never got the orders to the contrary. Neither was I actually in charge of the attack, though I had conceived, planned, and reconnoitered it.

You can't win.

I do not expect to win even today. Some modern-day Titophiles struggling to substantiate the *received wisdom* against all the evidence now piling up will no doubt claim that stopping sabotage on that line was necessary in connection with some "major strategic deception plan." But the same special pleaders will say in the next breath that the Loyalists were "collaborationists unwilling to do anything."

Kitted up and ready to go, Bora Manić was listening to the radio when I went to see him. As I told him my news, he turned up the knob so that I could hear the broadcast. After some preliminaries we heard, "The Partisans report that they have amassed a fund of reliable evidence of Četnik collaboration with the enemy." Manić smiled grimly. "The Allies are consistent, if only in changing their minds."

Sadly, because the SOE files available in the PRO only show signals to and from the missions from sometime early in September, I have not been able to trace the many messages that must have passed between SOE and Sehmer. But I have found my own signal decoded on September 15, serial 25 number 34, which states, "But I had Manić on road to break a bridge without orders Djurić when you stopped us. Djurić has now sent another order against sabotage and it will be difficult to get going against orders. If you want us to please state your wishes about all and will do my best Mike."

Not very grammatical, but the meaning is clear.

On September 17 Cairo replied, "Sorry misunderstanding your 34 of 15th and had no intention to stop you carry out sabotage. For your information stronger orders will be on way to Mihailovic soon to command him to order his subordinates to take action. Meantime stick it out and try to get sabotage carried out."

And they apologized again in another signal. Obviously,

someone was concerned lest it look as if something funny were going on, lest they be rumbled if something funny *was* going on.

As promised in my signal, I did indeed do my best. Signal Fugue 69 of October 4, 1943, reads, "Blew one Km East railway night 30th. Job done with 25 men sabotage group under English command and without Serb Officer or orders Djuric. Line will be out of action for ten days. The line was passing fifty trains per day troops tanks arms to Greece mostly arms continued Mike . . . each train about forty wagons. Must have immediately five planes one explosives four arms pinpoint Barje. To obtain sabotage have promised planes and must keep promise."

How naïve I was.

Dealing with the bridge affair, Major Sehmer's war diary, submitted when we came out at the end of May 1944 and which is now available in the Public Records Office (WO 202/162), states,

> Way [Lees] reported that one of his Serb commanders was prepared to start sabotage attacks against railway lines without orders from Djuric or Mihailovic. The writer did not wish to compromise any possible plans resulting from Wix's [Brigadier Armstrong's] arrival; Cairo was asked whether they wished Way to proceed or not. The result was a series of messages, Yes, No, Yes, No, Etc. Before Way got a final yes I had left for Kozjak when one of the first messages I received forbade all action which had not Mihailovic's or Djuric's approval. The writer received a signal in the middle of September apologising for keeping him in the dark for such a long time about the situation re. sabotage and reiterating no action without Mihailovic sanction.

Now, isn't that odd? Cairo telling me on September 17 that they did not intend to stop me from doing sabotage and at the same time telling Sehmer we had to have approval. And at the same time accusing the Loyalists of doing nothing.

My own Fugue report (WO 202/162) is more concise than Sehmer's about the incidents: "Major Sehmer sent through orders to stand by to blow the bridge I had reconnoitred. Djuric did not give permission and he [Sehmer] later ordered me to stand down."

So it seems that the "misunderstanding" was that Cairo had cleared the operation but had subsequently signaled to Sehmer equivocally about clearing actions with Mihailović or Djurić, and Sehmer had taken it upon himself to stop my operation because he knew we did not have Djurić's or Mihailović's permission. But he knew that beforehand. He knew that already when he first sent us Cairo's instructions to do all we could to block the line.

What a way to run a railroad. Or, rather, what a way not to blow up a railroad.

Maybe that was the explanation. Maybe someone somewhere along the chain of command did not want us to blow up that bridge, possibly because they did not want to disturb a deception plan or, possibly, for more nefarious motives or reasons. Like not letting anything interfere with getting the Loyalists abandoned for alleged noncooperation.

Some misunderstanding. Some cockup, some confidence trick, or some conspiracy?

The *received wisdom* has it that the Loyalists were collaborating and refusing to do anything. But in this and other cases they were doing nothing on Cairo's orders and thanks to Cairo's interference.

Maybe that too was intentional, because we are now moving into the period in which an increasing number of people at MO4 were less interested in action against the Axis by the Loyalists than in finding reasons to denounce and abandon them.

In order to protect Andrejević from possible trouble from Djurić, I had told Cairo that this major line demolition was carried out by a force under my own command without a Serb officer. Evidently this is why Cairo chose to include my operation in its fortnightly report to London. Thus the implication was that Loyalist officers were unwilling to do sabotage. My file searches failed to find my other sabotage success reports to Cairo mentioned to London.

It was SOE policy to exercise direct control over resistance movements. This was a standing tenet of faith. The idea—a very good one—was to be able to direct the sabotage to complement

Allied strategy. But working up a guerrilla band in enemy-occupied territory, and dodging cleanup drives by the Axis forces, and undertaking a major military operation is not something that can be subject to Yes-No-Yes-No-Maybe.

That was another factor in favor of Tito's Partisans. Mihailović was subjected throughout to the Yes-No-Yes-No-Maybe of chairborne warriors in Cairo, frequently without his best interests at heart. Tito, instead, insisted on sovereignty and got away with it.

Double standards. MO4 accepted ultimatums from Tito but not from Mihailović.

We waited for planes that never came. The fine weather held, and Manić, at first politely but later a bit more pointedly, wanted to know what ailed the Allies. First they promised supplies. Now none came. First they hailed Mihailović as the great hero of the resistance. Now they were talking more and more of the Partisans on the BBC. The Allies were consistent only in changing their minds, he repeated. Fiercely, he went on: "The Serbs are nationalistic. We love our king. Can you see our peasants in a communist state? Here each man has his *svojina*, his patch of land, his stock, his *rakija*. He is master in his own house. And I have shown my willingness to help you. Until you can show that supplies will come, I cannot agree to give you troops."

He had made his point. I did not need troops at that juncture because I was under instructions not to take action. But there was no point in staying longer with him on Kukavica. I had overstayed my welcome. I moved back to Oruglica, to Jovo Stefanović. I was still on good terms with him, and he did not complain about the lack of Allied support. He was glad and flattered that I had returned from Manić. He had written once again to Mihailović requesting permission to start operations.

Then suddenly again came a message from Sehmer to say that base wanted me to cut the rail line, adding, "Djurić refuses to move." No explanation of why Djurić's veto was no longer a hindrance. Odd. But satisfactory.

Stefanović, always the good soldier, would not act against orders, but Andrejević agreed to help on the condition that he would receive the whole of the next sortie when it came. It came that same night. He must have been fey.

We had a sortie. We even had a generator. I had an excellent operator in Johnson, and Jovo Stefanović came to tell me that Sofia had been bombed by a force of Wellington bombers that had started fires in the railroad yards. We had heard the planes while waiting for our own. It was a morale booster for us all. Our cup was full, metaphorically and actually too: the Loyalists kindly saw to that. According to the Partisan propaganda, after all, they were drunken womanizers. But the only woman around was Djurić's spy mistress, and she was not a factor until later.

So I went ahead. There was no time to set up another complicated bridge operation, and I was by no means sure that Manić would play again. My major failing is pride, and I did not want to be snubbed. In any case, he was a moody man, and the switching of the last sortie to Andrejević had not pleased him at all. So I avoided eventual complications and took thirty men from Andrejević's brigade, together with Tomlinson, to do a line-cutting job myself.

It was a long approach march from Oruglica to Barje to collect Andrejević's troops and then right over the top of Mount Kukavica. We kept on the Serbian side of the frontier and, staying in the woods, descended after dark into the meadows beside the line just where it emerged into the Leskovac plains to the north.

It was about midnight and the moon was not yet up. The commander of the men from Andrejević's brigade, a man named Pešić who held a rank equivalent to that of sergeant in the British army, was an excellent, aggressive leader. Taking him and two other men, I crawled forward toward the embankment to reconnoiter.

We heard the whistle of an approaching train and the rails vibrating. The headlights of the locomotive showed sentries, unarmed and in peasant dress, stationed in pairs along the track every hundred yards or so. Covered by the noise of the train rumbling away, we slipped back and joined the party.

I sent out one group of fighting men with orders to move

onto the embankment about 500 yards to the north, place a Spandau in position to protect our activities, and try to round up the sentries on that stretch of track before they could give the alarm. Another group set off to the south with the same task.

The demolition group, similarly, was split into two parties under Tommy's overall command. Pešić and I moved down to make sure that the starting point was clear, and Tommy followed shortly afterward with his men. They were to run out a length of Primacord explosive fuse in each direction. They carried a total of about a hundred charges of 808 gelignite weighing roughly one pound each. These were to be jammed against each joint on both rails and linked by a short length of Primacord to the main stretch of Primacord, so that detonating it at the starting point would explode all charges simultaneously.

I heard a voice raised and a soft thud to the left, then silence. Evidently one sentry had been accounted for.

The demolition parties were running out their Primacord rapidly in both directions and fixing the charges. All seemed to be going well for about five minutes. Then I heard a ringing sound. A sentry had seen us before he could be rounded up and was tapping the rail—the standard warning signal.

Then firing broke out, and I could pick out the deep, tearing noise of one of our Spandaus. That was a lovely noise. I can hear it now. I loved the Spandau; like all German weapons, it was beautifully engineered.

I ran up the line to the north and saw the flash of rifle fire coming from a small building a few hundred yards up the line. It was a blockhouse, obviously intended to guard the line. A group of Bulgars moved out of it, and it looked as if they were trying to move down toward our starting point through the fields on the far side of the embankment. I ran back to Tommy at our starting point and found that the group to the south had already run out their full length of Primacord and fixed their charges.

Waiting a couple of minutes more to allow the northern group time, I blew my whistle, the signal to disengage, withdraw clear of the line, and return to the collecting point where we had started. We waited a while to let all of the men get clear, and Tommy struck a match to light the fuse. It was slow-burning and fired a detonator taped to the Primacord. He fumbled and swore as he tried to light it and failed, and two minutes later he asked for a knife to recut the fuse. This time it caught, but as it burned, we were challenged from down the embankment to the north and the Bulgar group opened fire. Answering with Stens, we ran from the line to the collection point. Everyone was present.

It was a fuse cut to burn for three minutes. I began to worry at two minutes fifty, as I heard the Bulgars moving along the line toward it. At three minutes fifteen seconds I was worrying a lot. I whispered to Tommy, "Get out your second fuse."

Then the charge went up. The blast slapped our faces as a line of flame lit up the scene 500 yards each way. The sharp explosion was followed by the screech of flying metal and screams from some members of the enemy patrol who had caught the blast as they arrived to investigate. I was very pleased to see wooden sleepers (railroad ties) burning from the heat of the explosion. The full length of track would need replacing and many sleepers too. That was a big plus.

We wasted no more time and moved away as fast as we could. Behind us whistles shrilled and desultory firing continued, while the searchlights of an armored train wove patterns around the scene of destruction. When the moon rose, the railway was already a good way behind us.

On the return march we followed a course through the plains and foothills to the north of the Kukavica mountain range, heading for Andrejević's headquarters at Barje. In a village in the foothills Pešić suggested we stop for a rest and food. This sounded like a good idea. The lower-lying villages were richer and could offer better fare; and the men were tired, having been on the march for more than twenty hours. The inhabitants proved hospitable, and we were soon indulging ourselves with a magnificent meal and bountiful portions of fierce grape *rakija,* a specialty of the plains.

We were all in great heart. The demolition had been an unqualified success. Pešić reckoned that it would take a full ten days to repair the damage because the line, though the most important rail link in the Balkans, was only a single track. This would delay the work of clearing the damaged rails and sleepers and bringing up the replacements. We had used charges on every joint, and the line would have been totally destroyed for the full length of the demolition. It had been carrying a massive volume of traffic, which would now be piling up at junctions to the north right back to Belgrade and to the south to Salonika. Following the landing in Italy, the Germans were rushing troops south to Greece, presumably in anticipation of a further landing there. I don't know why, but they certainly were doing so.

The Serbs in the sabotage group were evidently very happy to have done something against the invader. Pešić in particular obviously relished his task.

As we were now well clear of the line and, we hoped, out of reach of German or Bulgar pursuit, I borrowed a horse to ride ahead of the group to Barje in order to make the midday W/T schedule. But I had hardly started work in Barje when we were interrupted by the noise of firing in the direction from which I had come. Andrejević quickly gathered together what men he could, and we retraced my steps. We had not gone very far before we met the party led by a very angry Tomlinson, with a wounded man in his column. The column had been ambushed shortly after leaving the village, and the attackers were not Axis troops but Partisans.

These Partisans came from the group of about 200 who had their base on Mount Radan on the other side of the Leskovac plains from Barje, to the north and west of Leskovac. The detachment had been doing political canvassing in the large villages in the plains. They hid in vineyards and maize fields by day and crept into the villages by night to requisition food and to hold political meetings spreading communist ideology.

According to our information, the political campaign—which was of course entirely directed at winning support for the Partisan movement and denigrating the Mihailović Loyalists—was having little effect on the peasantry. They wished to be left in peace to tend their crops while holding themselves ready to join Loyalist units for the *ustanak*. They also grossly resented the Partisan assumption that it was their duty to produce food without remuneration. The Loyalists had always paid for any food they took, and they were popular among the peasants for this reason, apart from the natural affinity of a prosperous peasant—and they were indeed prosperous in the Leskovac plains—for groups opposed to communism. Precisely because the plains were prosperous, the Partisans were using the area as a means of supply for their group instead of just consuming what they needed on their political visits.

Furthermore, the Mount Radan group of Partisans included a number of Arnautis, as well as Albanians and Macedonians from southwest of Skoplje, and their presence caused resentment among the Serbs, who considered internal politics their own affair and not that of Muslim "invaders."

The Partisans in the Radan group were a nuisance to us because their sorties into the plains created an additional complication for our sabotage operation. It was a long, hard march to the railway line in any case. Nevertheless, it was quite possible to leave our mountains one day, reach the line by darkness, carry out a line demolition or derailment, and return the same night. But there was little time to spare for reconnoitering as we marched, or for being held up by battles with Partisan groups, with the possibility of having wounded to hold one up subsequently. Their presence also forced us to take a larger party than would otherwise have been necessary. Later, after the British broke with Mihailović, I personally went to the line alone, chancing a contact with Partisans—but that's another story.

For about eight wonderful weeks through September until about October 24 I had some sort of W/T contact, though our motor charger ran a bearing fairly soon and we were back to a hand charger again. The previous drop had also brought a pedal charger, but this machine was a fiasco. It broke down almost immediately and was virtually irreparable.

I have been able to reread many of my signals from the operational files in the Public Records Office. The files are far from complete, but they coincide more or less with the period during which my wireless worked, and together with my report and those of the other BLOs, they have refreshed my memory.

An incident I had evidently forgotten when I wrote my previous book, *Special Operations Executed*, in 1949–50 was my Albanian adventure. Before our line-cutting expedition I crossed the new Albanian frontier, which lay to the southwest of our area, and made contact with a group of Albanians and Arnautis. They were right-wing Zogists—followers of the exiled King Zog—and they appeared to have considerable potential. They had put out feelers to me indicating that they wanted to form a guerrilla group and asked me whether I would come across and help them. I found a group of about 150 armed men awaiting me. They told me that they could call on another 1,000 to join in one or two days if we could get something going and that potential reserves were very large indeed; they even spoke of 4,000 within a couple of weeks and eventual reserves of up to 40,000. Although these figures were clearly wishful thinking or propaganda, to which we were becoming accustomed, I realized that it was nevertheless a significant grouping, and I traveled around a little and attended a series of meetings.

Very importantly, all of the men, who were Muslims, were armed already. Every man had a rifle, and many additionally had side arms and grenades. They were mostly peasants, though living more in hamlets and villages than those in our Serbian area. The houses too, while Muslim in character, were more sophisticated than the Serbian mountain peasant houses, and there were more signs of wealth around. The women were kept firmly in the background, and we missed our regular *rakija*. Most obeyed the Muslim custom of abstinence from alcohol. There was a rather sinister atmosphere about the whole area (not only on the abstinence account), but there was no doubt about the genuine guerrilla potential of the people who had contacted me.

I knew nothing of the local politics. Certainly I had had no briefing in Cairo about Albanian guerrillas or even about what an Arnauti was. The Serbs were inclined to be hostile to the Arnautis, and I was not at all clear where the ethnic Albanians fitted into the picture. But I was certain that the group was genuine in wanting to form a resistance movement.

With the benefit of hindsight I realize now that the movement may well have been motivated primarily by the desire to protect itself from the emergent communist movement in Albania of Enver Hoxha and from the Tito Partisans in Yugoslavia.

Neither of these movements had any viable guerrilla organization in the Kosovo area at that time, but they certainly must have represented a threatening cloud in the sky for the inhabitants of those parts still free from actual penetration by the communists. I would have thought the Arnauti peasant would be even less sympathetic to communist propaganda than the Serb peasant. None of that concerned me, however, and the politics of it was above my head at that stage. I saw it rather simply and from a military point of view. Here was a group eager to build a resistance movement, a group already armed with rifles, a group without a political ax to grind, a group that was just asking for a lead. What more could MO4 ask for?

What the Arnautis and Albanians wanted was contact with the Western Allies and a drop to demonstrate that they were recognized; they were then prepared to gather together as large a group as we asked.

I believe that war history has not given sufficient emphasis to the importance of Western Allied recognition in the Balkans. All of these various peoples, all of these different ethnic groups— many hostile to each other, confused and worried about the future— were eager above all for a lead from the Western Allies. Far more than we in the West, they all knew that the issue was communism. They all feared lest the Red Army reach the Balkans first, but at that stage they were still hopeful that there might be an earlier Western Allied landing. Any group that could show evidence that it was recognized by the Western Allies was in a very strong position to gather more recruits and build itself up.

My requisition for the drop reflected the situation. For a first drop—I asked for only one planeload—I wanted automatic weapons, along with clothing and cigarettes. The leaders insisted above all on cigarettes. The cigarettes, which would have been British army issue or American Lucky Strikes, were better than any propaganda leaflet, and two or three containers of cigarette packets—preferably ten in the packet, not twenty—could be distributed over a large area and have an enormous impact psychologically.

But these people were serious about fighting too, which is why they asked for automatic arms. They needed no rifles. Those they had already in abundance, but they could use automatics. I spent some days with the group and witnessed them in action against the Bulgars, who had heard something was up and who had crossed the border into the Albanian zone for a cleanup. My friends acquitted themselves excellently. Subsequently, the Bulgars made two more attempts to enter the area and failed on both occasions.

I stayed in contact with the group and tried repeatedly to arrange just that one planeload, which could have been instrumental in starting an important resistance movement. The surviving signals in the Public Records Office show my exchanges with Cairo. Cairo promised a drop two or three times, but each time it was postponed because of bad weather or some other excuse. The charade started sometime in August or early September and went on till late October, when my W/T finally went out of action.

My signal dated September 18, 1943, read, "Albanian situation first class. After capitulation Italy no occupying troops there. Bulgars have tried three times to enter and have been defeated. I have group up to seven hundred armed waiting and immediate reserves up to forty thousand all armed. Only must give them one plane for propaganda and have three times more men and arms than whole Djuric area. Dropping sheet 133 390330. Date must be 25th. Very urgent reply urgently Mike."

The signals in the SOE files about drops and promises and excuses in regard to my Arnautis go on until about October 25. In retrospect, it was a crazy situation. For the sake of one load Cairo let a really significant resistance potential wither away. But, looking back over the few signals in the operational log that came from Fugue mission, I am horrified to find how much was lost through MO4's failure to give us maybe half a dozen planes.

Following our line demolition on September 30, I signaled on October 4, "Am planning attack Leskovac power station and should be ready carry out shortly. Power station supplies light and power for factory, aircraft and tank parts. Do you want this. If you give me planes asked for can take party to attack and guarantee success. If I do not repeat not receive planes will go self under disguise but under these circumstances cannot guarantee success. Please send instructions urgently." The reply promised planes the next day and told me not to operate in civilian clothes.

The planes didn't come. Not the next day. Not the next week.

As for the cryptic instructions not to operate in plain clothes, I had been operating on and off in plain clothes for four months. How else could I have reconnoitered the bridges? In any case, we were so short of everything we frequently had to use local clothing or footwear.

In this context there is an entertaining, rather hysterical cable in the file dated November 7, 1943, from the mission call sign Neronian, which was the main mission in the Djurić area. Originally John Sehmer had been in charge. Then he was replaced by Lieutenant Colonel Cope and Major Raw. They signaled, "Things are very precarious here. After a month of waiting with last few days of frost and snow you still ignore our existence. Planes here will give you full returns. We English here are living like wogs with no clothing to keep out the cold, no decent food, no money. If you send no help before 20 this month you only support the German propaganda which says Britain cannot help with winter. For the love of Mike and all the Saints do something to support me here. I will not be responsible after the 20th. Almost in despair."

A cry from the heart. MO4 were set on undermining the Loyalists, but they could have done something for their own men.

On October 16 I signaled that I was preparing to attack a bridge and requested explosives and the five planes I had promised Andrejević in order to get started on sabotage. I also signaled that my motor charger had broken down and one W/T set was also broken. From then until October 25, when my communications ceased, my signals too became more and more desperate. But I, unlike Neronian, was bellyaching about lack of support to honor my commitments to the Loyalists and essential tools for sabotage and communications.

My demands were not unreasonable and were not for clothing, food, and money. I wanted five planes just to fulfill the promise made to Andrejević. The promise had been made in good faith on a clear understanding from Cairo that MO4 would support me. We had started sabotage without permission from Djurić or Mihailović and had made our little breakthrough. I only needed Primacord fuse, fog signals, detonators, and explosives. I also needed the motor charger. The only comfort I asked for was greatcoats for the mission. But the operational log shows a massive number of signals from all directions asking for all kinds of personal things. The Partisan missions got them, usually within a couple of days.

The operational log shows that Brigadier Armstrong had allocated the five planes to me as first priority of the Mihailović missions. So I was only asking for what I had promised, for what I had been promised, and for what was due. But the five planes did not come. The promise was not fulfilled. The Leskovac power station job was not carried out, and with my promise unfulfilled there was no question whatsoever of support from any of the local commanders for the major operation of blowing the Vladički Han bridge.

We all knew by then that *some* planes were going to the Partisans in preference to us, but it was only forty years later that I was able to read from the operational log in the Public Records Office that planes were by then actually pouring out to the British missions with the Partisans, that on nights we were being advised that weather had aborted our sorties the Partisans were receiving planes, and that fifteen sorties were dropped just south of us in November and December to a mission the very existence of which Cairo denied and the primary purpose of which was to prepare for the Partisan invasion of our area.

To cap it all, Andrejević complained to me that the BBC had credited my line demolition with his men to the Partisan group on the Radan. That group had to my certain knowledge carried out no sabotage of any sort other than burning the wooden bridge between Leskovac and Lebane in order to stop a motorized chase of their units by Bulgars from Lebane, purely a defensive action. They were not interested in offensive action against the Germans. Their activity was political, suborning all whom they could and turning them away from the Loyalist cause. They ambushed our sabotage parties on two occasions, and they made an attack on our positions near Barje in October when they sought to capture materiel from the sole drop we received during those weeks.

The Partisans on the Radan did, however, cause us very serious damage with their propaganda. Although everybody in the area knew that they were numerically insignificant, they spread rumors that the British were abandoning Mihailović. They spread rumors—at least we BLOs thought they were rumors—that massive support was coming to Tito from the British. Of course they were right, and this more than everything else really worried our Loyalist friends. Furthermore, the Loyalists knew far more about the scale of support to Tito than we did ourselves.

Things were not easy. But once we got started doing sabotage, between September 30 and December 13, leading parties of Loyalists, I personally carried out a second demolition of another thousand yards of line and four train derailments. In addition, two derailments were carried out by Serb personnel alone, sent out by my commanders and briefed by me. The details were clearly stated in the report on my mission that I submitted through Colonel Cope at the time of our evacuation. A general report about these activities was also made by Maj. Peter Solly-Flood, the intelligence officer from Brigadier Armstrong's headquarters who visited us early in December and stayed the winter at my mission headquarters.

Before losing communications about October 25 I reported three derailments and the first line demolition on my own signal series; and a further derailment and a second line demolition in November were reported on our behalf by Neronian (Cope and Raw) on their signal series. There can be no doubt whatsoever that Cairo knew that we were very active on that important railway line, and I specifically stated in signals that we could keep the lines cut permanently if we were given adequate support. The signals reporting my various actions and making this claim are on the operational log files in the Public Records Office (WO 202/131, 139, 140, 143, and 145).

Robert Purvis, who had the mission just south of me, had very similar experiences. He submitted a most vivid and interesting report about his adventures in a very difficult and dangerous area between Vranje and Skoplje on Kozjak Mountain east of the rail line near the old Bulgarian border in the part of Serbia annexed to Bulgaria. He lived constantly on the run, harassed by Bulgars, with Bulgar garrisons in all of the villages, and in two months he built up a force from scratch to 700 men under two excellent commanders named Krstić and Djordjević.

Purvis carried out two successful operations against the railway. The first was on October 15, when he blew up the line in sixty-five places spread over a length of seven kilometers. This was a different technique from what I had used but probably just as effective. Then, in early December, he mounted a very ambitious attack on a railway station near Kumanovo. In reporting these actions to Cairo, Purvis advised that given even a limited number of sorties, we could between us keep the line permanently out of action. He indicated an intention to send parties weekly.

Purvis received even less support than I did. He too was frequently out of communication, also with generator problems. He too needed fuse and detonators. This shortage could have been remedied so easily. Middle East Command was urging resistance movements to do sabotage. Yet in southeastern Serbia, with highly trained young British officers in position and leading guerrilla groups prepared to fight, we were held up by the need for a bit of materiel.

In his Roughshod mission report in the PRO WO 202/162 series dated June 1, 1944, Purvis tells of his attack on the railway line on (about) October 15: "We blew the line at about sixty-five places over a distance of seven km. The plan had been for Olden to derail a train in the middle but the guards spotted him and gave the alarm. We blew it between Bujanovce and Presovo and, according to peasant reports, no trains ran for four (4) days. On our way home we took away 800 yards of a new telephone line between the German H.Qs. in Vranje and Kumanovo. It was a start and everyone was most enthusiastic." But now comes the punch line: "We continued to wait for promised sortie as from about OCTOBER 18TH. It didn't come till NOVEMBER 28TH."

The report goes on to detail almost daily action against the

Bulgars. Purvis certainly had an active time. Then the report reads as follows:

ABOUT 2ND OR 3RD November heard report of British personnel held prisoner by party of Partisans. Thought they might be crew of AMERICAN aircraft which had crashed near VRANJE in October. Sent a note via peasants proposing escape channel and informed CAIRO. Received answer from a Capt. Mostyn Davies who was with party ALBANIAN PARTISANS making for Bulgaria. They were very short of all gear, had lost generator and batteries were flat. Tried to arrange meeting. Received assurance from GORGEVIC [Djordjević] that his party would not be attacked. CAIRO replied to have nothing to do with them as they were a very Special Mission. As contact already made and condition of his Mission already known tried to get his batteries for charging and informed CAIRO of his condition and whereabouts also guarantee during transit. PARTISAN Comdr must have got windy as they moved and we lost contact.

I question the lack of confidence CAIRO must have in its BLOS in not giving warning of a possible move through area. Feeling was very high against PARTISANS and an attack might easily have been made before we could intervene.

Later Purvis reports, "Sortie arrived that night [November 28]. DAVIES also had sortie same night only 5 km away and we could see glow of his fires. Feeling rather high. Told CAIRO could not keep up guarantee and he must move on."

Now, that is very interesting. In fact, as I explain elsewhere, the story about Albanian Partisans was untrue. It was a cover. Mostyn Davies' mission had two roles. First, and most importantly, it was getting into place to bring massive quantities of arms for Macedonian, Serbian, and Albanian Partisans who were to invade southeastern Serbia from the south. One of his closest henchmen, Vukmanović-Tempo, had been sent by Tito to command this undertaking and to build up the Partisans in the area south of Skoplje, though it is probable that Tito did not know about the Mostyn Davies mission. This was the "most secret" role, engineered probably by Keble guided by Klugmann. The other role of Mostyn Davies, also very secret, was to act as reception for Frank Thompson, a young, openly declared, and dedicated communist, who under the aegis of Klugmann and Seton-Watson was being infiltrated to organize the Partisans in Bulgaria.

Not only was the Mostyn Davies mission there with a definitely hostile role regarding the Loyalists, but supplies were being poured in to him. Operational-log signals show that a total of fifteen drops were made to him before the end of November, and Stowers Johnson's book *Agents Extraordinary* claims that twenty-four drops were made to them on one night in January. The Partisans with Mostyn Davies were attempting no anti-Axis sabotage at that stage.

Yet Purvis and I were frustrated in our sabotage endeavors for lack of a couple of loads of supplies. Moreover, if I had been given my promised five planes and one or two more, I could have sabotaged more of that line than was done by the Partisans in the next nine months.

On November 28, as we have seen, Purvis at last got a drop. On December 5 Dipper, another mission commanded by an Australian escaped POW, which was trying to penetrate to Crna Gora Mountain south of Skoplje, also received a drop. Purvis went on to write,

Having received more fuse on these two aircraft, we went on our second operation on the night of December 8th.

The plan of attack was OLDEN with Sgt. WALKER Pte. OPATOWSKI and guard were to blow road bridge 10 Km. North of Kumanovo. The DIPPER party had crossed it and reported it to be of wood. Charges were made accordingly. When OLDEN arrived, however, he found it heavily reinforced underneath with steel girders and concrete piers. He decided it was useless to attempt anything with the stores we had. The motive behind this demolition was to cover our attack on a railway station 15 km North of KUMANOVO, from motorised troops from KUMANOVO. This station was being used as a shunting yard since the bombing of SCOPLJE.

I, for my part, had charges for a derailment South of the Station. This would have been more successful had the train not been stopped by a distant signal, I did not know about and was only just underway when it went over the fog signals. The pont bogies came off but I think the drivers must have bridged the gaps. The engine driver put on steam and tried to lug his train on. Most of the trucks must, I think, have come off for there was a fearful noise and after a hundred yards or so the engine came off itself. When approaching the line, I could see a train in the distance a train in the station. Unfortunately, it started just as I was reaching the line and I had to take cover under a small bridge while it went over. This was a great pity as it was an S.S. troop train and going fast at my attack point. The train I did derail was only a goods, but it blocked the line for two days.

The derailment was a signal for GORGEVIC and his brigade to attack the station where it happened there was another S.S. troop train. They blew some of the points and some rail junctions North and South of the station. A big steam pumping plant was also demolished. While this was going on they opened fire on the troop train. Peasants reported next day that 4 had been killed and a great number of wounded were taken away by road to SCOPLJE. Later reports put the dead at forty but this may or may not be true.

The enemy put down pretty heavy tracer fire and also a wonderful fireworks display which was still going on when we were back in the hills.

No more troops went down the line for at least two days. Intelligence reports told us afterwards that these S.S. troops were going to ALBANIA.

After this we planned to send small derailment parties down each week at various points of the line, but *December 15th* ended that.

In his last two paragraphs Purvis writes,

The break was a great disappointment to us all, as we had raised the Korpus from less than 50 men to a good 700 with whom we were always on the best of terms. There was also no question of their not carrying out sabotage which they were keen to do. Given the proper supplies we could, I am sure, have managed to be more of a nuisance, and, with experience, have tackled larger targets. Reprisals were not feared as they were mostly ALBANIAN or mixed villages near the railway.

Had there been any question of a GERMAN withdrawal from GREECE, we should have been in a key position covering the railway and road into BULGARIA via KRIVA PALANKA which the GERMANS used frequently.

That report is written from the heart. Is that the report of an officer with collaborating troops? And were those troops doing nothing? Would that those who were sitting in armchairs, or pontificating their Marxist theses in smoke-filled rooms in Cairo, had accompanied Purvis and his band during those hard weeks dodging the Bulgars and striking back.

I find from the operational log that my first derailment took place about two weeks after our line demolition. We heard that our line job held up the line for seven days according to one report, and for eleven days according to another.

For the derailment I took Harry Lesar with me. He was an Australian sergeant who had been captured in the African desert and who had managed to escape from the train carrying him up through the Balkans to a POW camp. We took Pešić, Vlada (a sergeant from Andrejević's brigade), and sixty men because Andrejević had received a report that there was a strong force of Partisans in Miroševce, a village on the way down through the plains. We reached the line a couple of hours after dark. In October the nights were longer now and gave us more time, but the moon was already up and full. Vlada was in command of the covering party. This was deployed with a group each side of the point I had picked out from a distance, where the line had a slight curve and I wanted to derail the train. The covering party had orders to hold their fire until after the train came off.

The demolition party consisted of Pešić with a submachine gun, myself with the main charge, and Harry Lesar with a second charge in order to make sure. I was determined to do the key job myself. I wanted no mistakes, and if anything went wrong I would have only myself to blame. We were on uncharted ground. The instructors in Palestine had taught us how to make the charges. The theory was to use one pound of plastic, to cut the line on a curve, and—so they claimed in the school—the forward motion of the train would do the rest. I doubt anybody had tried the theory out. That system required a train with some speed and a point on the line with some curve. Some coincidence.

I am a careful man and I like to be sure. So I made up one five-pound charge and had Lesar carry another. I planned to place one on the inside of the outer rail and the other on the outside of the inner rail going around the curve. It was just a hunch, but I thought maybe it would be a good idea to introduce a bit of leverage.

Our line demolition had taught us that the line would be guarded with very closely spaced civilian sentries and that they would tap the line if they saw anything untoward. So we could not just go down and place our charges. Having sent Vlada off to position the covering parties some 100 yards back from the line under cover, Pešić, Lesar, and I crawled up along a ditch that led toward the bend in the line and settled down, waiting for a train to come. Knowing that the trains went by frequently, I planned to let one go through untouched, in order to spy out the land.

We had not long to wait. There was a whistle and a rumble, and then the headlights of the locomotive illuminated the scene.

Then we saw it. A galvanized iron hut with two soldiers outside. An emergency guardhouse. Located just on the other side of the line from the curve we had selected. We also saw soldiers and civilians on the line spaced out at intervals. There was nothing for it, however; we had to go ahead at this spot. To endeavor to withdraw and come down somewhere else was too risky. Once we were spotted, there would be no other chance that night.

The stationmaster was kind. He did not keep us waiting—it was only about ten minutes before the second train came. We had had plenty of opportunity to judge the distance to the line. We waited fifty yards away until the train was well in sight. We were learning all the time; the lights showed us the behavior of the nearest sentries. They were all turning to look at the approaching locomotive, a magnificent machine with a large cowcatcher in front. Obviously the sentries would do that, without thinking. It was a great help, and it was an important lesson.

Now! We started running. I led, closely followed by Lesar. Forget the sentries; forget the guardhouse. Concentrate on the job at hand. Up the embankment, onto the line. Fix the charge on the inside and wedge it with a stone. Take the other charge from Lesar and fix it on the outside. Knot Primacord between the two charges using the specially fixed length on each charge; clip the fog signal to the line. It is attached by orange, fast-burning fuse (ninety feet per second) to the first charge. Check everything quickly.

The train was maybe 100 yards away by then. Jump clear and run like hell. We tore back from the line. No sentry fired. They were all looking at the train. But the engine driver had seen us as he looked ahead along the line. He slammed on his brakes, screamed, and jumped clear of his cab. Too late. The train was right up to the charge. I shouted to Pešić and Lesar to get down, and the charge blew.

The train came off the tracks, but it slid along the line for quite a long way before it did so. In fact this was a good thing, because more of the line was damaged and the eventual pileup was satisfactory enough. But the theory was that the train should catapult straight off at the curve and come right off the embankment immediately. That it did not do. Still, we had done it. We had derailed the train. We had done a good enough job, but I would have to think some more about the technique.

I did. And I developed a technique using a substantial charge with a noninstantaneous fast-burning fuse to punch the front bogey wheels off even on a straight stretch of line with a slow-moving train. The technique, I believe, became standard practice later. It was taught in the battle school near Monopoli in southern Italy. In a conference on Italian resistance at Bologna University in 1985 I listened with amusement and gratification to two Britons who had been in northern Italy with the Italian partisans explaining how they had taught and carried out these methods. I doubt they knew that I had developed them.

But more about that technique later. Now we are near the railway line a few miles south of Leskovac in 1943, with Vlada's covering party pouring Bren and Spandau fire into the stricken train. A burst of Bren tracer exploded the boiler, and there was a fine scene of carnage all around.

That's enough. Let's go. It was a happy journey home. Back at Barje we found that there had been a drop at last, one of only two I received during that time. But sadly, there was no motor charger; and the Partisans attacked across the Veternica River in an endeavor to capture the stores. They were beaten off, but we suffered a couple of casualties. The day had started well. It finished badly.

CHAPTER
5
Tito Take All

■

It was about this time in October that I attempted to make a local deal with the Partisans. The thought was precipitated by the first ambush, when we were returning from our line demolition on September 30. If we were to carry out regular sabotage in the plains, it was essential that the Partisan ambush factor be eliminated. It had also seemed to me that I could put both MO4 and Djurić on the spot: if the Partisans agreed to a local truce, then base would have to make some gesture to encourage my local commanders, and that meant they would have to send me planes to honor my commitments. If the Partisans refused a truce, or my commanders refused to cooperate, at least the responsibility would be clearly pinpointed.

I was becoming more and more suspicious of the role Djurić was playing. First there had been the bridge incident, in which his attitude had been totally unconstructive and which had decided the issue adversely when Sehmer and Cairo got at cross-purposes. Then, when Armstrong dropped, there had been indications that Mihailović was being much more helpful in his attitude regarding sabotage. Yet Djurić continued to confuse the issue, first by maintaining a blanket veto and then by limiting approval to minor sabotage and train derailments; nothing major like a bridge.

At the time I only knew what the local commanders told me and what I learned from other British who happened to pass through, traveling from the Neronian mission en route to other areas. Cairo gave us virtually no information. This was just as well because, with our communications limitations, we could only handle short messages in and out. We needed all available W/T time for the more urgent signals concerning dropping grounds, fire plans, and our requirements.

John Sehmer had been followed at Neronian first by Maj. Rupert Raw and later by Maj.—subsequently Lt. Col.—Bill Cope. Whereas Sehmer had communicated reasonably well with Djurić in ungrammatical but relatively fluent German or Serbo-Croat—and they enjoyed a meeting of minds—neither Cope nor Raw spoke a word of Serbo-Croat. They had to use whatever interpreter was available, and there was no very good one there. Rupert Raw, a major in the guards and subsequently a distinguished civil servant and advisor to the Bank of England, had a strong political inclination. Bill Cope, a rather typical regular infantry officer, desperately wanted to do something to meet the demands for action by his friend and superior, Brigadier Armstrong. Studying the files forty years later, I found that this all led to a series of rather bizarre happenings.

There was the famous Cope signal, which I have already referred to, which found its way via SOE Cairo and the Minister of State's Office to the foreign secretary, to the prime minister, and even to the Commonwealth prime ministers and the American president. The signal alleged that Mihailović had ordered collaboration with the Germans. In fact, what Mihailović had ordered was, first, defensive action against the Partisans, who were at that time trying to penetrate his positions in the Sandžak to the west and, second, the encouragement of young folk to join the Nedić forces in order to desert with their arms when ordered to do so by Mihailović.

That signal, which was never corrected in London, was a major factor in the break with Mihailović. Or, perhaps, it might be more correct to say that the signal was not a factor but was used as an excuse.

Then there was talk from Neronian about Djurić making a local deal with the Partisans, when he actually had no personal contact with them at all. Indeed he never had such contact until he fled bare-bottomed, breaking his parole, after he had been arrested by Stefanović in May 1944, shortly after we had left the area.

There was also a lot of talk by Neronian about Djurić replacing Mihailović personally, which was political cloud-cuckoo-land, as Mihailović was personally revered in Serbia while Djurić enjoyed no personal standing at all. But all of this talk and the reports were seized on and magnified by the Tito protagonists in the British agencies and turned into "evidence" against Mihailović.

The famous Cope "collaboration" signal was in two parts. It was dated November 21, 1943, and is on File WO 202/143. The first part gave the alleged Mihailović "collaboration" instructions, which were misrepresented by Cope. The second part read that Partisan headquarters in Serbia had stated that no collaboration was possible with Djurić until he openly denounced Mihailović. The Partisans were willing to collaborate with any nationalist group that would succeed Mihailović. In Cope's opinion, Mihailović himself was the stumbling block to any agreement with the Partisans. As a soldier (Cope said) Djurić would obey Mihailović until King Peter and the Yugoslav government openly replaced Mihailović as minister of defense. Djurić's position was made more difficult by the fact that some of his commanders had direct W/T contact with Mihailović. Djurić stated that he would go to Cairo if possible.

I am convinced that Djurić was deliberately playing all ends against the middle so as to be able to profit personally, whatever direction political developments took. But the Cope report was material in the condemnation of Mihailović as a collaborator and in the ingenuous Bailey plan to replace Mihailović personally.

On September 14, 1943, under serial 18 Fugue number 31 (WO 202/131), I had signaled, "General mobilization here today against Partisans orders Djuric. Have persuaded all local commanders not to fight. Must have planes to support my control." This signal was not deciphered till September 21, 1943—a whole week later.

On September 15, 1943, I signaled (WO 202/131 sheet 13), "This friction is of great use to me and strengthens my hold over them. They all are loyal Djuric because they fear him but I had Manic on road to break a bridge without orders when you stopped us. Djuric has now sent another order against sabotage and it will be difficult to get going again without orders."

Later the same day (WO 202/131 sheet 14), I signaled, "Further about Djuric. He is far more interested in fighting Partisans than attending our interests. I am convinced that he adopts this attitude in hope of obtaining high office after the war. He could help us considerably if he wished but will not act. It would help considerably if he were replaced. Or pressure brought to bear. All information given LAKE [Sehmer] by Djuric highly unreliable. I have evidence to support all this and more."

That was, of course, all before Colonel Cope got into the act. More than forty years later, when I read the files in the Public Records Office, I was horrified to find that these earlier signals from me had been taken out of context and blown up to claim that the Loyalists in my area were rushing to fight the Partisans. In fact, it was the opposite. My three commanders were dragging their feet when called on by Djurić. The signals were written in good faith. As a young, reasonably straightforward, simple soldier, I did not anticipate that my signals would be taken out of context and used to prove something that quite evidently they did not say, or even imply. My signals were intended and written to give warning against Djurić's machinations, to ask for help, and to indicate that, given support by Cairo, I was hopeful of steering the local commanders in a direction in line with Allied policy. But my signals were used to make the case against Mihailović and the Loyalists as a whole. The files show that later in the

Foreign Office they were thinking they could use Djurić as a substitute for Mihailović. This was most reprehensible, for Mihailović at that time was showing a real determination to help, following the friendly message brought to him by Brigadier Armstrong from General Wilson.

My signals, I repeat, were directed against Djurić. They were not directed against Mihailović, not against the Loyalists in general, and above all not against my local commanders, who were by then showing every desire to cooperate with me provided they did not get into trouble with Mihailović or Djurić.

Djurić—in spite of his later "conversion" to communism—was much more rabidly anti-Partisan than, for example, Stefanović or Andrejević, but he presented himself to Cope as the contrary, with some success.

The situation became far worse when Djurić took up with Vera Pešić, who was captured on September 10, 1943. She exercised considerable influence until, sometime in November, under pressure from his subcommanders, he banned her and her mother from his headquarters and sent them to a subsidiary headquarters. Rupert Raw's report (File WO 202/162) shows that she had been an active communist before the war, and had become a Gestapo agent and the temporary mistress of a German general. Throughout she remained very friendly with a Partisan leader, Milivoj Perović, another prewar communist. Djurić's Partisan contacts—if he had any—went through Vera Pešić.

Once Vera Pešić started her affair with Djurić, there could be no doubt about his unreliability as an officer, an individual, and a patriot. Sadly, Stefanović, like Mihailović a gentleman, accepted Djurić's parole. Naïve fellow.

The manner in which the Partisans welcomed this rather despicable creature when he did his bunk, and used him, and promoted him, demonstrates not only the venality of Djurić himself but the utter ruthlessness of the Partisan principles.

Unfortunately, Colonel Cope and Major Raw were taken in by Djurić, in spite of knowing all about Vera Pešić. Their reports to Cairo regarding Djurić's tendentious misrepresentation of Mihailović's orders became a main constituent of the collaboration case trumped up in Cairo against Mihailović.

There is a reference in Rupert Raw's report to a signal from Cairo saying that sorties would be stopped to Neronian mission because Djurić was fighting the Partisans. Raw replied that, if supplies were stopped to Djurić headquarters, they should be stopped to all missions in southern Serbia. (With friends like that we sure needed no enemies.) I for one had told Cairo that I had managed to control my own commanders. Klugmann must have been laughing all the way to his office as he rushed to comply with Raw's suggestion. But it was all hypothetical. We were not going to get drops for a quite different reason, as I will shortly relate.

The three Loyalist commanders were by no means enamored of my ideas of a truce with the local Partisans. At that time, early October 1943, there was still only the group of 200 or so on Mount Radan and insignificant other groups in Jastrebac, Kozjak, and Crna Gora areas. In the light of their intensive political activity and the rumors of the support being given to the Partisans by the British, along with the anti-Mihailović tone of the BBC broadcasts, there was an entirely understandable school of thought among the Loyalists that favored cleaning up the Partisans before things got worse. Without our presence and our influence, the local commanders would have mounted an offensive against the Radan. I believe that the Loyalists could have cleaned them out at that stage— before British arms reached the group. Thus in one more instance we were unwitting tools in the move to destroy the Mihailović Loyalist movement.

I had first spoken with my three local commanders about my truce ideas immediately following the ambush after our line demolition. Manić was adamant; he for one would not consider a pact with the communists unless they agreed to place themselves fully under Loyalist command. It was a logical view; but I knew that the demand would not be accepted by the Partisans in that form, and I appealed to Jovo. But this time his sympathy, though unexpressed, tended to lie with Manić; and Andrejević thought likewise. After much argument I persuaded them to agree to back down in their demands. They would not insist on the

Partisans coming under command, only on cessation of all leftist propaganda.

We had left it that Andrejević would establish contact from his headquarters in the foothills in Barje. With our preparations for the first derailment and his annoyance about the BBC announcement that had credited our line demolition to the Partisans, however, he had done nothing. I think that it had been quietly agreed between the three commanders that they would not show adamant opposition to my ideas but that they would not help. Accordingly, I decided to try to arrange a meeting for myself.

I sent a peasant, the brother of the owner of the house where our mission was then established, to Miroševce, a village frequently visited by Partisans. In a note to the leader known to us as Crni Marko, I suggested that we meet. I received an answer very soon. It was written in English and suggested that I come to Miroševce at six the following night. Though naïve in those days, I was not plain stupid. I took our host, a man named Dragan, with me, and, promising Dragan a rather substantial reward if he would do what I asked, I briefed Tommy about my plans with full instructions about what he was to do if I did not return. If the Partisans kidnapped me, it was virtually certain that they would try to take me away to their headquarters on Mount Radan. If so, Tommy was to advise Andrejević and Manić to move rapidly to seal the route there. We fixed certain points where he was to have a covering party ready to help me if I had to make an escape.

It never came to that. We moved down early to a small hillock short of Miroševce from which we could see the village. Then I sent Dragan ahead to make a straightforward shopping visit, with the idea that he would wait till the Partisans arrived and then come back and tell me how many were there and how the situation looked.

We did not need Dragan's information. Shortly after he left us a Partisan column approached the outskirts of the village. A large man with a rifle over his shoulder collected a group around him and gave orders. The force split up and moved off in small groups in all directions, forming a cordon around the village. The men moved into concealed positions and only one route was left open, the route to Barje.

In my note I had informed Crni Marko that I would come without an escort and had asked him to do likewise. This cordon could mean only one thing: they intended to kidnap me. It was still not half past five. If I had arrived at the correct time instead of two hours early, I would have walked straight into a trap. We returned to Barje. Dragan did not get back until the following morning and told us that he had been locked up all night, not because they suspected him in particular but because he was from the mountains. Fortunately, he had bought some silk for his wife, and he showed it to them as proof that he was there on a purchasing expedition. But they took the silk from him all the same. That hurt.

The Partisan leader was evidently upset and had been asking about me and the British mission and the sorties we were getting. I forgot about trying to arrange a local truce. One can't do business with people like that.

Now I believe that it is possible that this incident was connected with a rather sinister figure variously described as Dragi Radivojević from Ub in Serbia and Branko Radojević from Valjevo. He is said to have been recruited by Captain Deakin in New York, and according to this account, he was a ship's radio operator contacted through Vane Ivanović. There are many gray areas in the story of this man, for others have it that he was recruited by Bill Stuart through Kovačević, the Yugoslav communist leader in Canada.

According to English W/T operators in Cairo, he had to be taught radiotelegraphy from scratch. This would be inconsistent with his being a ship's radio operator, most of whom were highly skilled. What does seem probable is that Radivojević or Radojević was brought in under the plan to recruit former Yugoslav members of the International Brigades in the Spanish Civil War who had ceased to be communist, in order to drop them into Yugoslavia and find out who Tito really was.

Certainly he had been in Spain, and certainly he claimed to

have ceased to be a communist. Some say that he was a Trotsky-ist—not a Stalinist—but that is another gray area and not really relevant. What is certain is that he claimed to have become disillusioned with the Reds. The plan in Cairo, when he arrived there in the spring of 1942, was to drop him in to spy on the Partisans, for which task he would have seemed admirably suited.

But it did not work out quite like that.

Between April 1 and July 25 there were eight unsuccessful attempts to drop him into Croatia. "Higher authority" then lost patience, dressed him up as an Englishman, Capt. Charles Robertson, and dropped him into Mihailović's headquarters. His cover story was that he was to help Captain Hudson, the head of the British mission, with his signals—a very important task. His secret brief from MO4 was to check up and report on Hudson and to find out about the Partisans in some way through Mihailović's headquarters staff.

Amazingly, Robertson was given full authority to use his own discretion about deserting from Mihailović to the Partisans. He was also advised to speak French with the Loyalists and not to let on that he knew Serbo-Croat.

I have pieced together Robertson's story from many sources, but the foregoing is spelled out clearly and unequivocally by the files in the Public Records Office (FO 371/59469 minute 11677/G). Regrettably, the minute does not specify who was the "higher authority." Neither does it tell us who gave Robertson his shameful brief to deceive Hudson and Mihailović, who at that time shared unquestioned British support.

The Foreign Office minute also tells us that Robertson took secret maps with him, drawn in invisible ink, showing where MO4 believed Partisan units to be located. Jasper Maskelyn of Maskelyn Devant, the famous London magicians, worked for MO4. He briefed me about secret inks, along with many other things. I had a fascinating couple of hours with him. Presumably it was Maskelyn who briefed Robertson too.

Robertson came to be suspected by Mihailović and his headquarters staff, who quickly realized that he was not what he made himself out to be but rather an outright communist spy. Furthermore, Hudson was tormented by Robertson, who caused him problems by sending denunciatory signals to MO4 Cairo behind his back: he could work the W/T, while Hudson could not.

I wrote earlier that Sir Harry Hinsley, the historian, refers to reports "still more critical of Mihailović from a Yugoslav officer who had recently joined Hudson after failing to make contact with the Partisans." This comment, derived no doubt from *received wisdom*, fails to mention the vitally important background I have provided. Robertson was in no way a "Yugoslav officer." He was a communist Yugoslav dressed as a British officer, and it is no wonder that he sent reports criticizing both Mihailović and Hudson. Hudson recently told me that he threw Robertson out of a first-floor window one day. Good for him! Yet Robertson's lies have, typically, become gilt-edged history.

Yet, in spite of entertaining great suspicions about him, out of respect for the British Mihailović took no action about Robertson until the latter fled from one of his units, taking with him a genuine British officer, Maj. Neil Selby. The two left Dragutin Keserović, a Loyalist commander, on Kopaonik in August 1943, with Bailey's full knowledge. They made their break with encouragement from MO4, supposedly in order to try to arrange a deal with the Partisans. Robertson made his way successfully to the Partisans on the Jastrebac, but Major Selby and his W/T operator were captured. Selby was later shot by the Gestapo while trying to escape. The Partisans tried to claim that the Loyalists had betrayed Selby, but no proof, circumstantial or otherwise, has been shown. The simple logic indicated that, if there was a betrayal, it was done by Robertson himself, precisely in order to discredit the Loyalists as a last action before finishing his spying mission on behalf of the communists and returning to the communist fold.

This version is further supported by an odd incident in Cairo, which occurred before Robertson dropped. He was beaten up one night. There were various versions of this affair. One was that he was the victim of royalist Yugoslavs who thought that he was a communist. The other version is that he was beaten up by the communists because he was a turncoat. But there were no overt Yugoslav communists in Cairo at that stage. The most likely version is that he had himself beaten up in order to strengthen his cover story, and this version is supported by his meticulous reporting of the incident to Col. John Bennet, the officer in charge. The really significant thing is that his "mother superior"—his minder—in Cairo was, of course, James Klugmann, and the devious brief to deceive the British head of mission and Mihailović was a typical Klugmann brainchild.

My searches through the 1943 records have recently revealed that Robertson wrote on August 24, 1943, to Captain Boon, a BLO near my headquarters, stating that Selby was taken by the Serbian Nedić state guards near Mali Jastrebac. Robertson did not say why he himself was not taken. All this is inconsistent with the alleged Mihailović-Nedić collaboration and with the tendency of the Nedić guards to turn a blind eye. Other reports had it that Selby was captured by Ljotić troops (a small Serbian quisling force), but Robertson's letter to Boon was specific that it was the Nedić guards. Finally, to my considerable surprise I find that Major Raw's report in the Public Records Office (WO 202/162) states that Robertson sent me a message asking me to establish a local W/T contact with him and thus to act as a W/T link between him and Cairo. At the time my own W/T was out of order. This mention by Major Raw establishes that Robertson was still alive in October 1943 and that, having failed to coerce Boon, he had tried to draw me into his spider's web too.

I was luckier than Selby. I often wonder what would have happened to me if I had made the contact. Would I too have disappeared? And in my case would there too have been allegations that the Loyalists had murdered me?

Another case is that of Maj. Terence Atherton, whose disappearance constituted another notorious mystery that has been exploited by Partisan propaganda. Atherton landed on the Yugoslav coast in 1942 with orders to join Mihailović. Like Hudson, he first established contact with the Partisans and was taken by them to Tito's headquarters in Bosnia, where he arrived at the beginning of March 1942. Atherton was a journalist who had lived in Yugoslavia, and he knew the area well. He stayed some time with the Partisans but then left without warning in order to get to the Četnik headquarters. He never arrived. He was murdered. The Partisan propaganda machine put up an enormous smoke screen about how Atherton was murdered by a Četnik. But it was a smoke screen. To this day there is no certainty that he was not murdered by the Partisans to stop him from joining Mihailović. That is the more logical explanation.

It is claimed by some historians that Atherton was murdered by an independent Četnik semibandit for his money. But these claims are not supported by proof, and they become all the more suspect when the alleged killer is linked with the Loyalists for propaganda purposes. As recently as February 14, 1988, Sir Fitzroy Maclean claimed in an interview with *The Sunday Times* that Atherton was murdered by the "Četniks," and there is a clear implication that he meant the Mihailović Četnik Loyalists. Not even the Partisans claimed that.

MO4 knew that Selby was making a break to the Partisans with Robertson. I told Cairo nothing of my plans to contact the Radan Partisans, either before or afterward. Maybe I was fortunate that I omitted telling Cairo. Everything seems to indicate that there were eyes and ears in Cairo—whichever ones they were—that were malignant to the Loyalists and even hostile to us British serving with them.

There is another interesting angle to these incidents. Until Mihailović was abandoned by Churchill on December 10, 1943, Tito insisted that no British officers be dropped to Partisan units in Serbia. The small Partisan units on Mount Radan and the Jastrebac would have benefited enormously from having a BLO. Tito was sensitive to the likelihood of BLOs with the two rival movements getting together, an eventuality that the British Foreign Office would have welcomed. But the last thing Tito wanted was British-sponsored truces between local groups of Serbs. He wanted the civil war to be fought to the finish. There is no doubt about Tito's policy, and it would fit very well with elimination of BLOs endeavoring to organize truces, such as Selby or Atherton—or me. It is interesting to speculate that even Robertson may have been liquidated for this reason.

When Brigadier Armstrong dropped on September 24 to take overall command of the mission, he brought a friendly and encouraging letter from General Wilson, the Middle East commander in chief, addressed to General Mihailović. The important sentence in that letter said, "It has now become logistically possible for me to send you military supplies on a much larger scale." In spite of all of his previous experience of British duplicity, it is evident that the decision to drop in a brigadier accompanied by a colonel, a chief of staff, and various others, together with this letter from General Wilson, must have made quite some impression on Mihailović. Certainly the spate of Loyalist activity, and the provision of forces for the bridge demolitions at Mokra Gora and Višegrad, appear to reflect a more trustful and constructive attitude on Mihailović's part. I believe that my own three local commanders sensed this or received some indication of it and that the problems in our area, insofar as there were problems, were created by Djurić and Djurić alone.

But the Venezia Division incident, when Bailey intervened to stop the Loyalists from disarming the Italians and let the Partisans move in and take the booty, evidently did enormous harm. Whether or not someone in MO4 set that up deliberately is something we, who have no access to the main SOE files, cannot tell. We can only suspect. As with the Glenconner signal ordering Mihailović to retreat to east of the Ibar on May 29—which was patently designed to open an escape route for Tito's hard-pressed Partisan headquarters troops—we cannot state here conclusively that cheating Mihailović was the purpose and that the whole Venezia Division affair was not just a coincidence. But if it was just another coincidence, it was one hell of a coincidence.

From Mihailović's viewpoint, however, these incidents were evident betrayals. And as the weeks passed following Armstrong's arrival and the "military supplies on a much larger scale" specifically promised by General Wilson did not materialize, Mihailović must have been getting very bitter. The reports from his agents in the Partisan areas will have told him of the arrival of Brigadier Maclean on September 17 and of the greatly increased supplies to the Partisans. As if that were not enough, he received constant reports of Partisan propaganda telling the population that Tito was now recognized by the British and that the abandonment of the Loyalists would follow shortly. Milovan Djilas, among others, was making public speeches to that effect. In reply to a question from Bailey through Cairo about this, Major Deakin at Tito's headquarters shrugged it off and wrote that he could not be responsible for what the Partisans said. Furthermore, the BBC was now making openly pro-Partisan broadcasts as well as attributing Loyalist successes to the Partisans.

At that point in time, Mihailović had to ask himself not only whether sabotage would cost reprisals but also whether he could afford the ammunition he was going to need in self-defense against the increasing Partisan attacks on his positions. This was a very important factor.

In retrospect, it is amazing to me that we were able to continue living with the Loyalists in total freedom and that we were able to obtain their support for the actions we carried out. That we were unable to obtain sufficient support to undertake larger operations in October-November 1943, though very frustrating to me at the time, is now entirely comprehensible.

I can write with firsthand knowledge only of the situation in my area, and with some authority in regard to Robert Purvis's area to the south of me. It is very evident from Purvis's report that his commanders were remarkably willing and tractable, perhaps even more so than my own. To the west of us in Keserović's Korpus area, Capt. George More was able to carry out a number of small demolitions too, and even working out of Djurić's head quarters, Captain Hawksworth attacked a railway station north of Leskovac. Then, of course, there was the very considerable activity by Archie Jack out of Mihailović's headquarters and the well-known, partially successful attempt to block the Danube by the Homolje group. All in all there was a lot of activity in the month of October 1943. Yet it was precisely at that time that our supplies dried up and it became quite obvious that our planes were being diverted elsewhere.

Looking back at the operational log of signals now in the Public Records Office, I found the signal that tells it all. It was addressed to all Mihailović missions and to them only. It was dated September 22, 1943, and read as follows:

Programme of flying disorganised this month due

(1) Demands on our aircraft for other purposes "owing to fall of Italy." [*sic*]
(2) Initial bad weather.
(3) Very bad start Bizerta which will have repercussions sorties.

Realise delicacy your position and doing best see no mission suffers out of proportion. Unwilling give any figure for remainder period. We regret very much.

Now, that signal was sent to the British and American missions with Mihailović. The one exception was Cavern, the signal name then used by Colonel Hudson. The transmission to him was canceled, apparently because of a signal from him a day or two previously in which he had exploded about the poor service given him since he was first in contact more than a year before. Evidently someone in Cairo thought it better to leave him in the dark and avoid getting an even more abusive signal back!

But this signal, saying in effect that we were being put out of action, was not sent to any of the missions with the Partisans. On the contrary, the signal traffic to them shows an increase in drops.

And why? The official policy was clear: full support for Mihailović units, provided that the arms were not used against other resistance groups. No one could claim that the Loyalists were so using the arms, because the operational log reports signals from Brigadier Armstrong specifically advising against drops into areas near Partisan units, which shows pedantic observance of this policy on the Mihailović side.

All of this occurred just when Armstrong was delivering the fulsome letter from General Wilson advising that "It has now become logistically possible for me to send you military supplies on a much larger scale." What gave?

I realize now that what gave was that Brigadier Maclean had dropped to Tito on September 17 and was already demanding that the drops to the Partisans be urgently stepped up. No matter that the commander in chief, General Wilson, had just written a letter promising substantially increased supplies to Mihailović. No matter that Mihailović was at last telling his outlying commanders that they could get moving on sabotage. No matter that Mihailović's own forces were going out with Armstrong and Archie Jack to blow up bridges. No matter that we were stating categorically and emphatically that we could carry out regular line demolitions and derailments on the vital Morava Valley line if given the tools to do the job; and that I could even do major sabotage such as the Vladički Han bridge if my promised sortie allocation was sent as an encouragement to the Loyalists. No matter that I was starting to establish an important new nonaligned resistance group over the Albanian border and needed just one plane for recognition and propaganda purposes. It had all stopped.

The vital clue lies in Maclean's signal of September 20, which reported on his "dinner with Tito" on the night of his arrival. The signal (FO 371/37612 number MA/9) starts by detailing a list of claimed Partisan successes and gives a first batch of tendentious Partisan statistics and territorial claims. In regard to these Douglas Howard, head of the southern department of the Foreign Office, noted in the margin "no longer" to the Partisan claim to hold the town of Split, and "that's a very unscientific statement" to the claim that "Partisans now have important forces in Serbia including the Vardar Valley and Srem which can therefore no longer be regarded as the preserve of Mihailovic."

It is incredible that only two days after arriving in the country Maclean was making these dogmatic statements of "fact," which can only have been based on what the Partisans told him. But then comes the crunch line: "Regarding supplies, I told Tito that he could count on a minimum of sixty sorties next month. He said that the quantities promised hitherto have no relation to those actually received and this and other questions were further complicated by apparent absence of reliable communications with Cairo. I replied that sixty was a firm figure and that steps were being taken to establish satisfactory communications."

That was on September 20. The message putting supplies to all Mihailović missions in question was sent on September 22.

Bang went our sorties, promised for sabotage done, certain to bring major sabotage results immediately if delivered. And bang went Purvis's and my motor chargers. The motor charger Cairo subsequently claimed to have dropped to me, but which never arrived, was obviously pulled out and sent to the missions to the Partisans in order to meet Tito's complaints about inadequate communications.

We were in a no-win situation. Cairo had got the message. Tito was Churchill's "great guerrilla," and Maclean had been anointed by Churchill. If Maclean demanded priority, he could have it. It made no difference that General Wilson, commander in chief, had promised Mihailović more supplies, not fewer.

After months of discussion backward and forward, after high-level consideration by the Foreign Office and the chiefs of staff of short-term and long-term policy, after every British agency getting their oar into the argument, it had been decided to send a brigadier each to Mihailović and Titó, to have them both report—and then to consider the reports together.

Armstrong had dropped to Mihailović, and at that stage things were at last looking up after the series of squabbles and setbacks between MO4 and Mihailović—which squabbles and setbacks were, as I have shown, substantially of British making. Now Armstrong's promising efforts were being nipped in the bud before he could even get started.

On whose authority were the Mihailović missions singled out for adverse treatment, even before Armstrong had time to study and report? On whose authority was the decision taken to effectively paralyze the emergent Loyalist action against the Axis and to switch all arms and supplies destined for them to the Partisans, who were making no pretense of adhering to the British policy of avoiding civil war? Was this switching done on the orders of the chiefs of staff, advised by the Foreign Office? Was it done on the orders of General Wilson, who had just promised Mihailović increased supplies? Or was it done quietly and surreptitiously by MO4? The files in the Public Records Office reveal nothing. That's odd, and sinister.

Rereading the operational log, I noticed the appalling delays suffered by the messages from the Mihailović missions in the decoding. Taking just my own case, there are two urgent messages from Fugue concerning recognition signals and fire plans for drops. One was sent September 3 and decoded on September 18. The second was sent September 14 and decoded September 21.

On September 13 a sortie failed to drop to us, and Cairo alleged that we had put out the wrong signal fires. They bludgeoned us with this accusation and demanded our explanation in repeated signals until our set went out of action about October 24. They diverted a drop away from us on the grounds that we had not explained. They at last told us what the plan should have been, and we confirmed again what we had already told them, namely, that our fires had conformed precisely to that plan. They did not apologize or even confirm, but forty years later in Kew Gardens in the PRO I found on the operational file a handwritten note: "R.A.F. mistake."

This same series of bludgeoning signals asked what had happened to two W/T sets dropped to us on September 8. None had been dropped. They also advised that a motor generator had been dropped, when it certainly had not. Obviously, it went to the Partisans, just like my malaria drugs, which landed up with Deakin. He mentions with surprise in his writings that malaria drugs were sent to him unrequested. I had asked for them two months earlier. No matter that I nearly died of malaria. The Maclean promise of sixty planes had to be fulfilled. All of this one finds decades later, and to me now it is remarkable that in the face of such difficulties we achieved anything at all.

But I do want to know *who* organized the switching of the aircraft to the Partisans in the face of the agreed policy. And on what authority, if any? Will the official historian tell us? These are the questions that really matter. The keys to history.

There is a postscript to Robert Purvis's report. It reads, "I should like a message we received to be recorded. It quoted a message that we had *never* sent and said it had too many 'D's.' It then stated that should this occur again none of our messages would be decoded for a week and it was only because of our tactical situation that this was not being put into effect."

The number of *D*s determined the priority.

In *Baker Street Irregular*, Bickham Sweet-Escott deals with the lack of planning at MO4 that resulted in insufficient cipher staff and near chaos. What seemed to have concerned him was the loss of reputation with GHQ when SOE had to ask for signalmen to help out. That speaks for itself. The fact that our vital signals, dealing with important intelligence and sabotage information from deep in enemy territory, were held up seems to have been of lesser importance in that staff officer's mind.

Yet more sordid was the nature of the signal sent to Purvis, which, incidentally, was copied to me and to other missions with Mihailović, trying to cobble together a justification for Cairo's shortcomings. They spent thousands of pounds and lost many lives putting agents into the field and then failed to read their messages. Then they blamed us. These despicable deceptions were, of course, used as smoke screens to hide the switch of all supplies and signal priorities to the Partisans.

When my own signalers could not cope with decoding, and even when they could, I sat down and worked with them. We were in a wartime situation, not a holiday. I would have liked to read another paragraph in Sweet-Escott's book saying, "We determined not to let our men at the sharp end down. All staff officers were ordered to put in two hours deciphering at the end of the day." There is no such paragraph, because there was no such decision. I guess that such a simple and decent solution would never have occurred to MO4. Gezira Club and the girlies called.

Oh, Micky Thomas, how right you were.

CHAPTER
6
The Coup de Disgrace
■

Telegram number 2360 of August 10, 1943, to the minister of state, Cairo, from the Foreign Office advised, "Lieutenant Colonel Maclean who has now been appointed Head of the SOE mission attached to General Tito leaves today for Cairo. On all political matters Lieutenant Colonel Maclean will report to you (or H.M. Ambassador) through SOE and will receive guidance from you. He will also consider himself as a member of your staff. Amendments to Lieutenant Colonel Maclean's brief necessitated by his change of status will be telegraphed to you."

They were referring to Maclean's new status as sole head of mission as opposed to the originally intended appointment as political advisor to Brigadier Orr.

Attached to this telegram was the original brief for "Captain" Fitzroy Maclean, political advisor–designate. This brief contained interesting handwritten amendments, which make it very clear that the original policy was maintained and that the brief envisaged work not only with Tito's Partisans but with "any other Partisan movements." It also clearly shows that the Foreign Office regarded work to cool the civil war as a priority.

Maclean flew back to Cairo on August 10, and he has told us in his paper delivered at the Auty-Clogg symposium that the prime minister wanted him to get into Yugoslavia as soon as possible. Yet he did not in fact drop till September 17. So what was he doing in the interim?

A fascinating memorandum contained in signal number 1994 of August 30, 1943, tells us something. The signal is from Maclean in the Minister of State's Office to Sir Orme Sargent in the Foreign Office. In the first paragraph Maclean reports his establishment of satisfactory relations with General Wilson. In the next he unleashes a broadside against the principals of SOE Cairo—Lord Glenconner; his chief of staff, Tamplin; and his director of special operations, Keble—claiming that all three had stated frankly that they were working "to reverse the decisions taken by the Prime Minister, the Foreign Secretary and the Commander-in-Chief."

The next paragraph alleged (correctly, it is almost certain) that SOE had been messing around with the messages directed to the minister of state from the political advisor to the head of the SOE mission in Greece. These messages had been subjected to the nondeciphering maneuver and had even been held up after being deciphered.

Next Maclean advised that these matters had been brought to the notice of the commander in chief, who had raised the whole question of the status of SOE Cairo and proposed that it come under GHQ. The signal went on to report a meeting of the commander in chief, the minister of state, various others, and Maclean himself, in which Maclean had stated that the attitude of SOE regarding his mission and the experience of Major Wallace (the political advisor in Greece) had caused him great concern. General Wilson had supported Maclean, and the status of SOE was to be discussed at a future meeting. Maclean went on in a final paragraph to pile on the agony about the horrors of being under the authority of SOE: "In any other circumstances I should not hesitate to tell the Prime Minister that I could not undertake mission with which he has entrusted me and give reasons. In view, however, of the urgency of the situation my responsibility, whatever obstacles are placed in my way, is clearly to carry out my mission."

Like his earlier move to get rid of poor Brigadier Orr with the spiel about unsuitable candidates, it worked wonderfully. Sir Orme Sargent sent it on to the foreign secretary, and in due course MO4 was brought under GHQ, becoming Force 133. Lord Glenconner and Keble were moved on some three months later. Tamplin had just died.

Having cleared the decks, secured his base, and incidentally arranged direct radio ciphers and links to bypass SOE if necessary, Maclean caught the next moon and dropped to Tito. But there can be no doubt that his month or so in Cairo gave due warning to all and sundry that he was no man to trifle with— and that maybe it would be wise to keep Maclean gruntled if one knew what was good for one.

Symptomatic of this situation was that the minister of state now decided to jump on the bandwagon with a long signal to the Foreign Office attacking Mihailović and pedantically questioning his assurances. This was evidently intended to hold up supplies to the Loyalists. The Minister of State's Office right throughout 1943 had been noticeably and aggressively antagonistic to Mihailović, but this signal excelled. In a memo analyzing it, Douglas Howard, the head of the southern department in the Foreign Office, stated,

The fact is, I am sure, that SOE Cairo (plus the minister of state) do not *want* us to come to a satisfactory arrangement with Mihailović. We have been on the verge of doing so many times, but on each occasion a spanner has been thrown in to prevent us. I recall the following occasions. We sent Bailey the directive. For various reasons or excuses it did not reach Mihailovic for many weeks. Just when Mihailovic was about to reply Glenconner sent his famous "bludgeoning" telegram. It took weeks to get that straight again. Mihailovic then replied to the directive (satisfactorily in our view and that of SOE here). Before we could reply to that effect, Bailey sends in his ultimatum, Mihailovic replies, again satisfactorily, but SOE Cairo find it unsatisfactory and now suggest another "showdown" on the grounds that he will probably refuse to cooperate with us. Would it not be more normal to tell Mihailovic that we accept his reply and will do our best to support him. If *then* it proves unsatisfactory and he fails to carry out his promises, we should re-assess our policy; but to do so on the *assumption* that he will not do so, seems to me typical SOE way of doing things.

Perhaps he was a little unkind to SOE. He should have said a typical MO4 way of doing things, thus drawing a distinction between SOE London—which had been correct all through—and SOE Cairo, alias MO4—which had hardly ever been correct.

Even so, the Keble epoch, as Davidson called it, was coming to an end with the knife thrust into MO4 by Maclean. Power had transferred from Cairo across the Mediterranean to Tito's Balkan headquarters with its British mission. Manifestly, power had transferred to Tito himself, because the files recording the events in the months ahead show Maclean using his remarkable powers of persuasion not so much to make Tito follow the commander in chief's wishes as to get the prime minister, the commander in chief, and everyone and his uncle to dance to Tito's tune, and to love doing so. But the transfer of power changed nothing politically. From January to November 1943 Keble firmly manipulated MO4 to sabotage Mihailović and build up Tito. From September 1943 Maclean's fantastic talent was dedicated to precisely the same ends.

In MO4 Klugmann was still moling away in the communist cause. Bill Deakin was still at Tito's headquarters compiling his dossier of evidence from the Partisans of Mihailović Četnik collaboration, while Bailey was still at Mihailović headquarters getting things snarled up. *Plus ça change . . .*

Poor Brigadier Armstrong, who dropped into Yugoslavia hoping to run a military operation, never had a chance. Poor Mihailović, who went into the woods in April 1941 to organize resistance against the Axis, never had a chance at all. We poor

BLOs trying to do our minor jobs blowing trains and killing the odd German or Bulgar never had much of a chance either.

SOE Cairo lost effective power and influence over British activities in Yugoslavia to the new Maclean mission and its Cairo link, the Minister of State's Office, as a result of the late August meeting. As I wrote above, however, Keble stayed in place a little longer. On September 29, 1943, he produced a paper at the request of the minister of state that was addressed to the chief of general staff of GHQ. This astonishing document (WO 201/1585) purported to "crystalise [sic] one's thoughts as at 28th September, 1943."

The paper started with a eulogy of Tito's forces, presenting them as communist-led but not really communist, very anti-Axis, and willing to fit in with Allied strategy. Keble then went on to denigrate the Mihailović forces, painting them as small, neither pro-Axis nor pro-Allied, ineffective, and only interested in postwar issues.

This prologue was followed by the most extraordinary dissertation on Tito-Mihailović relations. It was full of falsehoods and tendentious statements and clearly designed to please the pro-Partisan faction in the Minister of State's Office and to spread misinformation to the military. But he finished with a proposal that cunningly paid lip service to the official policy of trying to use the British presence in both camps in order to keep them from fighting each other.

He proposed as "SOE's suggestion" that a clear but temporary boundary be set by which Serbia would be recognized as Mihailović's territory and Slovenia, Croatia, Slavonia, Dalmatia, Bosnia, Herzegovina, and Macedonia south of Skoplje would be recognized as Partisan territories, with Montenegro and the Sandžak as "Tom Tiddlers ground" (no-man's-land). It was suggested that King Peter put this proposal to Mihailović and that the British, American, and Soviet governments put the proposal to Tito.

Following this scheme was a paper titled "Balkan Politico/Military Situation." This truly amazing document dealt with Greece, Yugoslavia, and Albania and pointed out quite correctly that the Soviets were endeavoring to build a communist bloc in the Balkans. It went on to recommend that this ploy should be countered by abandoning support for nonrepublican and royalist parties. The theory was that goodwill might thus be earned and that it might even be possible to bring back some monarchies afterward.

This was not simply a naïve document. It was very dangerous and sinister, and one cannot avoid the conviction that it was drafted by the communist Klugmann, who, as Basil Davidson told us repeatedly in *Special Operations Europe*, was Keble's special protégé. With the exception of Seton-Watson, he was also the only one in MO4 with sufficient knowledge and deviousness to cobble this paper together.

The proposal for the establishment of spheres of influence in Yugoslavia gave virtually the entire country to the Partisans except for the heart of Serbia. It was ingeniously devised to give the Partisans areas such as "Macedonia south of Skoplje" from which they could—and subsequently did—mount their attacks into Serbia. The proposal would have constituted the death sentence for the Mihailović movement. Even then it was not good enough for Maclean, who declined in an October 8, 1943 signal to MO4 to put it up to Tito on the grounds that it would prejudice the relations of his mission at that early stage. In this signal (PRO WO 202/131) Maclean made it quite clear in the first paragraph that Tito was determined to liquidate Mihailović and that Tito claimed that British arms alone had so far prevented him from doing so.

As the Allies had by then delivered to Mihailović arms for only about 1,500 men, either the Tito claim was false or the Tito forces were tiny. But Tito was already claiming an army of 180,000 men.

The British mission to Tito had just a few days earlier transmitted a "formal Partisan protest against news and propaganda from the BBC." This remarkably vitriolic protest, emanating from the Partisans but written in impeccable prose, listed complaints and threatened that unless BBC announcements presenting Mihailović as an anti-Axis resistance force ceased forthwith, a campaign against the BBC would be initiated by the Free Yugoslavia radio station. The protest went on to say that the presence of British senior officers with Mihailović would not alter the Partisan determination to wage war on Četniks throughout Yugoslavia and that no compromise with Mihailović would be considered under any circumstances. It gave notice of increasing strength of the Partisans in Serbia, who would soon be "in a position to liquidate the remaining Četniks and would not hesitate to do so."

Having sent that protest— whether or not they advised Tito on its drafting— it is indeed very comprehensible that the British mission was disinclined to pass on Keble's suggestion that the territory be divided into spheres of influence. Nevertheless, soldiers are supposed to obey orders, and the proposal by Keble was sent officially to the British mission on behalf of the Joint Operations Committee of the Middle East Command. The manner of its treatment demonstrated, if nothing else, that as of September 17 de facto power lay totally in the hands of Maclean and his rear link, the Minister of State's Office. The MO4 Keble era was over. Even the Joint Operations Committee counted for little.

It is ironic that the rear link was Ralph Skrine Stevenson (later Sir Ralph), who held the formal position of ambassador to the royal Yugoslav government. Yet in practice he seems to have been, after Maclean and Deakin, the major factor in advising Churchill to eliminate Mihailović, which of course, in turn, led to the end of the royal Yugoslav government to which he was accredited. It is even more ironic how Keble, who had been the major proponent of the Partisan cause since the end of 1942 and who had struggled to prevent Maclean's appointment, was being outbid by the latter in pandering to Tito. As Keble's professional demise came nearer, he must have felt very bitter. In fairness he kept on going, aiding Tito and sabotaging Mihailović right to the end.

The Foreign Office was shocked by the threatening nature of the Partisan protest about the BBC and signaled its displeasure. It urged very strongly that Tito not be allowed to get away with it. No one took notice.

The next chapter in the saga came with Maclean's return to Cairo and the circulation of his report, which came to be known in the trade as the "blockbuster."

After he dropped on September 17, Maclean spent a very short time at Tito's headquarters near Jajce in Bosnia. He was not involved in any action, so in fact he did not see the Partisans' fighting qualities. He then visited the coast to examine the possibility of bringing in seaborne supplies, for which purpose he visited the island of Korčula. He went back to Tito's headquarters, where he met Deakin, who had just returned from taking the surrender of Italian divisions, but he left again almost immediately in order to return to the coast and thence via Italy to Cairo, making his way via the island of Vis, where the Navy picked him up. It is not clear from his book *Eastern Approaches* precisely how long he was in Yugoslavia, because he gives no dates. Indeed, both this and his other book about Yugoslavia, *Disputed Barricades*, are notable for their lack of precision in such matters. According to Deakin in *The Embattled Mountain*, however, Maclean finally left Tito's headquarters on October 5; and Deakin is considered the primary historical authority on the whole subject. In the absence of any indication in Maclean's writings or signals of the precise dates, I assume October 5 to be correct. A few days one way or the other do not alter the argument materially. Thus Maclean seems to have had a total stay at Partisan headquarters of about three weeks, including one journey to the coast and back—not very long to determine the future of the country.

In *Eastern Approaches*, Maclean tells us that he was called back to Cairo and that he arrived there in time to meet with the foreign secretary, Anthony Eden, who was passing through the Middle East after visiting Moscow. The main purpose of Maclean's return, one might speculate, may have been to circulate his "blockbuster" report, which was dated November 6, 1943.

Another purpose of Maclean's visit to Cairo was to investigate the possibilities of obtaining aircraft to land in Yugoslavia, as well as to open up the sea route for stores. Furthermore, he was making arrangements for a Partisan delegation to come out and meet with the top people in the Middle East general headquarters. This in itself was anticipating major political decisions because it implied recognition of the Tito Partisans.

With his two journeys to the coast, where he spent quite some time preparing the arrangements for seaborne supplies, and his introductions to Tito and his headquarter's staff, Maclean had no time to see any part of Yugoslavia other than the headquarters in Bosnia and the country en route to the coast. From his own account in *Eastern Approaches* he saw no other parts, neither did he see any Partisan action or battles. Thus his "blockbuster" report—and the claims for the Partisans made in it—were based entirely on Partisan facts, Partisan figures, Partisan claims, Partisan arguments; that is, except for the input by Deakin, whom he met at Tito's headquarters after his return from his first visit to the coast.

Deakin had of course seen action in the desperate escape from the encirclement at Mount Durmitor, but I think it is correct to comment that, apart from that very rough and traumatic battle, he too had experienced only what he saw at Tito's headquarters and what he saw when he went down to the coast to help accept the surrender of the Italian forces. Neither of them had seen anything of any other part of Yugoslavia. Most importantly, neither had seen any part of Serbia.

But the Serbs—both the refugees from the minorities in Bosnia and Croatia and the heartland Serbs, the *Srbijanci*—were what resistance in Yugoslavia was all about. And Serbia was what the civil war was all about.

There may have been another rather sinister source of input for the "blockbuster." There was at Tito's headquarters a flight lieutenant named Kenneth Syers. Syers replaced Stuart and was working for SIS/MI6. His job was collection and collation of intelligence. Vladimir Velebit—who, together with Vladimir Dedijer, looked after the British mission at Tito's headquarters, who came on the delegation to Cairo, and who after the war became Yugoslav ambassador to Great Britain—wrote in his memoirs that Syers was a leftist "relatively active after the war in the British Communist Party." As ambassador for one of the most aggressively communist Eastern European governments in the immediate postwar years, Velebit must be taken seriously in his description of Syers. Syers—together with Deakin, of course— would logically have been one of Maclean's main sources for "blockbuster" facts and figures, particularly in view of the lightning speed with which that authoritative, on-the-spot, eyewitness account was prepared.

In Cairo, Maclean delivered his "blockbuster," and it is probably fair to comment that this report virtually sealed Yugoslavia's fate. In about 5,000 words of effusive praise Maclean presented the Partisan claims and pretensions far better than their best public-relations men could have done. In flowering Foreign Office prose he laid out the Partisan case without any wheretofores, howevers, or notwithstandings. He put their case without any serious consideration of any other viewpoint. He assumed the role of Tito's ambassador. But, even more, he assumed the role of Tito's prosecuting counsel in the case against Mihailović. All that after three weeks' experience at Partisan headquarters. That's mind-boggling.

The claims made in his report were quite preposterous. In the first paragraph it was claimed, "They [the Partisans] count on not losing more than one man killed for five of the enemy against Germans and ten against Ustasi or Cetniks."

Any soldier who has fought the Germans—and by "fight" I mean real fighting, not observing from a distance—knows very well that no army bests them to that extent under any circumstances, let alone a guerrilla rabble. Furthermore, the Loyalists were Serbs, the Partisans were largely Serbs also, and even if they were in some cases better led, it is clearly specious and indeed ludicrous to claim that one bunch of Serbs is going to kill another bunch of Serbs at a rate of ten to one.

And who says they were better led? The Tito propaganda machine said that, and it goes on saying that, in its broken-gramophone-record style. But I don't say so. Some of the Loyalist units were led by first-class regular officers. Stefanović, for example, was as good an officer as I have seen in any army. And the *ustaši*, though politically very nasty people, were German-trained and fierce fighters.

In the same flowery, romantic but dogmatic tone—which even brings in Lawrence of Arabia—Maclean goes on: "They have received the wholehearted support of the civil population. The savage reprisals of the enemy are not taken into consideration."

This is sheer rubbish. In Bosnia, where the Partisan columns lumbered back and forth, the poor, wretched peasants had no say. In Serbia, the largest province of Yugoslavia, where the savage reprisals had taken place at greatest cost, the peasants loathed and feared both the Partisans and the reprisals they had caused in 1941 and might well cause again. I know, because I was in Serbia at the time the report was written, because I was in touch with the population for a year without minders brainwashing me, and because I spoke their language. Maclean was not in Serbia. He was just writing down what Partisan headquarters told him on a visit lasting three weeks before he left again for the coast.

And so it went on. The report claimed that the Partisans had twenty-six divisions and a total of 220,000 men. Actually the divisions were much smaller in November 1943 than they were in the summer of 1944. Yet in the summer of 1944, each division counted only 1,700 to 2,500 men, as can be seen from the reports of BLOs with the Partisans filed in the Public Records Office (WO 202/154A, 162, 196). Thus a generous figure would be 60,000 total Partisans, not 220,000.

Stevan K. Pavlowitch, in his book *Yugoslavia*, gives an estimate made by the correspondent of a London weekly, *The Tablet*, entitled "Tito's Military Achievement: The Legend and the Fact 28th April, 1945." The correspondent, in an analysis based on Partisan communiqués of the time, cross-checked them against one another and against enemy communiqués, and arrived at a total of 60,000 to 80,000. Not 220,000.

In *Disputed Barricades*, Maclean claims that the Germans estimated 111,000 Partisans in December 1943. This figure supports Pavlowitch's figures, because there was massive recruitment between October and December 1943, encouraged by British recognition, the BBC propaganda, and the supplies visibly pouring in to the Partisans. There were also Italians who were recruited and used by the Partisans (particularly later, in the 1944 drive across the Drina against the Četniks). Italian Communist Party sources claim that eventually 60,000 joined the Partisans and 20,000 were killed. These additional recruits explain the increase in German figures for the Partisans from 60,000 or 80,000 in October 1943 to 111,000 in December 1943. But they make total nonsense of the "blockbuster" claim of 220,000 in October 1943.

The "blockbuster" went on to claim 30,000 Partisans in Serbia and Macedonia. Now, this claim was very important, because it was critical to the decisions that were going to be taken. The civil war for Serbia was what this charade was all about. Yet Dugmore, the BLO in Serbia who was with the Partisans from November 1943 until June 1944, stated in his report that the figure was 1,700 Partisans in January 1944—*not* 30,000.

And Maclean himself in a September 1944 report claimed that the Partisans had built up their forces in Serbia from a few scattered detachments "of only a few hundred men each in early 1944." Compare this with his claim in the "blockbuster" of 30,000 for Serbia and Macedonia made in November 1943. And British reports show that there were fewer than 500 men in Macedonia at that stage.

Churchill took his fateful decision of December 10, 1943, after reading Maclean's "blockbuster" figures.

The "blockbuster" refrained from giving specific figures for Mihailović forces—rather wisely—but it still claimed that the Partisans were "ten to twenty times more numerous." Taking the purely fictitious figure of 220,000 claimed for the Partisans, Maclean was saying that the Mihailović forces had 10,000 to 20,000 men in all of Yugoslavia.

In his voluminous report (WO 202/196), Maj. John Henniker-Major (now Lord Henniker), who commanded the missions with the Partisans in Serbia in 1944, gave a figure of 20,000 Četniks in Serbia alone for July-August 1944. That was a year later. It was nine months after we had abandoned Mihailović, three months after Djurić had defected and urged Loyalists to follow him. And it was when the unhappy king was being cajoled by Churchill to urge all Serbs to rally to Tito. It can in no way be reconciled with the "blockbuster" calculation of 10,000 to 20,000 Četniks for all of Yugoslavia in October 1943.

Pavlowitch states,

On a tour of Mihailovich's units in Serbia at the end of 1943 a group of British and American officers estimated that, given arms, he could throw into the battle at least two hundred and fifty to three hundred thousand trained men but that only seventy-two thousand were actually on active service *in Serbia* [emphasis added] of which ten thousand to eleven thousand were fully armed. These figures are slightly below those that can be gleaned from the accounts published abroad since the war by participants in Mihailovich's movement. The Yugoslav military encyclopaedia Belgrade 1964 puts the figure at sixty thousand.

Thus the scholars in Belgrade in 1964—scholars under the control and censorship of the Tito regime—gave a figure of 60,000 for Mihailović in Serbia *alone*, whereas Maclean claimed 10,000 to 20,000 in all of Yugoslavia.

Mr. Rose of the southern department of the Foreign Office wondered why, if the figures were correct, the Partisans had not already cleaned up the Četniks. I wonder why, if the figures were correct, the Partisans with twenty-six divisions comprising 220,000 men had not seen off, cleaned up, and massacred the mere fourteen German divisions of perhaps rather fewer than 100,000 men in Yugoslavia. After all, Maclean (who had not yet seen them in action) had said that the Partisans killed five Germans for every one of their men that they lost.

But seeing off Germans was not what it was all about. The civil war, and hoodwinking the Brits, was what concerned the Partisans.

The whole proposition was utterly ludicrous. It is incredible looking back now that this report was accepted and circulated, and that only Mr. Rose made that comment.

But Fitzroy served with the Special Air Service (SAS), the ultra-elite British raiding force, so he had already learned that "Who Dares Wins." All the same, what cheek.

It is a sobering thought that the people of Yugoslavia may have been subjected to the despotic rule of Tito, to full-blooded communism, and to all that has implied, to poverty and lack of progress—perhaps because of that report. But that may not be true. The whole swing to the Partisans may well have been an inexorable process begun in January 1943 by Churchill himself.

The object of the "blockbuster" is clearly seen by the first recommendation, that support of Mihailović should be discontinued. That was the number one, the vital, the key demand of Josip Broz Tito, the communist. It was the central point of his whole policy. He had to get rid of Mihailović, who was an Orthodox royalist Serb and who represented the major and only viable obstacle to an eventual takeover of Yugoslavia by the Communist Party. More immediately, Mihailović stood in the way of Tito's personal takeover and his despotic rule. In truth, the two resistance movements were probably about equally strong numerically and militarily at that point. But Mihailović controlled Serbia, the crucial arena in the war against the Germans and their communications. If the Allies had built up Mihailović and he blocked those communications, then they would have had to continue supporting him.

Serbia and the Serbs were what it was all about. As minister of defense for the royalist government, Mihailović had first call on Serbian loyalty, even though many Serbs from outside Serbia were already with the Partisans. Amazingly, Tito—that consummate politician—had managed to recruit and motivate the Serbian refugees from the Croatian *ustaša* genocide despite being a Croat himself and despite the tradition of prewar subversive cooperation by the outlawed *ustaša* and the communists. Tito had succeeded in presenting his movement as a national movement, and he thus overcame the ethnic problem as well as disguising his communist totalitarian aims. It was brilliant—typically Tito. Even so, it was not a secure situation until he conquered Serbia.

Tito knew that the only thing that mattered was to get the Western Allies to withdraw recognition from Mihailović and—later—to recognize the Partisans. The withdrawal of recognition from Mihailović was the vital first step. The second would follow as night follows day. Even the question of supplies and arms was secondary. The arms and supplies would be very useful against the Loyalists and also, incidentally, against the Germans if they attacked. But what mattered was to get the Western Allies to pull the ground out from under Mihailović's feet, because that would ensure ultimate Partisan victory in the civil war.

And Maclean, with his "blockbuster," did just that. No wonder Tito honored him so singularly.

The "blockbuster" was rushed out on November 6 so that all of the agencies and all of the key persons could see it before the prime minister's journey to Tehran and before his visit to Cairo on the way back.

The "blockbuster" was outrageous in its arguments. It can be torn to shreds. It was like some others of its author's writings, beautifully and entertainingly phrased but full of poetic license, weak on chronology, not terribly strong on accuracy. On such a technical subject what would a reader do? Glance through it, think what a good report, assume that the facts and the figures surely must be correct—otherwise Brigadier Maclean would surely not have included them—and turn to the recommendation. The first recommendation, of course. The one that mattered the most: sack Mihailović.

Six weeks later they did.

Maclean was not alone in his unqualified enthusiasm for Tito. Maj. Linn Farish, an American liaison officer who dropped in with him on September 17, wrote an equally effusive and sycophantic report, which, it is said, was shown to Stalin at Tehran. Farish, like Maclean and Deakin before him, seems to have been totally captivated by the Partisan propaganda at that stage. He was so excited that he exfiltrated himself to Italy as early as October 26 in order to report in person in Washington. He felt that there was too much to tell in writing. This whole happening reflects the air of Boy Scout unreality of it all. The romantic tone in the "blockbuster," with its reference to Lawrence of Arabia and its John Buchan–G. Henty literary style, built up the suspense. Vlatko Velebit, Tito's chief contact man with the British mission in 1943 and ambassador in London after the war, recently stated rather amusingly,

At Petrovo Polje I was appointed liaison officer with the British mission. . . . I tried to explain to Deakin the exact situation of the Partisan forces in Yugoslavia. Also one of my most important tasks, as I conceived it, was to convince him that the Četniks, the Mihailović people, not only did not fight the enemy but they actually collaborated with him in many various and different ways. My system of indoctrinating Deakin was to take him to a stream nearby, very nice cool and fresh water, where we used to bathe in the whole afternoon: I took always a bunch of captured documents with me, and I read them to him and translated them and I gave him many transcripts for his own use. I think this course of indoctrination, if I may call it that, worked very well because Deakin got more and more convinced that the Mihailović movement was really no good at all, and was really a kind of fifth column supporting the enemy rather than a resistance force.

Deakin stayed convinced, but, to his credit, Farish changed his tune radically after he had seen what the civil war was all about. In due course I will record an extract from a report that he wrote nine months and three drops later. On that occasion he expressed horror at the policies followed by the Western Allies in Yugoslavia. That was in June 1944, and the damage had already been done. His sickeningly gushing and irresponsibly naïve October 1943 report reflected the first glorious rapture. It is a tragedy for Balkan history that Farish was killed in a rather mysterious accident on a mission to Greece the following year. More than any other man, he could—and probably would—have exploded many Partisan myths. Nevertheless, with his first report of October 1943, which supported the "blockbuster" arguments so enthusiastically, he contributed substantially to the arbitrary switch of support from the Loyalists to the Partisans.

Brigadier Armstrong had been dropped to Mihailović about the same time as Maclean was dropped to Tito. Armstrong's job was to join Bailey, who would become his political advisor. Armstrong and Bailey together were the equivalent of Maclean with Tito. They were also charged with submitting a report, and as far as the Foreign Office was concerned, it was planned that they would come out to Cairo and report on the Mihailović movement so that the two sides could be represented in the upcoming policy discussions.

Sir Orme Sargent, the chief Foreign Office official concerned, had specifically indicated that this course of action should be followed. He signaled to Stevenson in Cairo, "We think it would be useful if Brigadier Armstrong and Colonel Bailey were both summoned to Egypt to arrive there at the same time as Brigadier Maclean and Partisan delegation and to be available for consultation during negotiations between commanders in chief and delegations."

It is not clear from the files precisely who told them not to come to Cairo. It seems probable that their journey was overtaken by events. Armstrong and Bailey signaled their report to SOE Cairo. It was dated November 7 and was sent in ninety-two parts. Yes, ninety-two parts. It too consisted of 5,000 words, more or less. It took till November 10 to come through to SOE.

But MO4—that is, SOE Cairo—did not circulate this signal until November 18. Someone in SOE held that signal up in the cipher department for more than a week—a critical week.

MO4 then passed the report to the Minister of State's Office, fiddling the date of origin to read not November 7 but November 18. Perhaps they used the "delay-in-deciphering" trick. In turn the Minister of State's Office sat on the report till November 23, when it was sent to London by slow "saving telegram." (An extremely brief summary was sent November 18.) It seems to have arrived on November 27.

The report was not acknowledged by the Foreign Office until December 10, and then only by a Mr. Nichols, a relatively junior official. Mr. Nichols wrote this analysis: "Armstrong's and Bailey's proposals are certainly a brave effort to solve our Yugoslav problem. They are, however, based on the assumption that the Partisans will be prepared to collaborate in some way or other with Mihailović. It seems to us that Maclean's report has put this possibility quite out of court. That being so Armstrong's proposal rather falls to the ground. Furthermore as you will have seen from our telegrams numbers 99 and 102 to Stevenson we are now convinced that it is necessary to get rid of Mihailović."

Game, set, and match to Maclean. He had been smart. Instead of wasting time fighting the Germans in Yugoslavia, he had gone back to Cairo, where the levers of power were, and made sure that the Foreign Office, through Anthony Eden, was well softened up already in November and that everything was set up for Churchill's blessing in Cairo on December 10. Even junior officials in the Foreign Office knew the score already.

In contrast, Armstrong had hardly hit the quick-release buckle of his parachute harness before he was off with Archie Jack and a force of 2,500 Loyalists on his bridge-blowing spree. Little good did it do him or Mihailović or the Yugoslav people. History should record the lesson to be learned.

I could find no discussion papers in the Foreign Office files considering Armstrong's long report and recommendations. Bailey was subsequently told by Anthony Eden that he had never even seen the report, though the signal had expressly addressed the report to the highest level. I have that story at second hand but see no reason to disbelieve it. The source is impeccable, and it fits.

Yet Brigadier Maclean's report had been seen by all and sundry. It had been printed as a Foreign Office "special paper," and it had been circulated to the Commonwealth prime ministers and even the president of the United States.

Armstrong and Bailey might just as well never have written their report. Indeed, Armstrong and his entourage might just as well never have dropped to Mihailović at all. It certainly would have been much better for the Loyalists if Bailey had not.

But what had happened at the Cairo end? What had happened in SOE when the Armstrong signals started coming through on November 7? Maclean's report had been dated November 6 and was probably just about to be circulated to all and sundry. Surely one would have expected all and sundry to have been advised that Armstrong's report was just coming through, that it would be sent out as soon as received in full, and that everyone should "hold everything" meantime. But this did not happen. What does seem to have happened is that, while sitting on the report for more than a week, MO4 rapidly cobbled together a memorandum intended to force and settle the Mihailović issue with the local Cairo military before the Armstrong report could be seen and studied.

On November 19, MO4 submitted a memorandum titled "Appreciation regarding the military situation in Serbia so as to determine what in the future should be our military policy." This memorandum, with its quaintly styled title redolent of the September 29 memorandum—the authorship of which I attribute to Klugmann though it was signed by Keble—contained Partisan claims and figures culled from Maclean's "blockbuster." It went a great deal further, however, and can only be described as outrageously mendacious. Not tendentious. Mendacious. Inter alia it used alleged statements in signals by British liaison officers with the Loyalists, abridged and out of context—wording that totally misrepresented their views as shown in their subsequent reports—and ended by recommending that support of Mihailović be discontinued, that the British missions be evacuated, and that BLOs be sent to the Partisans in order to arrange reception of supplies in Serbia.

While the Armstrong-Bailey report was simply held up by MO4 until November 18, and by the Minister of State's Office until November 23, this second sinister memorandum was submitted by MO4 on November 19 and was circulated the very next day by the brigadier director of military operations at Army Force Headquarters to the members of the Special Operations Committee. This was the committee in the Middle East Headquarters charged with making the necessary policy decisions. Effectively that action ensured that the ground was prepared in Middle East Headquarters for the abandonment of Mihailović.

The Armstrong-Bailey report seems not to have seen the light of day in Cairo either. Regrettably, the report started with a very long historical dissertation, which paid lip service to the criticisms of Mihailović, which was highly apologetic and quite unnecessarily defensive, and which even accused Mihailović of being pan-Serb. That was too much. The allegation simply was not correct; but it was a super hostage to fortune, with the Tito protagonists using the "integrity" of Yugoslavia as such an important argument. It was also irrelevant because at that stage, obviously, the issue was simply whether the Allies would continue to support Mihailović and the Loyalists in the heart of the country in which they operated—which was all Serbian territory—or help Tito take over the lot.

In summary, the Armstrong-Bailey report recommended that both Tito and Mihailović be required to put their two movements under the control of the Middle East commander in chief, that they be kept apart on the ground, that all political questions be postponed until after the Germans had been driven out, that substantial supplies at an equal level be sent to both movements, and, finally, that a conference to settle it all be set up between Mihailović and Armstrong on the one side and Tito and Maclean on the other, as well as a representative of general headquarters—presumably as mediator. In all logic, these recommendations should have commanded serious attention. After all, the British and American forces fought under joint control of Middle East headquarters. If they had agreed to do so, why should not Mihailović and Tito? If working under Middle East Command was not agreeable to them, why should the Western Allies indulge their foibles and supply them with arms to carry on a civil war?

It did not work out that way. Absolutely not. As Mr. Nichols of the Foreign Office had commented quite correctly, Tito's attitude excluded it. One might very fairly ask why that necessarily meant that the proposal should be summarily dropped. After all, it reflected Bailey's experience in Yugoslavia as the SOE Balkan expert with ten months' study, helped by Armstrong, who had been there nearly two whole months. By contrast, Maclean had written his report after three weeks at Partisan headquarters and little more than a month in the country.

But logical considerations like that do not seem to have been taken into account at all.

This scenario was typical of everything that happened. Tito had aroused the prime minister's curiosity and interest, and Churchill had introduced into play two young, highly talented, and intelligent British individuals he knew, liked, and trusted. These two individuals, Deakin and Maclean, were superb advocates of Tito's case, and they made it with enthusiasm, having seen or heard nothing of the other side of the picture. And their presentations were read avidly at the highest possible level.

In contrast, Mihailović's case was presented by virtually "faceless men" unknown to the majority of the decision-makers. Without regard to the merits of their case, Mihailović's advocates were in no way in the same league as those representing Tito, but it made no difference, because their report was not studied by the decision-makers. The Mihailović case lost by default. The Tito case was trumpeted to high heaven, as it has been ever since.

The Bailey-Armstrong report, though carefully worked out, evenhanded, and logical, was—like everything else Bailey wrote— intensely boring. One needed to be a rather considerable expert on the whole subject in order to understand what Bailey was getting at. Furthermore, he went to great trouble to be a devil's advocate, to include the wheretofores, howevers, and notwithstandings, and to set himself up as judge and jury. His style detracted from his advocacy.

The Maclean "blockbuster," conversely—whatever else it was—was certainly not boring! The Partisan facts and the Partisan figures, spiced with a bit of Lawrence of Arabia and other heroic allusions, made thrilling reading.

It all led inescapably and compellingly to the climactic conclusion: Mihailović had to go. The reader could not have helped being swept up in the current of Maclean's advocacy.

I am not the only one to have wondered what would have happened if Maclean had been dropped to Mihailović instead of to Tito. I reckon the Balkan map would look very different today. I for one would have loved to have Maclean running our show at Mihailović's headquarters, and I'm sure Mihailović would have loved it, too. We would have gotten the support we needed. We would have torn the enemy communications apart.

Maclean, in describing his first meeting with Tito, quoted Napoleon: "In war, it is not men, but the man who counts." He applied it to Tito, and was he right! He could equally have applied it to himself. I have enormous respect for Fitzroy Maclean. Physically, intellectually, and in determination he is outstanding; and he can be charming. But, with sadness, I have to express the opinion that he was an instrument of harm as things worked out in Yugoslavia, and particularly in Serbia.

Yet we cannot forget that, insofar as he was an instrument of harm, he was 100 percent the prime minister's instrument, or that the responsibility and the overriding directives were Churchill's. I believe that Maclean would claim that all of the Foreign Office briefs and military commanders' instructions were subjugated to the prime minister's demand that he report who was killing the most Germans and advise how to kill more. I believe that Tito bamboozled Maclean, but evidently the prime minister was happy with the way things went, and he seemingly did not ask too many questions. Insofar as blame attaches to anybody about anything, it attaches primarily to Churchill.

What matters too in war, as in life (but in war even more so), is being in the right place at the right time. Maclean wasted little time on his first trip to Yugoslavia, getting back to the locus of decision making in time for the foreign secretary's visit and to deliver the "blockbuster." Without waiting for a reply to his recommendations, he made arrangements for a Partisan delegation to be received in Cairo and, among many other things, prepared the delivery of supplies to the Yugoslav coastal islands by sea. He then flew into Yugoslavia to collect Deakin and a Partisan delegation, stopping only briefly before arriving back in Cairo just as the prime minister himself made a stop there on his way back from Tehran. That was quite a performance.

Churchill had a whimsical interest in the Balkans. His young friend Deakin had intrigued him in January with the doings of the shadowy "great guerrilla." That same young friend was now back from his narrow escape at Tito's side and from his stirring adventures on Mount Durmitor. He was accompanied by the new star, Maclean, with whom Churchill had been so impressed in July at Chequers. Maclean had even brought a delegation of real live Partisans with him. The prime minister was tired from his journey to Tehran and his tough talks with Stalin and Roosevelt. As he relaxed among his own in Cairo, it was inevitable that he would accept and welcome whatever was recommended to him by his earnest young protégés.

But it was not only his young protégés in the British mission to Tito who were baying for Loyalist blood. The mendacious MO4 paper of November 19, 1943, had been submitted on November 20 to the Special Operations Committee. No doubt the final recommendation of that committee supported the "blockbuster" and Deakin's "hostile brief" when he was required by the prime minister to spell out the Partisan allegations of Četnik collaboration in the dossier that he had been so assiduously preparing during his five months with Tito.

A memo by the director of military operations dated December 10, 1943, states in the first paragraph, "Since the P.M.'s statement to Mr. Stevenson today that he wanted Mihailovic removed by the end of the year and the King to associate himself with the removal, I think most of the Yugoslav problem, as it confronts the defence committee this evening, is out of date."

And that was that. It was all over, bar the shouting. Perhaps it would be better to phrase that "bar the shooting"—the shooting of the Loyalists by the Partisans, using British and American weapons, in the Yugoslav civil war that soon gathered force as the full weight of the Allies was thrown behind the Partisans and their campaign to "liberate" Serbia. The whirlwind that swept away Draža Mihailović and his work had been unleashed.

Maclean swung into action. With all Middle East headquarters systems "go" for him, the Partisan delegation was trundled around the chiefs of the air force, the chiefs of the navy, the chiefs of whatever. Arms, tanks, close-support training of pilots: they named it, they were promised it, and mostly they got it, because Fitzroy Maclean in full action, with the authority of the prime minister behind him, was an irresistible force.

CHAPTER

7

The Choice

(Between Loyalty to Allies and the Myth of Expediency)

■

I believe in a tragic choice between opposing forces the correct decision was made.

So wrote Sir Alexander Glen in a letter to Nora Beloff in the summer of 1988. Sir Alexander Glen, an eminent wartime naval officer, says that he knew Mihailović personally from pre-occupation days in Belgrade and had a high regard for him. He knew the Partisans from naval and land operations with them. His August 8, 1944, mission report (WO 202/196) shows that he was converted to their viewpoint and accepted their claim that the Četniks were "enemy."

Most eminent people who had to do with the Partisans claim that it was a question of making a choice. As I have already written, Sir Orme Sargent, the senior Foreign Office mandarin involved, insisted that there was a choice between the military "short-term policy" of backing the Partisans and the political "long-term policy" of backing the Loyalists and thus ensuring the return of the monarchy. That was precisely what Tito wanted them to believe and what his many allies insisted was the case; and that idea was fed indirectly into the position papers in the agencies by his dupes. Feeling his oats increasingly after Deakin, and then Maclean, dropped to him, Tito felt strong enough to start thumping the table and presenting the situation regarding Mihailović in "it's him or me" terms. When Deakin started collecting a dossier of evidence against the Loyalists, Tito knew he was on to a winner.

But there was no need for a choice. The Allies could have continued to insist on a policy of no support to aggressors in the civil war. There was nothing whatsoever wrong with that policy. What was wrong was the total absence of its application to the Tito side. No good having a policy if you do not carry it out. Don't get rid of the policy, sack the executives. But no one dared to suggest such a thing.

The Allies could have applied a policy of physical separation. Anthony Eden did not like that course, because it might have established a precedent for postwar decisions and he had an obsession about maintaining the integrity of the prewar Yugoslavia. Anthony Eden's objection was not very logical, because in accepting total support for the Partisans instead of geographical separation of the two movements, he established a far worse precedent for postwar decisions. From a practical viewpoint, the solution of physical separation of the two movements was difficult but possible, if there existed goodwill. Militarily it would have enormously increased the potential manpower reserves for the Allies, for the traditional martial peasant hordes in Serbia itself, the *Srbijanci*, were waiting to be, and were longing to be, mustered behind Mihailović and the Loyalists. This solution would certainly have presented the Germans with an increased garrisoning problem, both in Serbia and elsewhere, particularly if it led to the Partisans' effort being concentrated against the Germans instead of their brothers in the Serbian heartland.

In reality, the decision to abandon Mihailović meant that the main Partisan forces were immediately thrown into the war to wrest Serbia from the Loyalist Četniks. The Mihailović forces defended themselves. They held out on their own for a full year.

In the end, inevitably, some of them were pushed into the hands of the Germans. And for a year the Partisan effort was expended in civil warfare. Serbs were fighting Serbs, and the Germans got a breather.

Instead of promoting the civil war, the Allies could have kept out of the politics and out of the business of massive arms supply, just giving support to attack selected targets. This third possible solution, using Special Air Service or other commando types as liaison officers, could have been very successful indeed under Balkan conditions. I would have loved to take part in it, and I even suggested that policy for Hungary, where nothing else had succeeded. No one wanted to know.

Finally, it is arguable that, if there had to be a choice, if there had to be a "him or me," that choice could have been Mihailović. In any case, when someone says to you, "It's him or me," if you have any pride at all you say, "Thank you, dear sir, then it's him, not you." Any other course is the slippery slope of paying Dane-geld.

In fact, the choice of Mihailović was a viable one. The Loyalists got some moral support at the very beginning, but afterward nothing, either morally or logistically. Never at any time was Mihailović given good reason to drop his guard and trust the British. On a small scale—maybe, in fact, not so very small— some of the Mihailović BLOs did make the Loyalists fight, in spite of the misinformation to the contrary. We did it with virtually no support. Given support and real leadership I have no doubt whatsoever that the Loyalists in Serbia could have been made to fight on a grand scale once they had the arms to make German reprisals an expensive business for the Germans themselves. That was the key.

Churchill, I sincerely believe, made his decision on the basis of his confidence in Deakin and Maclean. But the rest of the hierarchy had to be carried along, and they were guided by the arguments. The mendacious November 19 Keble (Klugmann?) memorandum citing the reasons for recommending Mihailović's ouster epitomized the type of argument used by the Tito protagonists, though it went much further and was blatantly false. There were five parts to this line of argument.

The first was the numbers game. Relative troop strength is always a persuasive argument. So talk up the Partisans, talk down the Loyalists. Thus we had a claimed total strength of twenty-six divisions and 220,000 Partisans in October 1943, when the real figure was probably 60,000 to 80,000. The figure claimed for Mihailović forces by the Partisan protagonists was 10,000 to 20,000; the real figure was probably about 60,000, with reserves of 200,000 or more. As we have seen, for Serbia and Macedonia the claim was made at the time of decision that there were 30,000 Partisans and 15,000 Četniks, while the true figures were about 2,000 Partisans and 40,000 full-time Loyalists with 100,000 reserves. The point of the numbers game was, of course, to establish that Mihailović was a gone coon anyway and that the Allies were sacrificing nothing in abandoning him; but it was a pure confidence trick.

Milovan Djilas, one of Tito's closest colleagues, relates in his books how even Stalin commented on the Partisan exaggerations and warned against overdoing it. But the BLOs just passed on the figures given to them, and nobody at base thought to question them. Oh yes, Mr. Rose did. But none of the top brass even heard him.

Gestapo chief Heinrich Himmler himself said of Tito, in a speech at the Jaegerhoehe on September 21, 1944, "He has the cheek to call a battalion a brigade and we fall for it straight away. A brigade? In heaven's name. The military mind at once imagines a group of six or eight thousand men. A thousand vagabonds who have been herded together suddenly become a brigade." It is intriguing that Fitzroy Maclean, who was the chief victim of Tito's exaggerations, quoted this speech by Himmler, including this extract, in *Disputed Barricades*. Yet he accepted the exaggerations at face value when it suited his "blockbuster" claims.

The second point was the claim that no major sabotage was being undertaken by the Loyalists on the vital rail lines from Belgrade to Salonika and that supporting the Partisans would make the whole difference. The reality was the opposite. Sabotage was actually being done and had been reported through, and, more significantly, Cairo had been told that the line could be kept out of action if only a minimum of support was given. I told them.

Purvis told them. The signals are in the files for all to see in the Public Records Office. The abandonment of Mihailović had the opposite effect. It was not till the late spring of 1944 that the Partisans achieved the level of disruption that we had achieved already in the autumn of 1943. Six months' sabotage on that line was lost by our withdrawal.

The third point was that the population hated the Loyalists and loved the Partisans. I can only speak for Serbia, but there this claim is ludicrous. The Serbs in Serbia were individualists, Loyalists, and monarchists. It's hard to argue with Marxist dialectical materialists because they make their statements dogmatically even when they are claiming that black is white. I can only state what I know to be true.

The fourth point was that Mihailović was a pan-Serb. In fact this was not true at all, but it wouldn't have mattered if he had been. The question at issue in 1943 was whether to support Mihailović in Serbia and to utilize the enormous potential manpower reserve there against the Axis, instead of wasting it in civil war. But the Titoites argued that Yugoslav integrity mattered more and that only the Partisans would maintain it. I suppose the Soviets can claim that the communist rule has held the disparate ethnic groups in Russia together. But that was by force, not choice. And now, in the days of *glasnost,* as the iron fist of dictatorship relaxes its grip, ethnic pride and individualism are reasserting themselves. In Yugoslavia too there are ethnic stirrings.

The Foreign Office kept on about the integrity of Yugoslavia and the need to maintain it, but they had in mind the integrity under a democratic regime and the return of the monarchy. The Titoites exploited the Foreign Office's desire for integrity while covering up the fact that the integrity promised by the Partisans was simply total conformity under dictatorial rule.

The fifth point was that supporting Tito would result in tying down more enemy forces. This I believe to be the most fundamentally flawed argument of all. In fact, there were fewer enemy forces in Yugoslavia in 1944 than in 1941–42. The civil war and the massive diversion by Tito of Partisan armies to "liberate" Serbia from the Loyalists tied down Yugoslavs, not the enemy.

This last point rested on the allegations of collaboration by

Mihailović. I dealt with this question earlier in some detail because it is the main refrain that the Tito protagonists still keep singing. As I showed, collaboration by the Mihailović Loyalists up to the time of decision, that is, up to December 1943, was limited to collaboration with the Italians in Montenegro, specifically encouraged by SOE, and exploitation in a highly intelligent manner of the Nedić state guard in order to obtain intelligence, arms, and potential new recruits. As far as collaboration with Germans is concerned, the Partisan record was infinitely worse than that of the Loyalists. This is where chronology comes in, because in 1944, when the Partisans started their long and costly campaign to "liberate" Serbia, some Loyalists were progressively driven— literally—into the arms of the Germans. For the Tito protagonists today to bay about Mihailović collaboration after we abandoned him is humbug: pure, unadulterated, self-serving hypocrisy.

"Uncle Draža" Mihailović himself, though hunted and harried, actually avoided collaboration at any stage. Isolated and sick, he was eventually captured by a special Partisan task force created to hunt out the remaining Loyalists. And it took them a year after the Germans had gone. Poor exhausted old man. How disgusting can Perfidious Albion become in trying to justify its actions?

The collaboration accusations have been drummed up to justify the betrayal. It is scurrilous, ungracious, and unworthy. To make that point is the main purpose of this book.

It was about the time of the mendacious November 19, 1943 "Appreciation regarding the military situation in Serbia . . ." memorandum that Keble was finally removed from his position dominating MO4. Actually he gave up his post on November 27. The memorandum (WO 202/1581) is not signed, but the covering documents refer to it as having been presented by Keble to the Special Operations Committee. Like the sinister memo of September 29, also presented by Keble, it bears the literary style of Klugmann, his political mentor. Basil Davidson had gone off on his abortive mission to Hungary in mid-August, and Klugmann, though not formally head of the Yugoslav section, was the officer who knew it all and who logically would have drafted a detailed document for that section. Another Colonel Davidson appears in some documents about this time, as does Maj. Gordon Fraser. He was another left-winger who was later used by the BBC to sell the Yugoslav Partisans to the Western public. MO4 certainly seems to have attracted the budding left-wingers.

Colonel Davidson replaced Colonel Tamplin, and certainly he had no time to become an expert on Yugoslav affairs. He could hardly have drafted the memorandum. Gordon Fraser and a Maj. Roger Inman were both temporarily head of the Yugoslav section, but neither seems to have been active in policy matters in 1943; and Deakin took charge from December 13.

Basil Davidson tells us in *Special Operations Europe* that already at the end of 1942, Klugmann had been Keble's protégé and political mentor. Based on these facts, Klugmann had to be the one drafting those documents, conceivably helped by Seton-Watson in his role as political advisor.

Keble got up to one more vital maneuver. On the operational log dated November 17, 1943, there is a signal under the call sign Rapier from Major Seitz, the chief American liaison officer with Mihailović. It contains an assessment by American officers with the Loyalists of the Mihailović situation. The report, with great clarity and objectivity, draws much the same conclusions as the Armstrong-Bailey report, while also stressing Mihailović's distrust of the British. It states that if Mihailović is to perform effectively, he must have much greater support: "To have any effect the British must be able to fly MVITCH not a mere 30 sorties a month, but nearer to 300. . . . The United States now making 7,000 planes a month should be able to provide these planes. There must also be many DC-3s temporarily idle in Italy after Sicilian operations. These would be perfect here."

More significant than the contents of this report—far, far more significant indeed—is the way it was handled. Seitz says in a preamble to the report that it was completed October 25, but it appears on the operations log on November 17. What happened? Was it deliberately held up in the deciphering department of MO4, the technique used to sabotage Major Wallace in Greece, which also led to Keble's downfall?

Something very funny happened, because Keble wrote an

extraordinary letter to a Lieutenant Colonel West of OSS Cairo (FO 371/37618) that refers to the Seitz report and is dated November 14—three days before it appears on the log. So it had been sat on, probably for a long time; the total time lag is twenty-four days.

Keble's November 14 letter, just like the September 19 memo and the November 19 "appreciation," bears all the signs of Klugmann. It challenges the facts given in the Seitz report, and in its tone and style it could have been written by the Partisans' public-relations department under Djilas. The most sinister part of the letter is the last paragraph. It refers to a proposal by Seitz that he leave Mihailović's headquarters and make his way to the Adriatic Coast in order to proceed to Italy and give a full report in person.

That would really have put the cat among the pigeons. Keble (Klugmann?) wrote in this last paragraph, "We are unable to see how they can do this without the assistance either of Partisans or collaborationist Cetniks, both of whom lie between them and the coast. It is our firm rule that no officers with the Partisans or Cetniks shall ever on any account visit the opposite side. Were this to happen, distrust would immediately be sown, and in some cases, lives of officers would be prejudiced. Furthermore, it is clearly undesirable that any officers should have truck with collaborationist Cetniks, and these possibly provide shipping."

Now, that was quite some paragraph. First, Keble and Klugmann were quite obviously out to sabotage Seitz's coming out at that critical stage and telling the truth to the decision-makers. During the very same week MO4 was sitting on the Armstrong-Bailey report. It was also the very week that MO4 was not meeting the request made at the highest level by Sir Orme Sargent that Bailey be brought out to meet Maclean in order to make a joint report.

The second point in the paragraph referred to "our firm rule" that no officer with the Partisans or the Četniks shall ever on any account visit the opposite side. But it was MO4 Cairo that just three months previously had instructed Maj. Neil Selby to try to contact the Partisans, a journey that resulted in his death. Also, Fitzroy Maclean's firm instructions in July, when he was to be dropped to Tito, were to cooperate with Bailey at Mihailović headquarters and to try to bring the two sides together. This "firm policy" of MO4 keeping the two sides apart was something quite new.

And as regards shipping, what was wrong with the Royal Navy? The Royal Navy had picked up Maclean from the coast of Yugoslavia. Why not Seitz?

Clearly, what Keble and Klugmann were after was ramming through the abandonment of Mihailović in the forthcoming vital meetings without any Seitzes or Baileys or Armstrongs putting in their points of view in Cairo. And they succeeded. Whether they would have succeeded without the momentum built up by the Deakin-Maclean activities is something we will never know.

The Seitz report was a joint one with a Captain Mansfield. He was a lawyer in the same firm as "Wild Bill" Donovan, chief of OSS. He later became a distinguished judge. He was no light-weight, and he wrote a first-class report vindicating Mihailović when he eventually left Yugoslavia. He would have greatly em-barrassed the Titomaniacs in Cairo had he and Seitz gotten out in time.

The revolutionary policy advanced by devious methods at MO4 under Keble, with Klugmann at his elbow, was evident in a signal Keble sent on November 22, five days before he left. It was ad-dressed to a Major Dugmore, a BLO who had originally been selected to drop to the Mihailović Loyalists. It came on the heels of the infamous November 19 memorandum to the Special Op-erations Committee. The signal (WO 202/145 sheet X235) reads, in part,

Dugmore from Keble:

1. MVIC now given orders for collaboration with QUIS-LING NEDIC Government and troops.
2. This with clear indication that MVIC intention future collaboration with Germans and present proved collab-oration with Bulgars in resisting Partisans confirms our

appreciation now useless repeat useless send you to
MVIC missions.

3. There are Partisan groups at. . . .

4. MOSTYN DAVIES now en route to BULGARIA resting with group 300 PARTISANS in KOSJAK area . . .
adjacent to MVIC group with Captain Purvis.

5. Our intention if you willing to drop you and W/T operator to MOSTYN DAVIES ostensibly to go BUL-
GARIA with him.

6. He will be instructed to say on your arrival that he doesn't
want you after all.

7. Above story will be your cover to remain with PARTI-
SANS in South SERBIA without risking Tito's refusal if
permission asked.

8. Absolutely necessary we have BLO with W/T there before we make definite break with MVIC and you will
form dropping area later for reinforcement of BLO's.

9. See BLO with MVIC will be given safe passage by Tito
and evacuated by him which will mean you will be only
BLO left in that area.

10. Essential you keep clear of MVIC men and BLOs with
MVIC parties or Tito will evacuate you also.

11. We can only send you and await the events. . . .

Keble really was a man in a hurry. The signal was dated
November 22. It shows Keble, certainly advised by Klugmann,
acting in direct contravention of the established policy of continued support for the Loyalists in Serbia. That policy was not
changed even unofficially until the prime minister indicated on
December 10 that he wanted Mihailović removed. Keble's determination to scupper the Loyalists amounted almost to paranoia.

The signal also showed in paragraph 10 that there had already been discussions with Tito about evacuation of BLOs from
Mihailović, thus preempting all of the discussions supposed to
take place in Cairo with Churchill about future organization in
Yugoslavia. It is very real evidence of confidence tricks. The operational log shows that sorties poured in to Mostyn Davies when
we received none and when even Maclean was complaining that

Tito's headquarters were not receiving enough. It is clear circumstantial evidence that Klugmann, either alone or through Keble, was able to switch the planes to suit his nefarious purposes.

This cable should be framed and hung between Tito's and Mihailović's portraits in the Special Forces Club. It epitomizes the dirty side of Special Operations, which was, I insist, decisive in Tito's grab for power. As evidence of the activities of the dirty-tricks department in Cairo it is only equaled by the Cairo maps that were allegedly prepared from reports by people in the field but were quite simply cooked up.

Keble's head had already been on the block since Maclean's previous visit to Cairo. But with Klugmann at his elbow he still plugged away loyally in his campaign to destroy Mihailović. Thus, living on borrowed time, he prepared the ground for the Maclean coup de grace. That really is ironic. It was Maclean who had given him, Keble, the coup de grace too. On November 27 Keble disappeared from the scene.

On December 13, immediately on his return from Yugoslavia and having delivered to Churchill his "hostile brief" concerning Mihailović's collaboration, Deakin took over as head of the Yugoslav section. Klugmann stayed firmly in place. He was promoted to general staff officer grade 2 on December 15, and the following spring he took over as deputy head of the section. The same faces in the same key places. *Plus ça change* . . .

MO4 quietly disappeared and became Force 133, divorced from the sobering influence of SOE London and firmly under the military in the Middle East, with the Minister of State's Office handling the political side in Cairo for the Maclean mission. This arrangement was just what Maclean had requested.

On December 11, 1943, the day after the prime minister's fateful meetings and while signals warning Mihailović BLOs to get ready to run away to the Partisans were being prepared, Force 133 sent the most extraordinary signal, addressed to Armstrong and Bailey only. Like the sinister September 29 memorandum proposing the abandonment of all noncommunist groups in the Balkans and the MO4 November 19 "appreciation" memo preparing the Special Operations Committee for the Maclean-Deakin December blitzkrieg, this memorandum is written in the style I have come to associate with Klugmann's drafting. The extraordinary nature of this signal lies not so much in its contents—largely a rehash of the November 19 memorandum with "blockbuster" padding—as in the way it was addressed, in its length, and in the way it was covertly aimed at spying eyes. The signal must also be put into the context of the chaos that was about to engulf Mihailović. This chaos was about to be started by the call on Mihailović's sub-missions to defect. It would be intensified by a signal in the Villa Resta series, that is, the British W/T, from the Yugoslav prime minister pressing Mihailović to cooperate with the Western Allies even when they seemed to be acting strangely. And it would be climaxed—if chaos can have a climax—by yet another message, about the same date, on Yugoslav W/T telling Mihailović privately that he was being abandoned.

Here we must pause to consider the implications of a signal in the Public Records Office (WO 202/145 sheet 405A) that shows that all of the highly confidential "head of mission" messages were being deciphered by Yugoslav cipher clerks employed by Bailey.

What's so significant about that? The fact that these clerks would have advised Mihailović of everything immediately. So Mihailović had a pipeline into Bailey's communications. The Force 133 signal—regurgitating the November 19 memo—was bound to be seen by Mihailović. Presumably Klugmann knew this.

Another sinister aspect of the Force 133 signal is the fact that it was copied in full to London. This was a clever move by Force 133. In the absence of refutation from Armstrong and Bailey, the contents and conclusions of the signal would be presumed to have their agreement, and their tacit assent would go into the record. With everything that was happening at the Mihailović headquarters, Armstrong and Bailey would have no time or opportunity to digest a twenty-six-paragraph signal, let alone reply to it. Klugmann would have calculated that. And if Armstrong and Bailey did reply, the well-tested ciphering-delay technique could be used again.

Apart from being pure propaganda, the Force 133 signal was straightforwardly, impudently mendacious. Paragraph 11 stated, "In spite most constant and determined efforts WIX OLD

[Armstrong and Bailey] and other BLOs no repeat no effective demolition activity or important action against enemy has been reported by any BLO with Mihailović forces since OLD's arrival Mihailović's Headquarters last Christmas."

Now, that is ludicrous. The signal was addressed to Bailey and Armstrong, and they knew that it was a flagrant lie. Indeed, for Armstrong it was an insulting lie because he himself had attended the bridge demolitions. Armstrong's headquarters had reported five bridges blown, including one of the biggest in the Balkans. They had reported the action at Prijepolje in which substantial numbers of Germans and Bulgars were killed, prior to the treacherous treatment of the Loyalists at Berane at the time of the Italian surrender. They had reported the taking of Višegrad by 2,500 Loyalists fighting Bulgars, Croats, and Germans and killing at least 200 in one action alone.

Under my code name Fugue and through Neronian (Colonel Cope), I myself had reported three train derailments and two major line demolitions, and MO4 had repeatedly acknowledged my successes (WO 202/131 sheets 54 and 130; WO 202/140 sheets 61 and 62; WO 202/148 sheets 31, 36, 65, 187, and 263; WO 202/145 sheets 12, 23, 25, 30, and 68). Purvis at Roughshod had reported his extensive attacks on the Kumanovo railway station and another major line demolition.

There was a mass of other flagrant lies in the signal—about unfavorable reports from BLOs with Mihailović, about collaboration, and about BBC reporting. The shameful signal finished with a paragraph disclaiming criticism of the Mihailović BLOs' work and praising their "courage, patience and dignity in spite of difficulties caused them by Mihailović and local commanders."

This was a patronizing and disgusting signal by any standards. It was a classic communist-style brainwash combined with a very smart maneuver to put a totally false picture on record. It was very probably copied to the prime minister in Cairo at the time, and it almost certainly contributed to his quite uncharacteristic vitriolic animosity toward Mihailović, which shows itself in his exchanges with the foreign secretary in December and January.

From a historical standpoint the operational log of signals in the files in the Public Records Office is pure gold; the signals tell the truth of what really happened, and they explain a lot. Even then they do not tell our whole story. Significant numbers of my own Fugue signals are missing even though I had contact for only six weeks. The *received wisdom* cannot belie the operational log. Reports, assessments, memorandums could be written with hindsight. The signals could *not*. They show what was really happening. The BLO wrote the signal, and his NCOs and he himself put them into cipher. There was no way in which these signals could substantially misrepresent things. Similarly, the operational log and the geographical positions of the missions when they signaled cannot be fudged. They prove that the maps prepared in Cairo early in December 1943, allegedly from operational reports, were being cooked up. There is no way in which the *received wisdom* can override the facts that come out of the operational log. They give the lie to MO4.

CHAPTER
8
Making a Mess of Betrayal

In Serbia the nights were drawing in, the weather turned colder, and the planes still did not come. We were without greatcoats, and my boots were falling to pieces so that I had to use the local rawhide *opanake* all the time. To avoid unwelcome Partisan attention I switched my sabotage activities to the railroad east of Mount Kukavica, and I made a journey with Jovo Stefanović over the Bulgarian frontier and successfully blew another train. On the journey we caught three Bulgar soldiers in the act of stealing a pig from an old peasant in an isolated holding near the frontier. For two of them it was the last looting expedition that they would ever carry out. The third was disarmed and sent back over the border, where he was probably shot for losing his weapons. The owner of the pig, a gnarled but very agile peasant, who was under fire too as we dispatched the Bulgars, was absolutely delighted and regaled us with his best *rakija*.

With a party from Manić I demolished another length of

track in November, and with men from Andrejević I carried out a rather spectacular derailment in which the train crashed down a high embankment. There were various other minor actions carried out by my three local commanders. But the lack of air sorties and the difficulties in communicating became more and more depressing.

About October 25 we lost W/T contact for good and had to rely on couriers carrying messages to Colonel Cope's headquarters with requests that he send our messages on to Cairo. Looking at the signal files in the Public Records Office, I see that before my set finally expired, I had reported our first line demolition and two derailments. Subsequently, in November, Colonel Cope reported the second line demolition and another derailment on my behalf. Thus Cairo knew of two line demolitions and three derailments. In fact, I personally carried out one more derailment, which did not get reported through, and two others were done by Serbs alone. That should be recorded and underlined, as the Cairo memorandums stated that very little was done and that what was done was carried out by British. Not true. In fact, the reported sabotage, together with our comments, should have persuaded Cairo that there was quite a lot going on. I have traced the signals telling Cairo very clearly that if they sent just a few sorties, we could guarantee regular sabotage of that vital rail line.

Basil Davidson wrote in *Special Operations Europe,* "Against all the evidence of chetnik complicity with the enemy, high policy insisted on sending more British missions to chetnik groups . . . all of these tried to make the chetniks fight; none of them succeeded." Davidson was not the only Partisan proponent to write thus, unfairly vilifying the Loyalists, denigrating our efforts, and misrepresenting what really happened. Our BLO reports, notably those from Roughshod (Robert Purvis), Fugue (Michael Lees), and the second Kosovski area (George More), belie the oft-repeated contention that the Loyalists refused to cooperate. Moreover, those reports have been open to the public since long before *Special Operations Europe* was published. Apart from those three specific reports, there is a mass of signaled evidence of other Loyalist operations. As I have already written, five bridges were destroyed under the supervision of Archie Jack, Armstrong, and Hudson. When the Višegrad bridge was demolished, 2,500 Loyalist troops were involved, and they killed 200 Germans. There was the action when Prijepolje was taken, and again at least 200 Germans were killed in one skirmish alone. There was the ambitious though only partially successful Danube barge operation carried out by Greenwood and Rootham. On August 28, George More reported that Sergeant Belić of his mission had blown the railway line between Priština and Peć, and on September 24 Belić derailed a train in a tunnel. More himself carried out demolitions on three small bridges, with mixed success. But the attacks were made. These are just a few of the operations that were carried out by or with the Loyalists, under British supervision or with British observers. How can Partisan proponents say that we failed to make the Loyalists fight? Are we all liars?

A reading of any of the reports written by the BLOs at Mihailović headquarters, including the two American liaison officers, will show that more than once the headquarters came under enemy fire in their presence. Colonel Seitz paid special tribute to the Loyalist cover given to him when he was so close to the Germans that he "took pot shots with [his] luger." Is that complicity with the enemy? Is Seitz a liar too? There's not going to be room in hell for all of us liars.

The Loyalists did not fight as much or as frequently as we wanted them to. Of course they didn't. But in my area, in the period from September to November 1943, that was not so much because they were unwilling to fight as because of the tiffs between Bailey and Mihailović and the muddles between Djurić and his local BLOs, and because of the total lack of support given to us by Cairo. I can only speak for my area. I do not know about Homolje or Keserović's area other than from the BLO reports. Like me, those BLOs had problems with the Mihailović veto power over sabotage operations at first and with the stopping of supplies when the veto was lifted after Armstrong dropped. But, also like me, they did not know what was going on in Cairo. If they studied the files now, I think that they would understand the Loyalist viewpoint even better.

The BLO reports in the Public Records Office series WO 202/ 162, particularly those of captains Robert Wade and George More, reflect faithfully what was happening. The Loyalist leaders were in no way collaborating. In no way could they be charged with being neutral or inactive. But they were unwilling to commit themselves to all-out, large-scale offensive operations—and to consequent mass reprisals—without clear evidence of continuing British support. The Loyalists were daily receiving reports of increasing support being given to their enemies, along with propaganda that they were to be abandoned. They needed to conserve ammunition. The equivocal attitude of the British necessarily became reflected in an equivocal attitude on their part. If the Loyalists were less aggressive than the Partisans, the British had themselves to blame. The fighting material was the same on both sides. We BLOs have to ask ourselves in each individual case: Did we give them the encouragement they needed? The answer, thanks to Cairo, must be no. We also have to ask: Did we give them the leadership and trust and example they deserved and expected? But we BLOs did not grasp all of this at the time, because we did not appreciate the double game being played by our masters in Cairo.

The reports by George More and Bob Wade (WO 202 154A and 162) are important historically because they simply don't agree with the selective quotations from their signals that were pieced together by MO4 for the December 10 meeting with Churchill to damn the Loyalists.

Robert Purvis's report speaks of building up a force from 50 to 700. He was constantly under pressure from Bulgars, and when the break came he was just initiating a program to attack the railroad line weekly. Purvis gave his Serbs the leadership and example they deserved. I hope I gave mine some leadership too.

We had moved to winter quarters near Oruglica. The mission then consisted of myself, Tomlinson as second in command, Johnson as radio operator, and sergeants Faithful and Lesar. Lesar distinguished himself by cutting down our host Mirko's best plum tree when sent to get a pole as a W/T aerial. By the time we had placated Mirko, we had bought the *šljivovica* supply for an army, so luscious and rich and ever-yielding had been that tree.

It was a nice, friendly little corner, perhaps half an hour's march from the hamlet Oruglica, which was important enough to have a church. It was secluded, while offering a clear enough view of the approach routes. We had a subsidiary building to ourselves, a most unusual arrangement in those parts. It was about fifteen by fifteen feet and had a stove with a real pipe chimney instead of the normal hole in the roof. This was luxury indeed. The door was set above the ground, approached by steps, and there was even a cellar underneath. Mirko wisely kept that shut up with an enormous padlock.

Our simple needs were tended to by two giggling daughters of the house, Milunka and Zagorka, who seemed to greatly enjoy carrying over a pot of bean soup twice daily for our meals, plus our breakfast at dawn—according to Serbian custom, a double slug of double-strength *rakija*.

That plum tree might have been better left alone to go on producing the raw material for the elixir of life in the mountains. The W/T didn't need an aerial—the hand generator had broken down, and we were as far as ever from receiving a new one. Messages sent by courier to Sehmer or Cope for transmission remained unanswered. In the latter half of November, without supplies, without communications, and without any encouragement at all, we began to feel very depressed. The zest had gone out of it. The Loyalists, though still friendly to us, were obviously very concerned at the turn events seemed to be taking, and the increasingly hostile nature of the BBC broadcasts became a very sore and repeatedly raised subject. More and more the mission was withdrawing into itself.

Johnson had developed very nasty sores on his legs, known locally as "sugar." They seemed to be a form of scurvy and were very troublesome. So I decided to take him to Sirinska Banja, a spa in the mountains some two days' march to the west.

We had acquired horses for the expedition. Mine, a bay gelding of some fifteen hands, had belonged to Boon the Australian, and I took him over when Boon went south with Robert

Purvis. I named him Hitler and became very attached to him. He was indefatigable, very sure-footed, and he carried my 200 pounds easily. Together we covered great distances and at considerable speed. I would walk uphill and downhill to spare him and canter long stretches on the flat. Strangely, Hitler never trotted. It was walk or canter or gallop. I taught him to jump small obstacles. At night he would lie on the ground, and I slept with my head resting on his stomach.

We had many adventures together. On one entertaining occasion, when we were reaching the end of our journey to Pranjani, whence we were evacuated, I had had a few drinks, one thing led to another, and I had bet someone, Peter Solly-Flood probably, that I would ride my horse through Čačak and return to drink a toast to Draža Mihailović. Čačak was a town of some size and considerable significance, full of Germans. On entering the main street on Hitler, I encountered two German motorcycles with sidecars. Their riders leapt onto their machines to give chase, but I escaped through the town at full gallop and back into the mountains. Colonel Cope was not amused. Oh dear. Not at all amused. I collected a dressing-down, but I won my bet. Hitler did not let me down. He was fleet of foot at full gallop, and he needed to be that night.

In the intervening forty years I had entirely forgotten the incident until the story was told in the diaries of an American crewman from the bomber *Lucky Strike,* which had crashed near Skoplje. These diaries give a vivid picture of the unstinting help given to Allied servicemen by the Serb mountain folk.

I last saw Hitler standing disconsolately beside the runway with his new master, as I embarked on the plane taking us out. I loved that horse. We'll meet in his Nirvana one day. That day when the truth about everything will come out. It will be a shock for some people.

The other three horses we had acquired for the mission I named Goering, Goebbels, and Himmler. Goering was even shorter than Hitler, probably no more than fourteen hands, but jet-black, round as a barrel, very strong and sturdy. A superb packhorse. Goebbels was dull. I don't remember Himmler very clearly, so I suppose that, like his namesake, he was nondescript.

Anyway, here I was trying to take Johnson to the spas at Sirinska Banja to find a doctor for his sores. I think I picked Goebbels for Johnson. It was the end of November or beginning of December, and we traveled through snow at times. Sirinska Banja, when we reached it, was quite a shock. A paved road led to it from Medvedja, a neighboring village occupied by the Germans from time to time. It had a hotel. A real hotel with three stories—not just two, the sign of great affluence in our part of the world—but, wonder of wonders, three; and there were cafés and shops.

The hotel was closed, but we found lodgings at a café. We went to the spa and bathed in the sulfur baths, an unbelievable luxury, the first hot bath since we left Cairo. This oasis of civilization in the mountains was extraordinary, and apart from the empty hotel, life seemed to go on as it had in peacetime.

In one of the cafés we found a group of Loyalists in British battle dress, and outside we had noticed a very fine black horse with a good army saddle, festooned with leather bags, a rolled blanket, and other finery, which certainly showed up our rough-and-ready gear. The owner introduced himself as Peter Solly-Flood. He was a tall, heavily built Irishman with a handsome, round face and thinning black hair. He wore a major's crown on his British uniform's shoulders.

It transpired that Solly-Flood was on his way to visit us. He had dropped two months previously to the Mihailović headquarters as intelligence officer attached to Brigadier Armstrong and, after a month there, had been sent on a tour of all Mihailović Loyalist commands to bring back a report on their potential value as a striking force in the event of an all-out offensive being started.

Peter and I rode back to Oruglica the next day, leaving Johnson to complete his cure. He proposed to spend three days with us, studying our operations and our area, and then to cross the Leskovac plains in order to visit a Loyalist group on Mount Suva, northeast of Leskovac. Because of the danger of Partisan ambushes in the plains and the need to cross the railway line, which was ever more heavily guarded since our attacks had started, Peter needed a strong escort. He proposed to return to Oruglica, and I decided to accompany him myself in order to carry out an operation about which I had been thinking for some time.

Niš, a large manufacturing town, lay about thirty miles north of Leskovac. A few miles from Niš, at the foot of the mountain, there was an aerodrome with a squadron of Messerschmitts. The Germans used these fighters against the American heavy bombers that passed over en route to bombing the Romanian oilfields at Ploieşti. For some time I had been playing with the idea of carrying out a night attack to blow up, or set fire to, the aircraft on that field. It was not practical to mount such an attack from Oruglica, the distance to the airfield being far too great; but the aerodrome lay only about five hours' march from Mount Suva and was therefore well within the radius for a night attack.

The plan was our most ambitious yet. I planned to take a force from Andrejević's brigade and to cross the plains north of Leskovac, derailing a train as we crossed the line and crossing the Morava River at the foot of Mount Suva. Peter needed three days to conduct his business with the Loyalist commander, and I would borrow guides and, with a party of twenty men, attack the airfield on the second night. We planned to return by a route south of Leskovac and cut the railroad line for a second time on our journey back.

But, as usual, fate intervened. Peter and I were at Barje all kitted up and ready to go when my Serbian orderly, Mile, came galloping down the road from Oruglica riding Peter's black horse. He brought me a letter from Tomlinson enclosing a message from Neronian that was short and to the point. It advised us that the decision to break with Mihailović would probably be taken within the next few days, that we should cease operations, and that we should make a break to the Partisans if we could. It told us that Mihailović had not been informed of this decision.

Our immediate problem was that quite literally we were poised to go. The men were actually assembled. The railway charges had been made up, and the "sticky bombs" for attaching to the aircraft fuel tanks had been improvised and prepared. We had even had our last meal. Once again, with forty years' hindsight, as on the occasion four months before when we were ordered to call off the attack on the Vladički Han bridge, I now feel strongly that I ought to have gone ahead. It would not have altered anything in history, but at least I could have taken the memory of an airfield attack through life with me. The airfield-attack technique developed by the SAS in the African desert has always fascinated me, and I have always regretted never having done one.

I cobbled together an excuse to the effect that the major had received orders to return to Mihailović headquarters, and for that reason we would not go. But the Loyalists knew that something more had happened. After all the careful preparation that had taken place they had to ask themselves: Why does he not go ahead with the derailments and the airfield attack and let this major go back to Mihailović? Peter's presence was in no way necessary for the attacks, and they could hardly have forgotten the amount of pressure we had been putting on them to do sabotage.

Sheepishly we trekked back from Barje to Oruglica, feeling the mistrustful eyes of Pešić and his men on our backs as we moved off. For more than six months these Loyalists had been our allies, our companions, our friends; and that signal had changed everything irrevocably. We were used to living surrounded by enemies: the efficient Germans, the cruel Bulgars, the treacherous Arnauti bands, the small SS-style Ljotić forces, Serbian mercenaries, and even the Nedić state guard, who sometimes, but far from always, looked the other way when we passed; and, of course, the Partisans. We did not call the latter "enemies," though sometimes now I wonder why. Among all of these more or less hostile forces, the Loyalists had been unquestioningly on our side; and so too had been the local population. What was going to happen now?

It was my problem, not Peter's, because I knew the area. I was the BLO. I rejected a break to the Partisans. There was only the small band on the Radan, still about 200 strong, and there was no British officer with them yet as far as we knew. They certainly had courier links to other main Partisan groups to the west, but their routes passed through miles and miles of 100 percent Loyalist country. To trek from the southeastern corner through most of Serbia, a party of six with Johnson still very lame, with Partisan guides and escorts maybe, but through country hostile to them, would be a very hazardous undertaking. Indeed, outright impossible.

Add to that the ethics of it all. We had lived with these Loyalists, and we had been under enemy fire with them. We had enjoyed their protection and their assistance to undertake sabotage against the real enemy, risking reprisals against their compatriots. Those compatriots, the Serbian population, had shown us nothing but enthusiastic welcome and assistance.

Now some bloody Croat communist in the Bosnian wastelands, wanting to exploit the circumstances in order to create a despotic state, had hoodwinked the British into supporting him and selling out Serbia to the Soviets. The Serbs, the traditional allies of Britain, had already suffered the appalling genocide perpetrated by the Croat *ustaša*. That this Croat Soviet agent should get away with this was too much.

So it seemed to us in the heartland of Serbia in December 1943.

With hindsight, that was not totally fair. The Croat population of Yugoslavia wanted communism probably even less than the Serbs; and Tito's main source of cannon fodder was Serbian refugees from the *ustaša* genocide. But we were in no mood for hair-splitting in apportioning blame.

It should be recorded here that the Loyalists made no move whatsoever to put minders on us, either then or during the next three and a half months before we started our evacuation march. With the population totally loyal to them, no doubt they knew every move we made; but at least they behaved like the gentlemen they were. They never controlled us and never reproached us. Whereas Manić had been very blunt and outspoken at times during the summer and autumn—a roughness that was reciprocated by me—after the decision to abandon them was taken, there were never any hard words.

We decided to split up. Peter took Lesar with him and set off for the Neronian headquarters, where there was W/T contact. Tomlinson, Johnson, Faithful, and I started to bury equipment surreptitiously while holding our breath and preparing to tell any Loyalists who might see us that everything was wonderful. It was not easy and it was not convincing, and I must truthfully admit that there were moments that early dawn when I knew how those three Croat spies who had been taken prisoner by Djurić's men the day before the Bulgar attack in early June must have felt as they awaited their probable execution and, sweating, anticipated in their imagination the knives slicing through their jugulars.

Their throats were slit. That ours were not was by the grace of God— not thanks to the manner in which the affair was handled by Force 133.

Only more than forty years later did I come to know the almost unbelievable circumstances of that first move in the definitive break with the Loyalists. Missions that still had W/T contact had received some sort of questionnaire sent from Cairo a few days earlier, the purpose of which was to gauge the support enjoyed by Mihailović personally. This questionnaire reflected serious consideration in the Foreign Office of continuing support to the Loyalist local commands in Serbia while getting King Peter to replace Mihailović personally. This was an idea that may have emanated from Bailey; it certainly had his keen support later. It almost certainly arose from the messy Cope incident, when Djurić was playing politics and when Mihailović's instructions were translated incorrectly. It suffered from the disadvantage that the Serb population idolized Mihailović personally. Furthermore, his replacement would not have appeased Tito, who was intent on eliminating not only Mihailović but any independent Loyalist movement whatsoever.

Following that questionnaire came a signal to the missions dated December 7. The copy to Roughshod (Purvis) said, "Unlikely more sorties will reach you next few months than necessary for maintenance mission. Tell the Jugs this due bad weather which in fact principal reason. Continue attempts attack L of C [lines of communication] but do not rely on sorties in plans. Hope send you full explanation next few days."

This devious signal must have surprised Robert, because he knew by then that drops were pouring in just south of us to the Mostyn Davies missions with the Partisans. And forty years later I found the signals all about those drops in the PRO files.

Then, about the twelfth or thirteenth, came the fateful message passed on to us by Colonel Cope's headquarters. We had seen nothing of the previous messages, having been out of touch, and they had not been sent on to us by Neronian.

Bob Wade, a BLO with the Keserović Korpus to the west of Djurić's area, did indeed make a break with the Partisans, leaving December 14. He sent a message to Colonel Hudson, who was with Cvetić, another subcommander of Keserović's, and Hudson joined him. They traveled around with a Partisan group for quite some time before being evacuated. The Partisans, part of a corps commanded by the well-known Peko Dapčević, were delighted at this development and made great play of having the British with them as they tried to fight their way into Serbia. Bob Wade states in his report (WO 202/162) that Captain More had already "blown the gaffe" to Marković on December 14, and Wade's break too made it quite clear to the Loyalists what was going on. Marković was fairly close to Mihailović's headquarters, and Mihailović certainly knew everything by December 15 if not much sooner.

But Mihailović had not been informed officially. Indeed, Armstrong himself was not informed until about December 16. Cairo later excused this lapse on the grounds that they had been too busy. How Cairo reconciled telling us sub-missions to run away if we could, while not informing Armstrong or Mihailović, is an interesting mystery, but if Klugmann was involved, no doubt he was just adhering to the standard communist method of creating chaos. It is not clear to what extent Klugmann was in on the act. Deakin took over officially on December 13, and surely he was dealing with this literally life-and-death matter himself from then on. But the key messages were probably drafted on December 11 or 12. It's a mystery that only the official historian, with access to all of the secret files, can unlock.

The Yugoslavs in Cairo and the Loyalists locally were very apprehensive about what was going on, and they feared that they would be sold out to the Soviets in a deal made by the superpowers. Certainly they knew that high-level talks were taking place in Tehran. The BBC Yugoslav News reported it, and Manić mentioned it to me. Recently, Archie Jack wrote to me of how a Mihailović intelligence officer had told him at that time, without criticism or reproach, that the Allies had handed over Yugoslavia to the communists and Russia. "He hoped that we had achieved something of importance in return." He would have been horrified to learn that Yugoslavia was sold out gratuitously by Churchill, not in a deal with Stalin.

I can neither comprehend nor forgive the amateurish instruction that left the decision to run away or stick it out to individual sub-missions, thus ensuring that the Loyalists would know immediately that we were abandoning them while the majority of the British would have to remain in Loyalist hands.

The Tito proponents already claimed then, without any hard evidence whatsoever and against all logic, that Terence Atherton had been murdered and Neil Selby betrayed by "the Četniks." If the Partisan sympathizers in Cairo were sincere in believing that the Loyalist Četniks were murderers and betrayers, why, in heaven's name, did they create a situation in which some missions would run and others would stay hostage in far worse circumstances than existed at the time of the Atherton and Selby incidents? This demonstration of Perfidious Albion gave the Loyalists every justification to take us hostage, kill us, or betray us to the Gestapo.

Of course that would have given the communists more grist for their propaganda machines, and we would not have lived to tell the tale.

For some days there was no more news. No courier reached us in Oruglica from Neronian, and we could have been in another world. Finally I decided to move toward the Neronian mission headquarters through the mountainous country to the west. If we encountered hostility, we could turn south into the Kosovo area, eventually making for Albania—a last and unappealing resort.

After fourteen hours' hard marching we were already a couple of hours beyond Sirinska Banja when we met Peter Solly-Flood and Harry Lesar coming back. At first they pulled our legs— and we were hardly in the mood for a joke—by telling us that the Neronian party had all been shot by Djurić. Such was the situation that for a moment the news rang true.

The truth, however, was almost an anticlimax. It appeared that Mihailović had been informed and had agreed to the evacuation of the missions with only one proviso, namely, that any evacuation would be done through his channels and not by the Partisans. Brigadier Armstrong had given orders that we remain in southeastern Serbia for the time being and concentrate in Oruglica. So we trekked back the long march to Oruglica and back into Mirko's house, and Peter Solly-Flood moved in with us. It would be stretching things to say that our friends had hardly noticed our absence. But they were polite enough not to comment on it.

We settled into our winter quarters. The snow was constant now and at times so deep that movement was at best arduous and often nigh impossible. We experimented with homemade skis, but they did not function well. In any case, the hills were too intensely wooded and the snow frequently damp, and always powdery and heavy. We tried to make snowshoes, but that too proved a failure. So we just struggled about as best we could in boots—those lucky enough still to have boots—and in *opanake* for those like me who had none.

The other missions moved into the area. Purvis and Boon came from the south. Cope, Raw, and Sehmer set up Neronian mission nearby, and Hawksworth and a few others were somewhere around. We kept to ourselves in my Fugue mission in Mirko's house. Peter Solly-Flood, who had firmly attached himself to me and my mission, spent some time each day at the Neronian headquarters and told us what was going on and what we needed to know—at least that was what I thought, till forty years later I found from the files that there was plenty going on of which I had no knowledge. Once again I was reminded of Micky Thomas's remark that MO4 would let me down.

CHAPTER
9
The Truth about the Bridges Affair

■

I first learned of the bridges affair when I came to study the files in the Public Records Office forty years later. The bridge-demolition idea arose sometime in late November, before the abandonment of Mihailović, very probably in the Middle East Headquarters Special Operations Committee. It may have come from Ralph Skrine Stevenson, the ambassador to the legitimate Yugoslav government and (so paradoxically) political rear link in Cairo for Maclean's mission to Tito. From whom the idea came and when it arose are not material—suffice that it was seized on by all concerned rather quickly. It was also received enthusiastically in the Foreign Office and by the secretary of state himself. As a test of his sincerity, Mihailović would be asked to blow two bridges, one in the Ibar Valley and one in the Morava Valley.

While all of the agencies accepted the plan with enthusiasm, their approaches were not identical. The southern department of the Foreign Office under Douglas Howard was fair and objective as always. Howard evidently hoped that Mihailović might respond and that, at least, the air could be cleared of cant and propaganda. The southern department was constantly irritated by the anti-Mihailović attitude of MO4 and the Minister of State's Office in Cairo and had said so bluntly more than once.

Stevenson, conversely, cabled to the Foreign Office on December 3 that the Special Operations Committee, in considering future policy concerning Mihailović, had "agreed that, as most of the evidence regarding Mihailović's collaboration with the enemy could not be published, it was desirable to strengthen the case against him by calling upon him to carry out by a given date some specific operations known to be within his power, in the certain knowledge that he would fail to do so."

On December 8 Stevenson reported to the Foreign Office that the Special Operations Committee had agreed on the operations they wanted Mihailović to carry out and that Armstrong was being instructed not to admit to Mihailović that the request was intended as a test. Simultaneously King Peter and the Yugoslav government were being informed simply that Mihailović had been requested to carry out important operations, and it was suggested to King Peter that he might like to send a message asking Mihailović to do his best to comply.

The message from the commander in chief was received by Brigadier Armstrong on December 8, 1943. The message (WO 202/139 sheet 33) specifies the bridges to be destroyed and simultaneous subsidiary attacks, and requests Mihailović's *agreement* by December 29. The date, and the fact that it referred to his *"agreement,"* are totally clear in the message. Mihailović asked for time to study the message but refused Brigadier Armstrong an interview on December 9. That has no significance here, however, because by then the two were no longer on speaking terms.

Politics and diplomacy were not Armstrong's major qualities. Mihailović was not to know that Armstrong too was being cuckolded by Force 133. Inevitably he blamed Armstrong personally for the British deceit. No wonder they no longer spoke to each other.

Then in Cairo on December 10 the prime minister told Stevenson that he wanted Mihailović "removed" by the end of the month. No ifs or buts or maybes and not subject to performance in the bridge operations. That and nothing more, other than that the prime minister wanted the king to "associate himself with the removal." Perhaps Churchill did not even know of the proposed bridge operation. That could very well have been so.

The likelihood of this state of affairs is strengthened by a message to Armstrong from Force 133 dated December 17 (WO 202/145 sheet 384) stating, "C-in-C's request to MVIC re specific operation was sent with object getting first-hand and clearer evidence of MVIC's attitude. Wish to make it clear to you that decision to break [with Mihailović] is being considered on its own merits irrespective of MVIC's attitude toward these operations." In short, the real purpose of the bridges-operation demand was to strengthen the justification for the abandonment of the Loyalists, which was already a fait accompli.

Yet Mihailović had been requested by the commander in chief Middle East, by the Yugoslav prime minister, and by his king—who in turn had been urged by the British government so to request—to mount a major operation and to confirm that he could and would do so. The *confirmation* was to be given by December 29.

On or about December 12, Force 133 banged off the signals to the British missions telling the BLOs to prepare to desert to the Partisans if they could; and on or about December 14, George More blew the gaffe to Marković, and Bob Wade actually moved off. Hudson joined him, and they reached Peko Dapčević's Partisan unit on December 27. Dapčević was endeavoring to break into Serbia from the west. So by about December 15 Mihailović knew quite definitely that the curtain had gone up on the final act and that he was going to be abandoned; and the Partisans were making huge propaganda from it all. Actually, Mihailović may already have heard the news via the Yugoslav premier in Cairo, who had been given the word unofficially (WO 202/145).

In spite of this cataclysmic new development, Mihailović received Brigadier Armstrong on December 23, as previously agreed, to give him his reply to the commander in chief's request. Nothing passed between them in regard to Force 133's instructions to BLOs to defect or the disappearance of Wade and Hudson and why they had gone; or even about the intention to abandon him. Mihailović calmly asked Armstrong for a further fourteen days to enable him to move troops and explosives into position for the attacks. What was wrong with that? He needed every minute of that period, with the distances and logistics involved, through the mountains in the winter. The armchair warriors in Cairo would not have understood that. In any case, they were praying desperately that he would decline the request, thus falling for their ploy to use the refusal to justify the break.

The commander in chief's message had only requested Mihailović to *reply* by December 29. He had done so, and he had said in effect that he could carry out the operations as soon as he could move men and materials into position. The ploy had failed.

Accompanied by Loyalists, Archie Jack had already reconnoitered the Ibar bridge and was moving into position, preparing to blow it. Maj. Eric Greenwood, the senior BLO in the Homolje region, had moved up as observer for the other bridge demolition. Wade's report shows that, already before he set out for the Partisans, there had been discussions with Cvetić and Marković about blowing bridges; and the Angelica mission signal files show that Mihailović actually gave clear instructions before the December 23 meeting. He was therefore totally serious about complying with General Wilson's signaled request after studying the general's message.

Mihailović had a small problem, because the force that would have tackled the Ibar bridge had had to be sent to defend Serbian territory being invaded by Peko Dapčević's Partisans—the unit to which Wade and Hudson had moved. Archie Jack confirms, however, that even with the reduced force at his disposal his bridge over the Ibar could have been blown. But Cairo expressly refused permission when Armstrong sought the go-ahead in January. Whatever the situation regarding the northern Morava bridge, we in Oruglica could surely have organized the destruction of Vladički Han over the southern Morava.

After all, on December 12 Peter Solly-Flood and I had set out to blow trains and attack an airfield with sixty men from Andrejević. *We* stopped that operation, not the Loyalists. *They* were bitterly disappointed. In spite of their knowledge that they were being dumped, I believe sincerely that I could have gotten the necessary troops, particularly as Mihailović had definitely authorized the operation. I also had the explosives in my caches. Don't blame the Loyalists because Colonel Cope failed to get on with the job before Cairo called the operations off.

So evidently we were available, with forces sufficiently in position by about mid-January, and with Mihailović having agreed expressly in principle to blow the bridges well before his December 29 deadline for *agreement*.

Mihailović raised two more points with Armstrong. He pointed out quite correctly that he was very short of ammunition and had no heavy weapons, but he does not seem to have been attempting to use this as an excuse for refusal, merely to point out the difficulties and the possibility of failure in the event.

He also asked that ammunition expended should be replaced after the operations. This was a very reasonable request, because Mihailović knew by then that he was going to be abandoned whatever he did about the bridge demolitions. Ammunition had become his main worry because he knew that he would receive no supplies from the British in future, while his enemies were flush with Allied supplies.

Following the meeting with Armstrong, Mihailović signaled to Cairo on December 27, and in a personal message to General Wilson he made these points about ammunition and heavy weapons. The signal was positive and could only be interpreted to mean that Mihailović intended to carry out the attacks as soon as logistically possible. The signal (WO 202/136) is susceptible of no other interpretation. On the same day Armstrong confirmed in a signal to Cairo that Archie Jack had already left to watch the Ibar attack and assist in the demolition, and that he was sending Greenwood to watch the northern Morava operation. Armstrong asked for confirmation that arms and ammunition would in fact be replenished, though he stressed that he had not promised them to Mihailović. There is a shameful, flippantly written memorandum (WO 202/136) in which Force 133 ridiculed the idea of replacing ammunition used.

On December 28, Stevenson signaled to the Foreign Office in a totally negative manner. In the first paragraph he said that Mihailović had declined to discuss the commander in chief's message on December 9, pleading pressure of work. This was false. Mihailović declined to discuss it because he wanted to study the signal before committing himself and because he was no longer on friendly speaking terms with Armstrong. In the second paragraph, Stevenson expressed the opinion that Mihailović's intention was to "procrastinate." He had nothing except his own imagination and his evident animosity toward Mihailović on which to base this allegation. In the third paragraph he reported the interview between Armstrong and Mihailović on December 23 "when General Mihailovic stated that he could not undertake the operations until sometime during first half of January." In the next paragraph he stated that he thought it unlikely that Mihailović would make any really serious attempt to carry out the operations but that he might try to put up some kind of show "as it is clear that he knows that we are considering withdrawal of our support from him." Stevenson concludes: "We are therefore fully justified, despite his statement that he will carry out the operations requested sometime during the first half of January, in taking a decision now to withdraw our support from him. That decision as stated in my telegram number 212 is based on his attitude of non cooperation over a long period and on the fact that he has approved collaboration of his subordinate leaders with the enemy."

May the reader remember that this is the same Ralph Skrine Stevenson who was at the December 10 Cairo meeting with Churchill, Fitzroy Maclean, and Bill Deakin. The memorandum above bespeaks Stevenson's ill will toward Mihailović.

In a memo of December 30 (FO 371/37620) a Mr. Dew of the Foreign Office commented, "I cannot help feeling that Cairo is making up a case for the immediate break with Mihailovic in order that this may smooth the way with Tito. But if Tito won't play on the other issues then we shall have broken with Mihailović without any *quid pro quo* and may drive Mihailović into the arms of the Germans and alienate all those with him." It seems that the Foreign Office had not yet hoisted in that the break had effectively already taken place on December 10.

On January 1, 1944, Sir Orme Sargent added his assessment:

> I agree with Mr. Dew that we ought for tactical reasons to go slow over Mihailovic. . . .
>
> It is essential therefore that our evidence of his treachery should be unanswerable: it is not enough merely to denounce him for not having attacked the Germans more vigorously or as vigorously as Tito. In that aspect he after all is no worse than have been the Greek guerillas during all these months of civil war. Nor can we condemn Mihailovic because he fights the Partisans. It would be impossible to prove that Mihailović was the first to attack. . . . Lastly we come to the unfortunate test operation. Here, as I foresaw, we have got ourselves into difficulty, for Mihailovic has not refused, as Mr. Stevenson hoped he would but has merely asked for a fortnight's grace in order to make his plans. . . . On the strength of this reply Mr. Stevenson says we are fully justified in taking a decision now to withdraw our support from him: I beg to differ. I think it makes it increasingly difficult and is an additional reason for putting off our decision for the time being, in the hopes of some fresh development.

Sir Orme Sargent added a post scriptum:

> PS As we are obviously drifting to a position where we shall have to break with Mihailovic whatever he says or does, we ought I'm sure to clear this test operation out of the way as soon as possible. I would be inclined therefore to tell Mihailovic straight away that as he was not able to carry out the operation on the 29th December we no longer wish him to do so and therefore withdraw our request.

On the margin of this memo, Anthony Eden, the secretary of state, wrote, "There is force in all this. Perhaps we had better await final decision by the PM on his reply to Tito before we decide about above."

Sir Orme Sargent had overlooked the fact that Mihailović had not been requested to *carry out* the operation by December 29. That would have been logistically impossible, apart from anything else. He had been asked only to *give his reply* by that date, and he had given his affirmative reply in his signal of December 27. He had also indicated orally to Brigadier Armstrong on December 23 that he would carry out the operations.

More significantly, Mihailović had actually issued demolition-preparation orders to Marković and Cvetić immediately after receiving the request and before his meeting with Armstrong on December 23. This is very important, because the *received wisdom* has stated unequivocally that Mihailović was asked to carry out these bridge operations by December 29 and that he refused. This is almost a gospel tenet of the *received wisdom*, and it is totally and demonstrably false.

True to form, Force 133 had anticipated the Foreign Office. A signal of January 2, 1944 (WO 202/145 sheet 465), stated,

> Following is paraphrase of message sent to Brigadier Armstrong 31st December. The limit of 29th December imposed by C-in-C in his message to Mihailovic is considered reasonable and stores previously dropped are considered sufficient for tasks indicated. [Armstrong had not had a drop for three months.] These operations were considered with these considerations in mind and C-in-C's message was sent for purpose of securing further evidence of Mihailovic's procrastination and his general unwillingness to implement previous promises to operate against the enemy. Even if these operations had been successfully carried out within time limit this would not necessarily have influenced future policy of HMG towards Mihailovic which is being formulated independently on general grounds given below. No further supplies, therefore, will be dropped for these operations.

The signal went on with the usual spiel about Mihailović's collaboration. But Perfidious Albion made a grave error in talking about the December 29 "time limit." It would have been one degree less awkward to have said openly that everything had been changed by the prime minister following his meeting with Maclean, Deakin, and Stevenson on December 10, that the demolition of the bridges had become an embarrassing subject, and that action by the Loyalists was the last thing that London or Cairo wanted.

Both the Yugoslav premier and Tito had been informed around December 11 that the British government was abandoning Mihailović. King Peter was put in an invidious position in that, urged by the British, he had just signaled Mihailović pressing him to cooperate in the operations. Now he was being informed that the British government had decided to break with Mihailović and wished him, King Peter, to associate himself with the break.

Informing Tito on December 11 that the BLOs with Mihailović were being withdrawn had made the decision to abandon the Loyalists irreversible, whatever happened about the bridges or, indeed, about the king or anything else, for Tito's public-relations men immediately spread the news.

Prior to receiving the signal calling off the operation, Armstrong had moved off to join Archie Jack, and Mihailović had moved west to reinforce the defense against Peko Dapčević's Partisans. Shortly thereafter Armstrong was told definitely that any sabotage action by the British, with Četnik help or alone, must also cease.

After the war, an American liaison officer swore under oath that he had received a signal sent by the British from Cairo instructing him not to take part in the destruction of the antimony mine at Lisa, which was supplying about one-quarter of the total Axis requirements and for which he had obtained on December 12 a firm commitment from Mihailović to provide the necessary forces. He stated, "I never learned until later on the exact reason for that reply, but I was told by British officers to whom I had shown this cable that perhaps they were dropping Mihailović completely at that time, the British were going to evacuate and they felt that they just did not want to have anything more to do with any activity in that area." (This incident appears in David Martin's *Patriot or Traitor*.)

The break was by then open knowledge throughout the country. The Loyalists knew that they were on their own and that survival was the name of the game. They could not yet know that the British were not only abandoning them but preparing to throw massive resources against them—and even to bomb and machine-gun them.

In *Disputed Barricades*, Fitzroy Maclean states unequivocally that Mihailović was given three months to carry out the bridge demolitions and that he had to agree by December 29. The demand for *agreement* by that date is, of course, correct, and the deadline was met by Mihailović. The claim that Mihailović had three months to carry out the job and failed is clearly as inaccurate and specious as Sir Orme Sargent's understanding that Mihailović was asked to complete the demolitions by December 29. These totally contradictory statements are typical of the historical confusion arising from the desperate endeavors to blacken Mihailović and thus justify his abandonment.

CHAPTER
10
The Pawns in the Great Game
The British Missions to Mihailović

■

Forty years later in the Public Records Office I read the December 13 signal to Neronian about the impending break with Mihailović. The first paragraph said, "HMG may decide to drop Mihailović which would involve evacuation all British personnel." It added the order, "Burn this signal after reading."

The second paragraph said that the only method of evacuation was through Partisan territory. The signal then went on to give sketchy and erroneous details of where the nearest Partisan detachments were supposed to be. It said, "You must decide whether you can conduct your mission to Partisan territory with or without help local Mihailovic commanders. If this not considered possible with fair degree of safety remain at your HQ and we shall try arrange safe evacuation by pressure Jug government and BBC propaganda. Treat this as warning order. Will signal when decision made. Be prepared to move 15th if journey to Partisans considered possible." Force 133 advised Neronian that Tito had guaranteed safe-conduct. This confirmed that Tito had already been told that the BLOs were going to be withdrawn from Mihailović, or at least that withdrawal was under urgent consideration. Mihailović, the minister of defense of the royal Yugoslav government, had not been told, and he had just been asked to carry out a series of major demolitions. That was curious to say the least.

Tito, the Partisan leaders, and their masters the Soviets must have had a song of joy in their hearts. No doubt Stalin signaled to Tito, code-named Walter, "Push, boys. Keep pushing. One last push and we'll be there."

Logically Tito had to notify all of his local commanders down to individual detachment level—no easy or quick job—so that the guarantee of safe-conduct could be honored. But Force 133 had told Neronian, "Burn this signal after reading." That means the signal is top secret.

Top secret from whom? From Mihailović, of course. From our hosts and allies. How unworthy, and how unbelievably amateurish. The Partisans were laughing all the way to their propaganda megaphones and sending out their political agents to spread around the good news: "The Brits are pulling the rug out from under Mihailović. The Commies are coming. Hurrah! Hurrah!" But they would not have said "Commies." "The National Liberation Army" was the high-sounding name they used, though it meant the same thing. No doubt they added, "Put a good face on it because we are the masters now." Yet the Loyalists were not to be told by us BLOs. Cairo evidently wanted them to hear the bad news on the Grapevine. Or, maybe, Cairo just hadn't thought it all through.

But there was another funny little twist to this saga. Forty years later I find from the signal log that on December 15 Colonel Cope and Major Raw at Neronian had already had a chat with Djurić about it all, in spite of the order to burn the signal.

A signal to Neronian dated December 14 had asked specifically, "What are your chances of getting Djuric to agree to your moving over to the Partisans and of him possibly joining you later in the event of public declaration being issued?" So Cope and Raw, with their penchant for playing politics with Djurić, who was being advised by his mistress, the communist and erstwhile German spy Vera Pešić, were entitled to take this cable as an authority to talk to him. Amazingly, they did just that. The operational log (WO 202/145 sheets 350–520) contains a mass of signals on this very subject. The naïveté and irresponsibility, indeed childishness, of the Force 133 signals horrify me even today.

So there was a chaotic situation. The Loyalists all knew by then that the crunch had come. George More had told Marković. Wade had left. Cope, Raw, and Sehmer—who was by then back at Neronian, having been with Purvis in Kozjak and Boon in Crna Gora—were into another session of cozy chats with Djurić. In these meetings Djurić was once again playing politics while making soothing noises about the methods of evacuation. And dear old Brigadier Armstrong, a real fighting soldier who did not want to know about politics, poor fellow, was busy still organizing the bridge blowing and waiting to be received by Mihailović to talk about the demolitions as if nothing had happened. I'd have loved to be a fly on the wall in that December 23 talk. But there wasn't a wall. They were in the woods, *u sumi*.

A chaotic situation was just what James Klugmann—the high priest of communist ideology and methods—would no doubt have desired. Keble, his protector and political disciple, had now left SOE. Deakin was just back from Tito's headquarters and formally took charge as of December 13. According to letters from Deakin written in 1988, his second in command was a Major Wilson, one of the many transients in the Yugoslav section. He appears nowhere in the records I have found. Gordon Fraser was somewhere around, but it was Klugmann who was strategically placed. As of December 15, 1943, he was director of coordination, a key position.

Formally, Deakin was very much in charge. The prime minister signaled to the foreign secretary on Christmas Day 1943, "I am the more convinced that Maclean should get back as soon as possible to Tito. In Deakin you have a man who has eight months of experience of Tito and a bond with him through being wounded by the same bomb. Deakin is an Oxford don of great ability and, of course, is well known to me having helped me with Marlborough for four years before the war. You couldn't have a better set-up than Deakin in Cairo and Maclean with Tito."

Tito might well have expressed the same sentiment in even more effusive terms. No wonder that what Maclean wanted Maclean got. Moreover, the files show that—almost by definition— what Maclean wanted was what Tito wanted or what he thought Tito wanted . . . and Tito was nothing if not demanding. He wanted, and got, the jackpot.

This signal shows the prime minister's enormous regard for Deakin and, if further evidence were needed, constitutes yet another indication that Maclean and Deakin were reflecting the prime minister's wishes throughout and acting virtually as his agent, though they informed and counseled him.

Deakin is indeed a remarkable man. How could he be otherwise when he merited such confidence on the part of the outstanding statesman and war leader of the century? Although in my opinion he seems to have played a mistaken and weak hand with Tito, and subsequently to have been less than objective about Mihailović and the Loyalists, his outstanding personal qualities, his reputed bravery in action, and his patriotism cannot be gainsaid. On Durmitor and afterward he must have been a credit to the nation. The Partisans were incredibly brave, whatever else, and if—as Vane Ivanović has written—they made a point of commenting on Deakin's acquitting himself valiantly, then he must have been a very brave man indeed.

Deakin, like Maclean, was very much his own man and paddling his own canoe. His actions and words throughout are consistent with those of a conservative totally sold on the Partisans. A very gullible conservative perhaps. It is clear that the prime minister had complete trust in Deakin and respect for his views. He was and remains evidently a man of outstanding intellect and persuasive power, and his quiet influence undoubtedly played a great role in the prime minister's decisions and appreciations; and the regard he enjoys in historical circles ensures that his views continue to enjoy precedence. I feel that he was and is sadly wrong about Tito and Mihailović, but the views are clearly his own and held with total, indeed blind, sincerity.

My opinion of Deakin's political role when with Tito and of his influence on Yugoslav history—the *received wisdom*—is, of course, a personal view. It is never malicious. I write what I am sure is true, and I discount what I believe to be false. This book is written to fill a wide gap and paint the other side of the picture as regards Mihailović and Tito, but I want to be fair and absolutely truthful. Deakin, a historian, will appreciate this stance, and he will recognize my viewpoint, my purpose, and my sincerity even if he cannot radically alter his own, different, forty-year-old opinion. Maybe he has changed his views or will do so. Stranger things have happened. After all, Djilas and Dedijer, who were so close to Tito, have changed theirs radically. Even the Anglophobe and previously dedicated communist Koča Popović has now become a "democrat."

It probably was time for Churchill's "ambassador/leader," Maclean, to get back into Yugoslavia. He had been at Tito's headquarters for only about three weeks since his appointment four and a half months previously. Furthermore, Tito wanted to get on with the job of liquidating Mihailović and the Loyalists by any and every means as quickly as possible, and he wanted all the help he could get from the British now that the policy had been cleared with Churchill. The Loyalists knew this, and there we were with them, looking as if nothing had happened and discussing the unpleasant weather. It was all rather embarrassing. It would have been disturbing had we known what I know now and have recorded above about the chaos created by Cairo's messages. Charitably, I assume that Deakin had not had time yet to grasp the reins.

Although the *received wisdom* insists that the Loyalists were collaborators, they were still gentlemen. Nothing could alter that. With hindsight I do not remember any of us sitting around chewing our fingernails and wondering which execution technique they would use on us—the stab to the heart or the slit throat. At least everybody put a good face on it, and I for one only had that nasty thought in those drab and scary sleepless hours around four in the morning, after a good ration of *šljivovica* the night before.

I do not recollect worrying unduly, but we did an awful lot of sitting around. The winter was a hard one, and movement was very difficult. No doubt this was very fortunate, for it deterred Axis cleanup operations as well.

We sat around from Christmastime, when all of the south-eastern Serbian missions concentrated in Oruglica, until the news finally came through in the second half of February that the evacuation heralded on December 13 would go ahead. After letting him stew for just two months, Cairo finally sent Mihailović a signal signed by General Wilson advising him that the British government had decided to evacuate the BLOs and would he kindly so arrange. And Mihailović sent a very dignified reply that he would kindly so arrange provided the matter went through his own channels and not through those of the Partisans.

In the meantime Bailey and the American, Mansfield, had left and been evacuated via Mihailović's Loyalist channels—not "collaborationist Četnik" channels, as Keble would have it—to the coast, where they were picked up by the Royal Navy. The Loyalists organized it very well, and the Partisans did not get in the way, because they were not where Keble pretended they were. This was the journey that Keble earlier in November had declined to countenance for his own reasons. Keble's reasons were probably nefarious. Presumably he wanted to block Seitz and Mansfield from coming out with their report before the abandonment of Mihailović was a fait accompli.

Seitz came out with Wade and Hudson via Partisan channels. Colonel Hudson, the first British liaison officer to enter Yugoslavia two and a half years before, was held up in Berane while routine Partisan personnel movements took priority.

But what had happened to delay matters for those two months and to give us BLOs this nice, relaxing, winter-sports holiday in the mountains?

On November 29 Tito had called together the "Council for National Liberation" in Jajce, with delegates from all over Yugoslavia. While the meeting was stage-managed by the Communist Party, for cosmetic purposes it was designed so as to give it the appearance of a national assembly, a parliament. It issued resolutions repudiating the royal Yugoslav government and any other government created in the country or outside the country "against the will of the people of Yugoslavia." In Partisanspeak, "the will of the people of Yugoslavia" meant Tito's will. The resolutions held King Peter personally responsible for the actions of Mihailović and stated specifically, "King Peter Karadjordjević is forbidden to return to the country with the proviso that the question of the king and/or monarchy will be decided by the people itself by its own will after the liberation of the whole country." In straight language, that meant that the dynasty's days were numbered.

In Cairo the significance of these decisions was not understood at first, for a very odd reason. Stalin had been very angry about the Jajce resolutions because they contravened his advice to Tito. Stalin had been telling him, "For Pete's sake go steady, 'Walter.' You're going to blow it. You're going altogether too fast at it. The Brits will catch on." So Radio Free Yugoslavia had censored the report and toned it down. For not very clear reasons the British mission to Tito followed the same policy as Stalin, omitting to warn Cairo or London that the real resolutions were highly provocative and clearly designed to present a fait accompli as regards the Yugoslav government and the king.

Maclean had, of course, been away from the Yugoslav Partisan headquarters since October 5, delivering his "blockbuster" and keeping the pressure on Cairo for the elimination of Mihailović. But Deakin was at the mission. Why did he fail to tip off Cairo or London about the provocative nature of the Jajce decisions?

About December 18, Ralph Skrine Stevenson spoke officially to the Soviet ambassador in Cairo about the plans to evacuate the missions with Mihailović, letting the Russians know that Mihailović was being abandoned. Not surprisingly, Radio Free Yugoslavia, based in Soviet territory, promptly gave full support to the Jajce resolutions and came out with their full text, not censored and not toned down. The need to be careful about the provocative nature of the text had passed. They knew they had won concerning Mihailović. Now they went after the king, which put Churchill in a bind. Whereas he had not hesitated to abandon Mihailović, deposing King Peter was quite another ball game.

Incredibly, Churchill seems to have gotten the idea from somewhere that the Partisans could be tamed and dealt with. This was, of course, the Klugmann-Keble theme of the infamous September 29 memorandum. In sacrificing Mihailović, Tito's rival, Churchill seems to have thought that he could earn the gratitude of the "great guerrilla" and persuade him to have the king back immediately and free elections afterward; in other words, that he could educate the lifelong communist revolutionary and turn him into a democrat.

Stevenson told the Foreign Office in the first paragraph of a signal (WO 201/1599) dated December 20, 1943, that according to Brigadier Maclean the "Free Yugoslavia Broadcast was at variance with the attitude of Tito as known to him [Maclean] and to the Partisan Delegation now in Alexandria." Perhaps Stevenson advised Churchill to the same effect, that is, that Tito might be amenable to the king's return.

Maclean's *Disputed Barricades*, however, gives the text of a message from Tito to Moscow early in October that makes it unequivocally clear that the government and the king would not be allowed to return to Yugoslavia. Maclean cannot therefore have meant to tell Stevenson that Tito would tolerate the king's return. There must have been a misunderstanding between Maclean and Stevenson. If so, it evidently misled the prime minister in a crucial matter at a critical moment.

Furthermore, in the third paragraph of his signal number 194, Stevenson revealed that the Partisan delegation had brought copies of the Jajce resolutions to Cairo, which were sent on to London in the Foreign Office bag. Those copies were not censored or toned-down versions, and they made it very clear that Tito wanted to eat his cake and have it too. First he wanted Mihailović out, out, out. Then, for good measure, he wanted the innocuous Croatian Peasant Party leader Dr. Maček, then under house arrest in Croatia, out. And the Yugoslav government in exile out and, of course, King Peter out. In parenthesis they no doubt would have resolved to demand Cruise missiles and Thatcher out, if they had been able to look forward forty-odd years.

One can only suppose that Stevenson had not bothered to

read the resolutions before sending them off in the bag. Otherwise his statement to the effect that Maclean had said that the Radio Free Yugoslavia broadcast was at variance with the attitude of the Partisan delegation would have made no sense at all. But one also finds it almost unbelievable that Brigadier Maclean himself found the broadcast, which only reported faithfully what had happened at Jajce, at variance with Tito's attitude—because Tito presided at Jajce.

All of this seems to imply that, whereas Tito had made his position about the king totally and abundantly clear early in October and again at Jajce in November, Churchill had been led to believe at the December 10 Cairo meeting that, perhaps, if Mihailović were eliminated, Tito would accept the king back.

The prime minister appears to have been remarkably inconsistent during the course of his meetings in Cairo in December 1943. In his writings Maclean has made a great deal out of the exchange with Churchill in which he claims to have warned the prime minister that there would be a full communist setup in Yugoslavia after the war. The prime minister merely asked him whether he, Maclean, intended to live there and, on being told that Maclean did not, commented that he did not propose to do so either, and they shouldn't worry about what happened. Furthermore, Maclean himself seems to have given Tito considerable encouragement to be intransigent about the king. In *Disputed Barricades* he tells us that Tito, in passing the Jajce resolutions to Moscow, had stated that the British government would not insist on supporting the king and the Yugoslav government in exile. Maclean explains this rather surprising claim by Tito in a footnote. He says that, in accordance with his instructions, he had told Tito that the British government had no intention of trying to impose any government on the Yugoslav people against their will. The future form of government was a matter that they would have to decide for themselves after the war.

That is pretty clever semantics. The British government made it very clear to Maclean that it steadfastly wished the king to return and wished there to be free elections. Yet Maclean was quite clear in his own mind that the communists were going to rule and that their definition of "the people's choice" did not involve kings or free elections. Whatever he said to Tito, the latter had interpreted it in his own way, and it should have been fully clear to Maclean, and through him to the prime minister, that Tito had no intention whatsoever of having the king back.

Anthony Eden signaled Stevenson on December 20, 1943 (WO 202/138), "I have just received a communication from Soviet Government saying that they would favour action tending to unite the various elements in Yugoslavia against the common enemy." The Soviets may just have been fishing in troubled waters. They may have been angry with Tito for risking blowing it with the British. Milovan Djilas has told us that Stalin even advised Tito to restore the king and stick a knife in his back later. But Churchill and his Cairo team were in top gear in their determination to deliver the coup de grace to the Loyalists. Moscow's olive branch—if that is what it was—went unregarded. Without any need to placate Stalin, Churchill was determined to chop Mihailović for Tito's sake—an extraordinary attitude for an unrepentant right-winger like Winston Spencer Churchill.

Even Moscow wondered whether it made sense to waste the potentially huge Serbian Loyalist force waiting to stage their *ustanak* to coincide with the forthcoming Allied effort. But the British were totally sold on helping Tito win his civil war regardless.

On center stage of this whole charade was that superb political animal Tito, quietly pushing the British back step by step. First he had gotten Deakin to spend months assembling a dossier of Partisan allegations of Mihailović misdoings. Whether these were right or wrong, I contend that Deakin should have replied simply, "Shut up about all of that. I am not interested. Stop the civil war." Then Maclean arrived and the "blockbuster" emerged from his short visit to Bosnia, which he delivered in Cairo to the foreign secretary, who by coincidence happened to be there. Then the idea was sown of sending a high-level Partisan delegation to Cairo to participate in highest-level talks about logistical help to the Partisans, which visit happened to take place just when the prime minister was passing through; and Deakin, the prime minister's protégé, flew out to Cairo with them.

And at each stage the pressure came on a little harder.

From December 20 till early February there was a massive exchange of signals among the prime minister, the foreign secretary, Mr. Stevenson, Brigadier Maclean, and General Wilson. Even the frequently drunk Randolph Churchill, who had not yet dropped into Yugoslavia but who seems to have fancied himself a pundit, got into the act. And there was a shower of "for your information" signals to the Commonwealth prime ministers and the president of the United States. The prime minister wanted Tito to accept the king back. He even seemed to have a romantic idea of Brigadier Maclean, complete with kilt billowing around his ears, parachuting into Tito's headquarters with young King Peter—crown, Sten gun, and all—to fight alongside the Partisans. The king's return was a sine qua non, as was an acceptance by Tito that there would be free elections. Step by step he and the Foreign Office were pushed back, with Tito committing himself to absolutely nothing material. Maclean was kept busy devising formulas that committed Tito to nothing but kept the prime minister in play. At the end of the day Tito had everything he wanted. Later on, a straw man called Šubašić was inveigled to form a government acceptable to Tito and totally under Tito's control. It was inevitable, of course, that Šubašić got squeezed out too in the end.

It was a brilliant political performance by Tito. The smartest part of it all was that—while all of this was going on and while Tito was brushing aside the British efforts to hold on to something, anything, just any minute quid pro quo—everybody in Cairo was working away like crazy to harness all possible assistance for Tito and, with Maclean's fantastic drive and organizational ability, to create a support organization for the Partisans the like of which they could never have expected in their wildest dreams. The more obdurate Tito became, the more he got. But he was sophisticated and brilliant, because he operated so calmly, coolly, and politely—as long as no one mentioned the name Mihailović (or Maček). Furthermore, with Maclean smoothing the way with the British at every stage, everyone thought it was the British who were getting a good deal.

No one anywhere at any time seems to have stopped for

even one minute to ask, "Where else does Tito have to go?" The Germans had rebuffed him in the Zagreb talks, though the British did not know it at the time. He had to fight the Germans because they fought him. Just as simple as that. The Russians could not supply him yet. But everybody was conned into believing that Tito was doing the Western Allies a good turn by accepting their massive logistical support—in order to prepare himself for a showdown with Mihailović and his Loyalists, which was the only thing that interested Tito.

Anthony Eden dragged his feet. On December 29 he signaled (PREM 511/2) to Churchill, "I am doubtful whether we should tell Tito that we are prepared to have no further dealings with MVIC first because we have not yet got conclusive evidence of his misbehaviour and secondly because tactically it would seem better to keep this up our sleeves as a concession to Tito if he is prepared to discuss working with the King at all." But Churchill had been convinced otherwise. He replied, "Everything Deakin and Maclean said and all the reports received showed that he [Mihailović] had been in active collaboration with the Germans."

And where did we, the BLOs with Mihailović, fit into this? We became pawns in a game of international blackmail.

The ploy seems to have started in the Foreign Office, as the signal quoted above would indicate. This is surprising, because till then it was the Foreign Office that had attempted to play things straight and clean. In all probability it came not from the officials but from the foreign secretary himself: the idea that our continued presence with Mihailović could be used to blackmail Tito. Whoever it came from, His Majesty's Government decided to postpone our evacuation. The general idea was that, failing acceptance by Tito of the return of the king, the missions to Mihailović would be "reactivated." That point is quite clear. No equivocation or muddle in the signals. And they kept it up for two months.

So we sat there for that whole time, looking at the murk and the snow, playing bridge, drinking *šljivovica*, and waking at four in the morning, from time to time asking ourselves whether we would be dispatched in the merciful or the unmerciful manner when the time came.

With long signals flashing back and forth, no one seems to have thought out exactly how we could be "reactivated" and what they were going to say to Mihailović. Evidently the decision-makers were thinking that, just because Mihailović had not yet been formally advised of his abandonment, he could be told in a casual manner in due course, if appropriate, that His Majesty's Government had now decided to reactivate the British mission. Or that the mission had never been deactivated. "Forget everything that has happened in the past two months; forget the BBC propaganda that you are a collaborator; forget the Radio Free Yugoslavia broadcasts saying that you have been abandoned by the British; forget that 20,000 tons of supplies have been delivered to the islands and the mainland for Tito's forces; forget the twenty-four planeloads being dropped to one mission in one night in the south of Serbia to Vukmanović-Tempo in order to help him invade from the south; forget the BLOs now being dropped to the Partisans in Serbia proper. Just count your blessings and count yourself reinstated. Lucky you!"

This was precisely the unbelievably cavalier treatment Cairo had accorded Mihailović from beginning to end.

Of course, it was ludicrous to think that an old campaigner like Tito would have been impressed by leaving the BLOs as a means of blackmail. It was obvious that he would call the bluff. That it was a despicable way to treat an ally does not seem to have concerned anyone. And nobody seems to have worried much about us. Lip service was paid to concern for our welfare, but the chairborne warriors in Whitehall and Cairo shut their desks and went off to drink in their clubs without paying more than that. No doubt the lip movement improved their thirst.

To underline the irresponsible and incompetent nature of this whole episode, in *Disputed Barricades* Maclean tells us that already in mid-January he returned to Tito's headquarters carrying a letter from Churchill that confirmed that the British would give no further military help to Mihailović and would be glad if the royal Yugoslav government would dismiss him from their councils. So why were we waiting in the murk and snow, with those knives being sharpened around us?

Brigadier Armstrong signaled Cairo on February 7,

I had quite enough when you panicked my officers into deserting their sub-missions without knowing what was happening all the time and Mihailović thinking that I had issued the orders making me object of ridicule now you apparently want me to sit and do nothing sorry but that is not my idea of fighting the Bosh . . . can you please clarify sortie question I am completely bewildered. . . .

You inform me maintenance sorties will be flown to mission . . . we have now been without a sortie for three and a half months and the impression left in minds of all ranks who have spoken to me not only me but in other missions is one of complete lack of sympathy and appreciation by you of our conditions. Why should Sgt. Wren have only one shirt . . . why should Jill [Major Archie Jack] have to wear borrowed boots because his can only be sent by underground methods to enemy occupied town Raska for repair . . . surely you realise difference between slush and mud on a mountain track and a bus ride from flat to Rustem buildings . . . why should we have to seriously risk security by having to send Jugs to buy stores. . . .

Armstrong was no wimp. He was a gutsy fighting soldier with a remarkable record of service in action. But he had had a bellyful. When detailed to drop into Yugoslavia, he had made it clear that he did not want to go if politics was involved. He was no intellectual, no scribbler like Bailey.

Cairo had kept him, the general, in the dark when they advised the sub-missions on December 13 to be ready to take off. He was not told until about December 16, presumably so that he could not tell Mihailović. What a way to treat a general, and what a silly amateurish trick. If Mihailović was collaborating with the Germans, one might ask why we had not been handed over by then.

In correspondence in 1988 with me, Sir William Deakin wrote of what a big worry the evacuation of the BLOs had been and implied that a great job had been done. There can be two opinions about that. In my opinion a study of the signals in the operational log shows no great job, just an appallingly incompetent and unimaginative pouring-out of contradictory signals. Whether great job or incompetent muddle, we would have liked to have just one of the numerous planes being sent only a few miles south of us at the end of January to prepare Vukmanović-Tempo to invade our area. Could Cairo not have spared us just 2 tons out of the 20,000 sent to Tito in all?

There was absolutely no reason whatsoever not to send a plane; at least one would have kept us with boots on our feet. The hardships did not in fact happen to worry me personally. I am a peasant and a bit of a masochist, and I am used to being kicked in the teeth. But that really was a regrettable way to treat the troops.

We got a drop in southeastern Serbia in the end. I do not know whether Armstrong got one too after waiting three and a half months. I must remember to ask Archie Jack one day whether his boots ever came back from Raška.

That was the trouble with MO4 and the secret intelligence agencies. Everyone for himself and devil take the hindmost. And no esprit de corps. If the troops suffered, too bad! As Micky Thomas had said to me when I told him that I was joining SOE, "Don't cry if you get let down. They have a very bad reputation." I am not crying. I am just telling the world in the hope that it does not happen again. With the public sympathy for modern-day hostages, and the new positive attitude regarding the armed forces, it is hardly possible today to believe the attitude shown us by the policy-makers and our base in Cairo when they were trying to blackmail Tito, using us as the pawns.

CHAPTER

11

All Over, Bar the Shooting

■

Sometime in the first half of February, His Majesty's Government finally figured out that Tito could not be coerced, that he was the one who was doing all the coercing, and that he would go on doing so. So on or about February 17 the definitive order for evacuation came through. Tito, as usual, already knew it from Maclean. We sat around in Oruglica at least until sometime in March before starting the trek to Mihailović's headquarters near Pranjani, where the airstrip was going to be prepared.

I do not keep a diary, and the signals files do not tell me when it was that I went off and derailed a train single-handed, because it never got reported through. Looking back over the signal files and reading all of the chitchat between Neronian headquarters and Armstrong's headquarters about sabotage, and all of the ideas going back and forth, such as blowing the bridge at Vladički Han, I can now understand Colonel Cope's shocked reaction when one fine morning I wandered round to his headquarters and told him— treating it all as a bit of a lark— that, by the way, I had derailed a train just north of Leskovac the night before last. And that it had been rather successful. Silly me. I thought he would think it a big joke, as well as rather a good show. But not a bit of it. He was very upset. He squeaked aplenty.

After reading the signals in the operational log forty years later, I can see that it would have been highly embarrassing to him with all the talk that had been going on: Would they? Wouldn't they? Did they? Didn't they? But *I* did not know anything about the larger issues at the time.

Peter Solly-Flood might have told me, because he was in on some of the talks, though I do not believe he knew about all of the cloud-cuckoo-land signals going back and forth from Armstrong's headquarters through Cairo to Neronian and back. I see from sheet 616 on WO 202/140 that there was a Neronian message dated February 2, 1944: "Position British becoming delicate. Can now do no repeat no sabotage." I guess I blew the train a few days after that. So Colonel Cope's reaction is comprehensible, as is Neronian's failure to report it to Cairo.

Having been given quite a dressing-down, I was a bit sore. I had not expected it at all. My immediate reaction was to feel that jealousy might be involved. I had done a lot of sabotage prior to the break without any guidance, instructions, or help from Neronian— as had Robert Purvis, though he did get some help and encouragement from Sehmer. Actually, Sehmer had even tried to get Cairo to switch my sorties to Purvis; no matter, because there were no sorties anyway. Now here was I, with all of the missions together in Oruglica, being all of a sudden self-propelled again. Cope must have felt a bit awkward, I suppose. He was particularly sharp with me and less so with Peter— which was not correct, as Peter was senior to me. The discrepancy strengthened my feelings that jealousy was involved. As I say, I had not seen the signals.

Actually, it was Peter who triggered it all. He did not want to leave Yugoslavia without having seen some action, and he was as disappointed as I was when we had to call off our proposed operations against the railways and the Niš airfield just as we were

setting off for Mount Suva on December 13. All very comprehensible and commendable. When he suggested we might do
something, I jumped at the idea and said it would have to be a
train derailment and that we would have to go via the plains,
because the route over Mount Kukavica over the Bulgarian border would be quite impassable in the snow without guides. It was
bad enough even between Oruglica and Barje.

There must have been a thaw, because we were able to take
our horses to Barje and thence down to a large village in the
plains quite close to Lebane. We stabled our horses and enjoyed
a substantial and tasty meal with too much *rakija* and an excellent
pink wine. I had planned to march about four hours from our
halting place in order to hit the railway just north of Leskovac.
We had no guides. Although I had been in that area at night
more than once before on similar expeditions, it would be an
overstatement to say that I knew the country. But by marching
due north and aiming for the line a few miles beyond Leskovac
I could be guided by the lights of the town.

We crossed the Lebane-Leskovac road about an hour after
we started. It was there that Peter and I somehow became separated. As there was a Bulgar patrol moving up the road, I was
not going to hang around to wait for Peter. No matter. I had
made up the charge, I was carrying it, and I could manage very
well on my own. I guessed Peter would follow along hoping to
find me. He was not the type of man to give up and go back.
There was only one charge and only one person needed to fix it.
The purpose of a second person was, of course, mainly to provide covering fire. If we were unlucky and came up to the line
just beside an armed sentry, a companion would be useful, indeed rather necessary. There would be no time for me to deal
with sentries and get the charge fixed on the rail ahead of the
oncoming train. If Peter did not arrive in time, or if he missed
the direction I was following, I would just have to hope that I
did not encounter an alert armed guard at my point of derailment.

The railway line in the region toward which I was heading
was straight, so I was relying on my technique of punching the

front of the train off the rails. The charge was a fifteen-pounder, gun cotton blocks nailed to a board three blocks deep.

The going was heavy on that approach march. When I eventually neared the embankment, a line of telegraph poles loomed out of the gloom ahead. I guessed that the telegraph line would be placed within fifty yards of the permanent way, and the embankment seemed not that far off. I did not want to get too close. If I was spotted, that would be the end of the business for that evening. I was only prepared for a derailment. Without covering troops, explosives, detonators, or fuse there was nothing I could do to damage the line itself. I would be able to see precisely how distant the line was when the first train came through. It was my practice always to let one go through first, in order to plan the derailment spot and to spot the position of the sentries, block-houses, or other problems.

No train came. I was sweating profusely when I arrived, after struggling through the ankle-deep mud and slush in the fields, but after an hour of waiting in the drizzle I was becoming wet and cold. The hour lengthened to an hour and a half, then two hours. It was after midnight, and it was imperative that I get away by one o'clock. I had a four-hour trek back to the horses and several hours' riding before I reached the foothills; and I ought to be there by dawn. I felt cheated. What were the transport people up to? We reckoned on at least two trains per hour on that line, often much more. Dirty dogs!

At last I heard a train whistle. It came from the north. I would have to take this one. I could not risk waiting, and at any rate I was getting too cold. I slung my Sten over my back by the strap, took the charge in my right hand—the train was coming from the left—and the fog signal in my left. As the headlights twinkled in the distance, I crouched. The lights came nearer. It must be about 600 yards now. I started to run. I ran and I ran, but I had misjudged the distance and found myself literally racing the train, which mercifully had slowed down a bit because the station was only two or three miles ahead.

That locomotive looked enormous. Already it was towering over me, belching sparks and smoke from its tall, old-fashioned stack. The cowcatcher stretched out in front and to the sides. Just as well the charge board, which was placed on its edge, was narrow enough that it did not protrude over the rails. The cowcatcher had to go clear over the charge first without ripping it off the rail. The charge was timed to go off alongside the very front wheels. I tore across the path, scrambled up the ten-foot embankment, and slammed the charge against the rail. There was no time to wedge it, or even to pray that it would stick in position. I clipped on the fog signal—an easy, one-hand, half-second job, thank God—and leaped backward.

I hit the ground, and the charge blew over my head. It was as close as that. One stumble, one second of hesitation, and I would not have made it. But I did, and I was protected by the steep embankment. The tearing, wrenching metal went the other way. The charge unleashed a hail of stones, but the bulk went clear over my head. Only a few spattered around me, stones that had been blown straight up in the air and were falling back. I recovered my Sten, which I had dropped when falling down, and raised it as fire from an automatic opened up in front of me from the route on which I had come. It failed to fire; it had lost its magazine. My spare magazines from my deep hip pocket had fallen out too. I had only a handgun, an American-made .45.

I ran along the path below the embankment toward Leskovac but soon realized that the automatic fire was not following me. It had been directed at the derailed carriages.

After 100 yards or so I turned south toward the mountains but before doing so had a good look at the line. The locomotive had been thrown clear down the other bank. The leading cars were at a right angle to the tracks, telescoped into each other. It was a classically clean job, and there was nothing more for me to do. Half-running, half-walking, I struggled through the mud on the long, hard journey back.

Peter was not back with the horses. I fed and watered both and left without delay but saddled Peter's horse all ready for him. I was back at Oruglica by noon, but Peter did not arrive till midnight. He had pulled down the telegraph line but had been delayed borrowing a rope from a house in order to do the job. By sheer chance he had arrived just in time to open up on the train with his Sten—and nearly shoot me too. And on the way back he had learned that I had blown a *civilian passenger train*. That was something we could not have controlled, and it signified that at least there would be less likelihood of reprisals. The line, predictably, would not carry traffic for at least three more days.

At the time I was a bit sore at Cope's attitude. I did one more job, another derailment, adequately successful but not spectacular. We did not tell anyone, but I am pretty sure that Cope found out about it, and what with these incidents and my little equestrian performance at Čačak—when I galloped Hitler through the main street and got chased by German motorcyclists, all just for a bet—I guessed the source when later someone told me that an adverse report had been made about me, dubbing me a wild man. I was nevertheless disappointed because the main complaint about Mihailović had been that not enough sabotage was being done by the Loyalists. And I had a pretty good game bag. It was bigger than anyone else's, except perhaps Archie Jack's with his bridges. And that my game bag did not include the Vladički Han bridge and the Niš airfield was not my fault.

But the Yugoslav section of Force 133 did not want to know about my game bag, or any game bag, because it was claiming that we had done no sabotage. If I had been with the Partisans, my sabotage would have been trumpeted to high heaven. But if I had been with the Partisans, they would not have allowed me to go off and do sabotage. I would have had to do what I was told and send off signals about claimed Partisan successes that may or may not have been true. I do not think I would have lasted long as a BLO with the Partisans. When I dropped into the Piedmont area of northern Italy later, in September 1944, I dropped to a delightful man, Neville Darewski, who had previously been with the Partisans in Slovenia and who had experienced just such difficulties with them. He was forced to leave under a cloud.

Totally belying the claims in the MO4 memorandum of November 19, 1943, according to which the Partisans should already have mopped up the Loyalists in Serbia; also belying the Partisan "facts" given in the "blockbuster" report, we never saw a Partisan in our area in the months we waited in Oruglica. Everything in the Loyalist area was just the same as it had been since June 1943—except that the Loyalists were the enemy now, in the eyes of our Cairo base. And we were hostages.

Eventually we set out on the long trek to Pranjani in central Serbia. Even before we left southeastern Serbia, our large column of about twenty British was augmented with crashed bomber crews, and we collected more as we trekked. We traveled at the pace of the slowest, and we got held up for quite some time at one stage on the trek when Rupert Raw went down with pneumonia and nearly died of it. Finally the column moved on, and John Sehmer bravely stayed alone to look after him. We had one or two scares and diversions from German troops, and for a couple of days we were shadowed by two Fieseler Storches. Even farther north in Šumadija, however, we saw nothing of the much-vaunted Partisans, who, according to the "blockbuster" and the faked maps in Bari, should have been bounding down upon us out of every wood and spinney.

When we reached Mihailović headquarters and the dropping ground at Pranjani, we were delayed two or three weeks before we flew out at the end of May. The Loyalists held the area against the Germans, who were not far away at Čačak. For our evacuation the Balkan Air Force organized a special course in short-strip landing for two selected pilots, a wing commander and a flight lieutenant, and the two flew their Dakotas in to lift us out. The wing commander, a rather self-confident gentleman who looked like a perky sparrow, had landed first with amazing precision, grandly pronounced the air strip "Oh, a bit too long, too long," and taken a full load of twenty-three aboard. His confidence was misplaced. The strip was only 700 yards long, and we joked that it had been measured by Brigadier Armstrong himself pacing it—he was rather a small man. The official requirement for a DC-3 at that altitude was 1,500 yards. The plane was overloaded, and we held our breath as it failed to lift properly. It fell off the end of the runway, sank down a valley, and finally collected a nice big branch from a tree on a hill about a mile away as it struggled to get airborne. It carried the branch in its under-carriage all of the way back to Italy.

The next plane bogged down, and dawn was breaking when we got it unstuck. The pilot had been warned by radio of the first plane's problem, and the second took off with only six passengers abroad. I do not recollect precisely how many we were, waiting for embarkation, but there must have been nearly one hundred. Things looked black for a couple of days, and the word went around that the RAF was not buying that sort of job any-more.

Our organizers had been smart, and the first two planes had been packed with the more senior American crew. These officers kindly insisted that the U.S. Army Air Corps bring out the rest of us. And they did it in flamboyant style. Their pilots bumped in over the hedge for every sort of landing, banged their planes around, and took only eight per plane. But they kept coming. That's all that mattered. God bless them. They kept on coming. It was impressive.

In our relief to get out we did not realize an ironic twist of the situation. Those planes had earlier dropped arms to Partisan units, which arms would predictably be used against the Loyalists, who were holding the airfield and protecting the planes. What a shameful scene. The Loyalists suffered it all in dignity and courtesy. History should register that.

And that was that. We had written our reports and handed them to Colonel Cope in the field. I for one had absolutely no debriefing at all. No one in Force 133 was the least bit interested. The nice, sympathetic, helpful James Klugmann of MO4 Cairo, who in April 1943 had supplied us with magnetized fly buttons, was nowhere to be seen by the likes of us. No one wanted to know.

In December 1944 the Battle School at Monopoli in Italy paid me the compliment of asking me to write a report on my train-blowing technique, which they then adopted. That was the one lasting achievement of my one-year mission. A lot of blood, sweat, and tears just for that.

Summing up the whole Mihailović mission story in his highly regarded *Baker Street Irregular*, Col. Bickham Sweet-Escott wrote, "It was Bill Deakin who, helped by the encyclopaedic knowledge of Hugh Seton-Watson, finally convinced Cairo and London that there was truth in the stories that some of Mihailovic's lieutenants were collaborating with the enemy. It was mainly as a result of what he told us that we decided early in the new year to tell Mihailovic that unless he could satisfy the Allies of his bona fides by blowing up a bridge on the important railway running from Belgrade to Salonika, all supplies to him would finally cease. Mihailović was unable to comply."

Well, there's the *received wisdom* story for you. Bill Deakin, with his collaboration dossier collected at Tito's headquarters, and Hugh Seton-Watson—Klugmann's friend and erstwhile university left-winger—had "established" that "some of Mihailović's lieutenants" were collaborating. So the prime minister had decided to abandon the Loyalists, the king, and democracy for alleged peccadilloes.

"We decided," writes Bickham Sweet-Escott as if "we," that is, SOE London, still had some say. SOE London had been effectively out of power since September 17. And then, "stop supplies." What supplies? Armstrong had not had a drop for three and a half months.

Sweet-Escott's book is probably the most complete—and supposedly most objective—participant's account of SOE activities around Europe written by a senior officer. But in matters Yugoslav it is inaccurate and superficial. In this way the pervasive *received wisdom* has spread around and become history for lack of any contestation.

Sweet-Escott goes on: "Jasper Rootham has given a vivid picture in his book *Miss-Fire* of the frustration which our people on this mission had to suffer. It seemed to many of us unfair that most of them should go unrewarded, though the risks they took were neither fewer nor smaller than those taken by our men with Tito, on whom the fountain of honour played with such freedom."

Perhaps he could say that again. At least we got to know some rare and colorful gentlemen. And we did not make our experiences with overweening commissars blowing down the backs of our necks.

We all dispersed. Most went off on leave to Cairo. Peter Solly-Flood later dropped into Poland with "Marko" Hudson. John Sehmer dropped into Czechoslovakia and was captured, tortured, and shot. Robert Purvis dropped into France. Colonel Cope dropped into northern Italy. The others went off in their various directions. The Yugoslav section became—or rather, more correctly, remained—a totally Partisan affair, with James Klugmann the communist guru still firmly in place.

Yugoslavia was a British sphere of influence, but the Americans were not at all happy about the abandonment of Mihailović and the Loyalists. In the summer of 1944 OSS commissioned a professor of Balkan history from the University of Michigan, Robert McDowell, to do a study of the nationalist area in Yugoslavia. Dressed as a lieutenant colonel in the Rangers, McDowell—himself a linguist with many years' experience in the Balkans and the Middle East—took three Serbo-Croat–speaking officers with him and carried out an extensive study, traveling through large areas of Bosnia and Serbia. Traveling under the auspices of the nationalists (Loyalists), they moved with total freedom and talked to nationalist soldiers and Partisan prisoners, rich and poor peasants, shopkeepers, professional men, intellectuals, and students, including Bosnian Muslims and some Croats and Slovenes as well as Serbs from all parts of Yugoslavia. They also talked to nationalists and civilian leaders from areas they did not visit themselves—western Bosnia, Slovenia, Herzegovina, and Montenegro. The McDowell mission submitted a report in November 1944 that confirms all of the major points I have made in this book and constitutes a terrible indictment of the British policy of forcing Tito and the Partisans onto Yugoslavia. The McDowell report is conveniently ignored by the British *received-wisdom* historical school.

There were two other illuminating reports on 1944 Yugoslavia that you won't find in *received-wisdom* reading. One was from a British liaison officer with Tito, Surgeon Lt. Cmdr. D. S.

MacPhail, who was captured by the Loyalists in the middle of my old area on Mount Kukavica. He wrote a very fair and objective report (WO 202/196) of his experiences with both the Partisans and the Loyalists. He describes, in one passage, the attitude of the Četniks regarding the British:

> I have not the slightest doubt that the friendliness we met with was genuine, and the hospitality and kindness we received were more than could be accounted for by Serb tradition or the desire to impress. In spite of their loathing for the Partisans and our support of them, the Cetniks appear to be unable to think ill of us and admire and respect Britain as much as ever. A Serb who was at Salonika in the last war still swanks about it inordinately and is something of a local hero. Those Cetniks who were closely associated with B.L.O.s enjoy a special prestige and the same seemed to apply to our guards. Mobs of peasants came to see us anywhere, apparently just for the privilege of shaking our hands. Our journey to H.Q. was a triumphal progress. I could not help contrasting this with the situation in Partisan territory where any Partisan who became too friendly with the Mission was sent away in disgrace. The Serb is, of course, highly histrionic, and much of this may be explained by the desire to convert us to the Cetnik cause. But not, I think, all.

The final report I will cite here, a most telling and moving document, was written by Linn Farish, the chief American liaison officer with Tito, who accompanied Maclean when the latter dropped to Tito in September 1943. Farish, the reader may recall, is the man who actually wrote two reports—as different as night and day. Farish is mentioned very appreciatively by both Maclean and Deakin in their books. At the time of writing they had not, I'm sure, seen his second report. Indeed, Deakin only saw it in 1988, when I sent it to him. Farish wrote his first report on October 29, 1943. It was an American version of the "blockbuster." It was full of Partisan "facts," figures, and propaganda. It was sycophantic and gushing. It envisaged Yugoslavia under the Partisans emulating the United States: "It was in such an environment and under such conditions that the beginnings of the United States were established."

But after three drops and six months in the field Farish wrote another report, which he signed on June 28, 1944, entitled "Summary Report on Observations in Yugoslavia for the period 19 September 1943, until 16 June 1944." This paper, written just after the British missions from Mihailović were evacuated, is a most sober and impressive document. It is almost incredible that the two reports could have been written by the same man.

In his second report, Farish eats his own words. He issues a desperate plea for the Allies to intervene and stop the civil war between the Partisans and the Loyalists. Extracts from his report follow:

In all of this welter of confusion, of conflicting reports and misunderstandings, a few pertinent facts stand out:

The vast majority of the people in Yugoslavia, and we have seen them in Bosnia, Herzegovina, Dalmatia, Sandjak, Montenegro, Serbia, Macedonia and the Dalmatian islands, are neither Right, Left, Communist, Reactionary, or anything else. They are a simple peasant type of people, strong willed, hot blooded with tremendous powers of endurance and great personal courage. They love intrigue and gossip, and are the most profound liars I have ever met. I do not believe there is any tremendous urge for revolution among them. They love their mountains, their small homes, their farms, and their flocks. They want something better, but, measured by our standards, what most of them ask is not a great deal, a good government, their King and their Church, schools, more roads, shoes, clothing, a few modern conveniences, better modern farming equipment and some better livestock.

These people quite unique in Europe have the will and the environment with which to effectively fight the enemy. . . .

The senseless killing of these people by each other must be stopped. It is useless now to endeavor to decide which side first did wrong. Too much blood has been spilt, the feeling is too bitter, and too many men on both sides have uttered rash accusations and performed rash acts.

It does not seem to me that the allies have done well in Yugoslavia. . . .

However, as in the case of the primary issues between the Chetniks and the Partisans it does no good to report what we believe should have been done. What we must decide is, what shall we do in the face of conditions as they exist today. Is it too late to draw all the factions together into one group directed against the enemy under the guarantee of free elections without violence after the war? As far as the great mass of the people are concerned, it can be done, because they are weary of fighting each other, but eager to fight the enemy. There are thousands who have buried their rifles and refused to march with any group. There are thousands more who would volunteer if they could decide which side to support.

Only a few people on each side prevent a union from being formed—a few defeatists among the Nedic group who believed it was hopeless to oppose the German army—A few Croats who hated the Serbs worse than the Germans—A few Communists who would see their brothers killed to further their political aims—A few Serb Nationalists who classed as Communists all those who did not agree with them. . . .

. . . When I have called for aid to the Partisans, and officers with the Chetniks have called for aid to their group, we have had the same person in mind—a barefoot, cold, and hungry peasant farmer, a man whose courage and endurance must be observed to be understood. . . .

It is not now a question of whether the United States should send aid and representation to the Partisans—we have been sending them aid and have had representation with them for a long time.

During January, February, and March of this year we saw and received in Bosnia numerous night sorties, two mass daylight drops with fighter escort, one daylight glider sortie with fighter escort, and several night landings.

During April, May, and June, we saw and helped receive in Serbia approximately one hundred night sorties and one night landing.

Out of all these aircraft, something in the neighborhood of 300 with 60 in the air at one time, I have only identified 50 which were not American.

The Russian mission to the Partisans was landed by gliders, American gliders towed by C-47s flown by American pilots and escorted by American fighters. The Russian mission rode in the gliders and British pilots landed them. We have seen "Russian" aid drop to the Partisans from "Russian" planes, yet the planes were again the old C-47s and the goods were largely American packed in American containers dropped by American parachutes. . . .

Nothing stated here should be construed as anti-British, anti-Russian, or anti Anything. They are merely statements of facts intended to point out that we do have a very direct interest in what is taking place in Yugoslavia. It does no good to say that we are not interested in Yugoslavia and are not participating in the situation there, because we are, in a most material and effective manner.

I, personally, do not feel that I can go on with the work in Yugoslavia unless I can sincerely feel that every possible honest effort is being made to put an end to the civil strife. It is not nice to see arms dropped by one group of our airmen to be turned against men who have rescued and protected their brothers in arms. It is not a pleasant sight to see our wounded lying side by side with the men who rescued and cared for them—and to realize that the bullet holes in the rescuers could have resulted from American ammunition, fired from American rifles, dropped from American aircraft flown by American pilots.

At one time I worried because America was not getting the proper recognition for her participation in supply operations. Now I wonder—do we want it? I can only hope that the small round holes which I saw in those simple peasant boys in the guerrilla hospital in Lipovica village were not caused by cartridges stamped W.R.A., or fired from rifles marked "U.S. Property."

. . . Under any conditions, two things stand out, every effort must be made to end the conflict among the people of Yugoslavia, and the United States has a very definite interest in seeing that it is ended as soon as possible. . . .

Have you ever read poetry like that?

PART III
The Aftermath

CHAPTER
12
The Victor's History

■

James Klugmann, by then a major, stayed in the Yugoslav section until April 15, 1945, when he went to Yugoslavia to organize U.N.R.R.A. (United Nations Relief and Rehabilitation Agency) affairs there. He had done so much to help Tito into power in his subterranean way, but when Tito got into his row with Stalin, Klugmann promptly wrote a book denouncing Tito. He really was a prototype apparatchik. If there were any grounds for doubting that Klugmann's first loyalty was to Stalin, and to the British only insofar as it suited the Soviets, this switch against Tito must dispel those doubts; particularly as a year or two later he had to recant again, when Tito reestablished close links with the Soviets.

Klugmann made certain that everything was done to bury the last traces of the Loyalist movement. Already in the summer of 1944 steps were taken in Bari to start the historical assassination of Mihailović and the Loyalists, and this process has continued for forty-five years. Whether or not this systematic massaging of the record was originally Klugmann's brainchild I do not know. There were many others in Bari and Caserta with a strong vested interest in it. At an early stage, about August 1944, a pamphlet entitled *The Četniks* was cobbled together in southern Italy and edited by one Stephen Clissold. He was actually a charming individual, but he had always been left-inclined. *The Četniks* was prepared for circulation to all and sundry, particularly to the military, and it became a gospel source. It is shockingly tendentious, full of inaccuracies, and, in particular, it built on the technique of using misquotations of Mihailović BLO signals and reports.

The preparation and widespread circulation of *The Četniks*, published by Allied Forces Headquarters, foreshadowed the shape of things to come in the historical arena. Incredibly and inexcusably, there was no direct input for the document by any of the Mihailović BLOs. Yet we had arrived in Bari in the last days of May, and the pamphlet was not printed until August. If it was felt necessary or desirable to issue a pamphlet about the Četniks, would it not surely have been normal to ask one of those who had served with them to prepare it, or at least to act as consultant for an objective, independent author? We were British officers and prima facie objective and British in our views.

But no! Allied Forces headquarters gets hold of Stephen Clissold, a former BLO with the Partisans, who had seen only their side of the picture. He had worked briefly in Yugoslavia before the war and spoke Serbo-Croat, which would have helped him to absorb the propaganda. Above all, he was emotionally prepared to believe the whole Partisan picture as presented by their commissars. He only knew "Četniks" as "the enemy" of the Partisans. And for him the Partisans were "a good thing" by definition; all Četniks were bad eggs, and his job was to prove it. Though biased, he was competent and literate.

If nothing else proved the motivation behind the pamphlet, the choice of Clissold to edit *The Četniks* establishes that it was commissioned precisely in order to carry out a character assassination of Mihailović, to destroy the reputation of the Četniks, to explain their sudden overnight classification as enemy rather than ally, and—in case anyone should put two and two together—to salve Allied consciences about the massive support being given to Tito for his civil war and specifically for his liberation of Serbia and for the cynically named "Ratweek," starting about that time.

"Ratweek," thought up by the Maclean mission, really was a most unfortunate name. It was an exercise designed to catch the Germans on their retreat from Greece through the Serbian defiles. In fact, it failed in this aim, and an army of about 100,000 men carried out an orderly retreat. The real rats were the Loyalists. "Ratweek" for Tito was the autumn offensive to liberate Serbia from Mihailović and the Loyalists; and, incidentally, from any other opponents of the communists, actual or potential.

Inevitably, Deakin has played a major role in setting the trend for the British historical analysis of what happened in Yugoslavia. Himself a historian and a metaphorical blood brother of Tito, this was bound to happen. James Klugmann would have called it the dialectics of history. Deakin has made it clear in his writings that he was totally sold on the Partisans militarily. He did not specify his views on their politics. If their views were opposed to his own, he has done a fine job of putting his military opinions first.

In *The Embattled Mountain*, Deakin gives us a terrifying insight into the ways of the civil war in Yugoslavia and into the workings of even a highly cultured and civilized mind under those circumstances. In these paragraphs he relates honestly and sincerely how he had become totally involved with the Partisans. Describing how he rode over enemy wounded, he writes, "Pity had long drained out of us . . . a flick of the rein would have avoided the trampling of the imploring shadows. But in the triumphant wrath we crushed them. . . . I had taken on by stages a binding and absolute identity with those around me."

By writing and publishing those words in a book that came out in 1971, that is, twenty-eight years later, Deakin has surely associated himself indelibly with the Partisan movement. In my opinion, no man who even fleetingly felt that way and recorded that feeling without qualification a quarter of a century later can be regarded as an arm's-length observer. Yet Deakin has played a major—if not the chief—role in the historical record.

No longer can it be pretended that the whole Partisan struggle was anything other than a grab for power and that the methods were ruthless in the extreme, right up to Stalin's most cruel standards. Although the Partisans' methods were glossed over in the Titoites' postwar historiography, no intellectually honest person can paint the Yugoslav civil war as other than vile. I myself did not suffer from excessive scruples in my wartime career as a guerrilla, but I don't think I would have ridden my horse over wounded enemy, and certainly I would not have advertised it had I done so.

There is a massive bibliography that tells of the breathtaking wartime scenes in Yugoslavia. Some particularly evocative passages are to be found in Milovan Djilas's *Wartime*. He tells with evident great admiration of the "martial manhood" of the German Twenty-first Corps, joined by the Ninety-first Corps, carving their way through on the long and only road from Greece to the Drina River across Albania and Montenegro. He writes of how, hungry and half-naked, they cleared mountain landslides and stormed the rocky peaks; of how Allied planes used them for leisurely target practice; of how they had to kill their gravely wounded whom they could not get out; of how they seized farm animals to eat and took worn-out, shabby peasant clothing but did not molest civilians or burn dwellings; and of how, in the end, they got through. The German army could wage wars— "without massacres and gas chambers."

I loved that passage. It appealed to my own romantic military instincts. Milovan Djilas was no armchair warrior: he had been through it from beginning to end as Tito's major troubleshooter. He was in the political bamboozling business, but he was a real man nevertheless. My own experience of Germans was the same. They could wage war. That passage confirms too that in spite of close Allied air support and in spite of the Allies pouring arms into the Partisans, the German army beat an orderly retreat.

That passage also confirms how ludicrous was the claim in the "blockbuster" that the Partisans killed five Germans for every Partisan killed.

But Djilas tells more. He tells of massacres, of the murder of

35,000 Yugoslavs turned over to Tito by the British in Austria, of the purges in Zagreb, of the killings of Loyalists. He tells how Mihailović fought his way from Bosnia, trying to get back into Serbia in the winter of 1944–45. He writes how the Loyalists fought with great bitterness and "simply stomped over one of our brigades." In the ludicrous "blockbuster" it was claimed to be the other way around—ten Četniks dead for one Partisan. Djilas in *Wartime* was no longer writing for the Partisan propaganda machine. He was no longer in favor, and he was writing nearer the truth. He tells how no prisoners were taken. He explains the motivations and half endeavors to justify them. The facts are all there:

> Who issued the order for this extermination? . . . An atmosphere of revenge prevailed. . . . Once in a rambling conversation—after the clash with the Soviet leadership in 1948, of course—I mentioned that we had gone too far then, because among the executed also were some fleeing for ideological reasons alone. Tito retorted immediately "We put an end to it once and for all. Anyway, given the kind of courts that we had. . . ."
>
> Yet OZNA continued to carry out executions according to its own local and inconsistent criteria, until late in 1945, when at a meeting of the Central Committee Tito cried out in disgust: "Enough of all these death sentences and all this killing. The death sentence no longer has any effect, no one fears death anymore."

In his closing passage Djilas says of revolutions that their idealization is a coverup for the egotism and love of power of the new revolutionary masters. No wonder he fell out of favor in Tito's court.

So today the Titoites' great cry is very simple, it is the justification that was cobbled together by the agencies and even by the Foreign Office in the last two or three months of 1943. They recognized that Churchill was firmly hooked on getting rid of the Loyalists, so they set out to establish that Mihailović was a collaborator. There are repeated exchanges in the files of the Foreign

Office 371 series in the Public Records Office saying, in effect, "We must find justification. We must get some evidence that will stick." Not "Was he really a collaborator?" But "How do we prove it?"

No wonder that when Deakin turned up in Cairo with his dossier of Partisan allegations of Mihailović collaboration, amassed with help from Velebit and Dedijer, the dossier was metaphorically torn out of his hand. It was the justification they needed. Together with the Partisan mythology it formed the cornerstone of the Victor's History.

In war mistakes are always made, and some of them are very big mistakes. Also, in war, decisions have to be made for reasons of expediency. The decision to abandon Mihailović, the Loyalists, and the king was without question taken on those grounds. The subsequent justification is another matter. Is it not intellectually honest just to admit that a decision was taken for expedient reasons? One may not admit this in the heat of the moment; not perhaps for a year or two afterward; not perhaps in Churchill's lifetime to spare him the remorse. But, forty-five years later, do the surviving elderly widows and the descendants of those decent, patriotic Loyalists, who were slaughtered because of the political and material ambitions of Tito's clique, still have to hear the false vilification of their men? The proud Serb nation of old Serbia, the *Srbijanci*, Serbia as it was before and through the ages, has been emasculated. The harm is done. Does history too have to continue to be twisted? Do we just have to go on with the gramophone record stuck in the groove "Mihailović was a collaborator . . . Mihailović was a collaborator . . . Mihailović was a collaborator"? It is not only sickening, it is false.

According to SOE records, Deakin left Force 133 sometime in the spring of 1944. He was unwell for a period, and then he joined the resident minister's, Harold Macmillan's, staff in Italy, in the political advisor's office. There he was with Philip Broad, who had been sent to Cairo in August 1943 together with Fitzroy Maclean. Broad, who acted primarily as Maclean's man in the Cairo Minister of State's Office, had worked with Ralph Skrine Stevenson. Deakin also became advisor to the Balkan Air Force, and in that role he was still right in the thick of the Yugoslav scene. The Balkan Air Force seems to have taken over the administration of the whole Yugoslav operation and of the Maclean mission in support of the Partisans. It would be interesting to know whether he was also consulted about such things as the tactical and strategic significance of targets.

It is claimed today in some Serbian circles that the Allied air support was exploited by Tito to turn the people against Britain. The theory is that strikes by Western Allied aircraft of the Balkan Air Force were called down specifically against Serbian towns and villages, cynically choosing Serbian Orthodox religious holidays for the bombing. It is an undeniable fact that there was carpet bombing of Belgrade for three consecutive days coinciding with the Orthodox Easter in April 1944, the intensity of which surpassed even the Luftwaffe attacks of April 1941. On Saint George's Day 1944 the Montenegrin towns of Nikšić, Podgorica, and Danilovgrad were blasted by Allied planes, allegedly because there were strong Loyalist concentrations around those areas, but, in truth, to demoralize the pro-Mihailović populations. The same was done even to Zara to demoralize the Italian population. Maclean's book *Eastern Approaches* gives his impressive and horrifying eyewitness account of the devastation of Leskovac on the opening day of Ratweek, purportedly in order to destroy a concentration of German armor and motor transport. But fifty Flying Fortresses were used, and Maclean "tried not to think of the population of small farmers, shopkeepers and railway workers, of the old people, the women and children, who at this moment would be going about their everyday business in the streets. . . . the whole of Leskovac seemed to rise bodily into the air . . . the civilian casualties had been heavy."

Militarily it was using a sledgehammer to kill a gnat. Further, the vaunted Partisans were there in force—not the overwhelming force we were told about in the "blockbuster" report, because that was sheer Partisan misrepresentation, but force all the same. It surely was the Partisan guerrillas' job to cut the roads and railway lines and thus immobilize the armor; and then to go in with the bayonet and sticky bombs if need be. But to the Partisan leadership the purpose of that bombing and others was not military, it was political. It was to show the strongly pro-Loyalist population of the Jablanica who were the masters now.

The normal bombing procedure was that Tito and his commanders specified the targets through the British mission and their RAF advisors. One wonders why the BLOs, or the Balkan Air Force advisors at base, did not question the necessity of extensive bombings of Yugoslav civilian areas, of hospitals, and of churches—and on religious holidays too—if there was not some political motive. Why did Maclean not question the need to flatten Leskovac? Massive bombing of civilians in German cities was one thing. Germans lived there, and the German morale had to be broken. But bombing Belgrade or Leskovac on the odd chance of hitting a German barracks or tank and with the certainty of killing massive numbers of Yugoslav allies was surely something very sinister. I feel certain that the Allies would never have contemplated a blanket bombing of Paris, for example, on Easter Sunday—or any other day—however many German tanks were passing through.

But of course Tito had made it clear from the start that his was a sovereign army and that he would decide. Did that go for ordering out massive formations of allied bombers too?

The Soviets avoided bombing Serbian targets; they incurred no odium. The Western Allies incurred all the hate. Regrettably, the Balkan Air Force files are permanently closed like the main SOE files and those of SIS. One wonders why. What should be so secret about an *air force* operation? One hopes that the lock on those files is not so permanent that even those charged by the government with writing the "official" history of the war in the Balkans can't gain access.

In 1945 the newly formed Tito government and the Yugoslav Communist Party demonstrated that they had never for a moment intended to have free elections or any silly bourgeois nonsense of that sort. They started, as they had always intended, on an ultra-Stalinist course and, during the next three years, were without doubt the nastiest and most dictatorial of the Eastern European communist regimes. It surprises me that Deakin's emotional involvement with the Partisans, as reflected in *The Embattled Mountain*, survived this period after he moved from Italy to Belgrade and became first secretary in the British embassy. The next six months were the period of the massacres, and they surely must have had echoes in Belgrade.

In 1948 Tito broke with Stalin. It may be more correct to say that the Soviets broke with Tito and did so simply because Tito was getting a wee bit too uppity. It was the row with Stalin, not any gratitude to the British, that caused the Yugoslav regime to take a line independent of the rest of the Soviet bloc. To claim anything else is pure humbug.

Nevertheless Tito, the ultimate political animal, knew how to run to the West with a begging bowl and once more persuade gullible politicians that he was their friend. This did not inhibit him at all from burrowing away in the Third World, undermining the Western powers. As in the war, he pushed Western gullibility to the absolute limit.

It was a godsend for the Tito advocates that the Tito-Stalin row in 1948 coincided more or less with the intensification of the Cold War, the Berlin Airlift, and the erection of the Iron Curtain. These events created an atmosphere in which the West was looking for chinks in the Soviet armor, thinking wishfully as ever, and, lo and behold, there was Tito squabbling with Stalin. So Tito became a great vogue figure again. And again he was greatly helped by his British allies beating his drums. It was the same band as in 1943; only the tune had changed. Now it was: Look. We always said that if we supported Tito in the war we could woo him away from communism.

The scene has now changed. All but the ignorant and the deliberately blind have to recognize that Tito's "flawed legacy," as Nora Beloff called it, is indeed fatally flawed. And all of the euphemisms about the great national patriotic uprising have suffered a very severe jolt from the writings of revisionist Partisan leaders themselves, such as Djilas and Dedijer and Djuretić, the Belgrade historian.

The truth will always out (locked files notwithstanding). The British who still persist in trying to sell the idea that we "civilized" Tito are only deluding themselves. We helped bring Stalinism to Yugoslavia, and that's all there is to it. If the remaining traces of Stalinism come to be eliminated in Yugoslavia— as pray God they will be, maybe quite soon— it will be in spite of, not thanks to, what the British did in 1943–44. It may be forty years late, but that has to be said in unequivocal form. Cant and self-serving humbug. Out, out, out.

This central fact and sadness cannot be changed by events in recent years and by Yugoslav experiments in introducing a degree of economic and political liberalization. In his old age, when he was totally assured of his place in history, Tito seemed to mellow. The political temper of Yugoslavia reflected that. But Tito remained a despot at heart. The only difference was that, with all real opposition eliminated, his position was secure.

Even his friend and erstwhile advocate Fitzroy Maclean had come to criticize Tito before he came back into vogue again in 1948. In a report dated September 23, 1947, outlining discussions with him about displaced persons, Maclean wrote,

> I could not help wondering if he realised quite how unpopular he was in England. He had done himself incalculable harm in Western eyes by his political repression, by the execution of Mihailovitch and the imprisonment of Stepinac, by the shooting down of harmless American aeroplanes and, finally, by his consistently offensive attitude towards former Allies, who, as he and I knew better than anyone, had done a very great deal to help him during the war. The fact was that he had now made himself such a reputation as a blood thirsty ogre that large sections of British opinion would be reluctant to see even the worst war criminal handed back to him.

But that was, tragically, too late for the 35,000 Slovene, Croat, and Serbian surrendered personnel and refugees who had been shunted back to Tito from Austria in 1945 and massacred without any trial at all. And the 35,000 were only the tip of the iceberg. Other victims lay in unmarked graves, in quarries, rotting in riverbeds, and in mass graves they had been forced to dig themselves. Tito had served his apprenticeship under Stalin and Beria.

Vane Ivanović wrote in *Memoirs of a Yugoslav* that there has been no symposium or discussion in Great Britain or elsewhere in Europe on SOE's role in the last war in which Deakin has not taken a prominent part, and that in each of these meetings the version of events in Yugoslavia that has been aired is that of a victorious pro-Partisan faction inside SOE. Ivanović goes on to point out that on the British side he has come across no views or interpretations from the other side within SOE.

Why is that?

The British missions returning from Mihailović were hardly debriefed in June 1944. I have seen no evidence that our reports were read by anyone in the Yugoslav section—or anywhere else at the decision-making level. Maclean certainly did not read them, otherwise how could he have written in *Eastern Approaches* that there had been little or no interruption of traffic on the Belgrade-Salonika railway when we were there?

Bailey wrote no memoirs, and he was involved on the historical side hardly at all except insofar as he kept in touch with many SOE people and, in his last years, rather closely with Deakin. According to a number of independent sources (including John Cairncross, the alleged communist in exile in Rome, who knew Bailey well after the war), Bailey had collected a cache of papers and was going to start writing a book in early 1974. When he died shortly thereafter in his rented home near Arles in Provence, there were no papers at all. I have this directly from Deakin, who lived nearby and who came over to his place immediately in order to look after Bailey's companion. If there was such a cache of papers, it had disappeared into thin air at some stage, somewhere, even though Bailey had just written to Milan Deroc that he was about to start the book.

Though an alcoholic and a very sick man, Bailey did attend the 1973 Auty-Clogg symposium at London University, and he read a long-winded paper that, according to Deakin, he patched together at the last moment from memory. Like everything else Bailey wrote, it was muddled and harmful to Mihailović and the Loyalists while vaunting his own knowledge and importance. He

was, perhaps, motivated by a desire to please the other participants in the symposium and to pay lip service to their belief in
the sanctity of all Partisan claims. That would have been charac-
teristic of Bailey. Indeed, his desire to be all things to all men
was half of his problem. But at least he did insist—even in that
company—that Mihailović was not a collaborator, though in true
Bailey form he was equivocal about it.

Hudson is said to have destroyed all of his papers, and very
regrettably he too has not gone into print. There is a biography
of him in the pipeline, however. That is to be welcomed, because
in the *received wisdom* he has been quoted (and I suspect mis-
quoted) repeatedly. His story must be fascinating. He was a very
robust individual, and he saw and went through a great deal in
Yugoslavia.

Armstrong seems never to have published anything, and other
than the attractive personal memoir by Jasper Rootham (*Miss-
Fire*), nothing appeared in print from the Mihailović BLOs until
I published *Special Operations Executed*. That book too was a purely
personal memoir of which my Yugoslav experience formed only
a part. When I wrote it in 1949–50, I had little idea of all the
amazing things that had gone on in the MO4 headquarters, and
elsewhere, which I first learned about when I started researching
in the Public Records Office decades later.

A very tenacious and dedicated American, David Martin—
who happened to pass through London on his way to the East
when on service in the Canadian Air Force, got to know some
people interested in Yugoslav affairs at the time, and returned
through London when the Mihailović trial was making head-
lines—became secretary and prime mover of a committee that
was formed in the United States to try to ensure a fair hearing
for Mihailović. This committee took sworn statements from a large
number of Americans and endeavored to arrange for this evidence to be admitted in Belgrade. At the same time a number of
BLOs drew up a statement of evidence, which they tried to have
put forward by the British authorities. The Yugoslav government's riposte was typically Stalinist: Mihailović is guilty; there is
no need for evidence. That of course was even before the trial.

David Martin wrote several carefully researched books that,

other than Nora Beloff's work, *Tito's Flawed Legacy*, constitute the only real defense of Mihailović. Martin has been a lone voice crying in the wilderness for forty years. Hopefully he will get some response now in the era of *glasnost*.

Whereas the Mihailović BLOs disappeared into the woodwork, fighting other wars and making their living, some Partisan BLOs have made great names and quite a business out of their Partisan experiences. A number of books have poured forth. Fitzroy Maclean's beautifully written though rather fanciful *Eastern Approaches* came out in 1949 and was followed by *Disputed Barricades* in 1957. These two books became accepted as gospel, and the theories and contentions in them have been widely quoted. Even before *Eastern Approaches* came out, Basil Davidson, who claimed in his later book, *Special Operations Europe*, to have started it all in the MO4 Cairo office, rushed out *Partisan Picture* already in 1946. Thus Davidson, who had been first past the post in catalyzing the Partisan-Četnik war in Cairo, was also first past the post in getting into print, and whatever one thinks about his rather hard-left politics, he does write with tremendous sincerity, wit, and conviction. His books, with their convincing enthusiasm, like those of Fitzroy Maclean, made a great case for the *received wisdom*.

Then Stephen Clissold— author and editor of the pamphlet *The Četniks*—published a well-written book called *Whirlwind* in 1949. This was an account of events in Yugoslavia as seen from a purely left-wing viewpoint. These Partisan participant books, together with purportedly "historical" works by Seton-Watson and others—all of which carried a very clear and very strongly put political message—created a pro-Partisan climate in the general public as well as in scholarly circles, which was of course reinforced dramatically when, in due course, the lead figure and historical guru, Deakin, published *The Embattled Mountain*. Deakin, a prewar don, a researcher for the great man Churchill, hero of Mount Durmitor, and a postwar academic of distinction, quietly moved into a key position when he became chairman of the British Committee for the History of the Second World War—thus very much one of the Great and the Good. This position has enabled him, inevitably, to give extra weight and leverage to the Titoite side.

No one among the British participants has put forth the other point of view in detail. To my knowledge no one with direct participant experience on the Mihailović side has previously worked through the files in the PRO. Indeed, the nearest person to a participant to labor through these files in some detail was David Martin. It is only thanks to his recognition of the importance and significance of the SOE files, and, above all, of the operational-log signals, that I personally got involved.

British writing about Yugoslavia reflected the Partisan view. *Received wisdom* was, of course, being built up and reinforced in Belgrade by the Tito government's public-relations people. Where they could not scrounge up enough material to support the story they wanted to tell, they had a long list of scribes who would happily write anything they were asked to. People do that sort of thing under dictators. True or false, subjective or objective, the material from Belgrade has been drawn on heavily by academics studying, writing, and taking part in symposiums on the subject and has, in this manner, achieved gospel status. The "note on sources" in Deakin's *The Embattled Mountain* shows the extent to which he relied on Partisan sources. All of that Belgrade material—until the revisionists came along—had one underlying political purpose, namely, to smear Mihailović and the Loyalist Četniks and thus ensure that no ideas foreign to Tito's image, Tito's legend, and Tito's despotic rule could blossom. In the same way, Stalin destroyed Trotsky and all of his other rivals, and went on doing so all of his life; and, in the same way, Stalin ensured throughout his lifetime that his liquidated rivals continued to be denigrated and reviled in order to prevent any possibility of anyone ever raising the idea that maybe they were right and Stalin was wrong.

As this book bears witness, it is my firm conviction that, without British logistical help and recognition, Tito would never have been able to conquer Serbia, and in view of the traditional friendly attitude of the Serbs to the British, I count the de facto full recognition of Tito and his movement in December 1943 as possibly a more important factor than the thousands of tons of arms supplied to the Partisans, the extensive close air support, and the bombing of Loyalist areas. I suspect that, in their heart of hearts, most of the British Partisan supporters know this to be true. I believe that, subconsciously if not consciously, they recognize that Mihailović and his Loyalist Četniks were not collaborators but true patriots. And precisely in the subconscious knowledge of these facts lies the drive that forces them to go on and on trying to justify what was done, in the name of supporting the side that was allegedly "killing more Germans."

Precisely for that reason, in the Yugoslav Partisan victory, the British-aided victory over the Loyalists, there was no magnanimity. No magnanimity, no decency, no generosity or justice at all.

While they oiled the machinery, it was not the James Klugmanns who built the legends and myths. The James Klugmanns are not historians. They leave that to the other professionals, the dialectical materialists. Klugmann and his ilk, the out-and-out communist agents and apparatchiks, were quite clear about what they had to do before the war, during the war, and after. They knew that the name of their game was how best in their job to suit Stalin's needs and wishes from day to day.

The Stalinist myths and legends and, more importantly, the collectivist concept are being at least examined critically in the U.S.S.R. Oddly, it is in England, the country of freedom and democracy, that it is taking longer for the blind to see that in Yugoslavia, as in many other parts of the world, we were taken for a ride by the Marxist-Leninists. Regrettably, in England there was a massive and sinister penetration of both collectivist and elitist ideas, which gave birth already in the 1930s to phenomena such as the Cambridge communist set and the heavy penetration by communists of the secret services and even of the foreign service. In England the establishment is very much inclined to replace "My country right or wrong" with "My clique right or wrong." Thus the Blunts and the Philbys and the Burgesses and the Donald Macleans continued to be privy to highly confidential matters, even when their peers were getting suspicious about them. Even an outright, no-nonsense, no-cover communist like James

Klugmann was brought right into the secret work because he happened to be known by a colonel (later to become a general) from his school background.

The main stronghold in the United Kingdom of the *received wisdom* has been the School of Slavonic and East European Studies (SSEES) at London University. Hardly evidencing academic objectivity, this school even established a Tito fellowship, though for cosmetic reasons the name has since been dropped. Under the auspices of this school symposiums have been held to place on record Yugoslav wartime history. The school was greatly influenced by Seton-Watson, whose father was a very important figure there, and by Phyllis Auty, who held a position there.

Phyllis Auty was another dedicated Titoite who served in political intelligence in Cairo, where she worked closely with Seton-Watson and MO4. She stayed active in Yugoslav matters throughout the Partisan takeover and went to Yugoslavia later for U.N.R.R.A., serving under James Klugmann. Auty, who had considerable input into intelligence analysis and reports, wrote a biography of Tito that is tendentious and sycophantic to a nauseating degree. She gave her name to the Auty-Clogg symposium, the 1973 assembly of the Great and the Good of the British, Greek, and Yugoslav establishments organized by the SSEES. My comments about this symposium relate strictly to the talks about Yugoslavia, because I am advised that the discussions and papers about Greece, under the chairmanship of Richard Clogg, the well-known historian of modern Greece, were excellent and not controversial.

There is no room in this book to analyze and rebut the papers on Yugoslavia at this elitist gathering, which was organized to constitute the final and decisive word on the history of the British role in Yugoslavia—and would thus ensure that history reflected the *received wisdom*. It is also pointless to do so because none of the papers considered this basic, simple question: Was it correct to abandon Mihailović and the Loyalists and thus to promote the civil war, handing Yugoslavia over on a silver platter to the communists? All of the papers started from the supposition that this was no issue. In none of them was there any doubt that

Tito and the Partisans were "a good thing" and that Mihailović and the Loyalists were "very bad things indeed." As for the monstrous, brutal civil war and the slaughter and massacres by Tito, involving just possibly as many as a quarter of a million souls in all—well, all that wasn't much to talk about, really.

So the papers dealt mostly with bureaucratic office tittle-tattle. The charming and well-regarded Elizabeth Barker gave the main paper, which addressed Foreign Office internal politics exclusively. As this book shows, the Foreign Office views were irrelevant, because the Foreign Office became impotent in Yugoslav affairs in January 1943. Elizabeth Barker was another totally convinced Titoite. With no prior knowledge of Yugoslavia, its people, or its languages, she had occupied the Balkan desk in PWE and thus became the recipient and sorter of all of the information coming in about Yugoslavia, the vast bulk of which was influenced by Soviet misinformation. Because she was so civilized and so charming, she became regarded as an authority and was even considered a leading candidate to write the proposed official SOE history. This plan was aborted by her death. I am sure that Elizabeth Barker was no communist. In her post, however, she had been effectively brainwashed. There were many others like her.

The refusal to address the question of the basic decision to back Tito exclusively has been the pattern of the closed symposiums—with carefully picked participants—that have taken place in Belgrade and in the United Kingdom and have contributed substantially to the construction of the *received wisdom*. I believe that participants have been selected—whether deliberately or just because they made themselves available—among those who would not rock the boat, raise their hands, and ask, "But, ignoring the details, why did we underwrite a civil war against the king and the legitimate government and help out-and-out communists to gain power against the wishes of the majority of the people? What did it cost us, and what did we achieve?" Or, worse still: "Did not Comrade Tito hoodwink the British?" So the basic question has gone unanswered and unconsidered. It has been swept under the carpet.

In the immediate postwar atmosphere, anyone who dared question—even in the smallest detail—the heroic tale of Tito and his romantic Partisans was denounced as bad or mad. The myths abounded, and in due course they became accepted as history. It is easy to create a legend and so hard, half a century later, to give the lie to it.

The locks remain on the filing cabinets of the British wartime secret services. This helps to perpetuate many distortions of history. Only thanks to an administrative anomaly are some key SOE files now in the public domain. Without this bureaucratic foul-up this book could not have been written.

Our children and grandchildren are entitled to the full truth. It is a perversion of justice that the children of Loyalists should have to live with the slur that their parents were not true patriots.

The big lie of the Yugoslav civil war was perhaps best encapsulated in a recollection by R. H. S. Crossman (subsequently a senior cabinet minister in Harold Wilson's Labour government), who was involved in Special Forces affairs in the Second World War. Crossman wrote (quoted in Milan Deroc's *Special Operations Explored*), "I remember the awkward moment when the Government dropped Mihailović and backed Tito. 'In future' our directive ran 'Mihailovic forces will be described not as "patriots" but as "terrorist gangs." We shall drop the phrase "Red bandits", as applied to Partisans and substitute "Freedom Fighters".' "

Such is the stuff of history.

CHAPTER
13
Churchill's Charade?

■

Lord Alanbrooke, the wartime chief of the imperial general staff and close advisor to Churchill, wrote of Churchill in his diary after the Quebec conference, "He has an unfortunate trick of picking up some isolated operation, and, without ever really having it looked into, setting his heart on it. When he gets into one of these moods he feels everybody is trying to thwart him and to produce difficulties. He becomes more and more set on the operation, brushing everything aside, and, when planners prove the operation to be impossible, he then appoints new planners in the hope that the operation is possible."

That fits the pattern of the Yugoslav affair. Churchill had his planners—the Foreign Office, the chiefs of staff, the Joint Intelligence Committee, the director of military intelligence, SOE London—trying to get some control over a divided resistance, trying to coordinate its activities to suit the Middle East Command's strategic plans, and trying to discourage the civil war. But

Churchill, got at by MO4 in Cairo, horned in and appointed new planners—Keble and his MO4 team and the Minister of State's Office in Cairo. From January 1943, acting on his nod and wink, they set off on a course of their own, ignoring the requests and instructions of London except when it suited their policy of pushing through a program to build up Tito's communist Partisans, to put shackles on the Loyalist Mihailović resistance, and, later, to sabotage the Loyalists.

It was Churchill, through his implied encouragement of the de facto planning team in Cairo, who set the bandwagon rolling. It was he who, by his appointment of Maclean as sole ambassador/leader to Tito, overriding the wishes of the Foreign Office and SOE, made the ultimate outcome inevitable. It was he who made the fateful decision on December 10, 1943, that Mihailović had to go. Churchill was involved in and personally responsible for all of the key decisions.

Churchill got launched on many adventuristic schemes, ploys, and ideas, but Lord Alanbrooke usually steered him back onto course. Alanbrooke appears to have stayed out of the Yugoslav affair. Perhaps he let the prime minister have this little adventure. Yugoslavia was of secondary importance from the military viewpoint, and it was going to tie down a few German divisions whatever policy was followed.

In my view, everything that happened in MO4 in 1943 may well have been simply Churchill's charade. The actors played out their predestined roles and fulfilled their duty, secure in the conviction that the Great Man would pull whatever strings were necessary to bring the hierarchy into line with *what the actors believed* to be right and to conform to his wishes. Whether their judgment was correct is quite another question. That is what I think they believed. So they could go ahead and, if need be, anticipate the hierarchy coming into line. And that's just how it worked out.

The nod and the wink. Those, along with Maclean's weekend at Chequers in July, explain it all. We do not need to look any further. We only need to count the cost: to Serbia and Yugoslavia politically, in the waste of Allied resources in a civil war, and in terms of human suffering. In those terms above all.

Unlike the other actors, Klugmann was no doubt rejoicing

that his duty to his Soviet masters and his military duty as a British officer would be relatively easy to reconcile. I am assuming that there was a nod and a wink to Keble and to the minister of state in January 1943. If there was not, then the conclusions have to be different, and very nasty. I am sure that there was. The circumstantial logic is overwhelming.

I also have to recognize the probability that Churchill made it rather clear to Maclean at Chequers in July that he had already made up his mind to back Tito; that the Foreign Office brief was no more than a formality as far as he, Churchill, was concerned; that what he wanted above all was to have the switch in policy justified; and that if the deed were to be done—that is, if Mihailović were to be abandoned—it should be done swiftly and ruthlessly, like putting down a faithful hound that has ceased to be useful.

The Soviets must have been laughing their heads off. That the Soviets have always allocated huge sums of money and effort in order to spread communism by every means around the world is well known now, though it was not fully realized then. The war, bringing its alliance of necessity with the capitalist Western powers, changed that basic Soviet policy not one iota, as the subsequent nonobservance of the Yalta agreement proved. It merely caused Stalin to adjure his agents such as Tito to be wary of revealing too much of his revolutionary intentions to the Western Allies.

But in Yugoslavia, the Soviets needed do little more than grease the wheels. The British did their work for them. This has been commented even by Partisan writers, among them, I believe, Velebit. He should know.

Whereas the Soviets always regarded the capitalist system as the enemy to be destroyed by any means fair or foul, there was a substantial body of opinion in the West during the 1930s that was coming to sympathize more and more with the Soviet system. The Soviet propaganda penetrated the academic establishment and the intelligentsia to an extent that was not generally appreciated, particularly as public attention and concern were deflected more and more by what was happening in Nazi

Germany. The Cambridge communist set was only one symptom of Soviet penetration of the intellectual elite, and it took forty years before its true extent and significance became realized. Apart from the recruitment of the known moles— and certainly there were dozens of lesser ones who have quietly died off or disappeared without ever being uncovered— the carefully planned and organized dissemination of pro-Soviet propaganda by the Comintern ensured that, precisely at the critical time, the atmosphere in the intellectual classes was highly favorable to Soviet-inspired ideas. It only needed Barbarossa— the German invasion of Soviet Russia— and their time came.

Moreover, it was precisely the academic and intellectual ranks who gravitated into the British intelligence and political agencies. Spies, agents, and moles in MI5 and MI6 who are known about— and some of whom even penetrated that sanctum, the Foreign Office—were only the tip of the iceberg. SIS/MI6 was certainly deeply penetrated by out-and-out agents. But all of the agencies such as the Political Intelligence Branch, the Political Intelligence Department, the Political Warfare Executive, not to speak of the Army Education Corps and the BBC, were plentifully supplied with would-be intellectuals who were basically honest, decent patriots but who sympathized with left-wing ideas, were emotionally involved with the great Soviet ally, and felt strongly opposed to the capitalist system. Automatically in any situation they assumed that the left-wing views were right and any other views at all were reactionary fascist rubbish. Unfortunately, a culture developed wherein these intellectuals felt that they could make their own policies.

Perhaps the smartest thing the Soviets ever did was to propagate the concept of the "antifascist war." This and the other slogan, the "anti-Nazi war," permitted any adversary, whether conservative, apolitical, or even nonrevolutionary peasant party democrat (like the Croatian Peasant Party of Dr. Maček in Yugoslavia), to be classed with the real enemy as Nazi/fascist.

So the input into the decision-making process by the intelligence agencies reflected their strong left-wing bias. It was these people and their like who were influencing policy at the time.

Some SIS reports have found their way into the Foreign Office files in the PRO headed "From Most Secret Sources." Nearly all that I read showed left-wing bias, and many were full of straightforward propaganda. Furthermore, those which had to do with my area in Yugoslavia, or with subjects I know about and can judge objectively, tended to be inaccurate and slovenly in their presentation. The facts and figures given were often wrong or distorted. I honestly believe that many of the agents just wrote anything that came into their heads in order to justify their existence; but it had to have a left-wing bias.

That was the background in the agencies that were collecting and collating intelligence and feeding it to the decision-makers, the Foreign Office and the military. I have been impressed by the stance of the officials in the southern department. They were rational and consistent throughout—well, almost—and they endeavored to steer a straight path and hew their way through the jungle of propaganda and misinformation being fed in by the agencies. In the end they were simply overwhelmed by the pressure from all sides.

I would greatly prefer to leave Churchill out of this. As Vane Ivanović wrote, without Churchill's work we might all have ended up in a bar of soap. But I cannot do so, because he was deeply involved—in fact, he was the puppet master. The Foreign Office was simply bypassed by Churchill with his bandwagon.

It is interesting to note that the communist grab for power succeeded in Yugoslavia and Albania but failed in Greece. This outcome can be traced back to Churchill too. In Greece the reaction to communist political maneuvers in the resistance was immediate and violent, and SOE heads rolled. The Greek king protested, and things happened at once. But the Greek king had powerful leverage, and Churchill was not allowing that boat to be rocked. The Greek monarchy was unpopular at home but had clout in London. The king was cousin to King George VI. In Greece Churchill wanted quiet, and that was that.

The Yugoslav monarchy, like the government, had acted up a bit and caused the prime minister a few headaches. Churchill tried to save the king, but with the Churchill-Tito love affair the king lost out. Also, King Peter was not quite in the same power league dynastically as his Greek counterpart.

As regards Albania, the monarchy had no weight with Churchill at all. And Albania went to Enver Hoxha, a really nasty communist, without more ado and without fuss. I would love to see someone research the SOE role in Albania. I believe that they would find a very big can of worms there.

In her paper to the Auty-Clogg symposium, Elizabeth Barker commented very aptly, "There were four main factors in decision making: the Foreign Office, SOE under its various names, the Military and finally Churchill himself. There were also two or three jokers in the pack—by which I mean quite respectfully, Brigadier Fitzroy Maclean, Colonel F. W. D. Deakin and also, at one point, Randolph Churchill—who influenced decisions as individuals."

As we have seen, Fitzroy Maclean in his role as ambassador to his and Churchill's protégé Tito, exercised a disproportionate influence over the total British role from September 1943 onward. He was a truly remarkable man with an uncanny instinct for the levers of power. But the bandwagon was already rolling fast before he took over the steering.

Bill Deakin too quite clearly exercised a decisive influence, though in a much more indirect, discreet, almost shadowy way.

That leaves what might be called the half-joker in the pack. It is regrettable and rather shameful that Randolph Churchill got himself into a position where he exercised some, if limited, influence. Nevertheless he did. The prime minister gave Maclean the pick of the staff he wanted. It is hardly credible that Maclean recruited Randolph for his military qualities. Randolph served a rather useful purpose, however, by adding a cozy family touch to Maclean's signals to Churchill, which from time to time ended "Randolph sends his love." And this seemed to work wonders with the Old Man. Randolph was an unfortunate influence, malicious, overweening, and frequently drunk. His role is related very vividly by his companion, who increasingly became a reluctant companion, in his *Diaries of Evelyn Waugh*. The *received wisdom* has it that the Četniks were drunkards and womanizers, whereas the Partisans were good clean boys and girls, living and fighting together in sobriety and celibacy, avoiding the *rakija* and almost ascetic. As Waugh tells us, Randolph shook them. More's the pity that Randolph did not drop to the Loyalists, bringing his father's support and the dynamo Maclean with him; and maybe a crate of whiskey too. The map of the Balkans might look different today.

Before leaving the subject of Randolph, I have to tell my own story. In late April or early May 1945 I was carried back to the ward from an operating theater in a military hospital in Rome. In a miasma of excruciating pain from a bullet wound through my sciatic nerve I had been scrubbed and prepared for amputation of my leg, which was then totally paralyzed, but the American lady surgeon spotted a barely perceptible movement in one of my toes and—my eternal thanks to her—decided to give it a chance. They pumped me full of morphine and moved me back to my hospital bed. In my absence the next bed had been surrounded by screens. In spite of my half-conscious, befuddled state, I was appalled—and annoyed—at the heartrending moans, interspersed with uncontrolled outbursts of invective, coming from the occupant who had just moved in and who was being fussed over by practically the entire staff of the hospital from the colonel in charge downward. The patient—a rather inappropriate description—was Capt. Randolph Churchill, overwhelmed by alcohol and self-pity, and hospitalized for water on the knee.

Elizabeth Barker was nearly right. Randolph Churchill was a joker in the pack—a very sick joke indeed—and a tragedy for his father, who, regrettably, was inclined to supersede the hierarchy and run things in an almost family way. That became significant in Yugoslavia. Many opportunists climbed onto the bandwagon. Is it to be wondered that Tito treated his sponsors with contempt when he levanted to Moscow without even bidding them au revoir?

Churchill the prime minister, with his whimsical love of "great guerrillas," with his special interest in the Balkans, with his proclivity to support and rely totally on those he happened to know and trust, and with his propensity to brush aside the hierarchy, was the key figure. It was his charade. But he was only the ace of hearts. An ace of hearts with a huge heart himself.

Indubitably the ace of spades in the pack was Tito himself, and through his manipulation of Deakin, Maclean, and Churchill, he surely qualifies as the key factor in the British decision making in Yugoslavia. Tito made the British decisions for them. That was the heart of the matter.

From January 1944 on there were many direct exchanges between Churchill and Tito. These have been extensively and, dare I write, selectively and sycophantically collated in a scholarly work by Dušan Biber, a Yugoslav historian, titled *Tito–Churchill*. Biber was materially helped by Elizabeth Barker, using declassified material in the PRO. As I have already recorded, Elizabeth Barker ran in blinkers. Much of the relevant material remains classified. Some of us believe that this material contains details of secret deals between the two men that would not look too good today (PRE 3/511/1, PRE 3/511/8, and PRE 3/516–526).

This correspondence—all of it—is clearly of vital historical significance in light of the massaging of history that has gone on. We need to know what is being held back and why. In particular, we need to know the composition and style of Tito's communications. Tito evidently enjoyed enormous help from—and the total trust of—his British mission. Apparently it told Churchill what Tito wanted him told. Were the BLOs drafting communications to the British authorities on Tito's behalf? We British with the missions to the Loyalists were manipulated by MO4 in 1943. We were used as pawns by the foreign secretary in early 1944. Were our colleagues in the British missions to Tito manipulated by him as he played Churchill like a fish on a hook?

Earlier I referred to Himmler's speech at the Jaegerhoehe on September 21, 1944. There was one passage that shows what the Germans thought of Tito (and incidentally Tito's attitude regarding the Allies):

I would like to give another example of steadfastness, that of Marshal Tito. I must really say that he is an old Communist, this Herr Josip Broz, a consistent man. Unfortunately he is our opponent. He really has properly earned his title of Marshal. When we catch him we will do him in at once. You can be sure of that. He is our enemy, but I wish we had a dozen Titos in Germany, men who were leaders and had such great resolution and good nerves that though they were ever encircled they would never give in. The man had nothing at all. *He was between the Russians, the British and the Americans, and had the nerve actually to fool and humiliate the British and Americans in the most comical way. He is a Moscow man. He had arms delivered from there.* He was always encircled, and the man found a way out every time. He has never capitulated.

This quotation extolling Tito was used by Fitzroy Maclean in *Disputed Barricades*, but without the rather important italicized passage. That is a pity, because his book has become regarded as almost a classic on the subject.

Incidentally, this translation of the italicized passage rather softens Himmler's actual words, which are more earthy in the original German: "Er stand zwischen den Russen, Englaendern und Amerikanern und hatte die Nerven, praktisch die Englaender und Amerikaner gottvoll hereinzulegen, gottvoll zu bescheissen. Er ist ein Mann von Moskau. Er liess sich von dort die Waffen liefern."

Less vulgarly but equally succinctly, Tito himself boasted on the occasion of his election as an honorary member of the Yugoslav Academy in Zagreb on December 27, 1947, "I have outsmarted and deceived that old fox Churchill." This unequivocal statement by Tito, like the paragraph from Himmler's speech missing from the quotation in *Disputed Barricades*, is a matter of public record. Yet none of the allegedly authoritative works written by the Tito supporters have included these historically vital statements. Such is the one-sided nature of *received wisdom*.

It is argued that Tito was such an outstanding personality and ruthlessly competent operator that he had to come out on top in any situation and that, British help or no British help, the Partisans would have ended up as masters in Yugoslavia. It is true that Mihailović was hopeless as a politician and as a self-publicist.

He was certainly badly advised, he may well have been bumbling and bureaucratic, and his Loyalists lacked the rigid discipline and organization that Tito brought to the Partisans from the Communist Party. Nevertheless, infinitely more than Tito, Mihailović represented what the Serbs in Serbia wanted. The communists did not enjoy any real support in Serbia, whatever their propagandists like to pretend.

In spite of his failings, Mihailović was a very able guerrilla. If the British had left Yugoslavia to work out her own fate, or had limited support just to dropping in British teams for specific operations, then Serbia—or the mountainous area of Serbia at the very least—would never have fallen to the Partisans. Furthermore, the same number of Axis divisions would have remained tied down. The majority were there to guard against an Allied landing and to protect communications. They had to stay under any circumstances. And, had we not supported the Partisan invasion of Serbia, the Loyalists' planned large-scale uprising, the *ustanak*, would have done a much better job of harassing the German withdrawal. In this regard, the Partisans largely failed.

Unfortunately, guerrilla warfare was not what it was all about in Yugoslavia. It was all about a civil war and, as far as Tito was concerned, a civil war in which reprisals, casualties, chaos, and misery were of no significance or importance. But Mihailović, with his worries about saving the Serb nation from total extinction, was fighting with one hand tied behind his back.

If the British had not positively taken sides in Tito's favor, I do not believe that Stalin would have risked conflict with the West by providing Red Army help. That is really proved by Stalin's failure to support Tito in the row with the British over Venezia Giulia.

The Western Allied support was decisive not only militarily but also psychologically. The British denunciation of Mihailović and the Loyalist Četniks put the Serbian populace in an impossible position. They had prayed, hoped, and confidently anticipated that, in the end, the Western Allies, their traditional friends, would invade—in which case they would have risen to a man in the *ustanak*—or that at the very least they would be left to settle their own affairs. Instead, the Allies turned against their Serbian friends, and the full weight of the Allied propaganda swung behind Tito. There was then no longer light at the end of the tunnel.

Maclean himself tells us all about it in *Eastern Approaches*:

> . . . supplies to the Četniks had ceased and arms and ammunition were now being dropped to the Partisans in very considerable quantities . . . the change in our attitude had also an important psychological effect. All the prestige which the Četniks had hitherto enjoyed as a result of allied support was now transferred to the Partisans. The effect was increased by the news that Tito had come to terms with King Peter and by the King's proclamation calling on his subjects to support the Partisans. . . . Much play was made with the Tito-Šubašić understanding and with a proclamation made by King Peter calling on the people to support Tito, both of which carried a great deal of weight in Serbia, where Royalist feeling was so strong. Finally, Communist aims and policy were kept in the background, and very little was seen of the Red Stars, hammers and sickles, which were so prominently displayed by the Partisans in other parts of the country, but which would have had little appeal in this land of prosperous small holders.

There it is—the British betrayal of Serbia—clearly and succinctly described by Maclean himself.

In order to use the heaviest guns on the Partisan side, Maclean himself had flown to Serbia to oversee the Ratweek operations and presumably to show the Serbs a real live British general helping the Partisans, in case they did not know what was good for them. The bombing of Leskovac by the Balkan Air Force on the occasion of his visit shattered the Serbian heartland and demonstrated to any doubters that the British were firmly on the Partisan side.

All of this followed shortly after the meeting between Churchill and Tito in Naples, when the deal was struck with the strawman politician Šubašić in order to erect a façade of legitimacy. Yet Churchill and Maclean were fully clear between themselves that Tito was going to introduce a communist government after the war. Nevertheless, in the "liberation" of Serbia, Perfidious Albion lent itself fully to the manipulation of the king, the exploitation of his gullibility, and the use of the allegedly democratic government of the straw man Šubašić, in order to trick the Serbian people and beat them into submission.

It would not be so awful if we had been able to stop the massacres and liquidations that followed—which the British missions must have known might follow—as a quid pro quo for having greatly helped the Partisan victory. But Tito gave nothing, at any time, or in any way. And possibly he was not even pressed to do so.

In an article in *Encounter* ("A Conversation with Milovan Djilas," 1979), the writer states that "the British Military Mission knew what the Partisans were doing but preferred to shut their eyes." It might have been fairer to write that they were impotent. Tito was by then confident that he could do what he wanted, and the British could do nothing to stop him.

I repeat that I sincerely believe that the British cooperation was decisive in the conquest of Serbia by the communists and substantially helped Tito to carry out his revolution. And even if the Partisans did it all on their glorious ownsome, I cannot forgive the vilification of the Loyalists, just because they fought for their traditions and for their king, and the character assassination of Mihailović, just because he got in Tito's way and scared the guts out of Tito; and I cannot forgive the totally one-sided version of history that has been assiduously built up to justify what was done.

Mihailović was an officer and a gentleman in the old tradition and of the old school, one of the class that had made the Serbian fighting men such a wonderful example in previous wars. The Serbian leaders I personally knew and worked with—Stefanović, Andrejević, and even the ambitious and ruthless Manić—were cast in the same mold. The civil war was not only a war between communism and nationalism. It was a war between new upstart revolutionaries without any rule book, and the values that we British had previously prized. Tragically, we destroyed our natural friends. I think we did so because, after the British cultural revolution of the 1930s in the leading universities, our own values had been lost.

CHAPTER
14
The Cost of It All

■

In his report about his adventures when he was captured by the Loyalists, after he had been dropped to the Partisans, Lieutenant Commander MacPhail recounts a conversation with a Serb who had been educated at Oxford University. This Serb claimed— and very rightly too—that the Partisans were not grateful to us, that they used British help for propaganda, and that they would fight us tomorrow if Stalin told them to.

In fact, that Serb understated his case. The Partisans would have fought the British to assert their claims in Austria and Venezia Giulia in the spring of 1945 without any encouragement from Stalin at all. That they did not do so was thanks to the tough, no-nonsense New Zealander General Freyberg, who pulled them up sharp. But Tito was ready, willing, and anxious to fight his benefactors, the Anglo-Americans, in the spring of 1945, just as he had been ready and willing to join with the Germans in resisting an Anglo-American landing in the spring of 1943. Tito would have made a pact with the devil himself to gain power. It was certainly the devil's work that Tito and his clique carried out after the Russians and Bulgarians had helped him overrun the Loyalists in Serbia and the Germans had finally retreated.

I am not a historian, and throughout this book I have tried very hard to stick to what I know. I have written of my own eyewitness experiences from June 1943 to May 1944, and I have related these recollections to the can of worms that I found when I examined the files in the British Public Records Office and, in particular, those in the War Office section. These records contain the formerly classified SOE files, which evidently were released in error. I have not researched the happenings between June 1944 and May 1945, when the second wave of fratricidal horror hit Yugoslavia. (The first wave, of course, was the genocide operation carried out in 1941 by the Croatian *ustaša* against the Serbian minority in the Independent State of Croatia.) So I have to depend on the little that has been published. Even that small amount is horrifying.

Maj. Linn Farish, the chief American liaison officer with Tito, in his touching June 28, 1944 report, wrote of "a few communists who would see their brothers killed to further their political aims." I did not know Linn Farish, but he seems to have been thoroughly decent, as well as a highly perceptive and intelligent man. He was morally brave enough to recognize and report how things were going very wrong even as early as the summer of 1944. At that time Tito and Titoism were all the fashion. Anyone resisting the policy of total support for the Yugoslav communists was regarded in Allied circles in Bari as almost akin to a traitor. As I have recorded already, Farish wrote, "I personally do not feel that I can go on with the work in Yugoslavia unless I can sincerely feel that every possible honest effort is being made to put an end to the civil strife."

Farish did not live to see or learn what happened in 1945 when the new wave of horror hit Yugoslavia, as Tito set out to ensure that all possible opposition was ruthlessly crushed, and that the job was done so as to ensure that no opposition could possibly arise in his lifetime. One doubts that he worried too much about what was going to happen thereafter, beyond concern that his own personality cult would endure into history.

From what has been written about the massacres that occurred when Tito's minions had a clear field in which to operate, it is clear that a common feature of these horrors— particularly when refugees were tricked into a forcible repatriation by the British forces in Austria— was the utter determination of the specially recruited Tito extermination squads that no one should live to tell the tale. Some say that more than 30,000 died in the infamous pit of Kočevje in Slovenia, including many who had been told by the British, with whom they had taken refuge, that they were being transferred to Palmanova in Italy. They only discovered after they had been locked into trains operated by the British between Austria and Slovenia that they were being handed over to the Partisans. Milovan Djilas recently went on record with a figure of 20,000; he commented that the British "had made a mistake" in repatriating them and that the Tito government "had made a mistake" in massacring them.

Another 60,000 to 80,000 Croatians *ustaši* and Domobrans (home guard) tried to surrender to the Western Allies, but the surrender was refused; the Partisans captured them and herded them off on a march on which the vast majority perished. St. Vid, the transit center in Slovenia through which many of the victims passed, had already seen the passage of another 30,000 or so, who were taken out and slaughtered in order to make way for the Serbian Četniks, Croatian Domobrans, and Slovenian Domobrans from the British camp at Viktring. In Kočevje the death roll was at least 20,000, possibly 40,000. Another massacre site was Teharje. Yet another was in the Kamnik Mountains, where it has been rumored that 30,000 perished.

Few of those massacred at Teharje or Kočevje or in the Kamnik Mountains were *ustaši*. Most were Slovenian and Croatian Domobrans, together with Serbian Četniks. The *ustaši* had a bad record, but no civilized court in the Western world would have condemned the home guards as malefactors: they were simply defeated combatants. And the Četniks were our allies. Those massacres were not justified punishment ordered by courts. They were the arbitrary settling of old scores, without any pretense of trial, by communist execution squads.

In my first chapter I suggested that "about a quarter of a million" might be a realistic figure for the political killings by the communists. I was interested to read a suggestion by Ljubo Sirc in his memoirs just published (*Between Hitler and Tito*) that perhaps as many as 300,000 perished. Ljubo Sirc, a professor of political economy at Glasgow University and now director of the Centre for the Study of Communist Economies, served with the Partisan forces himself and is thus superbly qualified to write with restraint and realism on the subject.

Milovan Djilas, one of Tito's closest immediate circle, has also told us a great deal about these horrors in his writings. Furthermore, Stevan Pavlowitch, in *The Improbable Survivor*, underlines the significance of those writings. He records: "In fact all power emanated from the Communist Party under a quadrumvirate made up of Tito—whose cult was consciously organised—with Djilas, Kardelj, and Ranković." Djilas, now a revisionist and evidently remorseful about his personal share in the responsibility for all of this killing, tells us that Tito wanted the killing stopped only because "no one fears death anymore."

And while all of it was going on, Tito's Western Allied sponsors, who had enormously facilitated his grab for power but were now impotent to restrain him, either were hoodwinked some more or closed their eyes to the horrors.

The lack of information and discussion about the Tito massacres is amazing. Until the historian Count Nikolai Tolstoy became involved in a sensational court case over who bore the responsibility for the repatriation tragedy, very little had appeared in the West, and for obvious reasons historians in Belgrade were not inclined to enlighten us. The cozy British Yugoslav establishment symposiums talked about less disturbing things, about British Foreign Office internal squabbles and the like, and massaged the *received wisdom* so as to portray the takeover of Yugoslavia by Tito as the best outcome in the circumstances to maintain the integrity of the country. It seems that no one dared to stand up and ask: But what about the quarter of a million people it is rumored that Tito murdered?

There has been no hesitation about recalling the *ustaša* genocide. There has been plenty of talk about that. But for the past forty-five years there seems to have been astonishing amnesia about, or hesitation to dare to mention, the communist political killings. Even now, after Tolstoy, we have little record of the killings in other parts of Yugoslavia. But that they took place, massively, there is no shadow of doubt. It is possible, very possible, that Tito topped the *ustaša* record. Who knows? Who dared to count? But it was some performance if he did. The Partisan killings were certainly in the top league of communist butchery.

There were many massacres in Soviet Russia about which no one knew anything until *glasnost* started to dig into the dark corners. But there is no doubt whatsoever that in Yugoslavia, in Russia, in Poland, and elsewhere in communist territories, the butchery was horrifying. There is also no doubt that the leaders, *in every case*, were not doing their devil's work for ideological reasons. They were despots out for personal power and using ideology to justify their liquidation of all potential opposition. Even Milovan Djilas commented to that effect in his book *Wartime*, in which, obviously, he was referring to Tito specifically.

It is rather futile to speculate about what might have happened had the British not been hoodwinked by Tito, had the British stuck to their policy of support for Mihailović alone, and had the Allies given him real support in the autumn of 1943 and throughout 1944, when short-haul aircraft were available. Here we should take a look at some statistics. They are very revealing, and the *received wisdom* has ignored them for too long.

In 1942 SOE Cairo had only four Liberators available. They were augmented by four Halifaxes in March 1943 and by twelve more Halifaxes around June 1943. These planes had to service the entire SOE area in the Balkans, notably Yugoslavia, Greece, and Albania, and from May 1943 they were serving both sides in Yugoslavia. From late 1943 plentiful Dakotas were available to fly from Brindisi in Italy; they could reach the Partisan areas with ease but not the eastern Serbian area, where the Loyalists were located. Moreover, from September 22, 1943, when Fitzroy Maclean had his first dinner with Tito, supplies to Mihailović had been stopped in order to divert everything available to the Partisans.

From various sources I have calculated that Mihailović received a total of less than 150 sorties, 250 tons in all, from the autumn of 1941 till the end of 1943 when we abandoned him. Even this figure may be an overestimate. F. H. Hinsley, the foremost expert, gives total deliveries to Mihailović up to the Italian armistice, that is, till early September 1943, as 118 tons. Supplies sent after that were negligible.

The Balkan Air Force took over operations in the summer of 1944. Their official figures show that from June 1944 till May 1945—the precise period during which the civil war was at its peak—11,600 sorties totaling 16,460 tons were delivered to Tito's Partisans.

But the Partisans had been receiving the vast bulk of MO4/ Force 133 deliveries already since June 1943. They received approximately 500 sorties in 1943, equal to about 800 tons. Hinsley shows that in the first half of 1944 they received about 3,500 tons. Thus they received 4,300 tons in the first year, up to the end of May 1944, and 16,460 tons in the following year.

The 20,000 tons received by air by the Partisans compare with about 200 tons received by Mihailović. He got one percent of what they got. This shows up the ludicrous nature of the patter in the *received wisdom* about how Mihailović had our support and did not use it. What would the Loyalists have achieved had they received even a quarter of the arms sent to the Partisans?

But that's not all. Shipments by sea to the Yugoslav islands and the mainland for the Partisans in 1943 were 18,000 to 20,000 tons. I have no figures for January to May 1944, but from June 1944 to May 1945 a further 10,000 tons were shipped. Thus the Partisans got, probably, 40,000 tons by sea in all. Mihailović got nothing.

The Partisans in Yugoslavia—it has been said—received more supplies than the total of all other European resistance movements. And the vast bulk of those arms and supplies were used in the civil war, which served no useful purpose for the Western

Allies and brought communism, massacres, and misery to the people of Yugoslavia. The support of Tito in his grab for power was a disaster politically and morally. It also represented probably the least cost-effective operation ever mounted.

There is a letter from a Major Last to Mr. J. Reed of the Political Intelligence Department of the Foreign Office (FO 371/ 44278), which states that already between April 1943 and mid-September 1944 there were 5,000 air sorties of 6,900 tons and 22,000 tons by sea delivered to Tito. Incredibly, Major Last had to write this letter in order to answer an attack by Tito's Radio Free Yugoslavia broadcasting from Russia that alleged a lack of Allied support for Tito. Ironically, the broadcast was made just as Tito "levanted" off to Moscow, cocking a snook at his sponsors. Those sponsors really were patsies.

Sir Orme Sargent of the British Foreign Office contended that backing both sides would lead to civil war. The decision was accordingly taken to back Tito because it was believed that "he was doing all the fighting." That claim is certainly open to challenge. The information on which the claim is based came, of course, almost entirely from communist sources, communist propaganda, and sources indirectly influenced by the communists. But one thing is certain. By backing Tito, by putting in those massive supplies of arms, and by giving him our full recognition and every type of support, the British achieved precisely the opposite of what they were seeking. They scored the biggest home goal of all time. The arms deliveries precipitated the civil war. They went straight into battles in which Yugoslavs fought Yugoslavs. We have on our consciences not only those subsequently massacred but also the many, many thousands of Yugoslav patriots who fell on both sides as Serbs with the Partisans fought Serbs in the homeland using British and American weapons, delivered in American aircraft flown by British pilots. Have we no shame?

CHAPTER
15
The Morning After

■

Churchill got carried away in December 1943. His signals and minutes indicate that he was vitriolic about Mihailović and the Loyalists. Whatever the exact words of the cynical exchange with Maclean about not wishing to make Yugoslavia their home after the war, he was in a mood to allow himself to accept anything Tito wanted and to be manipulated by him. Eventually, however, that attitude changed.

As early as July 1944 (File PREM 3 513/8) Churchill had been asking questions about Tito's prewar activities and rumors that he had led demonstrations opposing resistance to the Germans. But it was not until the spring of 1945 that Churchill began to get the true measure of the dark forces that he had unleashed in the Balkans by his whimsical policy.

On March 11, 1945, in a memo to the foreign secretary (File PREM 3 513/6), he wrote,

My feeling is that henceforward our inclination should be to back Italy against Tito. Tito can be left to himself in his mountains to stew in Balkan juice which is bitter. But the fact that we are generally favourable to Italian claims at the head of the Adriatic will give us an influence over Italian internal politics as against Communists and wild men which may assist the re-integration of the Italian state. I have lost my relish for Yugoslavia which state must rest on the basis of the Tito-Subasic agreements etc. On the other hand I hope we may still save Italy from the Bolshevist petulance.

The above is for your eye alone. Pray let me know how you feel in regard to it.

On March 18, 1945, Churchill wrote in a letter to the foreign secretary, "I do not see how we could explain a change of policy to the Americans. The United States Government have never been enthusiastic about our pro-Partisan policy, and it has always been with great difficulty that we have dragged them reluctantly behind us. Are we now . . . to have to explain to them that after all Tito has not turned out to be what we hoped for."

On April 16, 1945 (File PREM 3 513/10), he wrote in a private office memo, "My inclination is towards the gradual but steady withdrawal of all our agents and missions from Yugoslavia except those at the Summit in Belgrade. Let me have an account of the numbers of British officers and men who are at present at the mercy of these wild people." Two days later he wrote to the earl of Halifax, ambassador to the United States (File PREM 3 513/6), "(1) You know my views about Tito whom I have never trusted since he levanted from Vis. (2) I therefore fully agree that all supplies to Tito should be shut down on the best pretext that can be found."

On April 20, 1945, he wrote to Sir Orme Sargent,

This is another proof of how vain it is to throw away our substance in a losing game with Soviet Russia in Tito land. . . .

The Russians are willing to aid the Yugoslav Air Force. Why have we to divert from our scanty store the valuable material in officers and men? The great changes which have taken place in the connections and centre of gravity of the Yugoslav government since we talked about providing them with an air force must not fall unnoticed. They have thrown themselves wholeheartedly into the hands of Russia. In these circumstances I should deprecate our making any serious sacrifice for the fight to play a losing game. As you know, my view is that a diplomatic and even perhaps a military front can be made between Britain, the United States and Italy in the disputed Adriatic territory. Nothing will wrest Yugoslavia from the Russian grip. In this particular theatre the policy is "dis-engage." On the contrary in Greece it is "hold fast."

Two days later he noted in a memo to his private office, "I propose to send a telegram to the Foreign Secretary, Field Marshall Alexander and Mr Stevenson appraising them of my changed attitude towards Marshall Tito. Please get together my various telegrams and minutes to Mr Eden on this subject, so that I can condense them into one secret message."

On April 25, 1945, he wrote another memo to his private office (File PREM 3 513/10): "In view of the way in which all our affairs are being sold down the counter in Yugoslavia and the mockery of the 50/50 agreement with Russia I really cannot write to King Peter except in the strain that it has not been within my power to alter the course of events and that I am sure that we have done all we could in the circumstances. I cannot however claim that the result is at all satisfactory."

One month later, on May 25, the prime minister wrote to the foreign secretary, "Be very careful that our missions are not cut off in Yugoslavia. They will be looking for hostages soon." And on the same day he wrote (File PREM 3 513/8),

Ask the Foreign Office for the fullest possible dossier on Tito. Is it true that he was educated at a Communist college? Is it true that he occupied part of his time organising strikes down the Dalmatian coast? Is it true that he did not move to fight for Yugoslavia when it was attacked by Germany but waited till June 22nd 1941 when the Comintern gave instructions to all its minions to help Russia? Has he ever been married and how many times? We know all about his running away to the island of Vis when it got hot on the mainland and levanting from Vis after three months of our protection to remake his contacts with Moscow. It is just as well to have all these things looked at to see what they amount to.

A lengthy Foreign Office memo confirmed the prime minister's suspicions fully. Still, it is deplorable that his trusted protégés, who had been sent to Yugoslavia to find out all about Tito, had not briefed him on these matters in December 1943 when they were telling him all about Mihailović's alleged shortcomings even without ever having met the general.

Not long thereafter, the British general elections removed Churchill from power; but evidently his resentment at the confidence trick carried out against him by Tito festered. In the winter of 1945 there was an occasion in Brussels on which he apparently spoke out at a dinner party. It was reported in the journal *Europe and America* on December 13, 1945, and in *Time and Tide* on December 29. Churchill was reported to have said, "During the war I thought I could trust Tito. He had promised me to observe the agreement he had concluded with Šubašić but now I am aware that I committed one of my biggest mistakes in the war."

The *received wisdom* has desperately tried to cast doubts on the veracity of these reports. But there is a note (FO 371/59517) from Sir John Colville, dated January 15, 1946, stating, "This certainly represents Mr Churchill's views and I don't suppose he would mind it being known: but I doubt if he will say so publicly except under provocation. He certainly won't accept any arguments to the contrary."

That surely is good enough.

Finally, the epitaph comes in a rather pathetic letter that Sir Winston Churchill wrote to Ernest Bevin, the foreign secretary of the Labour government, on April 9, 1946, asking that His Majesty's Government intervene to secure a fair trial for Mihailović. Not all of those British involved in helping Tito gain power were prepared to show magnanimity in victory. Churchill was; and Churchill, that really big man, showed his greatness by attaching two appendixes to his letter. They totally demolish any justification he could have thought he had for what he did that fateful December 10, 1943.

The first was a letter dated April 18, 1946, from a Capt. Maurice John Vitou, which stated,

1. To the best of my knowledge I was the first Allied Officer to contact General Draja Mihailovitch in this war.
2. I entered Yugoslavia on 22nd July, 1941, as an escaped prisoner of war.
3. I served with the followers of General Mihailovitch for a period of nearly nine months, and in the same H.Q. i.e. under the direct command of the General himself for three months.
4. I served a further period of ten months in political prisons and the Gestapo with members of General Mihailovitch's Chetnik Organisation.
5. I have full knowledge of the operations against the Germans by General Mihailovitch's organisation during the latter half of 1941 and early 1942.
6. I was in the town of Chachak in central Serbia, when *the forces of General Mihailovitch were attacked by the Partisans*, the nucleus of the present regime, thus enabling the Germans to retake the town.
7. I am prepared to swear an oath that General Mihailovitch's attitude was absolutely pro-British during the time I knew him and that all his efforts were concentrated on expelling the enemy from Jugoslavia.
8. I am further prepared to swear that these efforts were hampered by the attacks on his forces by the Partisans.
9. As an English Officer, an escaped prisoner of war, I was helped in every conceivable way by General Draja Mihailovitch.
10. During the time I spent in Yugoslavia General

Mihailovitch was as popular *with the people* as the Partisans were unpopular.

11. I know that Italian prisoners in General Mihailovitch's hands were exchanged for arms and field pieces to be used against the Germans.

12. I am aware that an Anti-Communist organisation (in no way connected with Gen. Mihailovitch) under Costa Pachamac calling themselves "Chetniks" and working under German control operated against the Partisans.

13. I was arrested and handed over to the Gestapo by the above organisation.

Nothing could be clearer or more positive than that.

The second was a statement by Capt. Vojislav Ilich, dated February 11, 1946. It read as follows:

WHY I AM NOT GOING HOME

This evening I am asked the question why I am not going home. My answer is, simply because I ran away. Why did I run away? That is what I am going to tell you.

The war in Yugoslavia found me a Captain in the Royal Yugoslav Air Force. I was a Pilot Instructor. In April 1941, serving as a fighter pilot, I had six German air-craft to my credit.

After the occupation of Yugoslavia by the Germans, I went to the mountains under the command of Draja Mihailovich. On December 15th, 1941, I was captured by the Germans, and, on February 22nd, 1942, I was condemned to death as a Chetnik. I was reprieved and sent to a Concentration Camp in Germany. I escaped from that camp and succeeded in rejoining Mihailovich in Serbia. I became Commander of a brigade of Mihailovich's Ravna Gora Corps under Captain Rakovich. From that time on, through 1943 and 1944, I fought with the Chetniks against the Germans, and sometimes also I had to defend myself from the Partisan Forces, which attacked us in the rear. I continued to fight against the Germans until the Russians came to Yugoslavia in October 1944.

When the Russian Army started their offensive in Yugoslavia, Mihailovich's forces were fully engaged everywhere in Serbia. Many towns and almost the whole of Serbia were in the hands of Mihailovich's forces. The most bloody fighting was carried on along the line of the withdrawal of the German forces from Greece and the Balkans. A great part of these forces, numbering about 30,000, had to pass through Chachak, where I was engaged with my Brigade. On October 14th, 1944, I liberated from the Germans a small place— Preljina—six kilometres from Chachak from all sides, when the Russian Army approached. The Russians were surprised to see us fighting the Germans, and in the beginning they thought we were Partisans.

We then arranged with the Russians for a common plan of action in the fight for Chachak. The negotiations were carried on in a little village called Brdjane, twelve kilometres from Chachak. I was present at these negotiations. We drew up a written agreement about joint action against the Germans. We fought for Chachak, supported by Russian artillery. Four times we took Chachak, and each time we had to withdraw in the face of constant fresh German reinforcements coming up from the south. Our losses were heavy. My Corps handed over to the Russians more than 2,000 prisoners. My brigade alone handed over 700 prisoners, for which I got a receipt from the Russians. In addition, we handed over another 4,000 German prisoners captured in our previous fighting with the enemy. When at last Chachak was definitely held by our troops, the Partisans of Tito arrived in small numbers and the Russians began to disarm Mihailovich's men, who would not recognise Tito as the Russians wished them to do. Only one part of our troops was disarmed, the rest of us went to the mountains immediately. Mihailovich gave orders for some units to move towards Bosnia and others to disperse in the country and await further orders. Dressed as a peasant, I entered Chachak, but was recognised by the Partisans and arrested. After three months in prison, I was condemned to death, together with 44 others. However, instead of killing me, I was sent to a camp near Shabatz to be used for clearing mines at the German front, north of Belgrade. This had to be done without any instruments for locating the buried mines. I succeeded in escaping and joining a Partisan fighting unit, and went to the front. After capturing some 20 lorries from the Germans I became a driver, and was later promoted to the rank of 2nd Lt. When the war ended I was taken into the Air Force as a transport pilot.

On October 11th, 1945, I was sent to London as a pilot, and I made use of this first opportunity to escape.

Why did I escape? Here are the reasons:—

1). I fought in Mihailovich's ranks for democracy and freedom in the Western sense and in the real meaning of these words. In Yugoslavia to-day, there is no democracy and no freedom, but only a dictatorial police state. The whole time I lived under suspicion and was shadowed by the OZNA—which is the secret Police in Yugoslavia exactly like the Gestapo used to be in Germany. This tyrannical police organisation sent regular reports about my conduct three times a month to the higher headquarters. Only those who have been there and have experience with OZNA—the Gestapo of Yugoslavia to-day—can know the true position. I lived in constant fear of sudden arrest without any cause.

2). When I was in prison in Chachak over 3,000 of Mihailovich's men were shot. My Corps Commander, Captain Rakovich, committed suicide to avoid being captured by the Partisans, who had surrounded him. All those who fought for real democracy and freedom under Mihailovich against the Germans, are to-day the opponents of Tito's regime, and they have to be destroyed in the spirit of this regime. I should like to mention here that my younger brother was also shot by the Partisans on January 17th, 1945, while my father, a Serbian priest, was murdered by Pavelich's Ustashis in 1941.

3). In Tito's army to-day, which is purely a Communist Party army: there is terrible propaganda against the Western Allies. Russia is the only friend, or, better said, the real boss of Yugoslavia.

4). How could I stay at home in such conditions? I had

to take this step. Some of my friends said "Remain and wait". Others said "Go to the mountains" and so on. As you see, we are still fighting for freedom.

That is the reason that I ran away, even though I had to leave my wife and child behind.

Those depositions, given by a British and a Yugoslav officer, are impressive and touching. But their primary significance here is that they represent a damning indictment of the British policy instituted by Churchill himself. It must have cost him dearly to have exposed his error so clearly to the Labour government's foreign secretary. He would never have done so had he not been totally convinced that, as he said in Brussels, he had made one of his "biggest mistakes in the war."

Churchill's approach to the Labour government evoked no favorable response from Clement Attlee, who feared that action on Mihailović's behalf would not be well received by the Labour Party. A plea by British officers to be allowed to give evidence at Mihailović's trial was rejected, and the testimony of some hundreds of American officers and aircrew was not admitted.

So, with no evidence in his defense, Draža Mihailović, abandoned by his allies, went calmly to his death on July 17, 1946. His last words at the trial were dignified, those of a gentleman: "Fate was merciless to me, when it threw me into the maelstrom. I wanted much, I started much but the gale of the world swept me and my work away."

ABBREVIATIONS

AFHQ   Allied Forces Headquarters

BBC   British Broadcasting Corporation

BLO   British liaison officer

CIA   Central Intelligence Agency (U.S.A.)

ELAS/EAM   Greek communist organizations, civil and military

Enigma   German cipher machine (see also Ultra)

Force 133   Successor to MO4 but under army command

GCHQ   Then secret government communications and signal interception center

GHQ   General headquarters

G1 (GSO1)   General staff officer grade 1 (colonel)

G2 (GSO2)   General staff officer grade 2 (major)

HMG   His (Her) Majesty's Government

ISLD   Another wartime cover name for MI6/SIS

JIC   Joint Intelligence Committee

KGB   Soviet secret service, successor to NKVD

ABBREVIATIONS

MI6	British secret intelligence organization for foreign intelligence, also called SIS and ISLD
MI5	British secret counterintelligence organization
MO4	Cairo office of SOE until November 1943
NKVD	Soviet secret police prior to KGB
OGPU	Soviet military intelligence organization
OSS	Office of Strategic Services U.S.A. Wartime intelligence and special force organization. Forerunner of CIA, it combined functions carried out by MI6 and SOE in British intelligence services
OZNA	Yugoslav secret police
PIB	Political Intelligence Branch, Cairo
PID	Political Intelligence Department of Foreign Office
PRO	Public Records Office
PWE	Political Warfare Executive
RAF	Royal Air Force
SAS	British elite raiding force (Special Air Service)
SD	Sicherheitsdienst, German security service
Section D	Predecessor organization of SOE
SIS	Another name for MI6 and ISLD
SOE	Special Operations Executive, British special force for undertaking both overt and covert paramilitary operations
SS	Schutzstaffel, German military political formations
SSEES	School of Slavonic and East European Studies, University of London
37 Military Mission	Rear base of Maclean mission to Tito under Balkan Air Force headquarters. It absorbed Yugoslav section of Force 133
Ultra	Organization that broke the German Enigma ciphers
UNRRA	United Nations Relief and Rehabilitation Agency
USAAC	United States Army Air Corps
USAAF	United States Army Air Force
W/T	Wireless telegraphy

CHRONOLOGY

April 6, 1941	Axis troops invade Yugoslavia.
April 10, 1941	New national state of Croatia is proclaimed by Axis.
April 14–16, 1941	King Peter II flees into exile eventually in London, where émigré government establishes itself.
April 18, 1941	Yugoslav forces capitulate.
May 12, 1941	Mihailović establishes headquarters of Loyalist resistance on Ravna Gora with cadre of army officers. He starts recruiting members of the Četnik home guards into a Loyalist resistance movement.
Spring 1941	*Ustaši* (SS-style Croatian fascists) launch extermination program directed at Serbian minority in new Croatian state,

	which continues throughout the summer and autumn.
July 1941	After the German invasion of the U.S.S.R., Tito establishes a second resistance movement, the Partisans, with headquarters in Užice. He draws heavily on Serbian refugees from genocide in Croatia for recruits. Leadership is communist.
Summer and autumn 1941	Uprisings in Serbia and Montenegro, by both Partisans and Četniks, lead to massive Axis reprisals. Partisans withdraw from Serbia; Loyalists disperse into scattered units, with many going underground or returning home, available for recall.
September 20, 1941	Capt. Bill "Marko" Hudson, the first of the British liaison officers whose function would be to organize resistance and sabotage in Yugoslavia, is landed by submarine on the Montenegrin coast. He makes his way first to Tito's and then to Mihailović's headquarters.
October 1941	Mihailović-Tito negotiations to coordinate resistance are interrupted by Axis cleanup sweeps following the abortive uprisings. Tito is forced to move headquarters to Bosnia. Mihailović, with a small staff, goes underground in Sandžak. Hudson spends winter alone, rejoining Mihailović in April 1942, but remains without adequate W/T communications with Cairo.
Throughout 1942	Mihailović, officially named defense minister of the Yugoslav government in exile, moves his headquarters around western Serbia, eastern Bosnia, and the Sandžak, where he maintains fairly

substantial mobile forces. He has large potential manpower reserves in Četnik formations throughout Serbia and Montenegro, as well as in Slovenia and Dalmatia.

In Britain, BBC starts hyping Mihailović. BBC claims arouse unrealistic expectations among Western Allies and encourage Axis reprisals. Britain's SOE and the Yugoslav émigré government counsel Mihailović to avoid reprisals and to conserve his strength for eventual major uprising. Loyalists do continue sabotage throughout 1942 but are increasingly deterred by reprisals and hampered by lack of support from British. During this period SOE specifically condones accommodations with the Italians by Montenegrin Četniks (Stanišić, Djurišić, and others) designed to facilitate eventual takeover of Italian positions and arms. Meanwhile, Tito builds up his Partisan National Liberation Army in Croatia, western Bosnia, Herzegovina, Dalmatia, Slovenia, and Montenegro. Responding to Axis cleanup sweeps, his headquarters and his main army shuttle backward and forward between Bosnia and Croatia, with forays south into Herzegovina and Montenegro.

February 1942   James Klugmann, known communist recruiter, joins SOE Cairo. Hugh Seton-Watson, Klugmann's friend and left-inclined academic specialist in Balkan affairs, becomes increasingly influential in political intelligence in Cairo and in MO4 (SOE Cairo) itself.

Spring 1942   Col. S. W. "Bill" Bailey of SOE and Capt. William Stuart of SIS start recruiting communist Croats in Canada for future use in Yugoslavia.

Allies become aware of Tito's Partisans; Dragi Radivojević (alias Branko Radojević), an International Brigade veteran, is recruited in United States to be dropped into Croatia "to identify Tito." Instead, after three months in Klugmann's charge in Cairo, hc winds up with Mihailović using the name Charles Robertson. His official task is to restore Hudson's W/T communications, but he has a secret brief to "report" on Hudson and Mihailović and to find out about the Partisans.

Early July 1942   Radio Free Yugoslavia, broadcasting from southern Russia, begins pro-Tito and anti-Mihailović campaign. Intensive communist misinformation campaign is instituted through neutral countries and via communist sympathizers in British secret services and other Allied agencies.

September 1942   Maj. Basil Davidson becomes acting head of the Yugoslav section of MO4, the Cairo office of SOE.

December 1942   Bailey, returned from recruiting communist Croats in Canada, drops to Mihailović headquarters as chief BLO.

Capt. F. W. D. "Bill" Deakin joins MO4 from SOE London.

January 1943   SOE starts dropping liaison officers to Mihailović. From January to September nine such missions are dropped.

ca. January 30, 1943   Following a personal social contact with

	Churchill made by Deakin, Brig. C. M. "Bolo" Keble obtains Winston Churchill's permission to contact Tito, in apparent contravention of SOE's official pro-Mihailović policy.
February 1943	"Christening party" speech by Mihailović condemns lack of Allied support and brackets communists with the *ustaša* as his worst enemies. Bailey stops supplies and reports speech to Cairo. Diplomatic exchanges over incident stretch out for four months.
March 1943	Battle of Neretva. Main Partisan army, driven south by Germans, enters Loyalist territory and defeats Montenegrin Četnik forces.
March–April 1943	"The March negotiations": Partisans and Germans negotiate in Sarajevo and Zagreb. Partisans agree to stop sabotage in Croatia; Germans agree to stop pursuit of Partisans. This truce frees Partisan main army to deal with Montenegrin Četniks.
April 20, 1943	Dropping of missions to Tito Partisans begins, using the communist Croats recruited in Canada. This follows formal approval in March by the chiefs of staff in London, and by military headquarters in the Middle East, of MO4 making contact with "other resistance movements in Croatia." The military thought that they were being asked to support apolitical Croatian Partisans. MO4 knew otherwise.
April 1943	Hitler rejects deal with Tito's "bandits." Germans renew cleanup operations with attack on Djurišić-Stanišić Četniks; 7,000

	men are captured. Axis then turns on Partisan army, which is encircled near Mount Durmitor.
May 27–28, 1943	Deakin and Stuart drop to Tito.
May 29, 1943	SOE Cairo dispatches infamous "Glenconner" signal. Seemingly designed to open an escape route for the trapped Partisans, the signal orders Mihailović to retreat into central Serbia, east of the Ibar River, abandoning all remaining Yugoslav territory to the Partisans. It is insultingly phrased and alleges that Mihailović forces are nonexistent or collaborationist outside the Serbian heartland. Ironically, the proposal demands a Partisan takeover of the Sandžak, which was what the Partisan negotiators had been discussing with the Germans in Zagreb.
June 2, 1943	Henbury mission (Capt. Michael Lees) drops to a Loyalist formation in southeastern Serbia and is immediately caught up in a German-Bulgarian cleanup sweep. Henbury mission and Roughshod mission (Maj. John Sehmer) lose four British killed in Bulgar dawn attack.
Early June 1943	The Algiers incident. Churchill signals minister of state, Cairo, asking that Deakin meet him in Algiers to report on Yugoslav affairs. Reply states Deakin was just dropped to Tito, forwards two MO4 memorandums drafted along lines of Glenconner signal. Desmond Morton, Churchill's intelligence advisor, intercepts and suppresses the memorandums after consulting with Foreign Office.

Mid-June 1943	Main Partisan army slips out of Mount Durmitor encirclement and moves north toward western Bosnia. Captain Stuart killed, Deakin and Tito slightly wounded by same bomb. About 10,000 of original 15,000 make good their escape.
Late June 1943	Foreign Office reacts with horror to Glenconner signal of May 29. Glenconner recalled to London; signal is eventually withdrawn.
July 19, 1943	BBC reports that *Novo Vreme* (an official news sheet) carried offer of 100,000 *reichsmark* reward for Tito while not mentioning identical offer for Mihailović printed in the same advertisement.
July 1943	British decide to drop brigadier-rank officers to both Mihailović and Tito, with Bailey to be political advisor to the former and Capt. Fitzroy Maclean political advisor to the latter. The two senior officer nominees are a Brigadier Orr, nominated by General Wilson to go to Tito, and Brigadier Charles Armstrong for Mihailović.
July 1943	Maclean is recalled to London to be briefed by the Foreign Office as political advisor. He is a former diplomat and a member of Parliament, and he gets to see the foreign secretary, Anthony Eden. He is invited to Chequers by Churchill, who decides to upgrade Maclean from advisor to head of mission to Tito. Opposition to this promotion by Foreign Office and SOE wilts under pressure from Churchill.
August 1943	Intercepted German Enigma signal indicates that Germans still regard

Mihailović as their main enemy in the Balkans and remain set on his destruction.

Following reconnaissance of main Belgrade-Salonika line, Vranje, Vladički Han, and Grdelica, Capt. Michael Lees prepares operation to demolish Vladički Han bridge with assistance of Capt. Bora Manić's Loyalist Leteći Brigade, pursuant to orders from MO4 to interrupt line. MO4 then countermands order at very last moment. Operation is canceled. (Subsequently, MO4 claims "misunderstanding.")

Capt. George More (Alkali mission with Loyalist leader Keserović) blows railway bridge in Ibar Valley, and a Yugoslav Sergeant Belić of his mission cuts another line between Priština and Peć. Both actions involve Loyalist troops.

Maclean flies to Cairo, crosses swords with MO4, and arranges direct link with Gen. Sir Henry Maitland ("Jumbo") Wilson, commander in chief Middle East, and with Churchill.

Mihailović's assurance that he will not attack Partisans is accepted, but very shortly thereafter Bailey becomes embroiled in new row with Mihailović. Bailey drafts a signal raising certain issues and again stops supplies, pending satisfactory reply by Mihailović. The signal, which purports to bear General Wilson's signature, details BLO complaints about Loyalist commanders. Foreign Office demands that Bailey withdraw signal immediately, but most of forty planned September drops remain canceled.

Yugoslav section chief Maj. Basil Davidson leaves MO4 on mission to Hungary (which proves impossible) and stays with Yugoslav Partisans in Vojvoda Bačka area.

Captain Robertson (alias Radivojević or Radojević), with consent of MO4 and Bailey, leaves Loyalist Keserović headquarters together with BLO Maj. Neil Selby in attempt to reach nearby Partisans. Selby and his radio operator are captured and fall into Gestapo hands. Robertson joins Partisans on the Jastrebac, then tries to contact first Capt. Danny Boon and then Lees, seeking to reestablish link with MO4. Robertson is subsequently reported shot by Partisans.

September 10 to October 10, 1943

Following news of Italian capitulation, Loyalists attack Priboj, Prijepolje, and Berane, killing several hundred Germans and Bulgars and accepting surrender of Italian Venezia Division. Actions are witnessed by Bailey, Hudson, and two Americans, Maj. (later Col.) Albert B. Seitz and Capt. (later Maj.) Walter R. Mansfield. Under orders from MO4, Bailey dissuades Loyalists from disarming Italians. Large Partisan army then force-marches into area, drives Loyalists back, and disarms Italians. Mihailović furious at British deception and loss of arms.

September 17, 1943

Maclean drops to Tito.

September 20, 1943

Maclean informs MO4 he has personally guaranteed Tito greatly increased deliveries, with "minimum 60 sorties this moon."

September 22, 1943 — MO4 advises all missions with Loyalists that supplies will be greatly curtailed because of bad weather, relocation of airfield, and other bogus reasons. From this date on, Loyalists receive nothing but minimum maintenance drops; all else is diverted to Partisans, but no mention of this policy decision is made in signals to missions with Loyalists.

September 1943 — BBC starts attributing Loyalist sabotage operations to Partisans, including major operations at Priboj and Prijepolje.

September 24, 1943 — Brigadier Armstrong drops to Mihailović with letter from Gen. "Jumbo" Wilson promising supplies "on a much larger scale" and asking for a special sabotage effort.

Late September through December 1943 — Mihailović forces blow four bridges at Mokra Gora. A major span over the Drina at Višegrad is blown by Maj. Archie Jack; the operation involves 2,500 Loyalists and leaves 200 Germans dead. Though witnessed by Brigadier Armstrong, operation is attributed by BBC to Partisans.

Lees's Fugue (previously Henbury) mission carries out major railway demolition September 30. This demolition is also promptly reported by the BBC as a Partisan success. Lees continues with line demolitions and derailments until end of November. Roughshod mission (under Capt. Robert Purvis) starts with line demolitions and a derailment and attacks a station north of Kumanovo. Homolje mission (Maj. Jasper Rootham

	and Maj. Eric Greenwood) attack Danube shipping. Other missions also active.
September 29, 1943	MO4 memorandum by Keble again proposes geographical division of territory along lines of Glenconner signal but allotting even more to Partisans. Maclean declines to put proposal to Tito, alleging it will impair relations. He signals that Tito is determined to "liquidate" Mihailović and the Loyalists and that he will shortly do so.
October–November 1943	Mission headed by Maj. Mostyn Davies appears in Bulgarian-annexed part of southern Serbia and starts receiving massive supply drops. Supplies are used to build up Partisan forces under Vukmanović-Tempo on edge of Loyalist territory. MO4 denies existence of this mission.
October 5, 1943	Maclean leaves Tito headquarters for the coast and Cairo to meet with Foreign Secretary Anthony Eden, to arrange a Partisan delegation's visit to Middle East headquarters in Cairo, and to propose additional massive support for Partisans.
October 23, 1943	American liaison officers with Mihailović, Seitz, and Mansfield dispatch objective report with policy recommendations designed to make best use of all Yugoslav resistance potential and stop fighting between Mihailović and the Partisans. They also seek permission to exfiltrate in order to take part in anticipated policy discussions. Their signal, addressed to William Donovan, head of OSS (forerunner to the CIA), is

	delayed in MO4 until November 14. Seitz and Mansfield remain in Yugoslavia, and their report remains unseen and unconsidered by policy-makers.
November 7, 1943	Maclean delivers what will become known as the "blockbuster" report. It relies heavily on figures and claims supplied by Partisans and recommends abandoning Mihailović. The report is passed on by Eden to the War Cabinet, Churchill, the Commonwealth prime ministers, and President Roosevelt.
November 7–10, 1943	Armstrong and Bailey signal 92-part report to MO4. It is along the lines of the more concise Seitz-Mansfield report and generally favorable to the Loyalists. It outlines detailed proposals to stop the internecine strife between Loyalists and Partisans and harness resistance efforts under direct Allied control.
November 11, 1943	Sir Orme Sargent of Foreign Office signals Ralph Skrine Stevenson, ambassador to the royal Yugoslav government in exile (now in Cairo), urging that Armstrong and Bailey be exfiltrated to take part in discussions with Churchill, Eden, and Maclean. Request is ignored in Cairo.
November 18, 1943	Armstrong and Bailey's long report, delayed for a week in deciphering, is passed to the Minister of State's Office in Cairo, which sends it to London by slow savings telegram November 23. It reaches the Foreign Office November 27 and is first acknowledged on December 10 by a junior officer, who comments that it has been superseded by decisions already taken. Neither

	Armstrong nor Bailey is exfiltrated. Anthony Eden later said neither he nor Churchill ever saw their report.
November 19, 1943	Keble submits to the Special Operations Committee of Middle East headquarters a paper that purports to be an appreciation of the military situation in Serbia and consideration of future policy. This shockingly mendacious and irresponsible memorandum concludes with the recommendation that support of Mihailović be discontinued, that the British missions to the Loyalists be evacuated (by making arrangements with Tito to that effect), and that new BLOs be sent to the Partisans in Serbia.
November 27, 1943	Keble leaves MO4, which is put directly under military control and renamed Force 133. Lord Glenconner, political head of SOE Cairo, also leaves.
November 28, 1943	Tehran Conference. Big Three agree to give all possible help to Yugoslav resistance but do *not* formally agree to concentrate all aid on Partisans.
December 2, 1943	Desmond Morton, Churchill's intelligence advisor, while preparing for the prime minister's arrival in Cairo, finds that MO4 maps differ substantially from London intelligence maps. The MO4 maps claim huge areas in hands of Partisans, Germans holding lines of communication only, and Mihailović forces limited to very small areas. Morton chooses to use the MO4 maps in briefing Churchill.
December 5, 1943	Maclean collects Deakin and Partisan delegation, bringing them to Cairo via Italy.

December 7, 1943	Force 133 instructs BLOs to sound out local Mihailović commanders about possibility of replacing Mihailović.
December 9, 1943	Through Armstrong, General Wilson asks Mihailović whether he will carry out specific bridge demolitions. This request is intended as a test of good faith. Wilson asks for a reply by December 29. At behest of British government, King Peter and the exiled Yugoslav government signal support for Wilson's proposal.
December 10, 1943	Churchill meets in Cairo with Maclean, Deakin, and Stevenson. No representatives from British missions with Mihailović attend. Maclean reports on Partisans, and Deakin presents dossier on alleged Mihailović collaboration. Churchill tells Stevenson he wants Mihailović "removed" by the end of the month and that King Peter be required to associate himself with the decision.
December 11, 1943	Tito is asked by his British mission to ensure safe-conduct for BLOs escaping from Loyalist units.
December 13, 1943	Force 133 signals BLOs with Loyalists to prepare to escape to Partisans. The signal is not sent to mission at Mihailović's headquarters, Brigadier Armstrong. Subsequently Force 133 signals that it had been too busy to inform him.
ca. December 13–15 1943	Lees and Maj. Peter Solly-Flood, setting out on expedition with sixty-man Loyalist force to blow Morava Valley rail line and attack enemy airfield near Niš, receive last-second order from Colonel Cope to abort mission and prepare to abandon Loyalists.

December 13, 1943	Deakin formally takes over Yugoslav section of Force 133.
December 14, 1943	Loyalist BLOs Col. William Cope and Maj. Rupert Raw discuss "prepare to escape" signal with Maj. Radoslav Djurić, chief Mihailović commander in southeastern Serbia. Capt. George More, also a Loyalist BLO, breaks the same news to Captain Marković, another Mihailović commander.
December 14–15, 1943	Capt. Robert Wade leaves Keserović to make a break to Partisans. He is joined by Marko Hudson December 23. About December 27 the two reach a Partisan division.
December 16, 1943	Brigadier Armstrong, chief BLO at Mihailović headquarters, finally learns that other BLOs are abandoning Loyalists.
December 23, 1943	Mihailović—never officially informed but by now undoubtedly aware that Allies are abandoning him—tells Armstrong he will comply with General Wilson's request regarding bridge demolitions. Mihailović says he needs a fortnight to get troops into position.
Late December 1943 to early January 1944	Brigadier Armstrong and Major Jack move out to Ibar Valley, and Major Greenwood to Morava Valley, for demolitions, as per General Wilson's request to Mihailović. Foreign Office London calls operation off at last moment. Eventually orders are given to stop all sabotage—with or without Loyalist help.
	Evacuation of remaining BLOs held up by Cairo while Churchill, Eden, Stevenson, and Maclean consult and negotiate with Tito about retention of

	King Peter's government and future of king himself.
Mid-January 1944	Maclean delivers to Tito letter from Churchill confirming that no further supplies will be sent to Mihailović and informing Tito that British want Yugoslav government to "remove Mihailović from their councils."
Mid-February 1944	Mihailović is at last officially informed of decision to abandon him.
Early February 1944	Captain Lees—one BLO not informed of Cairo orders to stop sabotage—carries out derailment near Leskovac on Belgrade-Salonika line, and follows with further derailment a week or two later.
Late May 1944	BLOs and crashed American aircrew are evacuated from airstrip Pranjani near Čačak, having concentrated from widely dispersed missions all over Serbia.
May 25, 1944	German paratroopers drop onto Tito's headquarters near Drvar in Bosnia. Tito is evacuated to Italy, thence to island of Vis.
Early June 1944	On return to Bari, BLOs who have just marched through large portions of Serbia without sighting Partisans see official British maps showing those areas in Partisan hands. Their protests are rejected, and they are forbidden access to the map room.
August 1944	Churchill and Tito meet at Caserta and discuss proposed new Šubašić government.
Late September 1944	Allied air attacks on retreating German army facilitate massive drive by Partisans into Loyalist Serbian heartland and demonstrate Western Allied support for Partisan cause.

September 21, 1944	Tito "levants" secretly to Moscow, soliciting Red Army help to clear Germans from Serbia and form alliance with Bulgarian army.
Autumn 1944	Churchill voices first disillusionment with Tito. Memos and signals over the next nine months show Churchill's increasing disappointment until, in June 1945, his party loses power and he leaves office.
Autumn and winter 1944–45	Partisans, initially with Russian and Bulgarian help on the ground, take areas of Serbia remaining in Loyalist hands. They get massive Western Allied logistical and close air support. Massacres by Tito execution squads begin.
April–May 1945	Partisans threaten Italian territory in Trieste, Venezia Giulia, and Austrian province of Carinthia. Massacres take place in Slovenia and Montenegro. A total of 35,000 surrendered troops, political refugees, and camp followers comprising principally Slovene and Croatian Domobrans but including some thousands of Serbian Četniks, are sent back forcibly from Austria to Yugoslavia by British forces. The vast majority of them are immediately slaughtered without trial and in great secrecy.
Winter 1945	At a dinner party in Brussels, Churchill describes his embracing of Tito as "one of [his] greatest mistakes of the war."
April 1946	Following Mihailović's capture on March 14, Churchill writes to Foreign Secretary Ernest Bevin asking that Britain intervene to ensure a fair trial for Mihailović.

July 10–15, 1946   Mihailović is tried in Belgrade for trea-
                        son. Evidence offered by Americans and
                        Britons is not admitted.
July 17, 1946   Mihailović is executed by firing squad on
                        a Belgrade golf course.

BIBLIOGRAPHY

Allied Forces Headquarters [Stephen Clissold]. *The Četniks: A Survey of Četnik Activity in Yugoslavia, April 1941–July 1944.* Bari, Italy: AFHQ, G2, September 1944. Paperback.

Auty, Phyllis and Richard Clogg, eds. *British Policy Towards Wartime Resistance in Yugoslavia and Greece.* London: London University Press/ Macmillan, 1975.

Beloff, Nora. *Tito's Flawed Legacy: Yugoslavia and the West 1939–84.* London: Victor Gollancz, 1985.

Biber, Dušan. *Tito–Churchill.* Zagreb: Globus, 1981.

Boyle, Andrew. *The Climate of Treason.* London: Hodder & Stoughton, 1980.

Clissold, Stephen. *Whirlwind: An Account of Marshall Tito's Rise to Power.* London: Cresset Press, 1949.

Davidson, Basil. *Partisan Picture.* London: Victor Gollancz, 1946.

———. *Special Operations Europe: Scenes from the Anti-Nazi War.* London: Victor Gollancz, 1980.

Deakin, F. W. D. *The Embattled Mountain.* Oxford: Oxford University Press, 1971.

BIBLIOGRAPHY

Dedijer, Vladimir. *Dnevnik 1941–44 (With Tito Through the War)*. London: Hamilton, 1951. English translation by Alex Brown.

Deroc, Milan. *Special Operations Explored*. Boulder, Colo.: East European Monographs, 1988.

Djilas, Milovan. *Wartime*. San Diego, Calif.: Harcourt Brace Jovanovich, 1977.

English, David. "Airlift from Pranyani: An American Flier Remembers." *Serb World* 1.3 (January–February 1985).

Herzstein, Robert Edwin. *Waldheim: The Missing Years*. London: Grafton Books, 1988.

Hinsley, F. H. et al. *British Intelligence in the Second World War: Its Influence on Strategy and Operations*, vol. 3. New York: Cambridge University Press, 1984.

Ivanović, Vane. *LX Memoirs of a Yugoslav*. San Diego, Calif.: Harcourt Brace Jovanovich, 1977.

Johnson, Stowers. *Agents Extraordinary*. London: Robert Hale, 1975.

Lees, Michael. *Special Operations Executed*. London: Kimber, 1986.

Leković, Miso. *The March Negotiations (Martovski Pregovori 1943)*. Belgrade: Nova Kniga, 1985.

Maclean, Fitzroy. *Disputed Barricades*. London: Jonathan Cape, 1957.
———. *Eastern Approaches*. London: Jonathan Cape, 1949.

Martin, David. *Ally Betrayed*. New York: Prentice-Hall, 1946.
———. Introductory essay in *Patriot or Traitor: The Case of General Mihailovich*. Stanford, Calif.: Hoover Institution Press/Stanford University Press, 1978.

Pavlowitch, Stevan K. *The Improbable Survivor*. London: C. Hurst, 1988.
———. *Yugoslavia*. New York: Praeger, 1971.

Penrose, Barrie and Simon Freeman. *Conspiracy of Silence: The Secret Life of Anthony Blunt*. London: Grafton Books, 1986; New York: Farrar, Straus & Giroux, 1987.

Pincher, Chapman. *Their Trade Is Treachery*. Revised edition, London: Sidgwick and Jackson, 1982.
———. *Too Secret for Too Long*. London: Sidgwick and Jackson, 1984.

Roberts, Walter R. *Tito, Mihailović, and the Allies 1941–45*. New Brunswick, N.J.: Rutgers University Press, 1973.

Rootham, Jasper. *Miss-Fire: The Chronicle of a British Mission to Mihailovich 1943–44*. London: Chatto and Windus, 1946.

Seton-Watson, Hugh. *The East European Revolution*. London: Methuen, 1950.

Sirc, Ljubo. *Between Hitler and Tito*. London: André Deutsch, 1989.

Stafford, David. *Camp X: SOE and the American Connection.* London: Viking, 1986.

Stevenson, William. *The Man Called Intrepid.* San Diego, Calif.: Harcourt Brace Jovanovich, 1976.

Sweet-Escott, Bickham. *Baker Street Irregular.* London: Methuen, 1965.

Tolstoy, Nikolai. *The Minister and the Massacres.* London: Century-Hutchinson, 1986.

Velebit, Vladimir. *Sjećanja.* Zagreb: Globus, 1983.

Waugh, Auberon. *The Diaries of Evelyn Waugh.* London: Weidenfeld & Nicholson, 1976.

Wheeler, Mark. *Britain and the War for Yugoslavia 1940–43.* Boulder, Colo.: East European Monographs, 1980.

Wright, Peter. *Spycatcher.* Richmond, Australia: Heinemann, 1987.

INDEX

INDEX

INDEX

INDEX

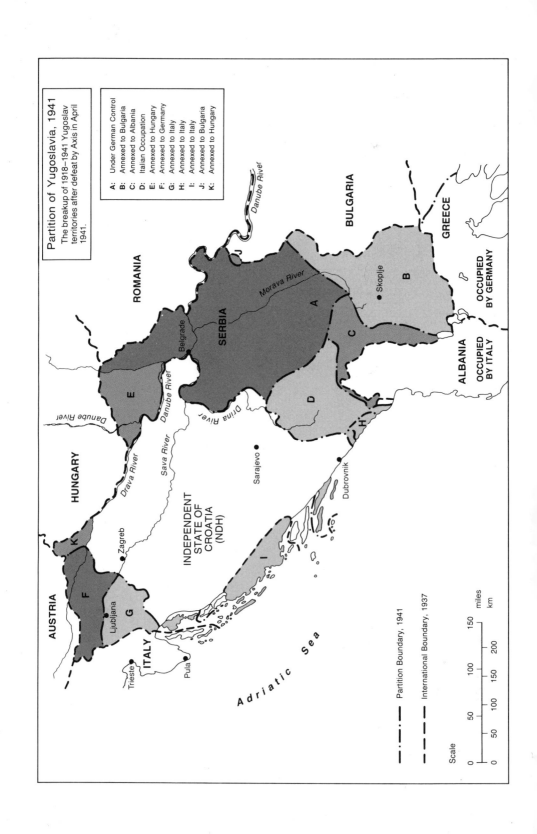

Partition of Yugoslavia, 1941

The breakup of 1918–1941 Yugoslav territories after defeat by Axis in April 1941.

A: Under German Control
B: Annexed to Bulgaria
C: Annexed to Albania
D: Italian Occupation
E: Annexed to Hungary
F: Annexed to Germany
G: Annexed to Italy
H: Annexed to Italy
I: Annexed to Italy
J: Annexed to Bulgaria
K: Annexed to Hungary

ROMANIA

BULGARIA

GREECE

HUNGARY

AUSTRIA

ITALY

ALBANIA

OCCUPIED BY GERMANY

OCCUPIED BY ITALY

Danube River

Danube River

Drava River

Sava River

Drina River

Morava River

SERBIA

INDEPENDENT STATE OF CROATIA (NDH)

Belgrade

Zagreb

Sarajevo

Dubrovnik

Skopje

Ljubljana

Trieste

Pula

Adriatic Sea

Scale

Partition Boundary, 1941

International Boundary, 1937

0   50   100   150   miles
0   50   100   150   200   km